twelfth edition

Building Classroom Management: Methods and Models

C. M. Charles

Emeritus, San Diego State University

Karen M. Cole

University of North Carolina, Asheville

D1710858

 Pearson

New York, NY

Director and Portfolio Manager:
Kevin M. Davis
Content Producer: Janelle Rogers
Media Producer: Lauren Carlson
Portfolio Management Assistant:
Casey Coriell
Executive Field Marketing Manager:
Krista Clark
Executive Product Marketing Manager:
Christopher Barry

Procurement Specialist: Carol Melville
Full Service Project Management:
Thistle Hill Publishing Services
Cover Designer: Cenveo® Publisher Services
Cover Image: © Addictive Creative
/Offset.com
Composition: Cenveo® Publisher Services
Printer/Binder: LSC Communications, Inc.
Cover Printer: Phoenix Color/Hagerstown
Text Font: 10.25/12 Sabon LT Pro

Credits and acknowledgments for material borrowed from other sources and reproduced, with permission, in this textbook appear on the appropriate page within the text.

Every effort has been made to provide accurate and current Internet information in this book. However, the Internet and information posted on it are constantly changing, so it is inevitable that some of the Internet addresses listed in this textbook will change.

Cataloging-in-Publication Data is available on file at the Library of Congress.

12 2022

ISBN 10: 0-13-444844-8
ISBN 13: 978-0-13-444844-2

Preface

NEW TO THIS EDITION

First and foremost, readers familiar with previous editions will notice a new title for the text. The text title and terminology have been updated to reflect a broader mindset with regard to schools, classrooms, students, and teachers. While discipline is an important element of classroom management, there are a myriad of other factors that affect teacher and student behavior. Broadening the scope of the text by including the commonly used term "classroom management" reflects the need for teachers to think broadly about the instructional and interpersonal factors that influence the way a classroom operates.

The chapters have been updated with the inclusion of new research about classroom management. We did some rearranging, added new material, and worked to eliminate any redundancy in the text itself.

Here is an overview of the way the text has been restructured. The first part of the text (Chapters 1–4) provides a general context for understanding classroom management.

In Chapter 1, the reader considers the teacher's role in managing the classroom with particular focus on the sorts of communication skills that set teachers (and students!) up for success. We discuss the professional obligations of teachers and factors that influence teachers' decision making about classroom management.

In Chapter 2, the reader explores developmental characteristics of students that inform their behavior. We then add a section emphasizing culturally responsive management; teachers and prospective teachers are given a chance to consider aspects of student diversity that influence the classroom management system.

In Chapter 3, we introduce terminology commonly encountered when reading and talking about classroom management. We then examine types of student misbehavior and take the reader through possible contributors to misbehavior—and to ways teachers can prevent inappropriate behavior or respond in the moment when a student is not meeting classroom expectations.

Chapter 4 describes the historical development of classroom management by discussing the work of different experts in the field from its inception through the present day. To help the reader better understand the significance of these developments, we identify a series of themes that classroom management systems may highlight to greater or lesser extents; throughout the rest of the book, we ask the reader to consider which themes are apparent in the work of the experts under study.

As in previous editions of the book, Part 2 of the text (Chapters 5–12) introduces the reader to different classroom management models, the authorities who developed them, and the recommendations they give for working with different groups of students.

Chapter 12 is a new chapter and covers the Positive Behavioral Interventions and Supports (PBIS) schoolwide model of management. The chapter includes examples of the sorts of data that schools consider when using the implementation framework as well as real-world examples of PBIS materials and strategies currently used in real schools.

Chapter 13 discusses learning differences and student disabilities that may affect the way the teacher manages the classroom.

Chapter 14 engages readers in a review of two real-world classroom management plans, allowing them to see how different teachers combine elements from the approaches under study.

MYLAB EDUCATION

One of the most visible changes in the twelfth edition, and also one of the most significant, is the expansion of the digital learning and assessment resources embedded in the eText and the inclusion of MyLab in the text. MyLab is an online homework, tutorial, and assessment program designed to work with the text to engage learners and to improve learning. Within its structured environment, learners see key concepts demonstrated through real classroom video footage, practice what they learn, test their understanding, and receive feedback to guide their learning and to ensure their mastery of key learning outcomes. Designed to bring learners more directly into the world of K–12 classrooms and to help them see the real and powerful impact of the classroom management concepts covered in this book, the online resources in MyLab Education with the Enhanced eText include:

- Video Application Exercises. Within each chapter, embedded videos provide illustrations of classroom management concepts and models in action. These video examples typically show students and teachers working in classrooms or teachers describing their thinking or experiences. The accompanying scaffolded analysis exercises challenge learners to use chapter content to reflect on classroom management in real school settings. Students respond to constructed-response questions; they then receive feedback in the form of model answers written by the text authors.
- Simulations in Classroom Management. These interactive cases focus on the classroom management issues teachers most frequently encounter on a daily basis. Each simulation presents a challenge scenario at the beginning and then offers a series of choices to solve each challenge. Along the way students receive mentor feedback on their choices and have the opportunity to make better choices if necessary.
- Self-Checks. In each chapter, self-check quizzes help assess how well learners have mastered the content. The self-checks are made up of self-grading multiple-choice items that not only provide feedback on whether questions are answered correctly or incorrectly, but also provide rationales for both correct and incorrect answers.

INSTRUCTOR'S MANUAL TO THE TEXT FOR UNIVERSITY AND WORKSHOP INSTRUCTORS

An instructor's manual is available for download from the Instructor Resource Center at www.pearsonhighered.com/irc. The manual includes a wealth of ideas and activities for use in teaching the course.

ACKNOWLEDGMENTS

C. M. Charles and I gratefully acknowledge the valuable contributions made to this and previous editions by the following teachers and administrators:

Roy Allen, Constance Bauer, Karen Barr, Linda Blacklock, Tom Bolz, Michael Brus, Gail Charles, Ruth Charles, Tim Charles, Diana Cordero, Keith Correll, Tom Daly, Barbara Gallegos, Nancy Girvin, Kris Halverson, Leslie Hays, Charlotte Hibsch, Charlotte Hipps, Elaine Maltz, Chris Martin, Colleen Meagher, Nancy Natale, Linda Pohlenz, Lillian Schafer, David Sisk, Deborah Sund, Mike Straus, and Virginia Villalpando.

We also want to acknowledge the valuable critiques provided by notable reviewers: Aubrey Fine, CA Poly University, Mandalina Tanase, University of North Florida, Margaret C. Torrie, Iowa State University, Deborah Burris, Southern Illinois University Carbondale, and Robert Harrington, University of Kansas.

I would like to personally thank the following individuals for their support and encouragement throughout this revision: Cale Burrell, Kevin Davis, Margaret Mahlin, Kendall Martin, Marquis McGee, Asia Pepper, Anne Marie Roberts, Janelle Rogers, Angela Urquhart, and Andrea Archer.

I dedicate this text to my nephew, Patrick Martin, who is embarking on his own journey as a classroom teacher, and to the memory of my mother, Nancy Martin, who taught me so much about what it means to be a caring, supportive teacher.

To Carol: Thank you for bringing me on board. I appreciate your confidence in me.

To my beloved husband, Dennis Lundblad: My commitment to this work has led us on a wild ride. Thank you for your patience, understanding, and never-ending support. As Mike says in Monsters, Inc., "You and me, me and you, both of us, together."

Brief Contents

PART I   Building a Foundation   1

1   The Teacher's Role in Managing the Classroom   1

2   Taking Student Diversity into Account in Classroom Management   29

3   Classroom Management Concepts and Terms   50

4   The Development of Classroom Management   71

PART II   Classroom Management: Models and Methods   97

5   Insisting on Compliance: Ronald Morrish's *Real Discipline*   97

6   Taking Charge in the Classroom: Craig Seganti   121

7   Getting Off to a Good Start: Harry and Rosemary Wong on Preventing Management Problems   146

8   Time Use in Classrooms: How Fred Jones Helps Students Stay Focused and On-Task   171

9   The Power of Positive Choice: William Glasser on Quality Learning   196

10   Fostering Responsible Behavior: Marvin Marshall on Motivation and Student Choice   221

11   Working on the Same Side With Students: Spencer Kagan's Win-Win Discipline   249

12   School-Wide Positive Behavior Supports: A Data-Driven, Evidence-Based Approach to Whole-School Behavioral Management   271

13   Classroom Management for Students With Learning and Behavioral Challenges   297

14   Striving for Personal Excellence in Classroom Management   318

Glossary   331

References   339

Name Index   345

Subject Index   346

Contents

PART I   BUILDING A FOUNDATION   1

1   The Teacher's Role in Managing the Classroom   1

Classroom Discipline Versus Classroom Management   1

Where Are We Going From Here and How Will We Get There?   2

     Fundamental Questions in Managing the Classroom   3

Let's Examine a Planning Guide for Building a Personalized System of Classroom Management   4

     The Guide and Its Contents   4

Classroom Management Is Complex: Five Realities   6

     Reality Number One   6

     Reality Number Two   7

     Reality Number Three   7

     Reality Number Four   7

     Reality Number Five   8

What Are the Main Objectives of Classroom Management?   8

     What Can I Do to Provide a Safe, Civil, Productive Learning Environment?   9

     How Can I Facilitate and Achieve Civil, Respectful, Cooperative Behavior in Class?   11

     How Can I Promote, Among My Students, a Sense of Personal Responsibility for Learning and Behaving Acceptably?   12

What Is the Legal Basis for Classroom Management?   13

What Are Schools' Obligations to Students?   14

What Are My Obligations to Students?   15

What About Student Obligations?   15

More About the Legal Obligations Associated With Managing the Classroom   16

What Are My Professional Obligations?   18

Who Establishes Professional and Ethical Expectations?   20

Communication Skills: Critical to Teacher Professionalism   21

     What Did Haim Ginott Say About Congruent Communication?   21

     What Did Stephen Covey Say About Frames of Reference?   23

     What Did William Glasser Say About Seven Connecting Habits?   24

     What Did Fred Jones Say About Nonverbal Communication?   25

Reflecting on Your Role as a Teacher or Future Teacher: What You Have Learned in This Chapter   28

2   Taking Student Diversity into Account in Classroom Management   29

    What Are Students' Obligations to Teachers, Fellow Students, the Community, and Taxpayers?   30

    Can I Anticipate How My Students Will Behave?   30

      Behavior in the Primary Grades (Ages 5 to 8)   31

      Behavior in the Intermediate Grades (Ages 9 to 11)   32

      Behavior in the Middle School Grades (Ages 12 to 14)   32

      Behavior in the High School Grades (Ages 15 to 18)   33

    How Do Students' Needs and Habits Affect Their Behavior?   33

      What Do Students Need and Want in Their School Experience?   35

    How Do Sociocultural Realities Influence Behavior?   36

      Values and Associated Behaviors: What Do Schools Emphasize?   37

      Areas of Conflict: How Do Group Values Differ?   38

      Economic Realities: Do They Affect Student Behavior?   42

      Ruby Payne: Teachers Should Understand the Culture of Poverty   43

      Paul Gorski: Let's End the Deficit Ideology   44

      How Can I Work More Effectively With Students of Various Societal and Economic Groups?   46

    Reflecting on How Student Characteristics May Affect Teaching and Learning: What You Have Learned in This Chapter   48

3   Classroom Management Concepts and Terms   50

      How Do I Get Students to Comply with These Expectations?   50

      How Do I Communicate When Students Don't Meet My Expectations?   52

    Let's Examine *Misbehavior*: What Exactly Is It?   53

    What Causes Students to Misbehave?   54

      Causal Conditions That Seem to Reside in Individual Students   55

      Conditions That Seem to Reside in Peers and Groups   59

      Conditions That Seem to Reside in Instructional Environments   60

      Conditions That Seem to Reside in Teachers and Other School Personnel   61

    What Additional Things Might I Do to Exert Positive Influence?   64

      Establish and Maintain a Positive Attitude   64

      Use Your Influence to Move Students in the Right Direction   64

      Avoid the Pitfall of Arguing with Students   65

      Replace Criticism with Positive Influence   66

    Reflecting on Behavior and Its Roots: What You Have Learned in This Chapter   69

4   The Development of Classroom Management   71

Chapter Preview: Why Does This Matter to Me?   72

A Timeline of Developments in Modern Classroom Management   72

Group Dynamics: What Did Fritz Redl and William Wattenberg Explain about Group Behavior?   76

Shaping Behavior: What Did B. F. Skinner Discover About Helping Students Learn and Conduct Themselves Properly?   77

Choice Theory: What Did William Glasser Say About Choices and Failure?   78

Lesson Management: What Did Jacob Kounin Discover About Teaching Style and Student Behavior?   80

Congruent Communication: What Did Haim Ginott Teach Us About Communicating with Students?   81

Needs and Democratic Teaching: What Were Rudolf Dreikurs's Contentions About Student Needs and the Best Way to Teach?   83

Taking Charge: How Did Lee and Marlene Canter Advise Teachers to Establish Control in Their Classrooms?   84

The Cooperative Approach: How Does Linda Albert Advise Teachers to Work With Students?   85

Positivity and Humaneness: How Do Jane Nelsen and Lynn Lott Help Teachers Bring Those Qualities into the Classroom?   87

Nelsen and Lott's Significant Seven   88

Inner Discipline: What Does Barbara Coloroso Say About Helping Students Accept Responsibility and Maintain Self-Control?   89

Learning Communities: How Does Alfie Kohn Suggest We Involve Students More Closely in Genuine Learning?   90

Approaching Management From a Schoolwide Perspective: How Do Students Benefit From a Program of Positive Behavioral Interventions and Supports (PBIS)?   93

Themes Across Time   94

The Foundations of Classroom Management: What You Have Learned in This Chapter   96

PART II   CLASSROOM MANAGEMENT: MODELS AND METHODS   97

5   Insisting on Compliance: Ronald Morrish's *Real Discipline*   97

Who Is Ronald Morrish?   98

What Is the Morrish Model of Discipline?   99

In Morrish's View, How and Why Has Modern Discipline Gone Wrong?   99

What Is the "Real Discipline" Morrish Advocates?   100

Which Maxims Help Us Understand the Nature of Real Discipline? 101

What Are the Three Progressive Phases Through Which We Should Guide Students? 102

Phase 1: Training for Compliance 103

Phase 2: Teaching Students How to Behave 106

Phase 3: Managing Student Choice 107

Specifically, What Does Morrish Advise in Regard to Planning and Implementing a Good Discipline Program? 108

How Does One Develop Positive Relationships with Students? 111

What about Consequences for Misbehavior? 112

What about Motivation and Rewards? 113

What Does Morrish Say About Fostering Self-Esteem? 114

What Should You Do When Students Fail to Comply with Your Directions? 114

Applying Morrish's Ideas: What Might They Look Like in Action? 116

You Are the Teacher 117

Reflecting on Morrish: What You Have Learned in This Chapter 118

6 Taking Charge in the Classroom: Craig Seganti 121

Who Is Craig Seganti? 121

The Seganti Model of Discipline 122

What Does Seganti Say About Discipline? 123

What Attitude Does Seganti Recommend for Teachers? 123

Rules: How Do They Promote Student Accountability? 125

Seganti's Rule 1 and Rule 2 126

Additional Topics Seganti Suggests for Rules 126

Leverage: How Do You Get Students to Follow the Rules? 129

Management: What Should You Do to Support Desirable Behavior? 132

How Might I Put Seganti's Ideas into Effect? 135

Use Effective Doorway Tactics 135

Watch for and Address Three Types of Behavior on the First Day 136

Assign Seats and Begin Learning Students' Names 136

Explain Leverage for Rules and Exclusion from Class Procedures 137

Outside Support: What Does Seganti Want of Administrators, Counselors, and Caregivers? 138

A Closing Comment From Mr. Seganti 139

Applying Seganti's Ideas: What Might They Look Like in Action? 141

You Are the Teacher   142

Reflecting on Seganti: What Have You Learned in This Chapter?   143

7   Getting Off to a Good Start: Harry and Rosemary Wong on
    Preventing Management Problems   146

What Is the Wongs' Model for Classroom Management?   147

Who Are Harry and Rosemary Wong?   148

A Quick Read of the Wongs' Principal Suggestions   148

About Roles and Responsibilities   148

About Classrooms and Procedures   149

About School   149

About Teaching   149

About Testing and Evaluation   150

About Student Behavior   150

About the First Day of Class   150

About the First Week of Teaching   151

More About Management Plans   151

About Planning and Organizing   152

Procedures and What They Entail   152

What Do the Wongs Suggest for Beginning a Class Successfully?   158

What Do the Wongs Say About the First Five Minutes of Class?   160

What Else Do the Wongs Say About the First Day of School?   161

What Do the Wongs Say About the First 10 Days of School?   162

What Do the Wongs Say About Procedures for Cooperative Work Groups?   163

Do the Wongs' Ideas Work for Secondary Teachers?   163

Applying the Wongs' Ideas: What Might They Look Like in Action?   166

You Are the Teacher   167

Reflecting on the Wongs' Ideas: What You Have Learned in This Chapter   168

8   Time Use in Classrooms: How Fred Jones Helps Students
    Stay Focused and On-Task   171

Who Is Fred Jones?   171

The Jones Model   172

What Five Management Problems Did Jones Bring to Light?   173

Massive Time Wasting   173

Student Passivity   174

Aimlessness   174

Helpless Handraising   174

Ineffective Nagging   175

How Would Jones Help Teachers Become More Effective?   175

Conserve Time and Don't Allow Students to Waste It   175

Arrange Class Seating to Facilitate Active Teaching and Close Proximity to Students   176

Teach Your Students the Meaning and Purpose of Your Management System   176

Assign Your Students Specific Responsibilities in Caring for the Classroom   178

Begin Every Class with Bell Work   178

Keep Your Students Actively Engaged in Learning   178

Use Visual Instructional Plans   179

Use Body Language to Communicate Pleasantly and Clearly That You Mean Business   180

Increase Motivation and Responsibility Through Wise Use of Incentives   182

Provide Help Efficiently During Independent Work   186

Have Stronger Backup Systems Ready for Use If and When Needed   188

What Is Jones's Study Group Activity?   188

In Review, How Might I Implement Jones's Approach in My Classroom?   189

Applying Jones's Ideas: What Might They Look Like in Action?   191

You Are the Teacher   192

Reflecting on Jones's Recommendations: What You Have Learned in This Chapter   193

9   The Power of Positive Choice: William Glasser on Quality Learning   196

Who Is William Glasser?   196

What Is the Glasser Model of Classroom Management?   198

What Were Glasser's Major Assertions About Noncoercive Classroom Management?   199

Why Is Boss Management Considered Futile?   200

How Can Schools Help Students Meet Their Basic Needs?   201

What Does Glasser Mean by the Term "Quality World"?   201

How Did Glasser Characterize a Quality Curriculum?   202

How Does Glasser Characterize Quality Teaching?   203

What Else Does Glasser Say About Boss Management and Lead Management?   204

How Is Choice Theory Applied in the Classroom?   206

How Does Quality Teaching Affect Classroom Management?   207

What Would Glasser Have Me Do When Students Break Class Rules?   208

What Does Glasser Mean by "Quality Classrooms," and How Do We Get Them?   209

What Are the Seven Deadly Habits in Teaching, and How Do I Avoid Them?   210

In Summary, How Can I Move Toward Building a Quality Classroom?   212

How Can I Go about Implementing Glasser's Ideas in My Classes?   214

You Are the Teacher   217

Reflecting on Glasser's Recommendations: What You Have Learned in
   This Chapter   218

10   Fostering Responsible Behavior: Marvin Marshall on Motivation
       and Student Choice   221

Who Is Marvin Marshall?   221

What Is the Marshall Model of Discipline?   222

Let's Begin With What *Not* to Do   223

So What Should We Do Instead?   224

What Is Internal Motivation, and Why Is It So Powerful?   225

What Are Motivational Theories X and Y?   226

What Is Marshall's Hierarchy of Social Development, and How Is It Used?   227

   Marshall's Hierarchy of Social Development   227

   How Does the Hierarchy Help Students Develop Self-Control?   228

   How Should I Teach the Hierarchy to My Students?   229

   The Butterfly Analogy: Another Way to Teach the Hierarchy to Students   230

What Other Tactics Does Marshall Suggest for Stimulating Students to Behave
   Responsibly?   232

   General Tactics   232

   Tactics for Interacting With Students   233

   Tactics for Motivating and Teaching   233

   Tactics for Influencing Positive Behavior   234

   Tactics for Empowering Students   235

   Tactics for Addressing Problems (or Meeting Challenges)   236

How Should Teachers Intervene When Students Misbehave?   236

How Does Marshall Suggest Teachers Evaluate Themselves?   239

Pertinent Comments in Dr. Marshall's Words   239

Summary of the Marvin Marshall Teaching Model   241

What Guidance Does Marshall Provide for Applying His System in the Classroom?   241

Applying Marshall's Ideas: What Might They Look like in Action?   243

You Are the Teacher   244

Reflecting on Marvin Marshall's Discipline Without Stress: What You Have
   Learned in This Chapter   245

11   Working on the Same Side With Students: Spencer Kagan's Win-Win Discipline   249

Who Is Spencer Kagan?   250

What Is the Kagan Model of Discipline?   251

What Is the Fundamental Proposition in Kagan's Approach?   251

   Irresponsible Behavior   252

   Student Positions   252

   Structures   253

   Structures for the Moment of Disruption   254

   Structures for Follow-Up   254

   Structures for Long-Term Success   255

   Structures for Promoting Life Skills   257

How Do I Match Intervention Structures to Various Types of Disruption?   257

   Interventions for Attention-Seeking Behavior   258

   Interventions for Attempts to Avoid Failure or Embarrassment   258

   Interventions for Anger   258

   Interventions for Control-Seeking Behavior   259

   Interventions for the Overly Energetic   259

   Interventions for Boredom   260

   Interventions for the Uninformed   260

What Else Should We Know About Win-Win Discipline?   260

What Does Kagan Say About Parent and Community Alliances and Schoolwide Programs?   262

How Do I Implement Win-Win Discipline in My Classroom?   263

   The Three Essentials   263

   Introducing Win-Win Discipline   264

Reminders and Suggestions   265

Applying Kagan's Ideas: What Might They Look Like in Action?   266

You Are the Teacher   268

Reflecting on Kagan's Recommendations: What You Have Learned in This Chapter   269

12   School-Wide Positive Behavior Supports: A Data-Driven, Evidence-Based Approach to Whole-School Behavioral Management   271

What Is PBIS?   273

   PBIS: Core Principles   275

   The Collaborative Nature of PBIS   276

Why Is PBIS Growing in Popularity?   276

The 3-Tiered Structure of PBIS   277

Tier 1 in Depth   278

Data Collection in Depth   280

Tier 2 in Depth   281

Tier 3 in Depth   288

The Role of Rewards in PBIS   290

What Does Research Say About the Effectiveness of PBIS?   292

Applying PBIS Ideas: What Might They Look Like in Action?   292

You Are the Teacher   293

Reflecting on PBIS: What You Have Learned in This Chapter   294

13   Classroom Management for Students With Learning and Behavioral
Challenges   297

What Model of Discipline Do I Use With Atypical Learners?   298

What Do We Know about Students With Learning and Behavioral
Challenges?   299

Scenario 1 Tyler   299

Indicators: What Would Suggest That a Student Might Have a Learning or
Behavioral Difference?   300

Two Common Diagnoses That Can Affect Learning and Behavior   300

Learning Disabilities: What Are They and How Can I Help Students with
This Diagnosis?   301

Scenario 2 Justin   302

Attention Deficit Hyperactivity Disorder: What Is It and How Can I Help Students With
This Diagnosis?   303

What Other Student Exceptionalities Am I Likely to Encounter?   304

Sensory Integration Dysfunction: What Is It and How Can I Help Students Who Have This
Diagnosis?   305

Scenario 3 Jimmy   305

Bipolar Disorder: What Is It and How Can I Help Students Who Have
This Diagnosis?   306

Oppositional Defiant Disorder: What Is It and How Can I Help Students
Who Have This Diagnosis?   307

Autism Spectrum Disorder: What Is It and How Can I Help Students
Who Have This Diagnosis?   308

Scenario 4 Tay   308

Fetal Alcohol Spectrum Disorder: What Is It and How Can I Help Students Who Have This Diagnosis?   309

Scenario 5 Sam   310

Brain Injuries: What Are They?   310

Rage: How Can I Recognize and Respond to It?   310

Scenario 6 Michael   313

What Are Some Specific Suggestions for Preventing Misbehavior Among Students With Special Needs?   313

What Are Suggested Ways of Redirecting Misbehavior?   314

Scenario 7 Abraham   315

Reflecting on Teaching Students With Learning and Behavioral Differences: What You Have Learned in This Chapter   317

14   Striving for Personal Excellence in Classroom Management   318

Identifying Themes in Action: Two Illustrative Management Plans   321

Example 1. An Approach That Emphasizes Rules and Consequences   321

Example 2: An Approach That Combines Prevention of Misbehavior and Cooperation Between Teacher and Students   325

End Word   330

Glossary   331

References   339

Name Index   345

Subject Index   346

1

The Teacher's Role in Managing the Classroom

As You Develop Your Management Skills, It's Important for You to Consider How Your Approach and Your Decisions Will Impact the Way Your Classroom Operates

LEARNING OUTCOMES:

1-1 Identify the main objectives of a classroom management system, consider the questions and sorts of information that you'll need to develop an effective classroom management system, and articulate ideas/strategies that move you toward your goal.

1-2 Explain why classroom management is important and why implementing an effective classroom management system is complex.

1-3 Articulate teachers' professional obligations with regard to classroom management.

1-4 Discuss the importance of effective communication in a classroom management system and make recommendations for how teachers can use communication to support their management goals.

CLASSROOM DISCIPLINE VERSUS CLASSROOM MANAGEMENT

Through much of the history of education, the term "discipline" was used to describe what teachers did to make students behave themselves in school. Frequently, teachers used two tactics: (1) Teachers would tell students what to do and what not to do; and (2) teachers would punish students who failed to comply with those directives. In that approach, misbehavior and discipline were largely treated as crime and punishment (Bear, 2015).

This historical approach might best be called "coercive discipline." As you might expect, the use of coercion in classrooms wasn't really very effective, so teachers began to modify their practices to avoid it (Brophy, 2010). For the most part, the way teachers approach classroom behavior has evolved considerably (thank goodness!). Coercive discipline, though still present in modern schools and classrooms, has generally been replaced by a different and better-considered approach—one in which teachers use organization, communication, and personal influence to foster and support proper behavior.

Interestingly, some researchers have asserted that we are moving backward in this area, and that some current management practices reflect a return to coercive discipline, treating behavior management as a form of "crime control." For further reading, refer to Hirschfield (2008).

Teachers invested in managing their classrooms without use of coercion carefully analyze student behavior (and especially misbehavior) to determine, as far as possible, its roots; teachers then take steps, often in negotiation with their students, to bring about a change in behavior. In fact, the term "discipline" is more appropriately replaced with the more inclusive term "classroom management"; teachers do far more than just disciplining students as they attend to setting up their classes in ways that facilitate student growth and learning.

Broadly speaking, classroom management reflects the ways in which teachers help students understand expected behaviors and comply with those expectations so that academic learning can take place; in many cases, the definition expands to include how teachers help students develop self-management and social-emotional competence (Bear, 2015). Classroom management is, without question, a form of teaching—the teacher helps the students understand the benefits of good behavior and provides a structure that encourages them to work and learn effectively. Classroom management is not about "making" students behave. It is about teaching them how to behave properly and influencing them to do so in a kind and positive manner.

WHERE ARE WE GOING FROM HERE AND HOW WILL WE GET THERE?

Are you nervous about what student behavior will look like in your classroom, and about how you'll manage and teach a large group of young people? If you are, it's understandable. Effective classroom management is considered by many educators to be the foundation of an effective learning environment—it makes all other aspects of teaching and learning possible. Fortunately, classroom management is a skill that can be enhanced through study and through practice, and student behavior can be improved through the use of carefully considered strategies and decisions. That's where this book comes in. As you work through its pages, you'll explore your own fundamental beliefs about how classrooms should operate, and you'll pick up many insights about how to ensure that your own classroom is a cooperative learning environment where behavior problems are few and student engagement is high.

The chapters that follow provide a great deal of information on classroom management approaches and experts who have developed them. You will almost certainly find much of the information enlightening and useful; you may find some of it challenging, or incongruous with your own personal belief system. As you read, you will begin to formalize your own personal system of management, one that is carefully attuned to your preferences and to the traits, realities, and needs of the students you teach.

Fundamental Questions in Managing the Classroom

When you begin thinking about classroom management, it can be surprising to realize that all the teachers you've had in your life have spent some amount of time considering how best to manage behavior and encourage learning. Classroom management can sometimes be "invisible" to students; in other words, it's such an expected and frequent part of classroom interactions that students often don't even realize the amount of time, thought, and preparation that go into encouraging and maintaining appropriate student behavior.

As you read this text, you'll begin to develop answers to some fundamental questions about classroom management.

- What is the purpose of classroom management?
- What does effective management require of me legally, professionally, and ethically?
- What attitude/approach toward classroom management will serve me best?
- What kinds of behavior should I expect of students?
- What is classroom misbehavior?
- Why does misbehavior happen, and how does it affect teaching and learning?
- What are the most effective things I can do to prevent or reduce the likelihood of misbehavior?
- What are the most effective things I can do to redirect misbehavior humanely and effectively?
- What are the most effective things I can do to support proper behavior and social-emotional growth in my classes?

Interestingly, your answers to these questions are likely to evolve throughout your career. As you gain experience, you'll realize that many factors influence the way you respond to each question. Your answers will be influenced by the ages and personalities of the students you teach, the location and demographic makeup of your school and classroom, the standards you're expected to help your students meet, the administrative leaders with whom you work, and many other factors.

The upcoming chapters will help you explore these fundamental questions and begin to develop your own answers to them. We will look at the questions from various points of view and will examine information and advice from experts in the field of classroom management. You'll find a wide array of belief systems covered in this book; keep in mind that some of the recommendations you'll see in later chapters may be in conflict with your own core belief systems and even with the advice given by other classroom management theorists and experts. It will be important for you to carefully consider your own belief systems and your teaching/school context as you decide upon your answers to the fundamental questions; remember, even if you encounter ideas in this book with which you vehemently disagree, you will be a better manager for having considered each one and actively decided whether or not to embrace it.

LET'S EXAMINE A PLANNING GUIDE FOR BUILDING A PERSONALIZED SYSTEM OF CLASSROOM MANAGEMENT

Like all teachers, you will need a system of management that works well for you and your students. You may find that you whole-heartedly embrace a ready-made approach provided by one of the various authorities in classroom management. It's more likely, though, that you will find that no single approach fully meets your particular needs and the needs of your students.

If you don't find an existing system that suits you well, you can construct one for yourself, using pieces of other models or developing your own strategies. This book provides guidance for you in the form of a planning guide, which you will soon see. Chapters in this book contain the information you need for completing the guide. You are certain to find many suggestions in later chapters that resonate with you, as well as some that don't. The guide presented here will help you select, modify, and reorganize tactics to bring everything in line with your students' needs, your belief systems, and your school's expectations and policies.

It is strongly advised that you keep a journal, either electronic or in paper form, as you develop your planning guide. Make journal headings that correspond to the topics in the guide. Allow space for notes. When you encounter appealing information related to the various topics, jot notes underneath the appropriate heading. When you have completed your studies, your journal will contain the information you need for articulating a personalized system of discipline. Then, you only have to organize that information as guided by the questions in the planning document.

The Guide and Its Contents

Here are several topics you will want to consider when formulating a personalized approach to classroom management. The remainder of the book will provide what you need for completing this task. As you proceed through the chapters that follow, please refer to this guide and make notes in your journal as you consider these elements.

Topic 1: My Philosophy of Classroom Management
- What is my definition of classroom management?
- How do I want my classroom to look and feel, behaviorally speaking? What aspects of classroom functioning are most important to me?
- What are my main responsibilities in classroom management?
- What are my students' main responsibilities with regard to behavior and classroom management?

Topic 2: My Theory of Classroom Management

- What are the necessary components of a classroom management system?
- What is the purpose of each component?

Topic 3. The Professional and Ethical Demeanor I Will Display

- How will I comply with the legal, professional, and ethical obligations associated with classroom management?
- What will I do to establish positive relations and develop trust with my students, my colleagues, and my students' caregivers?

Topic 4. The Kind of Behavior I Will Promote and the Rules That Support It

- What behaviors, generally speaking, will I promote in my classes?
- What specific rules, if any, will I use to guide student behavior?
- What procedures (routines) do I want to use to manage the complexity of the school day?

Topic 5. What I Will Do Proactively to Prevent or Reduce Misbehavior

- What steps will I take to prevent or limit the known causes of misbehavior that might otherwise influence my classes?

Topic 6. How I Will Support My Students' Efforts to Participate and Persevere

- How will I speak with and interact with my students?
- How will I make sure students know what they are expected to do?
- What types of activities will I emphasize in teaching?
- How will I engage students actively when I am providing instruction?
- How will I monitor and help students when they are doing independent work?
- How will I use my personal charisma to influence behavior?
- How will I use my body language to influence behavior?
- How will I influence students to do high-quality work?

Topic 7. How I Will Redirect Students When They Misbehave

- How will I use influence and positive tactics that preserve students' personal dignity?
- How will I stop misbehavior and help students return willingly to appropriate behavior?
- How will I deal with minor misbehavior such as talking or distracting others?
- How will I deal with more problematic behavior such as disrespect and apathy?
- How will I deal with students' refusal to comply with directions or do acceptable work?

Topic 8. How and When I Will Communicate My Classroom Management Approach to Students, Administrators, and Students' Caregivers
- How and when will I explain my classroom management plan to students?
- How and when will I communicate my classroom management plan to my administrator(s)?
- How will I seek administrative support?
- How and when will I communicate my plan to students' caregivers?
- How will I request support from my students' families/caregivers?

CLASSROOM MANAGEMENT IS COMPLEX: FIVE REALITIES

Classrooms are complex places. Teachers not only have to teach content and skills; they must also monitor student understanding, evaluate progress, provide feedback, and reteach when students haven't met the desired outcome. They must identify and meet students' various learning and social needs. Further, they must work to meet the expectations of their local school administrators; comply with local, state, and federal policies; and communicate effectively with students, colleagues, community members, and others. And in the midst of all these responsibilities (and others!), teachers must actively work to prevent misbehavior and to manage it when it occurs. No wonder teaching is so challenging.

Good news: Many students behave civilly most of the time. Bad news: Some do not, and those that don't can have significant negative effects on both teachers (think stress) and on other students (think distraction). In preparing to address the needs of both types of students, your first step is to acknowledge some important realities of classroom management. As we proceed through this text, you will decide how best to address them.

Reality Number One

All students misbehave at one time or another; the frequency and severity of occurrence can vary markedly among individuals, groups, and classrooms.

Before entering the teaching profession, many educationally minded people develop a mental image of what it will be like when they have their own classrooms. Commonly, these fantasies involve images of excited, engaged students; creative activities; delighted administrators and caregivers; and NO behavior problems. It's important for you to know, though, that even the very best classroom managers still encounter students who misbehave; there's no way to completely avoid management challenges in the classroom.

The reality is that while many students behave appropriately most of the time, every student is likely to have a bad moment, a bad day, or a bad week while they're in school. They are, after all, human beings, with the same sorts of quirks, flaws, and foibles that are common to all of us. And sadly, a few students are going to misbehave so frequently and/or severely that they negatively affect themselves, their classmates, their teachers, their parents, and the society that depends on their education as citizens. Teachers do well to acknowledge the reality that student behavior is likely to present mild to severe disruption throughout their careers. With careful thought, consistency, and planning, however, the scope and frequency of disruptive behaviors can be lessened.

Reality Number Two

To be successful in teaching, teachers must learn how to promote responsible behavior in the classroom.
You should be committed to figuring out, through a combination of study and experience, how to guide and support students so they behave productively, civilly, and considerately, even when they may not want to. Until teachers have developed classroom management skills, they will never teach to their full potential, and even students who want to learn in their classes will have difficulty doing so.

Reality Number Three

Fostering responsible behavior is likely to be the greatest challenge you will face in teaching.
Ultimately, your success and the well-being of your students depend on your ability to manage the classroom. The most creative, engaging lessons are generally doomed to failure unless they are delivered in an environment that ensures students know what to do and how to do it and in which cooperative, respectful interaction is expected, encouraged, and insisted upon. Unless you have exceptional natural talents, you will find that it takes work to develop the skills that promote good classroom behavior. This book presents you with many classroom management strategies that you can use as you develop a system that works for you.

Reality Number Four

Students who develop responsible behavior have a great advantage in life.
Most people cannot come close to realizing their potential unless they conduct themselves responsibly. Though some people admittedly would prefer it otherwise, conforming to basic societal expectations for the way we behave can smooth the path for us in school, in our work, and in our relationships with others. Individuals who recognize the need to cooperate, communicate effectively, and exert self-control are often those whom other people want to be around; the life lessons students learn as they internalize appropriate classroom behavior can be instrumental as they build a foundation for successful adult interaction.

Reality Number Five

You have to teach many students how to behave responsibly.
You actually have to teach your students, to varying degrees, how to behave, how to be successful, and even how to be likeable, all of which are very important if

they are to enjoy quality lives. With regard to learning appropriate behavior, some students receive the help they need only in school, with little support from home or community. When we talk to teachers these days, we hear that they frequently encounter students who haven't had the benefit of consistent behavior management in their home lives and who are not skilled at self-management; when this is the case, teachers can find classroom management highly challenging. Fortunately, we, and the teachers we've spoken with, have, through patient and consistent teaching, been largely successful in helping students learn to meet classroom behavioral expectations. So, even if your students don't start out knowing how and why they should behave appropriately in your class, they can develop both motivation and skills, ultimately ending up as well-behaved, cooperative, pleasant students. Even though leading them in this direction can be challenging (and at times frustrating), isn't it exciting to think that you can help them build such an important skill set?

WHAT ARE THE MAIN OBJECTIVES OF CLASSROOM MANAGEMENT?

Now that you have an idea of where you're heading with regard to learning about classroom management, let's talk about why we need and want effective classroom management in the first place.

Here are the outcomes teachers and administrators generally expect from effectively implemented classroom management systems:

Can you think of other objectives? Make a note in your planning guide.

- First and foremost, effective classroom management maintains a safe and positive environment in which high-quality teaching and learning can occur.
- Second, effective classroom management promotes civility and responsible behavior in classroom interactions.
- Third, effective classroom management helps students develop and use inner motivation and ongoing self-control.

Because you are expected to use effective classroom management for these three purposes, you would probably like to know how to prepare yourself to do so. As luck would have it, a plan for you lies just ahead in the next section of this chapter. It provides a picture of what skilled teachers do to establish and maintain an engaged, well-managed learning environment.

What Can I Do to Provide a Safe, Civil, Productive Learning Environment?

If our goal were to give you a complete list of things teachers can do to set a positive and productive classroom tone, this book would be ridiculously long. There's no way to list all the strategies that teachers use to create an effective learning environment, so we're not going to try. We will, however, give you some general suggestions to direct your thoughts toward the sorts of considerations teachers make when setting up a management system; we'll take you through *some* of the facets of building a healthy classroom environment, knowing that you'll think of others and that you will continue to develop your thinking over the years of your career.

Teachers can provide a high-quality learning environment for students by demonstrating effective class leadership and by being in charge democratically. Sometimes teachers jokingly refer to themselves as "benevolent dictators"—while they ultimately are responsible for how the class feels and functions, they prefer to engage students in ways that are compassionate and considerate, sharing responsibility and decision making to the extent that it's possible and practical to do so. Embracing your role as the leader doesn't mean you're power hungry; it means you acknowledge that, as the teacher, you're the captain of the ship, and are responsible for the safe journeys of your crew.

Effective teachers plan and adjust their instruction in accordance with students' varied traits, needs, and motivations. As you learn more about student behavior, you'll see that in many cases, misbehavior arises from an unmet need, a special learning challenge, or a lack of knowledge or motivation. If you are sensitive to these varied characteristics among your students, you can increase their engagement and willingness to work hard in school; when students are engaged and motivated, they tend to cause fewer management problems.

Effective managers teach students to abide by class expectations and routines. Students need to know what to do, how to do it, and when to do it. Good classroom management involves not just setting expectations, but actively teaching students how to become better and better at meeting those expectations. When students fall short of expectations, effective teachers ask themselves why. Was the expectation too high from the start? Do students need more instruction to be able to meet it? Do students understand the purpose of the expectation? One of the wonderful things about classroom management is that it engages teachers in solving puzzles; each day teachers have the opportunity to figure out what strategy—instructional, behavioral, or otherwise—will lead students to the desired outcome.

Effective teachers establish and maintain effective communication with and among students. Interpersonal connections are key in classroom management. Teachers who communicate clearly and sensitively are more likely to find that their students are more responsive to their expectations; teachers who help their students learn to communicate effectively with their classmates will likely move the entire group toward better behavior.

Effective teachers provide engaging instruction and interact with students in helpful ways. When students are interested in the material and activities in which they're engaged, they are less likely to be disruptive or off-task, so strong instructional planning is key to effective classroom management. And when teachers provide support and assistance to guide students over difficult spots, students develop an understanding that challenges are a normal part of the learning process. They also come to understand that the teacher will be there to assist them as they navigate the rough spots.

Being an effective classroom manager means monitoring student work frequently and effectively. Monitoring student work doesn't just mean attending to students' behavior as they engage in activities and complete assignments (though that's certainly part of monitoring!). It also means that teachers are reviewing student work, thinking about how well students are grasping the knowledge and skills presented, and giving students meaningful feedback about what they can do to improve.

Teachers who ensure that their expectations for work and behavior are clear and that they are consistent in helping students meet expectations are less likely to encounter disruptive student behavior. The teacher must decide what students should know and be able to do (academically, socially, and behaviorally). Expectations should be high but attainable, and the teacher should communicate clearly the belief that the students can and will rise to meet the standards. The teacher also needs to be able to adjust expectations if the situation warrants it and if new information becomes available.

Skilled classroom managers recognize and address the identifiable causes of misbehavior. Teachers who look for underlying reasons students misbehave can often work to prevent further instances of misbehavior (instead of just reacting to misbehavior in the moment). Prevention is key, as misbehavior has a tendency to spread and grow, much like the ripples that result when someone throws a pebble into a pond. Effective classroom managers try to stop the pebble from landing in the water in the first place; doing that involves thinking about *why* students might be disruptive or noncompliant rather than just recognizing that they are.

Classroom management is a form of teaching, and effective managers provide ongoing support for proper behavior in class. They teach and reinforce positive student behavior, helping students continue to work toward growth in their behavioral and interpersonal skills. Life would be so much easier for teachers if we could just set rules, teach them once, and expect students to comply—but unfortunately, classrooms (and people in general) don't work that way. As a teacher, you'll constantly be thinking about your students' behavior and how best to shape it so that your classroom is a smoothly functioning, emotionally healthy place.

When students do misbehave, effective managers redirect the behavior humanely and compassionately, preserving students' personal dignity. Students misbehave. Even the "best" students have bad days or bad moments. Effective managers understand the very humanness of their students, and they manage behavior in ways that do not deride, shame, or embarrass their students. No one wants to lose face in front of others; good managers develop strategies for preserving students' dignity even when behavior has been disruptive, annoying, or deliberately malicious. Does that sound like a challenge? It is! But you're on the road to developing a toolkit of strategies that allow you to respond humanely and effectively when students aren't at their best.

How Can I Facilitate and Achieve Civil, Respectful, Cooperative Behavior in Class?

Again, we could provide you with a lengthy list of steps and strategies for setting the tone in your classroom, but instead, we'll describe the sorts of considerations you'll make in developing your own classroom management style.

The most direct answer to the question in this section is that you achieve civil, respectful, cooperative behavior in class by teaching it and reinforcing it, and by carefully monitoring class interactions and dynamics to identify areas in need of change. Your own personal behavior is critical in establishing an emotionally safe classroom where students view each other as members of the same team. As the leader in the classroom, you must first expect, encourage, and model civil and considerate behavior with and among all members of the class and school community. What you do matters. Students will notice the ways in which you engage with others, and they'll make decisions about how effective your strategies are. If you're sensitive to the way your interactions unfold, you can provide students with one of the strongest possible models for effective behavior.

Maintaining a positive tone in the classroom means eliminating bullying, verbal put-downs, and social stereotyping. Easier said than done, we know, but this goal *can* be achieved if the teacher is committed to it. As you think about the ways in which you'll build cooperation and trust in your classes, it's important not only to think about what behavior is desired, but about how you'll react when a student doesn't meet that expectation; difficult or unpleasant interpersonal interactions can engender very strong emotion (both in your students and in you!), and you'll want to have made plans in advance about how to manage your own emotional responses when helping students manage theirs.

A positive classroom tone is quite often the outcome when the teacher fosters a sense of community in the classroom, emphasizing positive interaction and cooperation. So many aspects of schooling and society are competitive, and while competition certainly has its place, effective managers are committed to having their students view classroom interactions from a win-win (cooperative) viewpoint. Ideally, students will see any individual's progress as a positive outcome for all members of the group; at the very least, effective managers hope that students will support one another's efforts and respect each other's individual characteristics and skills. And while facilitating mature interpersonal behavior can be challenging, you will likely come to find that most students *want* to be part of a community and to be accepted; this basic human desire is one upon which you can build your classroom framework.

To reiterate, effective teachers continually model and reinforce the behavior they expect students to display. Your own interpersonal skills can have a profound impact on the tone in your classroom. Do you engage with students in positive and productive ways? Do they see you interacting professionally and positively with your colleagues? Do you show them your human side, explaining when you're frazzled, apologizing if you've been inconsiderate, and rolling with the punches when things don't go your way? Are you continually trying to improve and grow your own skill set? The model you set is key to their growth, as interpersonal and behavioral skills are learned both directly (through your expectation, teaching, and reinforcement) and indirectly (through your everyday modeling).

How Can I Promote, Among My Students, a Sense of Personal Responsibility for Learning and Behaving Acceptably?

You might have heard an angry child respond to a parent's direction by saying, "I'll do it because I want to, not because you told me to." We believe that this sort of response reflects the individual's desire to have as much autonomy as possible; let's face it, most of us would much rather *choose* to do something than be *required* to do something. In this text, you'll learn more about how human needs and wants influence behavior; for now, though, let's think about how you as the teacher can guide your students to *choose* to behave responsibly and to engage in learning.

Teachers can promote a sense of personal responsibility among students for learning and behaving acceptably by exploring with students the relationships and requirements of freedom, choice, and responsibility, and by providing developmentally appropriate opportunities for students to exercise choice and demonstrate responsibility. As students move through various phases of development, their ability to understand the nuances of choice and responsibility deepens, but even young children can understand that with choice comes responsibility. Effective classroom managers give students the opportunity to demonstrate responsibility with their choices. With a kindergartner, for instance, you might structure your learning centers in ways that let students choose the order in which to complete them; you might also, though, set the expectations that students will complete a certain number of activities by a certain deadline and that there can only be four children at any given center at one time. Students won't naturally know how to exercise their choice and behave responsibly; the teacher must teach the students how to make their choices and how to make sure they're fulfilling the obligations and responsibilities that accompany the choice.

These same core teacher behaviors are important regardless of the age of the students involved; as middle school students divvy up roles in a group project, choice and responsibility will be important to a successful outcome; as high school students settle on plans for their senior projects, they will be required to balance choices with responsibilities. In each case, the effective teacher helps the student identify, as is developmentally appropriate, the potential outcomes of the choice and the responsibilities associated with it. In the case of classroom management, your role will be one of helping students understand their range of choices, the possible outcomes (both positive and negative), and what it will take in terms of responsibility to achieve the outcome they desire.

It may sound a bit mushy, but effective managers play an important role in guiding students as they reflect on how to become the person they want to be. Complex factors are at play in this decision: Motivation and interest contribute to the outcome, as do goal-setting and self-management. Teachers can help students set short-term and long-term goals (behavioral and otherwise) and move toward them. And effective teachers help students understand not only the choices before them, but the potential outcomes of each one, and what to do if obstacles arise along the way.

And finally, effective teachers set up their management systems so that students gain experience, commensurate with their maturity, in making decisions and foreseeing and facing consequences. Teachers actively structure experiences so students evaluate their options ("What if I choose to hit Nick instead of to sit down?") and to think through what result might occur with each possibility. Teachers often, but not always, are the catalyst for behavioral consequences. In other words, sometimes the consequence of hitting Nick is that Nick hits back, but at other times, the teacher intervenes with or arranges for a consequence. In either case, effective teachers work to help students see how the consequence relates to the initiating behavior, and then to consider how they might choose differently next time to achieve a different outcome.

WHAT IS THE LEGAL BASIS FOR CLASSROOM MANAGEMENT?

Classroom management is not just something teachers *choose* to do; it has long been identified as critical to the educational process. In *Goss v. Lopez*, a U.S. Supreme Court case that was considered in 1975, Justice Byron White wrote in the decision that if learning is to occur in schools, teachers must be given the ability to manage student behavior. At the same time, teachers and schools are charged with protecting students' rights (Yell, Rozalski, & Miller, 2015). As you develop your classroom management system, you'll want to keep the notions of teacher obligations and student rights in mind.

You might be interested to know (or be reminded) that education is not considered a fundamental Constitutional right; in fact, while the federal government does influence how students are educated, it does not identify or regulate the ways in which U.S. citizens are educated. Rather, the states themselves are charged with setting policies regarding how they will provide for the education of their citizenry. States put policies, procedures, and expectations in place for their schools and teachers; state personnel work to ensure that schools and teachers are in compliance with these guidelines.

Yell, Rozalski, and Miller (2015) point out that, in general, behavior management systems are largely considered by the courts to be necessary (and thus likely to be upheld in cases of dispute) as long as they "serve a legitimate educational purpose, do not conflict with federal or state law, do not abridge a student's Constitutional rights, and are not discriminatory" (p. 439).[*] That statement is probably a relief to you. It's common these days to hear about lawsuits filed against schools and teachers. However, as long as your classroom management decisions and actions are consistent with the description in the last paragraph, and you can defend them as reasonable and purposeful, you're likely to find yourself supported by the courts should a question about your system arise.

That being said, in order to make sure that your system *is* reasonable and complies with state and federal expectations, you're going to need to be informed

---

[*]From Classroom Management and the Law in *Handbook of Classroom Management*, chapter 22, by Mitchell L. Yell, Michael Rozalski, and Jason Miller. © Published by Routledge.

and to constantly reflect on why you're making the decisions you're making, whether they are reasonable, whether they respect students' rights, and whether they are nondiscriminatory in nature.

WHAT ARE SCHOOLS' OBLIGATIONS TO STUDENTS?

In the United States and many other countries, schools by law and common agreement have the obligation to provide students with the opportunity for a free or low-cost well-rounded education, as well as with curriculum, instruction, and materials that enable them to acquire the knowledge and skills necessary for success in today's world. Further, schools are expected to provide a safe and supportive environment for learning, led by well-trained teachers, administrators, and other professional and support staff. Classroom management is often one part of these expectations, with some interventions being endorsed or forbidden at the state level. For instance, school personnel in many states are restricted in the use of seclusion, restraint, and corporal punishment; many states have instituted schoolwide zero tolerance policies that identify quick and decisive actions to be taken if a student exhibits a behavior of high risk or concern (Yell, Rozalski, & Miller, 2015). Though digging deeply into the myriad legal expectations of schools and teachers is beyond the scope of this book, keep in mind that the management of your individual classroom occurs in a broader context; without doubt, you will become very familiar with the expectations of local, state, and national constituents during your educational career, as you will have little choice but to abide by them.

WHAT ARE MY OBLIGATIONS TO STUDENTS?

Undoubtedly you have some ideas about what behaviors are expected of teachers; after all, you yourself have been a student for years, and have probably internalized the "rules of the game" to a greater or lesser degree. That's good. But it's not enough. Teachers must be intentional in considering their own responsibilities and obligations, both legally mandated and implied; failure to pay attention to what is expected is one way to end up in potentially problematic situations—and, perhaps, on the national news!

You undoubtedly know that teachers are supposed to do certain things, and to avoid doing other things. You've probably seen stories in the news about teachers who either decided not to adhere to their obligations or who didn't stop to think about the way their own behavior might affect them and their students. Please don't let this be you. Effective teachers are reflective teachers, and they carefully consider the possible outcomes of each decision they make and each action they take. A first step in being able to reflect in this way is to make sure you know what obligations schools and teachers have to their students.

Keep in mind that teachers are expected to adhere to certain professional standards, regardless of the classroom management system they utilize. Teachers are expected to maintain a safe, secure, and supportive environment for learning, and to recognize their own roles as professionals and as role models for their students. Teachers must be committed to being sensitive to and understanding of students' personalities, backgrounds, and needs, carefully considering the role of these characteristics in the classroom environment.

It goes without saying that teachers are responsible for helping students acquire important knowledge and skills; equally important, though more difficult to concretely define, are the behaviors and attitudes that teachers should foster among their students. Teachers are expected to provide their students with engaging, meaningful, and worthwhile activities that lead students to accomplish content and skill objectives. And, of course, teachers must help students learn to behave responsibly and, ideally, to strive for excellence. Piece of cake, right?

WHAT ABOUT STUDENT OBLIGATIONS?

It has probably occurred to you that students, too, have obligations when it comes to their education; these student obligations are integrally related to teachers' classroom management approaches and decisions. We'll go more into student obligations in Chapter 2, as part of our discussion about how students themselves figure into the classroom management equation. For now, though, we're going to proceed with more specific information about what is expected of teachers, because these expectations will directly impact your design and implementation of a classroom management system.

MORE ABOUT THE LEGAL OBLIGATIONS ASSOCIATED WITH MANAGING THE CLASSROOM

Certain teacher behavior is required by law, and certain teacher behavior is prohibited by law. For example, you are legally required to exercise due diligence in overseeing students under your care. You are prohibited by law from dating students below the age of consent (and we think it's generally good advice that you not date your students at all!). Further, you must not engage in illegal activities or immoral activities that might impinge on your teaching. (Unsurprisingly, the meaning of "immoral activities" is not entirely clear in the law; check your school district handbook and follow its guidelines.)

The "Don't Ever Do THIS" List

We've been in teaching for a long time. We continue to be baffled by the decisions some teachers make. We've asked ourselves, "Do teachers really need to be told that sending naked pictures to their students is NOT a good idea?" But since it keeps happening, we decided to include a list of things you should just avoid doing, no matter what—at least that way, we can feel certain the message is out there. So, here are some things that are really bad ideas:

Having sex with your students, dating them, sending them explicit messages, and sending or exchanging inappropriate photos. Sometimes even being alone with a single student is risky.	Restraining students, even in jest. Don't tape them to their chairs. Don't tie them in. Don't put tape over their mouths. Remember that things meant to be funny can evolve into real problems.
Isolating students out of your sight. Don't put them in a closet, or under your desk, or anyplace where they could be at risk, get into more trouble, or be forgotten about.	Writing on your students, especially with permanent marker. Students' skin is not a substitute for paper. If you need to make sure a message gets home, figure out a different method.
Shaming your students or humiliating them, especially if they wet or soil themselves. Don't make fun of their bodies, their hair, their clothes, or any other aspect of their person.	Threatening your students or touching them in anger. Responding aggressively is not okay, no matter what the situation. (Note: Though sometimes educators have to restrain students for safety reasons, they must adhere to strict guidelines.)

Now that we have gotten that off our chests, let's get back to what you *are* supposed to do.

The basic legal requirements you must be sure to observe relate to due diligence, negligence, breach of duty, and expectations associated with *in loco parentis*. Let's look at each of these terms.

Due diligence refers to paying close and reasonable attention to students who are under your supervision. You and other school personnel must oversee students at school and take reasonable care to protect them from harm (Goorian & Brown, 2002). Though of course it seems like common sense, many teachers are unaware they are required *by law* to keep a diligent eye on students. Your mere presence around students is not sufficient. You must watch over them carefully and follow established school policies. As a teacher, you're expected to conduct yourself as would a reasonable and prudent professional in similar circumstances.

Negligence is the failure to maintain careful watch over students under your supervision. It is considered to be a serious ***breach of duty***, meaning a serious failure to comply with one of your legal obligations at school. If a student is injured emotionally or physically at school and the teacher on supervisory duty did not exercise due diligence, the teacher and school may be sued for negligence (Drye, 2000). You can protect yourself against charges of negligence and breach of duty by adhering to the following guidelines:

- Perform your assigned duties ethically and conscientiously as directed by school policy, even when those duties might seem boring or unnecessary. Avoid assuming that "nothing will happen" or that you can trust even the best-behaved students always to behave safely and responsibly.
- Be attentive in monitoring student behavior. Do not leave students unattended in your classroom, shop, or instructional area. Managing your physical proximity to students can be tricky; there are undoubtedly going to be times when you'll want to leave your group (like when you have to go to the restroom!), but you'll need to figure out supervision for them, because if something were to happen while they were unsupervised, you could be held liable.
- For activities that involve physical risk, provide thorough precautions and safety instructions before you have students undertake the activities, and then monitor closely. This may seem like a no-brainer, but you can't always anticipate the ways in which students can get into trouble.
- Be vigilant for signs that students might be inclined to harm themselves. Pay attention to what they do, say, and write. Be alert to changes in behavior. If you have concerns, speak with your administrator or school counselor.
- Be alert to any signs that a student is being bullied or otherwise abused. Follow your school guidelines in these instances. Keep in mind that teachers are mandated by law to report any suspicions of abuse (physical, verbal, sexual, neglectful). Follow your school policies in any case where you suspect a student may be a victim of abuse.
- Exercise special caution regarding physical contact with students. Don't allow yourself to be alone in the classroom with a student unless you are in plain sight of others. Many teachers simply refrain, too, from touching students; those who do touch students are careful to do it in appropriate ways. Sometimes teachers get so frustrated that they are tempted to grab or strike a student, or to intervene through other physical means; it is very difficult to justify physical contact motivated by anger, and you should avoid it at all costs. Also, make sure you never throw pencils, pens, erasers, books, desks, or chairs, no matter how strongly you are provoked; your ability to manage your own emotional reactions is critical in performing your duties acceptably and in reducing your liability in any circumstance that goes awry.

As a teacher, you will act *in loco parentis*. In loco parentis is not an allusion to crazy parents; it is a legal term that means "in place of parents." It requires you to exercise the same duty at school as do parents at home in overseeing children's safety and security. In actual practice, you should watch over students even more carefully than their caregivers may.

The doctrine of *in loco parentis* is not limited to watching over students. It also gives you and other school officials *authority over students* in matters of academics and discipline. It permits you to take many actions that a reasonable parent would take under similar circumstances. Of course, some behaviors that parents might use on their own children are *not* acceptable at school; the key is to make sure you're behaving in logical, defensible ways. If you wouldn't take an action with the student's parent (or their attorney!) present, it's probably a safe bet that you shouldn't take that action at all.

WHAT ARE MY PROFESSIONAL OBLIGATIONS?

For teachers, the term *professionalism* refers to using the fairest, most considerate, and most ethical ways of fulfilling the duties of the teaching position. Where classroom management is concerned, your primary professional obligation is to establish and maintain a safe and productive learning environment for your students. That means keeping the environment physically and emotionally safe, keeping students on task, fostering positive relationships among members of the class, and minimizing behavior that interferes with your teaching or your students' learning. Take the following suggestions seriously, and make it your goal to abide by them completely:

Professional and Ethical Behavior: You must always conduct yourself ethically, treating your students and colleagues fairly, honestly, compassionately, and supportively. You must be honest with them, but at the same time avoid, when possible, saying or doing things that hurt their feelings or stifle their desire to learn or cooperate.

Effort: You must give your genuine best effort to the profession. Your obligation is to do all you reasonably can to help students benefit from their educational experience and find satisfaction in doing so. You should give that same effort to relations with administrators, colleagues, and students' caregivers.

Teaching: You must teach in a manner that is conducive to success for every one of your students. You will want to give careful attention to selecting appropriate subject matter, providing interesting and worthwhile learning activities, relating effectively and helpfully with students, adjusting instruction to students' abilities and personalities, and insisting on considerate, humane treatment by and for everyone in the class.

Helpfulness: Always do what you can to help students, collectively and individually. Help them succeed academically. Help them relate well with others. Help them find satisfaction in school and learning. As Haim Ginott (1971) said so many years ago, always ask yourself what you can do, at a given moment, to be most helpful to your students. He referred to continual helpfulness as "teachers' hidden asset."

Respect: Cultivate and demonstrate genuine respect for your students. Treat all of them as your social equals, worthy of your time and attention. Speak with each of them in a kindly manner as often as you can. Learn their names quickly and make an effort to remember significant things about them. Show genuine approval for effort and work done well (but skip insincere or undeserved praise). Spread your attention around evenly. Avoid causing students to lose face or to feel that you've taken away their dignity. As best you can, always treat your students as you would like to be treated in similar circumstances.

Cooperation: Help your students understand that accepting each other and working together benefits everyone in the class. Emphasize that you have a plan that will help them learn and enjoy themselves. Reassure them you will be considerate of their desires and feelings. Sincerely invite them to cooperate with you and each other, and give them some responsibility in making the class enjoyable and productive. Make sure they feel part of the process.

Communication: Students need to know clearly what is expected of them. Be helpful and encouraging, and avoid preaching or moralizing. Avoid grilling students about improper behavior or otherwise putting them on the defensive. When they speak, listen attentively and try to understand where they're coming from. When you reply to them, avoid criticizing their points of view. Frame your comments so that students recognize your intent to help them be successful in school.

Charisma: Charisma is a quality of attractiveness that makes others want to be in your presence and interact with you. You acquire charisma by making yourself personally interesting and by being upbeat and pleasant, using humor appropriately. You can let your students see your charismatic side by occasionally sharing information about your interests, experiences, and talents. Charismatic people generally avoid sarcasm; even when sarcasm may be intended to be humorous, it is easily misinterpreted and can be hurtful. Let students see your most positive qualities. Think about what you would want *your* teacher to be like, and then do those things. (Unless those things mean letting you watch TV all the time and never having to do any work—don't do that, please.)

WHO ESTABLISHES PROFESSIONAL AND ETHICAL EXPECTATIONS?

Professional expectations reflect agreements that have been established over time by members of various professions. They are made specific by groups that wish to promote and maintain high standards of conduct. Over the years, various individuals, groups, and agencies have worked to codify the professional conduct expected of educators. The most widely acknowledged of those efforts was set forth in 1975 by the National Education Association (NEA). Those standards are still in place. Summarized here, they stipulate, in part, that the educator should honestly represent his or her professional qualifications, use discretion when making statements about fellow educators, take care in accepting gifts, transparently report students' progress, and help students maintain dignity. See http://www.nea.org/home/30442.htm for a complete listing of the educators' Code of Ethics.

In addition to the NEA stipulations, it is generally agreed that, as a teaching professional, you should abide by the following:

- Dress professionally, as an adult in a professional situation. Your school will undoubtedly have policies about how you are expected to dress; you'll want to know what these are and abide by them. Different schools/systems have different policies, not just about clothing, but about piercings, tattoos, jewelry, and other forms of personal expression; investigate and follow these policies.
- Use appropriate language for the educational setting, with correct speech patterns and complete avoidance of obscenities. Again, remember that you are the leader in the classroom; what you do sets the tone for your students' behavior.
- Be attentive to others and treat them with respect and courtesy. This goal can be challenging in the rapid-fire flow of the school day, but it's critical that you develop your own classroom presence in such a way that it supports, rather than undermines, your classroom management efforts.

Today, much attention is also given to professional teacher competencies as articulated by the Interstate Teacher Assessment and Support Consortium, called InTASC (2013), which has formalized 10 standards that pertain to teaching in general. The standards are grouped into four categories: (1) The Learner and Learning; (2) Content; (3) Instructional Practice, and (4) Professional Responsibility. Classroom management is particularly relevant under Category 1, but arguably affects all four categories.

For each of the standards, InTASC provides recommendations concerning the essential knowledge teachers should possess and the related performances that characterize highly effective teaching. Most recently, InTASC has added progressions to the standards; these progressions operationally define/describe the standards, give suggestions for how teachers may improve their practice, and highlight the sorts of professional development experiences that might move teachers forward in their mastery of the standards. You can view the InTASC Standards at www.ccso.org.

COMMUNICATION SKILLS: CRITICAL TO TEACHER PROFESSIONALISM

Being an effective communicator is a vital aspect of being a professional educator. In classroom management—indeed in all teaching—the ability to communicate effectively is of critical importance. It always comes into play when we want students or others to feel welcome, be receptive to us, take in new information and make sense of it, follow directions, or stop behaving in a counterproductive manner. Both verbal communication and nonverbal communication play important roles. Our effectiveness depends on *what* we say or do, *how* we say or do it, how we *look* when saying or doing it, and how we *respond* to what the other person says or does. Let's see what some well-regarded authorities have said about these aspects of teacher communication.

What Did Haim Ginott Say About Congruent Communication?

Haim Ginott (1972) was the first authority to focus heavily on improving the effectiveness of communication between teachers and students. He identified *congruency* as the most important aspect of communication. He used the term **congruent communication** to describe communication that is harmonious with students' feelings about situations and themselves. For example, when third-grader Johnny disrupts your lesson by riding the classroom broom as his pony, Ginott would have you say, "Johnny, the broom belongs in the closet, please." Ginott also urged teachers to use **sane messages** when speaking with students. By sane messages, he meant messages that address *situations* rather than students' character or past behavior. Thus, with Johnny and the broom horse, he would *not* want teachers to say, "This is the fourth time today you've disobeyed our rule."

Intervening in age-appropriate ways is important. What might change about the way you would respond if you knew Johnny were a junior in high school?

Ginott emphasized that teachers *at their best*, using congruent communication, do not preach, moralize, impose guilt, or demand promises. Instead, they confer dignity on their students by respectfully treating them as capable of making good decisions. Ginott would suggest that you respond to Johnny's behavior by saying something like, "Johnny, would you help by putting the broom back into the closet, please?"

In contrast, according to Ginott, teachers *at their worst* label students, belittle them, and denigrate their character, as in this possible response to Johnny: "Johnny, you are disturbing the class again. I've had about enough of your rudeness."

Ginott added that effective teachers invite cooperation from their students. They do so, when a problem occurs, by describing the situation and what needs to be done. Further, they use *laconic language*—short and to the point—when responding to or redirecting student misbehavior. "Johnny, the broom belongs in the closet. Thanks." They do not dictate to students or boss them around—acts that sometimes demean students and provoke resistance. Ginott also said teachers should feel free to express their concerns, even anger, but when doing so should use *I-messages* rather than *you-messages*.

- A teacher using an *I-message* might say, "I'm worried about the way this disruption is affecting our class."
- A teacher using a *you-message* might say, "Johnny, you are being rude and disruptive."

You can see that the I-message is less likely to make the student feel defensive, leaving him more open to suggestions you might make or to redirection of his behavior.

How would Ginott have us correct a student's misbehavior? He says we should simply teach the student how to behave appropriately. That might require reteaching the student two or three times or more. Even though the process might take time, it is much better than causing the student to react negatively or hostilely. Once a negative or adversarial tone has been set, management problems are more likely to escalate; the teacher's goal should be to de-escalate each situation to the greatest extent possible.

One more thing: Ginott especially urged teachers to refrain from asking *why questions* when discussing behavior—for example, "Why did you get that broom out again?" or "Why in the world can't you follow instructions?" Ginott asserted that such questions almost always make students feel guilty and put them on the defensive. Instead of asking *why* questions, simply request that the student do the appropriate action.

Commentary From an Anonymous Teacher: Why I Avoid Some Types of Questions When I Address Student Behavior

In my teacher education program, I was exposed to the idea that asking students "Why" questions about their behavior could result in power struggles. Not only do I agree with Ginott that such questions, especially when asked publicly, put students on the defensive, I also believe that many times, students, especially younger students, don't have any idea what has really led to their misbehavior. For instance, I love imagining asking a sixth-grader why he keeps ignoring the expectation that he read quietly without disturbing those around him. It's such a pointless question, because there's almost no chance that he will come up with a reasonable "real" answer—"I am not a very good reader, and it makes me uncomfortable to think that all the other students are able to read easily and fluently. So I decided that instead of struggling with the words on this page, I would find another way to amuse myself, and to get some attention from you, Teacher. I mean, negative attention is better than feeling bad about myself and my reading abilities, right?" Once you realize that there is probably some underlying reason for misbehavior, you begin to realize that questioning it is a tricky proposition.

That's not to say that I never ask my students questions about their behavior. I just do it carefully. I might say, "What do you think would make this work go better for you?" or "What is causing you and Tao to have difficulty getting along?" The key is to make sure that the questions are ones that students have a real chance at answering, and that the questions serve a purpose—moving students forward in their behavior.

What Did Stephen Covey Say About Frames of Reference?

Stephen Covey (2004) says one of the most important things he ever learned about communication was that in order to communicate well, you have to understand your listener's *frame of reference* as well as your own. The listener's frame of reference, he says, is often different from yours.

For teachers, that means being perceptive of students' deeper hopes, fears, realities, and difficulties. When you understand those things, you adjust what you wish to communicate so it aligns with the student's child or adolescent frame of reference, rather than your adult or teacher frame of reference. What the student sees as reality often differs substantially from your perception of reality; matters you consider important may be trivial in students' view. And, of course, both of those statements are also true in reverse. Covey suggests that to work well with students, you need to know not just their thoughts but what those thoughts mean in their personal existence.

Covey wrote that highly successful people attempt to understand their listeners *before* they try to make listeners understand them. As he put it:

> If I were to summarize in one sentence the single most important principle I have learned in the field of interpersonal relations, it would be this: Seek first to understand, then to be understood. This principle is the key to effective interpersonal communication. (Covey, 1989, p. 237)[*]

Covey uses the term *empathic listening* to refer to attempting to read and understand the emotions of others. He acknowledges that empathic listening

[*]From *The 7 Habits of Highly Effective People* by R. Covey © 1989. Published by Simon and Schuster.

takes time, but not nearly as much time as does having to back up and correct misunderstandings and unexpressed and unresolved problems. Students want to be understood, and you influence them much more strongly when you understand them.

What Did William Glasser Say About Seven Connecting Habits?

Renowned psychiatrist and educational authority William Glasser (2001) put great emphasis on communication between teachers and students. He identified seven deadly habits that inhibit teachers' ability to establish optimal relationships with students. The deadly habits are *criticizing, blaming, complaining, nagging, threatening, punishing*, and *rewarding students to control them*. He said that if teachers are to establish and maintain good relationships with students and gain their willing cooperation, they must eliminate these deadly habits.

Glasser contends that as teachers stop using the seven deadly habits, their relationships with students will begin to improve. The improvement continues further when teachers replace the deadly habits with *seven connecting habits*, which Glasser identifies as *caring, listening, supporting, contributing, encouraging, trusting*, and *befriending*. Glasser believes—and the success of his Quality Schools supports his conviction—that all students who come to school can do competent work. In order to ensure acceptable competence, teachers must connect strongly with their students. This means you use the seven connecting habits and *give up* trying to use external controls to make students behave.

Glasser makes his point by describing how we relate to friends (and he does indeed urge teachers to befriend their students). He notes that we do not criticize, blame, or speak harshly to our friends. Rather, we use connecting habits when relating with them.

Please take a moment at this point to do the following, preferably with a partner:

For each of the following, think of a specific example in a realistic situation. Then indicate what you might say instead, using a connecting habit.

Give an example of <u>criticizing</u> . . . what might you say instead?

Give an example of <u>blaming</u> . . . what might you say instead?

Give an example of <u>complaining</u> . . . what might you say instead?

Give an example of <u>nagging</u> . . . what might you say instead?

Give an example of <u>threatening</u> . . . what might you say instead?

Give an example of <u>punishing</u> . . . what might you do instead?

Give an example of <u>rewarding students to control them</u> . . . what might you do instead?

What Did Fred Jones Say About Nonverbal Communication?

Fred Jones (2007a), a widely followed psychologist and expert in teaching and discipline, believes nonverbal communication—which he refers to as *body language*—is even more effective than verbal statements in promoting good behavior in the classroom. He puts special emphasis on eye contact, physical proximity, body carriage, and facial expressions, as follows:

Eye Contact: Suppose Miss Remy is explaining the process of doing a complex mathematical proof. She sees Jacobo has stopped paying attention. She pauses. The sudden quiet causes Jacobo to look at Miss Remy and discover that she is looking directly at him. He straightens up and waits attentively. Jones says few physical acts are more effective than eye contact for conveying the impression of being in control. He adds that turning and pointing the eyes and the feet toward students who disengage or disrupt shows teacher commitment to discipline.

Physical Proximity: Miss Remy has finished her demonstration and has directed students to complete some exercises on their own. After a time, she sees from the back of the room that Jacobo has stopped working and has begun talking to Jerry. She moves toward him. When Jacobo senses her presence, he immediately gets back to work, without Miss Remy having to say anything. Jones emphasizes that teachers who use physical proximity rarely need to say anything to the offending students to get them to behave appropriately. In many cases, a teacher can move close to students without interrupting the lesson itself; proximity, like eye contact, is a very powerful strategy.

Body Carriage: Jones also concluded that posture and body carriage are effective in communicating authority. Good posture and confident carriage suggest strong leadership, whereas a drooping posture and lethargic movements suggest resignation or fearfulness. Students read body language and are able to tell whether the teacher is feeling in charge or is tired, disinterested, or intimidated. Teachers should be mindful of what their body language communicates, and use their physical presence to their advantage. For instance, if you're talking with a student in hopes of resolving a behavioral issue, sitting or squatting near their desk may reduce the feeling that you're towering over them in an authoritarian style; they may be more receptive to your message if you approach them on a more-or-less even level.

Facial Expressions: Teachers' facial expressions communicate a great deal. They can show enthusiasm, seriousness, enjoyment, and appreciation, all of which encourage good behavior; or they can reveal boredom, annoyance, and resignation, which may prompt lethargy or misbehavior among students.

Facial expressions such as winks and smiles demonstrate a sense of humor and personal connection, traits students appreciate in teachers.

Commentary From Anonymous Teacher 1

I am an elementary teacher with 18 years of experience in grades 2, 3, and 5. I prepared for teaching at a large reputable university and later earned a master's degree there.

I was asked if, during my training and graduate studies, I had heard of, or had experience with, any of the teachings of Ginott, Covey, Glasser, or Jones. I'm not absolutely certain, but I don't remember ever hearing or reading about Ginott, Covey, or Glasser, although I realize now they are widely recognized. A few years ago, I attended an in-service workshop directed by Dr. Jones. He influenced me a great deal and I now regularly use his suggestions on eye contact, physical proximity, and facial expressions to help my students stay on task and conduct themselves properly. For me, Jones's nonverbal tactics work about 90% of the time.

Source: Used courtesy of Timothy C. Charles.

You're probably beginning to see, by our emphasis on it in this chapter, that we believe that teachers can and should think carefully about the ways in which they communicate with students, colleagues, and all members of the school community. Your communication skills can augment your professionalism, or they can detract from it. Communicating clearly, respectfully, and well is, we would argue, as much a professional obligation as is providing effective supervision.

Classroom Management in the Big Picture

Classroom management doesn't occur in a vacuum, despite our focus on it in this book. It's critical that you understand that in practice, it's virtually impossible to think of classroom management without thinking of lesson planning, instructional delivery, assessment, school context, and other elements of the school experience. Further, classroom management is affected by many other factors that, while *related* to the classroom experience, are more appropriately described as coming beyond a teacher's personal control. The way we manage classrooms can be affected by local, state, national, and international trends and issues. Think about it—the way schools work, and ultimately the way students and teachers function in the classroom, can be strongly affected by

- decisions made by federal, state, and local policymakers, such as
  - funding and defunding of school programming and initiatives
  - decisions about teacher pay
  - accountability and testing requirements

- local and state curricular decisions
- zero tolerance disciplinary policies

■ societal trends and issues such as

- harsh, inconsistent, or lackadaisical parenting
- gender, sexuality, and identity considerations among students
- diversity, equity, and poverty issues
- drug and alcohol use and abuse among students and families
- mental health concerns and suicidality among students
- family trends (divorce, dysfunction, homelessness)
- community and family violence, child abuse, and neglect
- technology access and use
- media violence
- bullying and cyberbullying

If you spend some time thinking about it, you can probably come up with other factors that either directly or indirectly affect the ways schools operate and the ways in which teachers and schools work to manage student behavior and learning. Although a thorough discussion of each of these issues is beyond what we're able to cover in this book, it's important to keep in mind as you read that the way you and your students move forward together is a function not just of your own planning, but of how you consider and respond to the particular mix of trends and issues that affect you and your students at any given time. You'll want to remember that trends and issues ebb and flow, and what works with one student or one class may not work for another student or another class; when that happens, you'll want to spend some time reflecting on which *outside* factors might be contributing to management challenges, which *school* and *classroom* factors might be contributing to management challenges, and which *individual* factors (for students *and* for you as the teacher) might be having an impact on how your management system is working.

REFLECTING ON YOUR ROLE AS A TEACHER OR FUTURE TEACHER: WHAT YOU HAVE LEARNED IN THIS CHAPTER

In this chapter, you learned how your own behaviors, obligations, and responsibilities are likely to affect the way you manage your classroom. We introduced you to the notion that teachers absolutely must think carefully and critically about how they are going to manage their classrooms and promote positive, civil behavior among students, and we gave you some information to get you thinking in that direction. (Much, much more is coming in later chapters in this text!) We gave you some questions that should guide you as you read the rest of the text and as you begin shaping your own classroom management system. We encouraged you to be mindful of your professional and legal obligations, and to consider your own style of communication and how it might help or hinder your classroom management efforts. We pointed out that effective managers are constantly reflecting, not only about their in-class experiences, but about what factors (individual, school, and societal) might affect some or all of their classroom management experiences and decisions.

Roadmap for Advanced Learning

Do some independent reading on the topics below, each of which directly relates to classroom management:

Zero Tolerance Policies: How do consistent and severe consequences affect student success?

Testing and Accountability Procedures: What impact does frequent high-stakes testing have on the way teachers teach their students and manage their classrooms?

Mental Health Challenges Among Children and Adolescents: How do teachers respond effectively when working with students with behavioral/emotional health issues?

Meeting the Needs of LGBTQI Students: What do classroom teachers need to know to support these students in the classroom?

MyLab Education **Self-Check 1.1**
MyLab Education **Self-Check 1.2**
MyLab Education **Self-Check 1.3**
MyLab Education **Self-Check 1.4**
MyLab Education **Application Exercise 1.1** Identifying Guiding Questions in Action
MyLab Education **Application Exercise 1.2** Identifying Classroom Complexities
MyLab Education **Application Exercise 1.3** Thinking Like a Teacher: How Will You Handle Bullying?

2

Taking Student Diversity into Account in Classroom Management

LEARNING OUTCOMES:

2-1 Identify developmental and need-based factors that influence student behavior

2-2 Describe how students' and teachers' sociocultural contexts affect classroom learning and behavior

As we indicated in Chapter 1, educators now generally endorse the idea that it is very difficult to promote desirable behavior in today's students by using criticism, admonishment, or punishment. They realize that they have a better chance of getting the results they want by using "influence tactics" that are positive and helpful. Such tactics attract students, encourage cooperation, and make learning more enjoyable. Some of the tactics activate students' internal inclination to do what they know is right. You will encounter many such tactics as you proceed through this book.

Reading about these approaches is of limited value unless you understand and master their application. It will be important to grasp the ideas, understand their purposes, and become comfortable with them. When possible, discuss the approaches with others and practice applying them in realistic situations. Watch what teachers do when you visit schools and classrooms. Think about the decisions they make and the actions they take.

The strategies you will be learning also help students move toward "self-management," a term we use to describe what is happening when students voluntarily conduct themselves in ways that bring success in school. As you learned in the last chapter, teachers exert positive influence by demonstrating the behavior they expect, speaking with students in a kind and helpful manner, teaching students how to follow routines, having students practice kindness and civility, and providing feedback that is helpful rather than punitive.

You've learned about teacher obligations; we're now going to do a quick overview of student obligations. None of this will surprise you, but it can be helpful to remember that teaching and learning require action on the parts of both students and teachers.

WHAT ARE STUDENTS' OBLIGATIONS TO TEACHERS, FELLOW STUDENTS, THE COMMUNITY, AND TAXPAYERS?

Students who attend school are expected to meet many important obligations, yet they rarely think of them as such. They often look upon education as something expected of them or forced on them—something to be endured, rather than enjoyed as one of the greatest opportunities of their lives. When you speak with students about the roles they are expected to fill in class, consider stressing these points:

- Students have the obligation to make a reasonable effort to learn. They fulfill this obligation by attending classes, paying attention, cooperating with the teacher, participating considerately in class activities, and doing the assigned work.
- Students are obliged to refrain from interfering with class work or the progress of others. They must not unnecessarily disrupt the teacher or instructional activities, or interfere with other students' efforts to learn.
- Students are obliged to display acceptable behavior, which includes abiding by class rules, behaving civilly, and showing consideration for others.

When students meet these obligations, their behavior is considered appropriate, and they are almost always successful in school. When students do not meet these obligations, their behavior is considered to be misbehavior or improper behavior, and a great many of those students do poorly in school. You might wish to emphasize this point in your classes.

CAN I ANTICIPATE HOW MY STUDENTS WILL BEHAVE?

Yes. With effort, you can gain quite a good understanding of how students at various age levels in various segments of society tend to behave individually and in groups. Virtually all conscious behavior, proper or improper, has a motive behind it. Some of those motives are genetically determined and reside within us, some occur and change as part of the maturation process, some are learned, some are triggered by environmental and social situations, some are set off by emotion, and some occur because we become able to make better choices as we develop intellectually. A bit later, we will examine a number of conditions that underlie student misbehavior, but first let's review what is considered typical or "natural" behavior at different levels of development. Keep in mind that these depictions are general and do not always apply. They describe what is typical for various age groups, but at any time, a student may be ahead of or behind peers in terms of development.

Behavior in the Primary Grades (Ages 5 to 8)

Have a look at primary-grade children on the playground. They are generally full of life and eager to learn. Most of them have loving dispositions. They particularly enjoy stories, music, and rhythmic activities. They have an enormous facility in learning language, which often makes them appear intelligent beyond their years. Children at this age don't like to sit still for long—in fact, you can hardly make them do so.

And yet these students, precocious though they seem, have limited capabilities in some regards, a fact that has important implications for teachers. Between the approximate ages of 2 and 7, most function intellectually at what Swiss psychologist Jean Piaget called the *preoperational stage*, where they reason not on the basis of logic but rather on impressions obtained from their surroundings (Charles, 1974; Piaget, 1951). Piaget found that during the preoperational phase, students are poor at remembering the order of events, understanding rules, explaining cause–effect relationships, comprehending number relationships, and understanding other speakers accurately, including their teachers. Socially, they get along reasonably well with each other, although they often squabble. They tire easily, get fussy, and require frequent rest. They make little distinction between work and play.

From birth to approximately age 2, children are in what Piaget called the *sensorimotor period*, in which learning occurs through sensory and motor interaction within their environments.

An important change occurs in children at around age 7, give or take a year or so. They move into an intellectual stage Piaget called *concrete operations*, where brain development enables them to begin understanding concepts that they interpreted differently only weeks earlier. Importantly, they become able to consider the relationship of parts to a whole and to reason in terms of cause and effect. Where previously they reasoned and explained on the basis of appearances or intuition (e.g., "The sun moves because the wind blows it along"), they can now understand number relationships and many concepts in science, such as the cause of day and night.

Socially, they are learning to play well together. By second grade, they are enjoying games such as tag and hide-and-seek. They like puzzles, riddles, and guessing games. Although able to learn rules for games, they are not so good at following them. They typically accept adult authority with little question. They tell fabrications routinely but seldom in a malicious way. They are highly imitative of each other. For them, misbehavior is whatever adults don't like, and guilt is understood in terms of getting caught.

By the time they complete grade 3, students are usually well socialized to understand that raising hands, standing in lines, taking turns, and waiting patiently are expected behaviors. They continue to respond well to affection and personal attention. All through this stage, students tend to enjoy music, art, rhythms, stories, and activities that have to do with plants and animals.

Behavior in the Intermediate Grades (Ages 9 to 11)

As students move into grade 4, they become increasingly able to function independently, although they still want attention and affection from teachers. Their interest in animals and the natural world continues to be strong.

Intellectually, they continue to use concrete language and images for thinking (as indeed do many adults). Teachers need to realize that students cannot yet think by using pure abstractions. For example, they do not conceptualize negative numbers per se, such as –4, but can think of four real items being removed from a group.

Socially, these students increasingly want to share each other's company. They like group names and begin to form cliques and clubs. Their individual behavior begins to reflect peer norms. They recognize the need for rules and rule enforcement, both in games and class behavior. They like to play group games. And they are beginning to enjoy competition, provided they win. Losing, which they find difficult to accept, is a different matter; losing causes many to cry and lose their tempers.

Verbally, these students tend to be highly argumentative. Many are loud and vocally aggressive, yet increasingly they rely on reason and efforts to persuade others. No longer is teacher authority blindly accepted. Students may argue with the teacher, talk back, and be uncooperative.

Ethically, they show a growing awareness of honesty and its importance in relationships. Although most stretch the truth frequently, they see that the more a lie intends to deceive, the worse it is. Conscience is developing along with respect for others. A growing sense of right and wrong is evident.

Behavior in the Middle School Grades (Ages 12 to 14)

As adolescence begins, students move toward Piaget's *formal* operations stage. Intellectually, most students have acquired a great new power—the ability to think abstractly. Their minds work as quickly as do those of adults, although they lack adult perspective and wisdom. Students can make use of concepts such as love, hate, honesty, loyalty, negative numbers, force, speed, time, and atomic particles. They have become *metacognitive*—able to think about and actively control their thought processes. Being metacognitive means that students can figure out how to approach an assignment or how well they're understanding information that they're reading.

However, at the same time, student behavior tends to become somewhat more erratic, and teachers require great skill in order to teach well and build supportive relationships. Bodily changes worry, perplex, excite, and dismay these students. New realities associated with sex stir and baffle them. Psychological weaning from parents leaves them feeling lost and cut off. They crave adult support, yet the emerging need for independence leads to conflict with adults. These realities often act as serious distractions to school learning.

At the same time, students are becoming increasingly rebellious and disposed to probing the boundaries of rules and customs. Their awe of the teacher has waned, but has been replaced with respect and affection for teachers who show understanding and helpfulness.

Behavior in the High School Grades (Ages 15 to 18)

Before entering high school, students have developed the capacity for deeper thinking. They now show a proclivity for theorizing. They try to find a cause, a purpose, and a place for everything. They think about the *possible* as much as the *actual* and have acquired a strong concern for right and wrong. Their rational power produces the idealism that is characteristic of adolescence. Propositional thinking emerges: "If I do *x*, then *y* will result." Interest in people and society in general is growing rapidly.

Lies are now seen as anything intentionally false. Punishment must take into account factors such as intent to break a rule, age of the violator, and previous record of behavior. Many rules and laws are seen as unfair or irrelevant, so breaking them is no longer considered absolutely wrong. Socially, these students can see various groups' points of view, which they like to weigh, clarify, and evaluate against each other. They can't see why everything is not ideal—politics, institutions, human relations, and so forth—which makes them overly critical of the way institutions and people actually function. Students may scathingly reject existing social arrangements and values, but for the most part their personal behavior complies reasonably well with social norms.

As they near the end of high school, students begin to settle down emotionally. They understand themselves better and have reached a truce with their bodies and feelings. They have begun to think about what they hope to do in the future. Some, lamentably, become further alienated from the educational mainstream.

A new relationship with adults also emerges. The love–hate attitude of earlier years fades, while respect for adults grows as students recognize their own interdependence with the community. Teachers can interact with these students as fellow adults, and students see teachers as mentors and role models.

HOW DO STUDENTS' NEEDS AND HABITS AFFECT THEIR BEHAVIOR?

All people have needs that prompt them to behave in certain ways. A ***need*** is a vague condition within us that strongly and persistently urges us to seek out certain satisfactions. We cannot directly observe a need—that is why psychologists refer to needs as mental constructs, meaning imaginary "somethings" that help us explain motivation and behavior. A desire that is long-lasting, recurrent, and seemingly part of the human psychological makeup is deemed to reflect a "need." A need is a bit different from a "want," which is more societally influenced and transient. When we are unable to satisfy a need, we feel more than disappointed—we feel uneasy, distraught, or incomplete over longer periods of time.

Psychologists generally agree we have inborn **basic needs** for safety, comfort, and positive relations with others. Abraham Maslow (1954) provided the first widely acknowledged model of needs, which he depicted hierarchically. Figure 2.1 will give you an idea of Maslow's levels and some of the needs associated with each level.

For teachers, the following list of needs may be more useful than Maslow's hierarchy because it identifies what students require in order to benefit fully from their educational program. This list is drawn from ideas set forth by Rudolf Dreikurs and P. Cassel (1995), William Glasser (1998b), and C. M. Charles (2008), among others:

- *Security:* to feel safe without worry
- *Association:* to be with and interact with others
- *Belonging:* to feel a part of things, be valued, and have a place in the class
- *Dignity:* to feel respected and worthwhile
- *Hope:* to believe that experiences in school and elsewhere are worthwhile and that success is possible

Figure 2.1 ▪ Maslow's hierarchy of needs

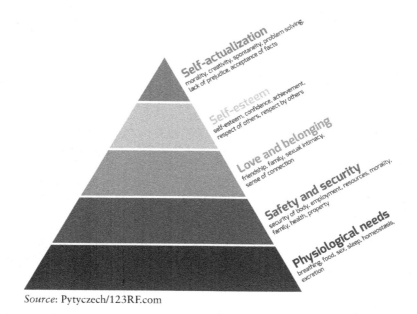

Source: Pytyczech/123RF.com

- *Power:* to have some control over and input into events in which one participates
- *Enjoyment:* to experience pleasurable emotions of anticipation, intrigue, fun, and interest
- *Competence:* to feel capable of doing many things well, including expected schoolwork

Educators can help students meet these basic needs by removing threat from learning activities and social interactions, permitting students to work together, insisting on courteous treatment of others, involving students in planning and making decisions, ensuring that learning activities and personal interactions are satisfying, and making sure students learn important information. When teachers do these things well, student behavior is less likely to be a serious problem.

Habits also play strong roles in student behavior, but they are different from needs and wants. Habits are patterns of willful behavior, ingrained through practice to the point that we repeat them without having to think. Habits are quite useful when they help us behave considerately and productively, but are harmful when they interfere with our progress or offend others. Thus, we hear the expressions "good habits" and "bad habits."

In teaching, we try to help our students establish productive habits, such as automatically sitting down and getting to work, following directions, treating others with consideration, and striving for high quality. Classrooms become efficient and relatively free from disruption when students learn to follow class routines automatically. You will hear these routines referred to as *classroom procedures*; teachers who establish and teach their procedural expectations are setting a strong foundation for their classroom management system.

What Do Students Need and Want in Their School Experience?

Now let's turn more specifically to what students need and want from their teachers and schools. When students receive these things, their behavior improves. Although preferences vary somewhat from group to group and change steadily with maturation, virtually all students want the following:

- a sense of safety and importance as a class member.
- a teacher who is friendly, interesting, helpful, and supportive.
- interesting learning activities on topics of obvious value.
- camaraderie or enjoyable association with classmates.
- opportunity for and likelihood of success and accomplishment.
- acknowledgment for what they do right and help with what they do wrong.

Provide these things and it is quite likely you will be a successful teacher.

On the other hand, many students (but not all) dislike the following, which they will avoid if they can:

- sitting still for long periods of time.
- keeping quiet for long periods of time.
- working alone.
- memorizing facts for tests.
- completing lengthy reading and writing assignments.
- doing repetitive work.
- engaging in competition when they have no chance of winning.

We suggest that you discuss these matters with your students and explain how you will, as often as possible, match classroom conditions and activities to their preferences, while keeping to a minimum those they dislike. (Remember, however, that students vary somewhat in preferences. Some students like activities such as working alone and memorizing information. They will tell you if you ask.) Effective teachers figure out how to best meet the needs and preferences of the group while also attending to the needs and preferences of individuals. Doing so is challenging, and you will likely never feel as though you've done it perfectly, but we hope you'll always work to move toward the goal.

HOW DO SOCIOCULTURAL REALITIES INFLUENCE BEHAVIOR?

You know that today's rapidly changing demographics bring together students from many different economic and cultural groups, and you undoubtedly already know that various groups of people tend to display certain values, outlooks, habits, customs, aspirations, and ways of interacting. You may also know that teachers are frequently criticized for using strategies that are not culturally neutral, but that instead reflect the values and behaviors of white, middle-class culture (Cartledge, Lo, Vincent, & Robinson-Ervin, 2015). It's important for you to become as informed as possible about sociocultural trends, and to let that knowledge inform your teaching and your management of the classroom. It's also important that you reflect regularly on the decisions you make and how they may be received by your students, and it is *critical* that you work to develop sensitivity and to avoid stereotyping students in any way.

A term that you'll likely hear frequently as you study classroom management (and teaching in general) is ***culturally responsive teaching***. Teachers who are culturally responsive recognize that their students' backgrounds and experiences may differ from their own; these teachers are committed to treating all students fairly and respectfully, embracing differences, and working to meet all students' needs (Ford & Kea, 2009). Effective classroom managers use sociocultural considerations as a way to inform their practice, merging what they know about best practices in classroom management with what they know about their students' backgrounds, home lives, interaction patterns, and experiences.

One step in becoming a culturally responsive teacher is to learn as much as you can about the traits and mannerisms of students from various backgrounds, especially backgrounds different from your own. Then you'll need to apply this information sensitively and reflectively, remembering, as is true with any group of humans, that some people will be exceptions to the "rule."

Let's take a moment to examine a few of the general differences you may encounter among your students and how these differences may play out in terms of the way you manage your classroom.

Values and Associated Behaviors: What Do Schools Emphasize?

The majority of schools and teachers in the Western world reflect values, beliefs, and behaviors that stem from the Judeo-Christian ethic, influenced by a capitalistic outlook, future orientation, and interpersonal equality. They emphasize individuality and competition over belongingness and cooperation (Cartledge & Johnson, 2004). Following are examples of such beliefs and behaviors.

- *Time orientation.* Promptness is valued; orientation is toward the future.
- *Planning ahead.* Plans are made ahead of time to serve as guides for action.
- *Relations with others.* A general sense of equality prevails; other people are to be treated with consideration and respect.
- *Personal achievement and competition.* Individuals are urged to aspire to personal achievement; it is considered good to compete and try to rise above the norm.
- *Child-to-adult relations.* Adults are shown respect but are not seen as infallible.
- *Adult-to-child relations.* Children require guidance but are not to be treated as subservient.
- *Opportunity.* Potential advancement in life is available to everyone; one has only to seize the opportunity and follow through.
- *Verbal learning.* Much learning in school is expected to occur through the verbal mechanisms of listening, reading, and discussing.
- *Success.* Success in life is seen as performing well, getting a good job, providing a good home, and acquiring a degree of wealth.
- *Personal behavior.* We are all responsible for our own behavior; most people behave ethically, and laws and regulations are to be obeyed.

As you read the list of values that have traditionally been emphasized in schools, did you find yourself agreeing with them? Arguing with them? Doing some of each? Let's look further at some of the tension points that can occur when the values system of the school doesn't coincide precisely with the values system of the teachers who work there, or the students who study there.

Areas of Conflict: How Do Group Values Differ?

Human behavior and values across all groups are far more similar than different, yet students from various cultural and economic groups may display certain values and behaviors that seem to be inconsistent with expectations in school. Sometimes those differences are misunderstood by teachers, and sometimes teacher behavior is misunderstood by students and caregivers. As a classroom teacher, you'll want to think critically about the role that differing cultural values can play in school and classroom interactions, and the effects they may have on how you need and want to manage your classroom.

For example, some cultural groups do not prize individual achievement and recognition; although they want the group as a whole to do well, they consider it improper for individuals to stand out. Some groups place strong emphasis on traditions from the past. Some see little purpose in working at school activities that do not appear useful or are not inherently interesting. Students in some cultures are made uncomfortable by eye contact and some show respect by being quiet and nonconfrontational. Some groups do not think it proper to voice ideas that disagree with the teacher's, and some groups use very direct communication styles that teachers may interpret as disrespectful or forward. Failure to recognize and adjust to such differences can lead to misunderstandings between teachers and students, making teaching and learning more difficult than anticipated.

For more information on this topic, check out Morgan, H. (2010). Improving schooling for cultural minorities: The right teaching styles can make a big difference. *Educational Horizons*, 88(2), 114-120.

Culturally responsive teaching helps teachers avoid some of the pitfalls associated with a narrow view of student difference. You'll be interested to know that a narrow view of difference among students is, unfortunately, correlated with many negative school outcomes: Students who are culturally or linguistically diverse are disproportionally represented in referrals to the office for behavioral issues and in suspensions and expulsions from school (Kaufman et al., 2010). They are also overrepresented in placement in special education classrooms (Chamberlain, 2005). These trends persist, despite the fact that culturally responsive teaching has been encouraged for more than 20 years (Ladson-Billings, 1995).

Figure 2.2 shows some tension points that teachers and students may encounter when the expectations of the dominant school culture aren't aligned with students' cultural backgrounds and experiences. As you study it, please remember that any effort educators make to characterize group responses has to acknowledge that students who are members of a particular group may not exhibit the characteristics described; we must not overgeneralize. Instead, we should be aware that *some* students in these groups may experience conflict between their own ways of operating and the expectations of the school.

Figure 2.2 ▪ How the Behavior of Students From Various Cultural Groups' Behaviors May Differ from What Teachers Have Been Taught to Expect

The following table will help you explore some aspects of the school/classroom situation where cultural differences may affect learning and behavior. Keep in mind that the table reflects *trends* in behavior; you may encounter individuals, classes, schools, and perhaps even whole communities where these descriptors are *not* illustrative of behavior or approach. Nonetheless, these ideas are worth considering as you develop your classroom management system (and your approach to instruction and assessment). To understand the ideas deeply and fully, you will need to do much deeper reading of the source material; a summary table like this is designed to whet your appetite for more information.

Dominant Emphasis or Expectation in Schools	Approaches and Experiences Among Other Cultural Groups That May Differ	Potential Impact of the Difference	Reference(s)
The teacher is the authority figure and deliverer of consequences.	Many students experience discipline through teachings at home.	Students can be thrown off by punishment at school.	Dykeman, Nelson, & Appleton, 1995
The approach taken to many tasks is competitive/individualistic.	Students' home environments may reflect a collectivist/mutually supportive society.	Students may not work as well individually or competitively.	Ledlow, 1992; Chamberlain, 2005
	Students may show group focus with regard to motivation and stage-setting, but may be individualistic in actual task completion/solution delivery	Students may struggle when expected to work individually; may balk at the idea of group grades.	Gay, 2010
	Student focus may tend to be collaborative and social.	Students' emotional expression and strong need for social interaction may be viewed negatively.	Gay, 2010
The typical discourse pattern is direct but mutually respectful communication in which one person at a time shares thoughts or ideas.	Students may come from an environment that relies on nonassertive language use.	Students may not be comfortable answering questions or expressing ideas, particularly in management-related situations.	Chamberlain, 2005; Cartledge, Gardner, & Ford, 2009

Figure 2.2 ▪ *(Continued)*

Dominant Emphasis or Expectation in Schools	Approaches and Experiences Among Other Cultural Groups That May Differ	Potential Impact of the Difference	Reference(s)
	Students may demonstrate louder, more exuberant expressions and participatory-interactive discourse patterns.	Student responses may be misunderstood as aggressive or disrespectful when their language does not match the typical passive-receptive discourse pattern.	Chamberlain, 2005; Cartledge, Gardner, & Ford, 2009; Gay, 2010
	Dialectical differences may present themselves in verbal and written expression.	Students' linguistic/dialectical style may be deemed inappropriate to the school setting; the speaker may feel his or her language patterns are denigrated. Students' oral facility may go unrecognized.	Gay, 2010
	Students may engage in "co-narration" or talking together to convey ideas or complete a task.	Students' talk may be interpreted as contributing to classroom noise and chaos; it may also be seen as reducing the voice of the individual.	Gay, 2010
Indirect, socially veiled language (e.g., "I like the way most of you are sitting quietly") is used to shape behavior.	Students may be socialized to respond to direct language (e.g., "put your pencils down and put your notebooks away").	Students may miss the intended message of the indirect language; the teacher may view students as uncooperative.	Delpit, 2005
Eye contact is interpreted as a sign of engagement and respect.	Failure to make eye contact reflects respect in some groups.	Students may not show eye contact, leading teacher to assume defiance or lack of engagement; they may be uncomfortable when a teacher says, "Look at me."	Gay, 2010
Listeners affirm the speaker through eye contact, nonverbal expression, and appropriate verbal interjections.	Students may have been taught to show deference to the teacher out of respect for position and knowledge.	Students may be seen as unengaged or unwilling to participate.	Brown, 2003

Figure 2.2 ▪ *(Continued)*

Dominant Emphasis or Expectation in Schools	Approaches and Experiences Among Other Cultural Groups That May Differ	Potential Impact of the Difference	Reference(s)
	Students may affirm the teacher with loud or obvious verbal interjections	Students may be seen as attention-seeking or boisterous.	Brown, 2003
Communication is topic-centered and to the point; only enough context is given for the listener to understand the message.	Students may communicate more episodically, setting the context for the listener with many details.	Students' communication may be viewed as poorly organized or difficult to follow.	Cazden, 1998, in Delpit, 2005
Personal space is to be preserved and respected.	Students may have a smaller personal space "bubble" and may move closer to others than expected.	Students may be seen as invading space and inattentive to boundaries.	Morgan, 2010
Classroom interaction often involves convergent (one-answer) questioning and deductive reasoning.	Problem solving may involve a phase of social "stage setting" that precedes the actual work of problem solving.	Time spent as students "get started" may be deemed as dawdling or time-wasting.	Gay, 2010
	Students may prefer that questions, even convergent ones, be posed to the group; problem solving may involve extensive collaboration, expression of ideas, and consensus building.	Tasks that focus on competition rather than cooperation may be challenging; time and resource allocation may have to be reconsidered in light of stylistic preferences/ behavior patterns.	Gay, 2010
Speakers tend to relate to materials, issues, and topics under study as "reporters"; objective positions are valued.	Discourse dynamics may include a strong position of advocacy; opinions may be strongly expressed during discussions.	Speakers may be seen as impulsive and impassioned rather than objective and rational.	Gay, 2010
Authorities/experts are generally recognized as credible based on education, certification, or accomplishment.	The validity of alternate viewpoints may be challenged directly.	Speakers may be seen as challenging authority and expertise.	Gay, 2010

Figure 2.2 ■ *(Continued)*

Dominant Emphasis or Expectation in Schools	Approaches and Experiences Among Other Cultural Groups That May Differ	Potential Impact of the Difference	Reference(s)
Dialogue occurs in ways that minimize conflict and opposition to ideas; participants are expected to be open-minded, consider information from a variety of perspectives, control impulses, and manage their emotions effectively.	Expression may involve direct confrontation or criticism of ideas.	Speakers may be perceived as impulsive, overly emotional, and unable/unwilling to control their personal investment in a particular stance.	Gay, 2010

What do you think of the information in this table? What aspects of it might be helpful to a classroom teacher? In what ways might this sort of information be problematic?

Economic Realities: How Do They Affect Student Behavior?

Today, large numbers of our students come from economically disadvantaged backgrounds. *Economic disadvantage* is a term used synonymously with *living in poverty*. Students are considered to be living in poverty if they are members of households that must spend more than one-third of their disposable income for food adequate to meet the family's nutritional needs. According to information from the National Center for Children in Poverty (NCCP), in 2014, more than 15 million children under 18 years of age lived in poverty (http://www.nccp.org/publications/pub_1145.html). If that statistic doesn't distress you, here's a different way of conveying the information: Roughly 21% of all children live in poverty, which was defined by the U.S. Census Bureau in 2015 as having a household income of $24,036 or less for a family of two adults and two children (https://www.census.gov/topics/income-poverty/poverty.html). Poverty calculations are complex, so other metrics are used to assess economic hardship; the NCCP indicates that in 2014, roughly 44% of people under the age of 18 were considered to be living at "low income" levels—that is, they lived in households whose income was less than twice the federal poverty threshold.

Students who live in situations where access to material resources is limited face many challenges in school. Although many educators, researchers, and activists have written about the impact of poverty on student learning and achievement, this quotation from Rebell and Wolff (2012) clearly enumerates the effect that financial disadvantage has on our educational system:

> In reality, America doesn't have a general education crisis; we have a poverty crisis. The effect of poverty on children's learning is profound and multidimensional. Children who grow up in poverty are much more likely to experience conditions that make learning difficult and put them at risk for academic failure. Moreover, the longer a child is poor, the more extreme the poverty, the greater the concentration of poverty, and the younger the child, the more serious the effects will be on the child's potential to succeed academically. (p. 62) [*]

There has been much debate about how we can best think about and work to mitigate the effects of poverty on students. In the next segment of the chapter, which we're presenting as a Point and Counterpoint argument, we'll explore the views of two well-known authors who focus on poverty and student success: Ruby Payne and Paul Gorski. As you read their very different ideas about how we view poverty in the educational spectrum, consider the extent to which you agree or disagree with each position. The goal of this exercise is not to have you endorse one set of ideas over another, even though you may; it is instead to illustrate the complexity of the problem of socioeconomic effects, not just on students and how they learn, but on teachers and how they teach.

Ruby Payne: Teachers Should Understand the Culture of Poverty

Ruby Payne's experiences have led her to conclude that each economic class has its own set of *hidden rules* by which people in the group operate. In this case, Payne refers not to classroom rules, but patterns of how people approach their work, their interpersonal relationships, their entertainment—how they live their lives. According to Payne, the hidden rules for schools, teachers, and about half of the school population mesh well with the predominant middle-class school values we listed earlier, focusing on time orientation, planning, competition, verbal communication, etc. Payne goes on to say, though, that the hidden rules for students from *generational poverty* (defined as long-term familial poverty, as opposed to temporary or situational poverty) are different, and that students from low-wealth homes often struggle in school because they operate from one set of "rules" at home but are expected to follow an unfamiliar set of rules in school. Payne articulates these "rules" and urges teachers to learn them as a way to understand, communicate with, and work productively with students.

Payne (2001) asserts that for people in poverty, the major driving life forces seem to be survival, personal relationships, and entertainment. She believes that students in poverty tend to value relationships more than achievement, and that it can be disquieting for an individual from a low-wealth situation to acquire too much education, because the educated person might then leave the community.

[*]From *Educational Opportunity Is Achievable and Affordable*, by Michael A. Rebell and Jessica R. Wolff. © Published by SAGE Publications.

Payne suggests that in poorer homes, conflict is often resolved by fighting, and respect is accorded to those who can defend themselves. School discipline, she says, is more about penance and forgiveness than behavior change, and students often save face by laughing when they are disciplined, particularly because their senses of personal value are aligned with the ability to entertain others. Money is to be used and spent, not saved. Destiny and fate are believed to determine most matters; individuals feel they have relatively little control over their lives, according to Payne.

Payne adds that students in poverty often use a casual, informal style of speech that contrasts with the more formal style emphasized in school and business. She indicates that teachers will need to clarify the difference between formal and informal speech and help students learn to use language that is appropriate for given situations.

Payne goes on to say that noise level among people of poverty may tend to be high, and they may frequently display strong emotion, something she believes is less typical of individuals from middle-class backgrounds. At home, the noise from the television may mix with participatory conversation, and multiple people may be talking at the same time; the classroom, in contrast, is expected to be quieter, with speakers taking turns. Payne believes that this juxtaposition of home and school expectations causes students disequilibrium in the classroom, and that teachers who are sensitive to students' tendencies to engage in these behaviors can respond to them appropriately and teach students the behaviors (hidden rules) commonly expected within schools.

Payne's work has been widely embraced by many school systems. Teachers who read her work often find that her descriptions of students and their behavior seem to reflect their own classroom experiences. Many teachers point to Payne as the person who made class differences "make sense," and who led them to realizations that ultimately helped them be better teachers and manage their classrooms more effectively.

Paul Gorski: Let's End the Deficit Ideology

Paul Gorski (2011, 2013) is one of many educational researchers who assert that frameworks such as Payne's lead educators down a dangerous path: that of viewing student differences, and particularly ways students differ from their teachers, as deficits. When approaching teaching and management from a deficit perspective, teachers view their students, and respond to their behavior, in ways that suggest that something is lacking in the student's personality, circumstance, or culture; whatever is thought to be lacking is seen as a within-student or within-family/within-community problem to be solved, an obstacle to be overcome, or an immovable barrier to student success. Gorski asserts that approaching any aspect of education from a deficit perspective is a form of bias, and is a gross oversimplification of the impact of circumstance on educational achievement.

Gorski, fiercely critical of deficit ideology, describes it as an institutionalized worldview that essentially allows its holders to rationalize why achievement outcomes vary so widely across different groups of students. In other words, if teachers see the problem as situated within people and communities, then they don't have to address the larger sociopolitical context that is, Gorski asserts, responsible for much of the disadvantage that students face societally and educationally. Deficit thinking becomes a justifying stereotype that teachers use, either blindly or intentionally, to explain away instances of low expectations for some students, or to rationalize why students from marginalized groups perform less well than their majority peers.

Gorski would be inclined, we believe, to describe deficit thinking as leading to a sort of teacher paralysis—providing a seemingly reasonable rationale for a teacher to reject a model of teaching (and classroom management) that builds on students' strengths and conveys the belief that all students can learn. He is fiercely critical of Ruby Payne's work, because he believes that her class-specific generalizations, particularly the ones about people living in generational poverty, perpetuate the idea that something is wrong with students from low-wealth backgrounds, and that teachers must identify the "wrongness" and then work to compensate for it. Gorski maintains that such a perspective leads to low teacher expectations, disparity of treatment of students based on race or class, disproportional rates of disciplinary actions among students of marginalized groups, and institutional structures that keep education from being universally accessible, meaningful, and supportive.

Head to Head: Payne and Gorski

Payne seems to suggest that teachers view socioeconomic differences formulaically—that if you have poor students in class, you can rely on a basic set of assumptions about what matters to them and to their families, how they interact, and what sorts of behaviors you can expect from them in your classroom. She gives seemingly practical suggestions for teachers to use to help students overcome the differences between expectations at school and at home. Teachers and school systems have endorsed her ideas and many indicate that by approaching their students according to Payne's suggestions, they have improved their students' overall educational experience.

An interesting article about the idea of a "culture of poverty" is found at http://www.ascd .org/publications/ educational- leadership/apr08/ vol65/num07/The- Myth-of-the-Culture- of-Poverty.aspx.

Gorski encourages educators to take a broader view of the problem, considering the sociopolitical context in which students and schools exist and operate, and resisting the temptation to oversimplify the impact that poverty has on students, families, and communities. He calls attention to the fact that multiple studies point to all the ways in which schools in high-poverty areas are disadvantaged: fewer resources, less-qualified teachers, and insufficient facilities, to name a few. Children from low-wealth homes and areas have less access to healthcare, more difficulty getting basic nutritional needs met, and less access to safe housing. In general, the deck is stacked against these students, Gorski asserts, not because of any "hidden rules," but because they do not have access to the same resources that most teachers take for granted. Gorski believes that if teachers buy into deficit ideology, they will be complicit in reducing even further the opportunities for poor children.

What's Your View?

Now that you've read summaries of the perspectives of both Payne and Gorski, what do you think? What ideas resonate with you? What ideas, if any, do you reject? How do these two viewpoints figure in to your developing philosophy of what it means to manage a classroom full of students?

As you move through your career, you'll likely be faced with opposing viewpoints such as the ones we've presented here from Payne and Gorski. Over time, you'll continue to develop your own strategies for navigating any disequilibrium you may feel when you encounter well-known ideas that are in conflict with one another. We encourage you to read widely, question deeply, discuss vigorously, and be ready to revisit and revise your viewpoints as new information and experiences come your way.

How Can I Work More Effectively With Students of Various Societal and Economic Groups?

Most teachers ask themselves this question; many of them seek information to help them develop an answer. We've put together some ideas here that will get you thinking about the ways you can increase your cultural responsiveness and weave it into your classroom management system.

The following list contains suggestions from various authorities on working more effectively with students from diverse backgrounds.

- Learn as much as you can about students from backgrounds different from your own. Pinpoint what those students consider important, how they relate to each other and to adults, and how they relate to teachers and school in general. As you plan and teach, think about how your decisions and actions may be received not only by the group, but by individuals within the group.
- Show acceptance of your students, their families, and their lifestyles. Work toward not just tolerance, but toward appreciating differences. Consider students' contexts as you plan, teach, and manage. Consider the degree to which students' backgrounds of experience may impact their understanding of new content and skills; think about how their access to resources may play into their success at meeting your expectations.
- Show solidarity with students and be eager to help them learn and find success. Help your students celebrate one another's successes, and help them develop resilience and grit. Give them agency when you can, so that they feel

they have some level of choice and control about how their school experiences unfold.

■ Emphasize the knowledge, skills, and values needed for school success while at the same time encouraging students to develop strong personal and cultural identities.

■ Communicate your genuine conviction that all students can succeed in school and indicate how you will help them do so. Consider your expectations for them; set your standards to be high but attainable, and provide enough support and scaffolding so that students can hit the target. And when students aren't able to meet the target even with help, set an intermediate target that moves them forward toward the ultimate goal.

■ Link your curriculum content to students' out-of-school experiences. Focus on what is relevant and meaningful to your students. Help them understand why they're learning what they're learning and how the new knowledge and skills will help them as they navigate their lives. And when you have to teach something that you can't really correlate directly to students' lives, be honest about that. Let them know that sometimes, learning for the sake of learning is a meaningful exercise, and that sometimes, we find a use for knowledge or skills at a time or in a place we weren't expecting.

■ Provide mentoring and guidance for your students. Scaffolding them as they learn and work is an especially effective tactic for improving motivation and building personal relations. (*Scaffolding* refers to providing support and assistance that is gradually withdrawn as students gain mastery of knowledge and skills.) Focus on your interpersonal relationships with them, and on the relationships they have with one another. Communicate that you are all on the same team, and that when one succeeds, everyone benefits.

■ Establish standards of class behavior that are sensitive to all cultures. Emphasize responsibility and respect. Consider where students are, developmentally and culturally speaking, and meet them there as you work to move them toward higher levels of academic achievement, self-management, and interpersonal skill.

■ Demonstrate for students the behavior that helps them succeed in school; have them practice that behavior, and give them feedback about how well they're meeting classroom expectations. These teacher behaviors are particularly important in classroom management; you can't always assume that students come to you knowing what to do, how to do it, or why it matters.

■ Teach your students to adjust their language use in different situations. Help them understand that in school, expectations for language use (spoken and written) may differ from expectations at home or in their neighborhoods. In the same way you almost certainly would use different language to text your best friend than you would to communicate an important message to your professor or your school principal, students should be able to consider the appropriateness of their word choice and communication style for their audiences.

■ Keep family members informed about their child's performance and behavior and ask them to work with you for the child's benefit. Work to establish collaborative relationships with your students' caregivers; many teachers make it a habit to, at the start of the school year, communicate positive news to their students' parents. Some call parents in the first weeks to say things like, "I just wanted to tell you how glad I am to have Aisling in my class; she did a great job today as discussion leader, and I knew you'd be happy to know about that." Teachers who make this sort of effort often find that if they should have to contact a caregiver later to ask for help with an academic or behavioral issue, the parents are more willing to be supportive.

■ Be mindful of, but not intimidated by, language differences. You may have students whose home language is not the same as yours. Talking with the students or with their parents may make you feel a bit awkward—just remember, they likely feel awkward, too. A sense of humor helps in these cases, as does accessing resources (human, technological, or otherwise) that can help you bridge the language barrier. And when you're feeling out of your element interpersonally, do your best to retain your focus on why it's important to build relationships. Push through any awkward feelings; persist. Communicate that you want to work alongside students and their families for everyone's benefit, and the awkwardness will likely fade; even if it doesn't, you can feel confident that you gave it your best effort and that you didn't avoid a situation that was potentially challenging.

REFLECTING ON HOW STUDENT CHARACTERISTICS MAY AFFECT TEACHING AND LEARNING: WHAT YOU HAVE LEARNED IN THIS CHAPTER

In this chapter, you've learned a great deal about influences on student behavior. You've considered how student needs affect their behavior, and how teachers can work to keep unmet needs from being the cause of misbehavior. You've learned about sociocultural and economic influences, not just on student behavior, but on teachers' responses to student behavior. You've considered the fact that you will likely be working with peers or administrators whose educational priorities and beliefs differ from yours. Hopefully, you're beginning to develop a strategy for how you'll respond in those situations, as well as a commitment to learning as much as you can about what classroom management options will be most effective with your students.

Signpost: Further Readings About Cultural Considerations and Classroom Management

Bondy, E., Ross, R, Gallingane, C. & Hambacher, E. (2007). Creating environments of success and resilience: Culturally responsive classroom management and more. *Urban Education, 42,* 326–348.

Cartledge, G., Singh, A., & Gibson, L. (2008). Practical behavior management techniques to close the accessibility gap for students who are culturally and linguistically diverse. *Preventing School Failure, 52*(3), 29–38.

Gay, G. (2010). *Culturally responsive teaching: Theory, research, and practice* (2e.) New York: Teachers College Press.

Delpit, L. (1995). *Other people's children: Cultural conflict in the classroom.* New York: New Press.

Weinstein, C.S., Tomlinson-Clarke, S., & Curran, M. (2004). Toward a conception of culturally responsive classroom management. *Journal of Teacher Education, 55,* 25–38.

MyLab Education **Self-Check 2.1**

MyLab Education **Self-Check 2.2**

MyLab Education **Application Exercise 2.1** Assessing a Teacher's Strategy: Identifying Ways Students' Needs Are Met

MyLab Education **Application Exercise 2.2** Simulation: Understanding "Triggers" for Unproductive Student Behavior and Preventing Such Behavior

Classroom Management Concepts and Terms

As we proceed, we will introduce a number of concepts and terms that are used in the conversation about how teachers manage their classes. Whenever you see a new term in bold type, it is listed and defined in the Glossary near the end of the book.

Classroom management refers to teachers' efforts to establish and maintain four standards of fundamental importance in all classrooms:

1. Teachers are allowed to teach in a professional manner without being disrupted.
2. Students are allowed to learn without being hindered by others.
3. Students learn how to cooperate, appreciate, and get along with each other and to manage themselves and their behavior.
4. Teachers and students experience satisfaction and pleasure in their school experiences.

How Do I Get Students to Comply With These Expectations?

Effective teachers discuss these four expectations with their students. They help students see the difference between appropriate behavior (which helps them succeed) and inappropriate behavior (which hinders their progress or the progress of others). Helping students see the rationale for your rules, procedures, and management decisions is one way to invite their appropriate participation in class experiences; when students understand *why* they're asked to do something, they're more likely to do it.

How do you communicate with your students about these expectations and why you find them to be important? In the early days of public education, teachers told students they were to "act like civilized human beings" or "behave like ladies and gentlemen." Laudable as those suggestions sound, they're not very helpful. To help students know what you want from them, you will need to be specific about your expectations. Students need to see, understand, and practice various behaviors that will help them be successful, which means you need to be able to articulate clearly what you'd like students to do and how you'd like them to behave.

Carolyn Evertson and Edmund Emmer are well-known classroom management experts who encourage teachers to develop both rules and procedures for their students (Emmer & Evertson, 2012; Evertson & Emmer 2012). It's helpful for teachers (and prospective teachers) to be able to distinguish between rules and procedures, because they address different aspects of classroom management and are used in different ways. As you read further in this text, you'll read different authorities' opinions on rules and procedures: how many there should be, what they should cover, and whether or not to involve students in developing them. You'll need to think carefully about what approach is going to work best in your particular teaching situation, and adapt as you find what does and doesn't work for you. For now, though, let's think about how Emmer and Evertson describe rules and procedures.

According to Evertson and Emmer (2012), *rules* are expectations for how students engage with people, time, space, and materials; they're applicable in all situations (with the possible exception of times when a student's learning challenges mean that there needs to be some flexibility until the student masters the expected behavior). Rules include ideas like "Treat yourself, others, and class materials with respect" and "Speak at appropriate times in appropriate voices." Rules may need to be operationally defined, so students understand what you mean by "respect"—some teachers involve their students in the development of class rules, and include a discussion of why a given rule is important and what it looks like when that rule is being followed in class. Consistent enforcement of class rules is critical; if a behavior or set of behaviors is important enough to be included in a rule, the teacher should be prepared to take action each time it is broken.

Emmer and Evertson (2012) describe *procedures* as routines that cover how things get done in the classroom; procedures can vary depending on the situation. Questions that guide sample classroom procedures include:

- What should students do upon arriving in the classroom? (put away materials? begin a start-of-class assignment?)
- How and when can students move about the room/school? (When and where do they get materials, sharpen pencils, go to the restroom, etc.?)
- What should students do with their work when it is completed? What if they're not finished when it's time to move to another lesson or class?

■ How should students ask for assistance? (raise hands? ask a peer?)

Classroom procedures are quite often numerous, and, when they're well developed, taught, rehearsed, and reinforced (as appropriate for the grade level), they provide a solid foundation for smooth classroom functioning. Some procedures should be in place from the first day of the school year; others can be introduced as they're needed.

Evertson and Emmer recommend that teachers at all grade levels develop a small number of rules and a large number of procedures, and that they spend time at the start of the school year teaching students these expectations, letting students practice, and reinforcing students' success at meeting them. Teachers should work to make their rules developmentally appropriate. Younger students need rules that are clearly stated and taught directly and then reinforced both at the start of the school year and after holiday breaks. Older students are likely to need less instruction in what rules mean and how to comply with them; nevertheless, teachers of students in high school should make sure they've communicated rules clearly and that students are consistently following them.

How Do I Communicate When Students Don't Meet My Expectations?

In addition to clarifying expectations, you need to have in mind several helpful comments or questions to use when students fail to display acceptable behavior. Those comments and questions *do not scold or criticize*, but instead call on students to reflect and make choices. Here are examples of questions you might ask and statements you might make, all while using a pleasant facial expression and neutral tone of voice:

That is against our rules. Would you do it again, please, correctly this time?
Is that what you intended to do (or say)?
Let's remember to give everyone a chance to speak.
Which of our class expectations does that violate?
Is that in keeping with the kind of person you truly want to be?
How would your parents or caregiver want you to conduct yourself in this situation?

As we move ahead, we will examine many such ways of responding to misbehavior, and none of them scolds the student. Being scolded tends to make students defensive; it's hard to simultaneously make someone defensive and expect them to move toward you and your expectations.

Behavior is the totality of one's physical and mental activities. Although it includes everything we do, in classroom management we are only concerned about actions over which students and teachers have *voluntary control*. We will be working toward influencing students to *choose* to behave in ways that benefit themselves and the class.

Misbehavior (also called ***disruptive behavior*** and ***inappropriate behavior***) refers to actions that disrupt teaching, interfere with learning, demean others, or otherwise violate the moral codes of society. We can make sure students understand the meaning of misbehavior by using examples to which they can relate.

Appropriate behavior (also called ***acceptable behavior*** or ***responsible behavior***) refers to student behavior that is consistent with class expectations and does not interfere with learning, demean others, or violate the moral codes of society.

Limits are the imaginary boundaries that separate acceptable behavior from misbehavior. Those boundaries are generally established by cultural traditions and are made explicit by teachers. In actual classrooms they vary somewhat from teacher to teacher. To be fair to your students, you should make very clear just where your limits are set—that is, where the lines are that separate acceptable behavior from misbehavior.

Positive influence is what we do, noncoercively, to invite or entice students to conduct themselves in accordance with class expectations. It is exerted through various acts and comments, positive in nature, that open up possibilities and provide helpful assistance rather than criticism. Positivity is important because it minimizes student resistance while supporting appropriate actions. Better yet, it often activates students' inner motivation to do what is proper.

LET'S EXAMINE *MISBEHAVIOR*: WHAT EXACTLY IS IT?

Misbehavior in school is behavior that violates class rules, demeans others, or is otherwise incompatible with the legal or social norms of the society. Most student misbehavior in the classroom falls into two categories—unwillingness to work as directed and causing unwarranted distractions. Within those two categories we can identify several specific kinds of misbehavior that require teacher attention. You will encounter many of them on a daily basis. Some are far more serious than others, yet even the benign ones require attention because they hinder learning. Here we list 13 types of misbehavior, presented generally from less serious to more serious:

1. *Inattention.* Daydreaming, doodling, looking out the window, thinking about things irrelevant to the lesson
2. *Apathy.* A disinclination to participate, sulking, not caring, being fearful of trying or unconcerned about doing well
3. *Needless talk.* Chatting during instructional time about things unrelated to the lesson
4. *Moving about the room.* Getting up and wandering around without permission
5. *Annoying others.* Provoking, teasing, picking on others, calling names (These behaviors can be, but aren't always, associated with bullying.)

6. *Disrupting.* Calling out during instruction, talking and laughing inappropriately, using vulgar language, causing "accidents"
7. *Lying.* Falsifying to avoid accepting responsibility or admitting wrongdoing, or to get others in trouble
8. *Stealing.* Taking things that belong to others
9. *Cheating.* Making false representations for personal benefit or wrongly taking advantage of others
10. *Malicious mischief.* Doing intentional damage to school property or the belongings of others
11. *Defiance of authority.* Talking back to the teacher, ignoring the teacher, or refusing to do as requested
12. *Sexual harassment.* Making others uncomfortable through touching, sex-related language, or sexual innuendo
13. *Aggression and fighting.* Showing hostility toward others, threatening, shoving, pinching, wrestling, hitting, bullying

All of these types of misbehavior have a dampening effect on teaching, learning, personal feelings, and motivation to learn. Many of them occur regularly. Psychologist Fred Jones (1987a, 1987b) reported the frequency of misbehavior in hundreds of classrooms he studied. In the better-behaved classes, one or more of the above misbehaviors occurred every 2 to 3 minutes. In less well-behaved classes, the frequency was more in the order of three or more misbehaviors per minute. You can imagine the amount of time teachers must spend dealing with that amount of misbehavior.

As you consider these behaviors, keep in mind one favor you can do yourself: Don't take it personally. Do your best to set aside your own emotional response to student misbehavior, remembering that most of the time, misbehavior is *not* intended as a personal affront to the teacher. (Yes, sometimes students *will* misbehave to get under your skin, but you'd be surprised at how often you can identify a cause that has nothing to do with you.) Once you reject the idea that a student is misbehaving specifically to upset you, it becomes easier to identify why a student might be misbehaving and to react in ways that de-escalate the situation. Teachers who become good at figuring out reasons for student misbehavior are more able to prevent it and more able to react reasonably and compassionately when misbehavior does occur.

WHAT CAUSES STUDENTS TO MISBEHAVE?

Many conditions promote misbehavior among students. By identifying and addressing the causes, you can significantly reduce inappropriate behavior in your classes. At this point, we will note a longish list of conditions that tend to correlate with misbehavior in school. You will see that you can take steps proactively to limit, or even eliminate, many of these conditions.

Causal Conditions That Seem to Reside in Individual Students

Ten conditions that often promote misbehavior seem to reside within individual students. Those conditions are: unmet needs, thwarted desires, expediency, urge to transgress, temptation, inappropriate habits, poor behavior choices, avoidance, egocentric personality, and neurological difference or disability. Here we note each of the 10 conditions and indicate how you can address them.

1. *Unmet needs.* Both in and out of the classroom, students continually try to meet strongly felt needs for security, association, belonging, hope, dignity, power, enjoyment, and competence. Everyone, almost without exception, strives to meet these needs. When unsuccessful in doing so, students become unsettled, distracted, and more likely to behave inappropriately.

    Suggestions: Keep student needs in mind, and plan in advance how you will address them. Write them on an index card you keep on your desk to remind yourself they are in play all the time. By observing students and talking with them, you can usually identify needs that are prompting misbehavior; often, you can help the student meet the need in an appropriate way, thus resolving the problem.

2. *Thwarted desires.* When students fail to get something they want, they may complain, become destructive, sulk, pout, or act out.

    Suggestions: When appropriate, discuss with students the fact that all of us occasionally get to have things the way we want them, but very often we do not, and that managing our reactions to disappointment is an important skill. When students show keen disappointment, compliment them for whatever positive behavior you've seen from them, such as making a strong effort. Ask them what might help them in the situation. Be sympathetic, but don't dwell on the problem. Promote an attitude of "Let's move ahead and keep trying." Take action to draw them back to productive work, such as by changing up assignments, posing a challenge, or offering them a choice.

3. *Expediency.* Anticipate that all students will, on occasion, look for short-cuts to make their lives easier or more enjoyable. In doing so, they will break rules and sometimes behave dishonestly.

    Suggestions: Discuss this behavior openly, while stressing that the best procedure for all of us is to do things correctly, even when it is inconvenient; that's how we make genuine progress and get others to trust us. Ask students why they sometimes take the easy way, such as reading book summaries or reviews rather than the assigned book, rushing through a writing assignment, or copying the work of others. If they are comfortable enough to answer honestly, they will probably say they do so because they don't like the work, don't see the point in it, or don't want to spend the time it requires. Help them understand the longer-term benefits of trying hard. Ask them what would encourage them to give their best effort. Listen to their suggestions and make use of them if you can.

By the way, expedient behavior is not so evident in classes that students find interesting, but it appears often in classes they find difficult or boring. (Can you adjust assignments, curricula, or workload?) And remember that teachers, too, sometimes exhibit expedient behavior; when we remember that students aren't the only ones who take shortcuts or fail to give 100% effort, it makes it easier to not take the behavior personally.

4. *Urge to transgress.* Many of us have a natural aversion to rules imposed by others, and we seem to find it a challenge to break them, despite knowing there is a chance we'll get caught or even harm ourselves or others. Students succumb to this urge frequently, especially when class activities are not appealing, and they cheat, take shortcuts, tell lies, break class rules, and annoy others.

   Suggestions: Anticipate this urge and plan ways to counter it. When talking with your students about expected behavior, discuss the urge, its effects, and how it can be controlled sensibly. Tie this in with the reasons for rules and their value in keeping us comfortable, equalizing opportunity, and helping us live together harmoniously. If students are old enough, discuss ethics, ethical conduct, and personal character.

5. *Temptation.* Students regularly encounter objects, people, situations, and behaviors they find powerfully attractive. This phenomenon is evident in students' taste in relationships, ways of speaking, and behavioral decisions. Although students know they are sometimes misbehaving when succumbing to these temptations, they nevertheless find them so attractive they often adopt, mimic, acquire, or tolerate them, even when the acts are not condoned by adult society.

   Suggestions: Conduct discussions with your students to analyze temptation and seek to understand why certain behaviors and opportunities are so seductive. Help students foresee the undesirable consequences of giving in to temptation when they know a choice is questionable. Help them clarify the lines that separate appropriate behavior from inappropriate and urge them to resist involvement in activities likely to do them harm.

6. *Inappropriate habits.* Inappropriate habits are ingrained ways of behaving that transgress established standards and expectations. Jason uses profanity at school. Maria is discourteous and calls others names. Larry shirks his assignments. Some of these habits are learned in school, but many become established outside of school.

   Suggestions: When first discussing desirable behavior/rules in school, raise this topic. Tell your students there are certain requirements for behavior at school, even though those requirements might not prevail outside of school. Let them know that there are certain ways we must conduct ourselves and treat others in school. (Be careful not to single out individuals as examples in this conversation; use hypotheticals instead.) Identify unacceptable behaviors such as cursing, calling names, and showing disregard for others. If necessary, show students how you expect them to act. When they fail to comply, call it to their attention and ask them if they remember how that particular thing is done in school. Ask them courteously to show you that they know.

7. *Poor behavior choices.* The behaviors students use in attempting to meet their needs are sometimes acceptable, sometimes not. In most cases, students choose to behave as they do, sometimes with unintended consequences. For example, Alicia, when seeking attention, pesters others so much they avoid her. Max, seeking to augment his sense of power, refuses to do what his teacher requests. Assuming those behaviors are under their control, we say that Alicia and Max are making poor behavior choices.

   Suggestions: Help your class recognize that when they choose to misbehave, they are hindering the likelihood of being successful in school. To help such students, you might address the class as a whole and pose the following questions:
   - What are some of the things you have seen students do to [get attention, be acknowledged, get better grades than they deserve, get out of work, become members of certain groups]?
   - Does their behavior usually get them what they want?
   - What could those students do that would probably bring better and more satisfying results?

8. *Avoidance.* No one likes to face failure, intimidation, ridicule, or other unpleasant situations. One way to escape those things is to avoid activities or places where they might occur, or if that is not possible, simply refuse to participate. But in school, students' reasons for avoidance are not always evident to teachers. For instance, when Norona refuses to participate in a group assignment, she seems to show disrespect for the teacher, but her real reason may be that she doesn't want to appear inept in front of her peers.

   Suggestions: To help students such as Norona, show your class how to face unpleasant situations and work through them. You might ask them to work in pairs or small groups and together answer questions such as the following:
   - Are there things you try to avoid in school, such as people, events, or activities you find frightening or embarrassing?
   - Which of those things could best be dealt with through avoidance (e.g., staying away from a clique that is maligning other students)?
   - Which of those things cannot be dealt with through avoidance (e.g., giving an oral report in front of the class)?
   - What is the worst thing that can happen in class if we make a mistake? What is the value in making mistakes?

- What could we do as a class to keep others from feeling embarrassed when they make mistakes?
- What might a person do to reduce fear of making mistakes or being involved in unpleasant situations?

9. *Egocentric personality.* People with egocentric personalities focus primarily on themselves, believe they are superior to others, and usually think they do little wrong. Most classes contain one or more students with such personalities.

  Suggestions: To help these students behave more appropriately, ask questions of your entire class such as the following:

- Are the needs and interests of all students important, or do only certain students deserve attention?
- Is one person often entirely right and everyone else entirely wrong?
- Is everyone entitled to an equal opportunity in the class? How should you and I react to a person who always wants to dominate, be first, be right, and quarrel with those who don't agree? (Make sure the proffered suggestions are positive in nature, not negative.)

10. *Learning difference or disability.* A few students behave undesirably not through intent or thoughtlessness but because their brains call forth behavior they cannot fully control. In Chapter 13, you will see a discussion of certain diagnoses that may increase the likelihood that a student will have difficulty complying with behavioral expectations. For instance, it's possible that students with learning disabilities, attention-deficit hyperactivity disorder (ADHD), or other challenges will exhibit a higher level of behavioral non-conformity. You may find that students with these diagnoses respond less reliably to typical classroom management tactics, or you may find that they have more difficulty managing their impulses and actions. Chapter 13 will give you more information about these designations and provide information to help you teach students with learning and behavioral differences.

  Suggestions: Teachers who have students with learning and behavioral differences often benefit from seeking out colleagues who are specialists in working with such students. But "regular" classroom teachers should understand that they aren't powerless to help shape the behavior of these students, and to help others in the class understand differences that may be exhibited. Levine (2003) urges teachers to explain to the class that some people's brains function in ways that make self-control more challenging, meaning they may misbehave more frequently than others do. Other authorities ask teachers to (1) consistently model the calm, de-escalating behavior we want students to display; (2) make sure students feel cared about and respected as human beings; (3) be careful about making eye contact, which stimulates upper-cortex activity and is often interpreted as a challenge or threat; (4) react to situations without escalating them; and (5) provide considerable structure to activities (meaning directions and procedures) because a lack of structure often makes learning difficult for students with these learning differences.

Conditions That Seem to Reside in Peers and Groups

Two significant causes of misbehavior—*provocation* and *contagious group behavior*—seem to reside in class peers and groups. Here are suggestions for dealing with them.

1. *Provocation.* Much misbehavior results from students' provoking each other through teasing, petty annoyance, put-downs, sarcastic remarks, and aggression or bullying. For instance, Otisha is trying to study, but Art is bent on teasing her incessantly until she reaches the bursting point. Marty calls Jerry a name and Jerry responds hotly.

   Suggestions: Provocation often produces strong emotions that overwhelm self-control and increase combativeness. Discuss this phenomenon with your class. Ask:
   - Is provoking others or teasing them consistent with the class character we are trying to build or with the kind of people you truly want to be?
   - Can you name some things people say or do that upset you so much you want to retaliate? What presses your buttons?
   - If you retaliate, what do you think will happen? Will that put an end to the conflict?
   - What are some positive things we can do to stop provocation in the class?

2. *Contagious group behavior.* Students sometimes succumb to peer pressure or get caught up in group emotion and as a result may misbehave in ways they would not consider if by themselves. It is difficult for students to disregard peer pressure; it is easy to get swept up in group energy and emotion, and easy to justify one's misbehavior as "only what others were doing." For example, because Kerry and Lee want to look cool to their peers, Kerry defaces school property, and Lee bullies a weaker member of the class. Neither of the boys does those things when alone.

   Suggestions: Discuss this phenomenon with your class. For example, tell the class about some event in which a friend of yours, let's say Sarah, behaved badly just because others were doing so. Indicate that Sarah is now very embarrassed about her behavior and wishes that no one knew about it. Ask your students if they know any stories like Sarah's they would be willing to share, without mentioning names the class might recognize. (Tell them they must not mention family matters or members—doing so is a sure way to get parents upset with you.) If they share stories, guide the class in analyzing one or two of them. If they don't contribute a story, have a fictional one ready for their consideration. After hearing or recounting the story, ask questions such as:

- Is the behavior something the person will be proud of later?
- Why do you suppose the person behaved that way (e.g., for fun, comradeship, testing limits, being seen as clever or cool)?
- What do you think the long-term results will be for that person (e.g., an unpleasant story to remember, regret, guilt, getting caught, being found out, worry, disappointing one's family, possible punishment, living with knowing you did the wrong thing)?
- How do you believe the possible benefits compare with the probable risks?
- If you are caught doing something you are truly ashamed of, is there any way to make amends and save your reputation?
- How can you stay away from, or keep out of, group activities that are unlawful, hurtful to others, or against the rules?

Conditions That Seem to Reside in Instructional Environments

Four conditions that promote misbehavior are associated with instructional environments. They are *physical discomfort, tedium, meaninglessness,* and *lack of stimulation.* All are easily avoided.

1. *Physical discomfort.* Students often become restless when made uncomfortable by inappropriate temperature, poor lighting, or unsuitable seating or workspaces.

   Suggestions: Attend to comfort factors in advance and ask students about them. Make modifications as necessary. Build in some chances to move around if class periods are long.

2. *Tedium.* Students begin to fidget after a time when an instructional activity requires continued close attention, especially if the topic is not appealing.

   Suggestions: For such activities, break the work into shorter segments or add something that increases the level of interest. Try to plan your day so highly engaging activities are interspersed with lower-interest ones; moving from one low-engagement topic to another is likely to increase tedium and may escalate misbehavior.

3. *Meaninglessness.* Students grow restless when required to work at topics they do not comprehend or for which they see no purpose.

   Suggestions: Make sure the topic is meaningful to students—that they understand it and see its relevance and importance in their lives. Also, make sure they know how to do what is expected.

4. *Lack of stimulation.* The topic and learning environment sometimes provide little that is attractive or otherwise stimulating. Students may take no interest in the lesson.

   Suggestions: Select topics and activities in which students have natural interest. When that is not possible, introduce elements students are known to enjoy, such as novelty, mystery, movement, group work, group competition, and role-playing. Make sure that the work you're asking students to do is developmentally appropriate. Extend choices to students when possible, either about the topic to be studied or the ways in which students will show that they understand the material.

Conditions That Seem to Reside in Teachers and Other School Personnel

You won't hear it discussed often, but teachers and other school personnel sometimes misbehave in school and in so doing influence students to misbehave. Here are 10 examples of *teacher misbehavior* (and school personnel behavior) that sometimes promote student misbehavior:

1. *Poor habits.* Personnel in the schools sometimes use inappropriate ways of dealing with students or each other, such as using unseemly language and speaking in a sarcastic or bossy manner.

   Suggestions: Reflect regularly on how you interact with and speak to your students. Self-monitor your behavior and make sure it is as you want it to be. If you see or hear colleagues treating students in an unprofessional manner, and if you believe it is having a harmful effect on the students, consider speaking about the matter in private with your school administrator. Describe the situation, remaining as objective as possible. The administrator may or may not wish to follow up.

2. *Unfamiliarity with better techniques.* You may have heard the old expression, "I did then what I knew how to do. Now that I know better, I do better." These words are relevant for teachers as they learn to manage their classrooms; some educators have not had occasion to learn some of the newer, more effective ways of teaching and relating with today's students.

   Suggestions: It is important that you keep yourself informed about topics and activities that are well received by students. Reach out to popular teachers at your school and ask them what seems to work best for them. You can also find innumerable outstanding ideas and suggestions on the Internet and in professional books and journals that might be available at your school.

3. *Presenting poor models of behavior.* At times, all of us behave inconsistently and irresponsibly, especially on days when, for whatever reason, we are short on self-control. On those occasions, we sometimes treat students discourteously. We can't expect to be perfect, but we must realize that when we treat students poorly—which is to say, in ways we would not want to be treated—we leave a lasting impression that not only damages relationships but also encourages students to imitate our bad behavior.

   Suggestions: Always be the best model you can for your students, who watch you very closely and often pattern their behavior after yours (especially when you misbehave). If you do something that is inappropriate, call attention to it, explain why it was wrong, and apologize if necessary.

4. *Showing little interest in or appreciation for students.* We sometimes fail to show interest in students or appreciation for them as individuals, despite knowing they want our attention. If we disregard them repeatedly, students become hesitant to approach us or may seek our attention in disruptive ways.

    Suggestions: Give each student as much personal attention as possible. Greet them by name, exchange a friendly word, and show you are open to discussing any challenges they might be facing in school. Acknowledge their accomplishments and try to help them feel at ease. Time and effort invested in developing relationships is often returned in students' willingness to work productively because of connection and mutual respect.

5. *Succumbing to personal frustration.* Some educators get beaten down from continually having to deal with misbehavior, inconsiderate parents, or an abundance of meetings and paperwork. The stress may at times make it difficult for them to work with students in a kind, helpful manner.

    Suggestions: Regarding professional stress, especially the type that arises from concerns outside the classroom, figure out what works for you to process the situation and move beyond it. Talk to colleagues if it helps, but avoid repeatedly wading through all the frustrations, as continuous focus on the negative is unlikely to help shift your stress levels. Exercise. Join a study group or learning circle. Get involved in school leadership. Focus on the positive things that happen each day. Do your best to give each student (and yourself) a clean slate at each available opportunity.

6. *Reacting badly to provocation.* Though most misbehavior isn't personal, sometimes students may do and say things intentionally to get under your skin. You know you should keep your composure, but find yourself becoming upset and saying or doing something that is not professional.

    Suggestions: When students try to provoke you, disregard their comments and actions and proceed as if nothing has happened. If you feel the need to respond, only say, "Something is causing violations of our agreement about being considerate of others. I don't like that in our class. I'm wondering what we can do so that won't happen." Being able to manage your own strong emotions is very important in this situation.

7. *Providing ineffective guidance and feedback.* In the absence of guidance and feedback, students sometimes do not understand what is expected of them, how much progress they have made, or how they can improve.

    Suggestions: Make sure students understand clearly what they are supposed to do and how they should go about it. During and after assigned activities, tell students what they have done well and what they can do to improve. Emphasize that making mistakes is almost always a part of learning. Ask them for their appraisals of the activity and the efforts they have made. When you give feedback on student work, remember to focus on both the positive aspects of their performance and the things they can do to improve. Help them understand that your feedback on their work is not feedback about them as people, and that it's designed to help them build their skills rather than to judge them or criticize them.

8. *Using ineffective personal communication.* Some educators are not adept at communicating with students on a personal level. This may result in students becoming uneasy and hesitant about approaching their teachers.

    Suggestions: Speak regularly with students in a friendly way. Students want you to know their names and exchange pleasantries with them. Often they want to tell you their views on various matters and would like to know yours. Speaking with students as social equals (i.e., in a friendly manner) validates them personally, though you'll want to ensure that you set reasonable boundaries in action and conversation. Avoid comments that hurt feelings or dampen enthusiasm. Without overdoing it, say things honestly that increase students' optimism and bolster their confidence. If you need to have a difficult conversation with a student and are uncomfortable about it, run through it with a peer first so you can figure out how to communicate your message in a way that doesn't make the recipient defensive.

9. *Failure to plan proactively.* Many educators do not adequately plan their instructional program in advance or try to anticipate problems that might arise. Then, when unexpected things happen, they are not prepared to respond effectively.

    Suggestions: Think carefully about your curriculum and instructional activities and how your students are likely to respond to them. By anticipating difficulties, you can avoid most problems and prepare yourself to deal with whatever might happen. Investigate relevant school policies. Think through what you will do when people are injured or become suddenly ill, grow defiant, or otherwise misbehave. Decide what you will do and say if an unauthorized visitor approaches you, if a parent berates you, if the class groans when you announce an assignment, and so forth. Determine how you can respond decisively to such eventualities, yet maintain your composure and ability to relate positively with others.

10. *Using coercion, threat, and punishment.* Students don't like to be threatened or forced to do anything. (In our experience, very few people do.) If you treat your students abrasively, they will keep a watchful eye on you, fearful of being scolded, embarrassed, or demeaned, and will very likely develop negative attitudes toward you and school.

    Suggestions: Give up coercion and threat and replace them with considerate helpfulness, personal attention, and good communication. Explain to students how they should behave, demonstrate those behaviors, and have students practice the behaviors. When you see students behave responsibly, thank them for doing so. For older students, express your appreciation privately or to the class as a whole; singling students out in front of the group (even for positive reasons) can sometimes have unintended negative consequences.

WHAT ADDITIONAL THINGS MIGHT I DO TO EXERT POSITIVE INFLUENCE?

There are many suggestions for exerting positive influence on students in a systematic way. Here we briefly examine those four ways to positively influence your students.

Establish and Maintain a Positive Attitude

You will probably love dealing with students who are nice to you, but you may find it distasteful and troubling to deal with those who misbehave. But doing so is necessary, and you need to do it well. Following are some suggestions.

First, look at your misbehaving students. Allow your mind to sweep across them and see them as individual human beings, many of them striving for recognition from you and from their classmates, perhaps showing off or pestering others or causing disruption as opposed to being involved in the lesson.

Second, think this thought and do your best to truly mean it (paraphrased from an unknown source): *I am grateful to each and every one of my students for being here, for trusting themselves to my care, and for enabling me to have this important job. I appreciate the challenge of helping them. I appreciate the opportunity to assist them in becoming better persons. I appreciate their testing and strengthening my capabilities. Because I am truly grateful for this opportunity, I will do the very best for them I can.*

Third, occasionally remind your students that you're glad they're in your class, and that you're committed to doing your best for them. You might add that you will support them in school and would like for them to support you in return.

Use Your Influence to Move Students in the Right Direction

Teachers are encouraged to give their best effort on behalf of their students, but today many teachers do not understand fully how to do so. Let's look at this matter for a moment. Suppose you take the most brilliant scholar in a given field and put her in charge of teaching students who have virtually no interest in the subject she is to teach. What does that scholar need to do in order to teach the students well? Which of these three things do you think should be at the top of her list?

1. Emphasize her strong knowledge of the subject matter.
2. Organize a structure that will help students understand the subject matter, see how its main points are interconnected, and understand what it is good for.

3. Influence students by using personal charisma, intriguing questions, interesting demonstrations, and personal attention.

All three of those aspects—knowledge, structure, and influence—are essential for successful teaching. But of the three aspects, the one for which teachers usually receive the *least* preparation is the last of the three. Occasionally a teacher knows intuitively how to approach and work with students—teachers with that ability are often called "natural teachers." But many beginning teachers have focused mostly on learning their subject matter and deciding how to organize it for student learning. Unfortunately, they may not have been taught very much about how to interact with students and influence them in a positive manner. You'll find many recommendations in this text for helping you hone your influence skills and interact with students in ways that invite cooperation and effort.

Avoid the Pitfall of Arguing With Students

It is self-defeating to argue with students, or anyone else for that matter. It is worse than a waste of time, because telling them (or anyone) they are wrong doesn't change their minds. It often makes them even more resistant to your point of view. They will typically clam up or get defensive or angry, and after a time so will you. Remember this adage:

> *People convinced against their will*
> *Are of the same opinion still.*

Dale Carnegie included that saying in his marvelous book *How to Win Friends and Influence People* (1981 revision), in which he pointed to the pitfalls of arguing. He said he had listened to, participated in, and analyzed thousands of arguments and had concluded that arguing was invariably detrimental to your cause. You should avoid it, he said, as you would avoid rattlesnakes. Why? Because you can't win an argument. It is impossible. If you make the weaker case, you lose. If you make the stronger case, you also lose, because you have made the other person feel inferior and have wounded his or her pride. Wounded pride does not seek to cooperate. And arguing with students can escalate problems and lead to power struggles, often introducing an additional level of complexity and emotionality to the situation.

Carnegie says that when you disagree with another person but need to discuss a situation, here's what to do: Control your temper, listen, look for areas of agreement, and promise to think carefully about what the other person has said. He further advises that when you express your view, try saying, "I may be wrong. I often am. Let's see if we can examine the facts together." Never tell the other person he or she is wrong. If it turns out you are wrong, admit it quickly and sincerely.

Replace Criticism With Positive Influence

Let's suppose you are teaching a lesson and come face to face with the moment of truth in classroom management: A student, or group of students, has misbehaved—perhaps even offended you personally. You feel you can't overlook this behavior; you must respond. What do you do?

Here is a suggestion: At that point in time, hesitate (with a neutral expression on your face) long enough to hold in check any natural reaction to find fault, criticize, admonish, or lash out. Those reactions won't accomplish anything positive, nor will they ever convince the student that she was wrong. They may well make the student shut up or answer back, but that student will never thank you for the correction. She will not consider that she might be wrong. Or he will think you are browbeating him. Students who become embarrassed or resentful or angry are far more inclined to withdraw or subvert your efforts than to cooperate.

Instead of scolding or criticizing, select a response that does not threaten or demean the student's sense of self. Your actions or comments should lead the offender back to positive behavior, with no damage to the fragile ego. How, exactly, do you do so? Following are two suggestions.

First, if the misbehavior is relatively benign, just pause a moment and look at the offenders, making eye contact if you can. If the misbehavior seems to stop, continue on with your lesson in a smooth flow.

Second, if the misbehavior continues or is repeated, follow the suggestion of either Marvin Marshall or Diane Gossen. Marshall (2001/2007), whose work you will encounter later, might ask the misbehaving student,

> "At what level is that behavior?" He would have taught students the characteristics of four different levels of behavior. Merely asking the student to identify the level of his or her behavior is not very threatening. By honestly categorizing the level of behavior, the student is influenced to return to an acceptable level.

Or Gossen (2004), an authority on restitution theory, might ask the offending student,

> "Is that behavior in keeping with the kind of person you want to be?" If the student answers "yes," ask him or her to stay for a moment after class to speak with you (at which time you might say, "If that is truly how you want to be, we need to do some thinking. It is simply not acceptable for anyone in the class to interfere with the lesson and other students' learning"). If the student says it is not how he or she wants to be, Gossen would ask, "What could you do that would be?"

Such questions do not criticize the student or ask students to criticize themselves, especially if they are delivered in a neutral tone of voice. Remember: Criticism almost never works. Who among us seeks it? Or appreciates it? Although we may enjoy criticizing others, we hate being on the receiving end.

Then what *do* we like to receive from others? How do we like to be made to feel? In five minutes, you could make a list that would fill the next two pages, but one thing stands out above all the others. It is this:

We want to feel appreciated and important.

It's as simple as that. If you want to draw students to you, if you want them to cooperate with you and support you, say and do things that genuinely make them feel appreciated and important.

One way to make students feel appreciated is to ask them privately if they will help you with something. Another way is to offer them support and encouragement. Another is to give them individual help. Another is simply to listen to them when they confide in you. Another is to learn and remember something of importance to each student—their siblings, pets, or favorite activities outside school. And a surprisingly powerful one is simply to find a minute or two each day to chat with them individually about anything at all *except* their behavior. But what you say to them must be genuine. Insincere conversation doesn't do the job, at least not for long. Students see through it, and their trust in you is negatively affected.

Commentary From Anonymous Teacher 2

I have learned that just as we encourage our students to develop scholarly habits to make learning easier, we can develop "teacherly" habits that make teaching and learning easier and more enjoyable. Three of my favorites are:

1. *Greet students as they enter the classroom.* I stand at the door, smile, use first names, and offer a quick comment or question to each student. This is quick, easy, and fun. It helps students feel "seen" and valued, and I can model friendliness and caring. I see less misbehavior arising from students who otherwise feel unnoticed.
2. *Use lesson planning as a key tool in behavior management.* Variety is the name of the game to keep students interested, engaged, and just a little off-balance. I like to use different groupings of learners, offer choices in activities and tasks, and feature assignments using all learning modalities. Planning carefully for variety makes the class more fun and cuts down on misbehavior stemming from boredom.

3. *Keep students and caregivers informed of expectations, assessments, and evaluations.* In my experience, parents don't like surprises at report card time and students are poor at guessing how they are doing in a class. For all projects, reports, oral presentations, and the like, I use grading rubrics. I design the rubric to reflect my expectations, then spend time teaching it to the students before they begin the assignment. I have students practice peer evaluations using the rubric. They soon understand what is expected and how to go about meeting the requirements. My district, and all others that I know of, uses a Web-based computer grading program that offers parent access. I make it a priority to keep up with my grading and to post grades at least once weekly. In addition, I print out monthly progress reports for all students. This habit ensures students receive guidance in successfully completing assignments and that they receive accurate and timely feedback.

I'd also like to tell you about my struggles with a student I'll call Brendan. Our ongoing battle started the first day of school. He and all other students in our French class were asked to choose French names from lengthy lists. They would be called by those names in class. Brendan insisted on "Mozambique" for his name. I asked him to consider a normal name such as "Philippe" or "Guillaume" or "Jacques." He refused and began chanting, "Mozambique! Mozambique! Mozambique!" I relented, smiling, in order to avoid an unpleasant standoff on the first day.

That was the beginning of my unending difficulties with Brendan. I soon saw him not as a quirky kid but as an absolute contrarian. You'd have thought his mission in life was to plague me by doing the opposite of what I asked or expected. Hardly a threat to the eye, he was cute with dark brown curls, bright eyes, and a cheerful smile, liked by his peers, especially girls. But his actions and attitudes flustered me and put me off my game. Worse, the two of us produced a negativity that affected the entire class. There was nothing explosive or violent from him, but before long his ceaseless resistance wore me down.

To illustrate with but one example, we began each class with 5 to 7 minutes of bell work. Once the procedure was established, all the students except Brendan complied without grumbling. Brendan didn't grumble, but he stalled. "I don't have a pencil/study guide/piece of paper." I would supply him with what he needed, accompanied by a frown or look of exasperation. Those exchanges sometimes lasted through bell work. If any time was left, he would say, "I don't understand this." If the assignment was to practice French greetings and good-byes with table partners, Brendan was certain to remark: "I don't speak French." And "I don't know these people."

If the assignment was to respond with correct answers about days and months, Brendan would call out, "Paris! Notre Dame! Haiti! New Orleans!" We had a rule to keep chair legs flat on the floor with no leaning back: Brendan would lean back as far as he could, balancing precariously. If I said, "Please don't lean back in your chair," he would say, "My bad." In less than 3 minutes he'd be leaning back again.

I didn't know how to handle that or relate to him. I nagged, complained, criticized, reasoned, counseled, muttered, and shook my head in disgust and resignation. None of that changed Brendan. But it changed me. I retreated behind clenched jaws and grinding teeth. I suspended bell work for that class. I used fewer and fewer groupings for oral practice. I started to pretend I didn't see when he leaned back in his chair. I came to dread that class and rejoice when he was absent.

I soon learned Brendan was not motivated by grades, good or bad, or by parent phone calls, good or bad. He didn't care about privileges or the loss of same. He was not intimidated by threats, by referrals, by chats with the assistant principal. He was always smiling. He kept me frowning and itchy. He won. I finally asked to have him removed from my class.

I think now I could do better. But back then, I took his behavior personally. His defiance offended me and kept me on the defensive. I wish I would have just smiled and chatted with him about his pets and his music, the two most important things in his life. I got that information from him the first day on "inventory" sheets I use for students to introduce themselves to me. I wonder, too, if we might have chatted about geography or French history or anything he liked in school. But I didn't think of it. I was stubborn. My pride was on the line. I gave it priority over taking the time to get to know a bright and challenging student in my care.

Source: Used courtesy of Timothy C. Charles.

REFLECTING ON BEHAVIOR AND ITS ROOTS: WHAT YOU HAVE LEARNED IN THIS CHAPTER

In this chapter, you've learned about various causes of misbehavior, and you've begun to develop a set of strategies for considering and responding to each. And you've learned a lot of new terminology that educators use as they discuss classroom management. You now have a basic understanding of classroom management that can serve as the lens through which you view ideas presented by the experts discussed in each of the later chapters of this book. Remember, it's a good idea to make notes in your planning guide of those ideas that resonated with you.

Roadmap for Advanced Learning

Do some independent reading on the topics below, each of which directly relates to classroom management:

Teach Without Touching: How can teachers avoid allegations of inappropriate contact with students?

Charisma for Teachers: What is charisma, and how can teachers build their own?

Teacher Power Styles—Authoritarian, Authoritative, Permissive: What are the effects of adopting each approach to classroom control and teacher identity?

MyLab Education Self-Check 3.1

MyLab Education Self-Check 3.2

MyLab Education Application Exercise 3.1 Simulation: Responding to Mildly Disruptive Behavior

MyLab Education Application Exercise 3.2 Maintaining a Positive Climate While Managing Inappropriate Behavior

MyLab Education Application Exercise 3.3 Discussing Reasons for Inappropriate Behavior With a Student

The Development of Classroom Management

Which 20th-Century Authorities Set the Foundations for Today's Classroom Management, and What Did They Advocate?

LEARNING OUTCOMES:

4-1 Identify individuals who have made significant contributions to the study of classroom management and articulate the basic tenets of each individual's recommendations.

4-2 Identify themes from historical approaches to management that are still prevalent in the field today.

Prior to the 1950s, classroom management was thought of as an ongoing struggle between demanding teachers and disobedient students. The teachers' job was to make students learn, and although many students complied with that expectation, many others resisted work and caused disruptions. Altogether, classroom management was a mélange of demands, rules, misbehavior, insubordination, punishments, detention, suspension, and corporal punishment. No one really objected. Those conditions were accepted by students, parents, and teachers, often smilingly, as natural and necessary in schooling.

That picture began to change around the middle of the 20th century. With the end of World War II, newer attitudes toward behavior and classroom management became evident. Society was growing more tolerant of behavior a bit outside the norm, and with that tolerance came an inclination to treat students more considerately and humanely. Over time, threat, corporal punishment, and other forceful means of controlling behavior fell out of favor.

At the same time, society began asking schools to assume a stronger role in teaching students to be civil, responsible, and self-controlled, traits that were traditionally taught in the family and sometimes in religious institutions. The schools accepted the challenge, more or less by default, and by the end of the 20th century, the sternly coercive teacher had almost disappeared, replaced by teachers of gentler demeanor who relied on "friendly persuasion" to get students to behave themselves. In this chapter, we review the nature of those changes and see how they came about.

CHAPTER PREVIEW: WHY DOES THIS MATTER TO ME?

In this chapter, you will see a sequence of major developments in classroom management, beginning with the first systematic classroom management approach set forth in 1951 and running up through the present. It will give you a picture of the historical transformation in classroom management. Incorporated into the sequence are commentaries about contributions from great educators, psychologists, and psychiatrists, showing how classroom management evolved in the last half of the 20th century. Those powerful ideas, which opened new lines of thought about classroom management, are then reviewed succinctly in this chapter. Newer contributions that appeared or grew in strength in recent years are included in the overall timeline and then are described in greater detail in later chapters in this book.

You might wonder why we are dedicating so much of this chapter to classroom management ideas that originated many years ago. After all, isn't it more important for 21st-century teachers to know the newest and most current information about what works in classrooms? Well, while many of the approaches we're covering in this chapter are no longer in vogue, they reflect themes that are still critical to classroom management in the 21st century. As you read about each historical contribution to the evolving field of classroom management, think not just about what those systems would have looked like in practice, but how their basic ideas are still reflected in our management systems of today.

A TIMELINE OF DEVELOPMENTS IN MODERN CLASSROOM MANAGEMENT

1951 *Understanding Group Dynamics*—Fritz Redl (psychiatrist) and William Wattenberg (educational psychologist) presented the first systematically organized approach to classroom management. It was based on their identification and analyses of forces they called "group dynamics" that affect people's behavior when in groups.

1954 *The Role of Reinforcement in Shaping Behavior*—B. F. Skinner (psychologist) expanded on the discoveries of Russian physiologist Ivan Pavlov and for many years studied how reinforcement (what happens *after* a behavior) affects both animal and human learning. His conclusions led to tactics for shaping behavior through a process now popularly called "behavior modification."

1969 *Understanding Behavior as Student Choice*—William Glasser (psychiatrist) turned his attention to educational theory and practice after becoming convinced that personal choice—as distinct from reinforcement—was pivotal in human learning and general behavior. The teacher's role was to help students make choices that served them better in school.

1971 *Managing Students and Lessons*—Jacob Kounin (educational psychologist) discovered that classroom behavior is very strongly affected by how teachers present and manage lessons, which opened yet another line of thought about classroom management.

1971 *Using Congruent Communication*—Haim Ginott (teacher and psychologist) set forth a number of new conclusions about how communication and teacher actions affect student behavior. His realizations still feature prominently in most of today's approaches to classroom management.

1971 *Emphasizing Democracy and the Need for Belonging*—Rudolf Dreikurs (psychiatrist) became convinced that students are continually motivated to pursue a primary goal in school, which is to achieve a strong sense of belonging. Misbehavior is often manifested in their unsuccessful attempts to do so. Dreikurs co-wrote *Discipline without Tears* with Pearl Cassel in 1971; his daughter, Eva Dreikurs Ferguson, has assumed co-authorship of the book since his death.

1976 *Assertively Taking Charge*—Lee Canter and Marlene Canter (educators) provided a tactic that teachers of the day sorely needed—a means of easily and effectively taking charge in their classrooms and dealing with misbehavior. Their approach, called "assertive discipline," dominated classroom management practice for 20 years thereafter.

1986 *Applying the Principles of Choice Theory*—William Glasser (psychiatrist) returned to prominence with new thoughts on helping students make better behavior choices.

1987 *Keeping Students Actively Involved*—Fred Jones (psychologist) discovered that the major problem in classroom management was "massive time-wasting." He developed several tactics which remain popular today, for conserving time and keeping students involved.

1988 *Maintaining Student Dignity*—Richard Curwin (educator) and Allen Mendler (psychologist) introduced the concept of *discipline with dignity* (Brian Mendler, educator, now participates in the work). They insist that for classroom management to be effective, it must allow students to maintain a personal sense of dignity (self-respect), a concept now emphasized in virtually all modern approaches to classroom management.

1989 *Cooperative Discipline*—Linda Albert (educator) presented a number of strategies for improving class behavior through structures that help students relate positively with each other and with the teacher. She focused on teacher management styles and encouraged the use of teacher influence in managing student behavior.

1992   *Self-Restitution Theory*—Diane Gossen (educator) developed and emphasized the concept of self-restitution, in which she asked students who misbehaved to reflect on their behavior, identify the need that prompted it, and then create new ways of behaving that are consistent with the responsible persons they want to be.

1993   *Emphasizing Positivity and Humaneness*—Jane Nelsen (educator) and Lynn Lott (educator) provided additional positive classroom tactics that promote cooperation and enhance personal relations.

1994   *Building Inner Discipline*—Barbara Coloroso (educator) promoted the growth of "inner discipline" in students, meaning they are helped to realize that proper behavior leads to a better existence than does improper behavior.

1997   *Real Discipline*—Ronald Morrish asserted that student discipline is the result of compliance training, and that teachers must insist on correct behavior from students. Morrish went on to say that students are often not mature enough to be able to handle having choices and that teachers must teach students how to behave appropriately.

1998   *On Classroom Roles and Procedures*—Harry Wong and Rosemary Wong (educators) insisted that proper class behavior is much more likely when students know exactly what is expected of them—hence, they advocate establishing and teaching clear procedures for all class activities. Their work, which is strongly impacting present-day teaching, is reviewed in Chapter 7 of this book.

1999   *Learning to Meet Needs Without Harming Others*—Ed Ford (director of Responsible Thinking Process, Inc.) developed a noncontrolling approach in which students learn to meet their needs without infringing on the rights or comforts of others, thereby reducing conflict in the classroom.

2000   *Promoting Synergy in the Classroom*—C. M. Charles (teacher educator) advocated reducing misbehavior by energizing classes through use of teacher charisma, topics and activities of high interest, group competition, cooperative work, and recognition of genuine accomplishment.

2001   *Building Moral Intelligence*—Michele Borba (educator) provided suggestions to help students differentiate between right and wrong, establish ethical convictions, and act on those convictions in an honorable way.

2001   *Classrooms as Communities of Learners*—Alfie Kohn (educator) lamented the failure of schools to promote in-depth learning. His remedy was to convert classes into "communities of learners," with give and take and in-depth exploration of meaningful topics.

2002   *Promoting Civility in the Classroom*—P. M. Forni (director of the Civility Initiative at Johns Hopkins University) launched a push to popularize civil behavior in schools and society.

The works noted up to this point have been pivotal in the development of modern thought on classroom management. Those that follow depict today's strongest influences in classroom management. Most, but not all, will be discussed in separate chapters, as indicated.

1997 to present   *Positive Behavioral Interventions and Supports*—PBIS was introduced in the reauthorization of the Individuals with Disabilities Act of 1997 as a way of providing more effective interventions for students with behavioral disorders. (Unlike most other works presented in this chapter, its genesis is not attributable to a single author, though many individuals have developed expertise in its use. You'll read much more about them in Chapter 12.) Over time, it has evolved for schoolwide use and is currently one of the most prevalent management approaches in the United States. The program provides a framework for making data-driven decisions about evidence-based behavioral practices and is intended to move all students toward academic, behavioral, and social growth (Sugai & Simonson, 2012).

1998 to present   *How to Be an Effective Teacher*—Harry Wong and Rosemary Wong's ideas grow in popularity. Their book *The First Days of School: How to Be an Effective Teacher* (revised edition, 2009) is the best-selling education book of all time. The Wongs' highly influential teachings are presented in detail in Chapter 7 of this book.

2001 to present   *Every Student Can Succeed*—William Glasser (psychiatrist and education consultant) established yet another major approach to classroom management, which promoted high levels of student learning and positive behavior. His contribution is described in Chapter 9 of this book.

2001 to present   *Raising the Level of Student Responsibility*—Marvin Marshall (educator) developed and disseminated a highly popular approach to humane classroom management that he calls *Discipline Without Stress*. As described in Chapter 10 of this book, Marshall's approach makes strong use of a four-level "Hierarchy of Social Development," with teachers helping students learn to function at the highest level.

2001 to present   *Teacher-Student Same-Side Approach to Discipline*—Spencer Kagan (psychologist and educator), in collaboration with Patricia Kyle (educator) and Sally Scott (educator), explained the strategy and tactics of *Win-Win Discipline*, which called on teachers and students to work together on the same side, learn to identify states of emotion in students who misbehave, and employ appropriate "structures" that help students conduct themselves appropriately. Win-Win Discipline is described in Chapter 11 of this book.

2003 to present   *Fred Jones's Tools for Teachers*— Fred Jones enjoyed growing popularity for his tactics in keeping students meaningfully involved in lessons and managing classrooms more efficiently. His ideas are examined in detail in Chapter 8 of this book.

2005 to present — *What Is Real Discipline?*—Ronald Morrish (behavior specialist and consultant) answered this question in a website article (see references) and two popular books. He described basic tactics for promoting responsible behavior. His ideas are presented in detail in Chapter 5 of this book.

2008 to present — *Discipline Through Clear Expectations, Leverage, and Student Accountability*—Craig Seganti (teacher) worked for 20 years in inner-city Los Angeles schools, where he developed tactics for getting the best from students who are often considered to be difficult to manage. His work is described in Chapter 6 of this book.

Now, we proceed to review in a bit more detail the earlier 20th-century contributions in classroom management (1951–2001) and note the specific influences they have had on today's classroom management.

GROUP DYNAMICS: WHAT DID FRITZ REDL AND WILLIAM WATTENBERG EXPLAIN ABOUT GROUP BEHAVIOR?

In 1951, psychiatrist Fritz Redl and educational psychologist William Wattenberg developed and disseminated the first theory-based approach to humane classroom management. Their conclusions, described in their book *Mental Hygiene in Teaching* (1951), helped teachers understand group behavior and how it affects individual behavior. Redl and Wattenberg contended that much student misbehavior is caused by forces detectible only in larger groups. They called those forces **group dynamics** and said if teachers are to understand student behavior, they must first understand group dynamics. Their ideas marked the beginning of what we now think of as "modern classroom management."

Redl and Wattenberg explained that group dynamics account for phenomena such as group spirit, group norms and expectations, imitative behavior, desire to excel, scapegoating of certain students, and providing hiding places for nonachievers. They said students take on **student roles** such as leader, follower, clown (who shows off), instigator (who provokes misbehavior), and scapegoat (on whom blame is placed even when not deserved). They urged teachers to be watchful for these roles, bring them to the class's attention, and be prepared to encourage or discourage them as appropriate.

They also pointed out that students expect teachers to fill certain **teacher roles**, such as role models, sources of knowledge, referees, judges, and surrogate parents. Teachers must be aware that students hold these expectations and should discuss the implications with students.

Redl and Wattenberg urged teachers to behave toward students in a helpful manner, remain as objective as possible, show tolerance, keep a sense of humor, and help students maintain positive attitudes toward school and the class. All these things, they said, should be thought of as *influence techniques*, to be used instead of threat and punishment to promote desirable behavior. They also advised teachers to involve students in setting class standards and deciding how misbehavior should be handled, both of which are now widely used practices.

The Redl and Wattenberg Model To control misbehavior, (1) identify and soften typical causes of misbehavior; (2) clarify and discuss student roles and teacher roles; (3) involve students in deciding how misbehavior should be handled; and (4) maintain responsible student behavior by using "influence techniques" such as encouragement and support of self-control rather than demands and reprimands.

SHAPING BEHAVIOR: WHAT DID B. F. SKINNER DISCOVER ABOUT HELPING STUDENTS LEARN AND CONDUCT THEMSELVES PROPERLY?

In the 1940s and early 1950s, Harvard behavioral psychologist Burrhus Frederic Skinner (1904–1990) was investigating how our voluntary actions are influenced by what happens to us immediately after we perform an act.

Skinner reported his conclusions in a number of publications, two of which were his book *Science and Human Behavior* (1953) and his article "The Science of Learning and the Art of Teaching" (1954). His findings convinced him that much of our voluntary behavior is shaped by reinforcement (or lack thereof), which we receive immediately after performing an act. Simply put, when we perform an act and are reinforced immediately afterward, we become more likely to repeat that act or a similar one and even to try harder in the future.

For purposes here, reinforcement can be thought of as reward, although reward is a term Skinner never used. The term he used was *reinforcing stimulus*. He learned that a stimulus (something the individual receives) can strengthen a particular behavior, but only if it is received very soon after that behavior occurs. In the 1960s, teachers frequently used reinforcers such as candy, popcorn, and tangible objects, but that practice died out once teachers learned that students often worked mainly to get the reward, leaving unsatisfactory residual learning once the rewards were removed. Reinforcing stimuli now commonly used in classrooms include knowledge of results, peer approval, awards, free time, and teacher smiles, nods, and praise.

Constant reinforcement, given every time a student behaves as desired, helps new learning become established quickly. *Intermittent reinforcement*, given occasionally, is sufficient to maintain desired behavior once it is established, whereas behavior that is not reinforced tends to disappear over time.

Shaping behavior is accomplished through *successive approximation*, in which behavior is reinforced as it comes closer and closer to a preset goal. This process is helpful in building skills incrementally.

Although Skinner did not concern himself with classroom management per se, his discoveries affected it strongly. In the early 1960s, his followers organized his principles into the procedure called *behavior modification*, which became very popular in classroom management and teaching. By the mid-1960s, many primary-grade teachers were using behavior modification as their entire classroom management system, rewarding students who behaved properly and ignoring those who misbehaved. (Skinner did not use punishment in shaping behavior. He considered its effects unreliable.)

But before many years passed, teachers abandoned behavior modification as a main approach to classroom management, considering it akin to bribing students to get them to behave acceptably. Moreover, teachers found the process cumbersome to use and inefficient in teaching students what *not* to do. Teachers quickly realized it was far easier just to teach students how they *should* and *should not* behave.

That said, it is nevertheless true that teachers still use reinforcement tactics dozens of times every day, principally through praise and approval to motivate and support students.

The Skinner Model When students conduct themselves acceptably, provide immediate reinforcement to increase repetition of good behavior and shape behavior in desired directions.

CHOICE THEORY: WHAT DID WILLIAM GLASSER SAY ABOUT CHOICES AND FAILURE?

William Glasser is unique among the authorities featured in this book in that he was both a pioneer in the earlier movement toward modern classroom management and, later, the contributor of an exemplary approach in modern classroom management. In Chapter 1, you saw descriptions of the "seven deadly habits" he observed in teachers and the "seven connecting habits" that produced much better results.

Glasser gained instant fame in educational circles with the publication of his blockbuster *Schools Without Failure* (1969). That was his second major book in four years and was later acclaimed as one of the most influential education books of the 20th century.

Glasser was already widely known for his prior book, *Reality Therapy: A New Approach to Psychiatry* (1965). In that book, he urged psychotherapists to move their main focus away from probing into what had happened to troubled individuals in the past (the classical approach) and toward helping individuals resolve their problems within the context of present reality.

Glasser, when counseling delinquent adolescents, found that they responded especially well to reality therapy. That experience led to a long career of writing about education, working with educators, and striving to apply his ideas in schools. Glasser believed a great many of our personal problems are due to unsatisfactory or nonexistent connections with people upon whom we depend. Reality therapy provides a means for troubled people to connect or reconnect with others who are important in their lives, such as teachers. Glasser's suggestions for working effectively with students include:

- *Focus on the present.* Time spent dwelling on the past, complaining, or discussing symptoms is wasted. Instead, focus on the here and now and seek ways to resolve problems.
- *Avoid criticizing and blaming.* These are harmful external control behaviors that destroy relationships.
- *Remain nonjudgmental and noncoercive.* Appraise everything in terms of results. If actions are not providing the desired results, the behaviors are not working. New ones are needed.
- *Don't get bogged down in excuses.* Whether legitimate or not, excuses prevent one from making needed connections with others.
- *Put together specific workable plans for connecting with people important to you.* Implement the plans and evaluate your efforts and the results. Be ready to revise or reject plans if they do not work (The William Glasser Institute, 2009).

In addition to the principles of reality therapy, Glasser introduced three new ideas that gained educators' immediate attention:

1. *The Problem with Failure.* Sense of failure is one of the most disheartening things that can happen to students. School should be organized to promote genuine success for all.
2. *The Power of Choice.* Students choose to behave as they do. Nothing forces them to misbehave and no one can force them to learn. Teachers must recognize that all they can do is *influence* students to make better choices in how they behave, which leads to greater success in school.
3. *The Value of Classroom Meetings.* Classroom meetings are a superb vehicle for interacting with students and involving them in meaningful discussions. At a class meeting, the teacher and students share their thoughts and identify and resolve classroom issues.

Glasser also proposed an approach to classroom management that emphasized rules of behavior linked to consequences for breaking them. The students themselves were to assume responsibility for proper behavior. When students misbehaved, they were asked in a friendly tone to state what they had done and to evaluate the effect their actions had on themselves, their classmates, and teacher. They were further asked to identify and commit themselves to subsequent behavior that would be more appropriate.

Glasser acknowledged that this process was a bit tedious. But he insisted that students who saw themselves as failures were not likely to improve unless they had ongoing supportive involvement with successful people, such as teachers, who provided positive influence and accepted no excuses for improper behavior.

The Early Glasser Model (1) Involve students in reflecting on difficulties they encounter in school. (2) Have students suggest how they might help resolve the problems they face. (3) Ask them to take positive action by consciously choosing how they will behave in various circumstances. (4) Remove the notion of failure; judge students in terms of their positive efforts.

Commentary from Anonymous Teacher 1

From what I have seen in the past several years, I'd say most of the teachers at my school pretty much follow Glasser's principles when interacting with students. However, I doubt that many of us, if any, credit those skills to Dr. Glasser. We have picked up on them somehow or another. Maybe they have become part of the climate of teaching. Anyhow, most of us have good rapport with our students, and best I can tell most of the students seem to have a feeling of connectedness with teachers.

Personally, I think Glasser's ideas are right on the mark. I, for one, find that using them makes my teaching days go more smoothly and leaves me with fewer behavior problems to deal with.

Source: Used courtesy of Timothy C. Charles.

LESSON MANAGEMENT: WHAT DID JACOB KOUNIN DISCOVER ABOUT TEACHING STYLE AND STUDENT BEHAVIOR?

In the late 1960s, Jacob Kounin, an educational psychologist at Wayne State University, conducted an extensive investigation into how highly effective teachers dealt with classroom misbehavior. But as reported in his 1971 book *Discipline and Group Management in Classrooms*, he didn't find much at first, as his research failed to uncover the information he was seeking.

And yet it remained evident that some teachers seemed to promote excellent class behavior while others did not. Kounin analyzed his data again and this time made a surprising finding—that good classroom management was not so much dependent on what teachers did when misbehavior occurred, but on how teachers presented lessons and dealt with various groups in the class. *Their success came from what they did before misbehavior occurred, rather than from what they did to correct it after it occurred.* Kounin captured the need for classroom managers to anticipate and work to prevent misbehavior.

Specifically, Kounin noted that the more effective teachers managed their lessons so that students were kept alert, on task, and involved. He found that those teachers used identifiable procedures for gaining student attention and clarifying expectations. Of particular interest was what he called *group alerting*, where teachers obtained students' full attention before giving directions or making explanations. Then, during lessons, the teachers maintained student *accountability* by calling on students from time to time to respond, demonstrate, or explain.

Kounin also found that teachers of well-behaved classes displayed a constant awareness of what all students were doing in the classroom at all times. He used the term *withitness* to refer to such awareness. Teachers with higher levels of withitness were able to monitor and interact with students doing independent work even while those teachers were presenting lessons to smaller groups. Kounin used the term *overlapping* to refer to teachers attending to two or more classroom events simultaneously. He concluded it was one of the most important of all teaching skills.

Other important qualities Kounin discovered included lesson *momentum*— referring to a forward movement of the lesson, with no confusion or dead spots; *smoothness*, meaning a steady progression in the lesson without abrupt stops and starts; and *satiation*, meaning students getting their fill of a particular topic or activity and becoming bored or frustrated, causing them to disengage from the lesson.

The connection Kounin identified between teaching and student behavior led to a new line of thought concerning how teaching style affects student behavior. Most systems of classroom management now place heavy emphasis on that connection.

The Kounin Model Know what is going on in all parts of the classroom at all times. Learn to attend to multiple issues simultaneously. Carefully organize and conduct interesting lessons that (1) move forward smoothly without dead spots or abrupt changes, (2) hold students accountable for attention and participation, and (3) stop before reaching students' point of satiation.

CONGRUENT COMMUNICATION: WHAT DID HAIM GINOTT TEACH US ABOUT COMMUNICATING WITH STUDENTS?

In the same year that Kounin published his work, another small book appeared that had immediate and lasting influence on teaching. The book was Haim Ginott's *Teacher and Child* (1971), in which Ginott explained the critical role of communication in teaching and classroom management. One of Ginott's main contentions was that learning and behavior are greatly influenced by the way teachers talk with students. His teachings had enormous effect in establishing the personal, caring tone that prevails in classroom management today. In Chapter 1, reference was made to Dr. Ginott's views on "congruent communication," which are revisited and elaborated on in this chapter.

Ginott, a classroom teacher early in his career, later held professorships in psychology at Adelphi University and New York University Graduate School. He also served as UNESCO consultant in Israel, was resident psychologist on NBC's *Today*, and wrote a weekly syndicated column entitled "Between Us" that dealt with interpersonal communication.

In *Teacher and Child*, Ginott reminded us that learning always takes place in the "present tense" and is intensely personal to students. He said teachers must not prejudge students and must remember that each learner is an individual who requires much personal attention.

Ginott coined several terms to help convey his messages about communication. Those terms included *congruent communication*, meaning communication that is harmonious with students' feelings about situations and themselves; *sane messages*, which address *situations* rather than the students' character or past behavior; *teachers at their best*, as when they use congruent communication and do not preach, moralize, impose guilt, or demand promises, but instead confer dignity on their students by treating them as social equals; and *teachers at their worst*, as when they label students, belittle them, and denigrate their character.

Effective teachers also invite cooperation from their students by describing the situation when a problem occurs and indicating what needs to be done. They do not dictate to students or boss them around—acts that demean students and provoke resistance. Above all, teachers have a hidden asset on which they can always rely, which is to ask themselves, "How can I be most helpful to my students right now?"

Ginott had a great deal to say about praise as well, and his contentions came as a surprise to most teachers. He insisted that *evaluative praise* is worse than no praise at all and should never be used. An example of evaluative praise is "Good boy for raising your hand." Instead of evaluative praise, which comments on student character, teachers should use *appreciative praise*, which comments on effort or improvement (e.g., "Thank you for remembering to raise your hand.")

With regard to correcting inappropriate behavior, Ginott advised simply teaching students how to behave properly, instead of reprimanding them when they misbehave. He urged teachers to avoid asking *why* questions when discussing behavior, such as, "Why did you do that to Thomas?" *Why* questions make students feel guilty and defensive.

Ginott acknowledged that his suggestions do not produce instantaneous results. They need to be used repeatedly over time for their power to take effect. Ginott said that misbehavior can be squelched, but genuine discipline (meaning self-discipline) rarely occurs instantaneously. Rather, it develops as a series of small steps that lead to genuine changes in student attitude. He placed great emphasis on the teacher's role in the overall process:

As a teacher I have come to the frightening conclusion that I am the decisive element in the classroom. It is my personal approach that creates the climate. It is my daily mood that makes the weather. As a teacher I possess tremendous power to make a child's life miserable or joyous. I can be a tool of torture or an instrument of inspiration. I can humiliate or humor, hurt or heal. In all situations it is my response that decides whether a crisis will be escalated or de-escalated, and a child humanized or dehumanized. (1971, p. 13)

The Ginott Model Use congruent communication and sane messages when helping students with their behavior. Sincerely confer dignity on students and invite them to cooperate with you. Use appreciative praise and avoid tactics students might see as punishment.

NEEDS AND DEMOCRATIC TEACHING: WHAT WERE RUDOLF DREIKURS'S CONTENTIONS ABOUT STUDENT NEEDS AND THE BEST WAY TO TEACH?

In 1971 (the year before he died), psychiatrist Rudolf Dreikurs put forth two ideas that were new to classroom management. The first was that students—indeed all humans—have a powerful inborn need for belonging. He believed that when students in school are unable to satisfy this prime need (the genuine goal of their behavior) they turn by default to certain mistaken goals such as attention-seeking, power-seeking, revenge-seeking, and withdrawal.

Dreikurs's second major idea was that learning occurs best in *democratic classrooms* that emphasize active student involvement, promote a sense of belonging, and foster self-discipline. He characterized democratic classrooms as those where students participate in class decision making and are treated as social equals by their teachers.

Dreikurs said the best way for teachers to deal with misbehavior is to identify and address the mistaken goal it reflects and then discuss with students, in a friendly and nonthreatening manner, the faulty logic in that goal. Dreikurs suggested calmly asking, "Do you need me to pay more attention to you?" or "Could it be that you want to show that I can't make you do the assignment?"

Dreikurs also had much to say about the nature and importance of democratic classrooms. In such classrooms, teachers help students develop self-control based on social interest, which includes showing responsibility to oneself as well as to and for members of the group in matters of work, friendship, and self-significance. Students gain self-control as they become able to show initiative, make reasonable decisions, and assume responsibility in ways that benefit themselves and others.

*From *Teacher and Child: A Book for Parents and Teachers*, by Haim G. Ginnott. © Publisher by Scribner.

Dreikurs contrasted democratic classrooms with autocratic classrooms and permissive classrooms as follows: In *autocratic classrooms*, the teacher makes all decisions and imposes them on students, which does nothing to help students show personal initiative and accept responsibility. In *permissive classrooms*, the teacher overlooks students' failure to comply with rules or conduct themselves humanely, which suggests the teacher accepts those behaviors. In democratic classrooms, teachers

- speak in positive terms.
- encourage students to strive for improvement, not perfection.
- emphasize students' strengths while minimizing their weaknesses.
- help students learn from mistakes and recognize them as valuable elements in the learning process.
- encourage independence and responsibility.
- show faith in students and offer them help in overcoming obstacles.
- encourage students to help each other.
- show pride in student work; display and share it with others.
- are optimistic and enthusiastic.
- use encouraging remarks such as, "You have improved." "Can I help you?" "What did you learn from that mistake?" (Dreikurs & Cassel, 1995 [originally published in 1971], pp. 51–54)*

The Dreikurs Model Help all students meet their need for belonging in the class. When they misbehave by pursuing mistaken goals, discuss the fallacy in a non-threatening manner. Strive to maintain a democratic classroom that emphasizes group well-being, promotes a sense of belonging, and helps students make positive choices and exercise responsibility.

TAKING CHARGE: HOW DID LEE AND MARLENE CANTER ADVISE TEACHERS TO ESTABLISH CONTROL IN THEIR CLASSROOMS?

In 1976, Lee and Marlene Canter, both classroom teachers, published a book entitled *Assertive Discipline: A Take-Charge Approach for Today's Educator*. In that book, they introduced a classroom management approach called Assertive Discipline, which took education by storm and for the next 20 years was far and away the most popular classroom management system in American schools.

As the title of their book suggests, the Canter approach urged teachers to "take charge" in the classroom and showed them how to do so—just what teachers were looking for at a time when permissiveness throughout society seemed to be fostering student behavior that made teaching ever more difficult. The Canters

*From *Discipline Without Tears* by R. Dreikurs and P. Cassel © 1995.

provided a simple but well-structured plan that enabled teachers to interact with students in a calm, insistent, and consistent manner. In the rationale for their plan, the Canters insisted that students had a right to learn in a calm, orderly classroom, and teachers had a right to teach without being interrupted by misbehavior.

Assertive Discipline prompted students to make positive behavior choices. Its approach required

1. a clear set of rules for class behavior;
2. positive consequences such as recognition and praise applied intermittently when students comply with the rules;
3. negative consequences applied consistently when students break the rules.

In the Assertive Discipline model, the negative consequences were organized into a hierarchy that became progressively more unpleasant if students continued to break rules. The Canters asserted that misbehavior ends when teachers apply a consequence that is distasteful enough that students would choose to comply with class rules rather than endure the consequence.

The Canters wanted all teachers to function as assertive teachers who clearly, confidently, and consistently model and express class expectations, build trust, and teach students how to behave appropriately.

Assertive Discipline was enthusiastically accepted at first, but over time it was criticized for being overly controlling. To address that complaint, the Canters added provisions for talking helpfully with students and working to establish mutual trust and respect. After some 20 years of dominance, Assertive Discipline as a major classroom management strategy faded away, but vestiges of it are still seen in classrooms everywhere.

The Canter Model Establish five or six rules for class behavior. Make a list of positive consequences you will apply when students comply with rules. Make a list of negative consequences you will apply when students break the rules. Organize the negative consequences from less severe to more severe. As students continue to break rules, apply more severe consequences until the misbehavior ceases.

THE COOPERATIVE APPROACH: HOW DOES LINDA ALBERT ADVISE TEACHERS TO WORK WITH STUDENTS?

Linda Albert, author and disseminator of *Cooperative Discipline* (1989/1996/2002), has been a counselor, syndicated columnist, university professor, and classroom teacher. She has worked nationally and internationally with educators and parents.

In her work, Albert's main focus was on helping teachers and students cooperate with each other in a manner that removes most of the adversarial relationship that so often exists between teacher and student. Albert believed cooperation occurs more easily when students truly feel they have an important place in the class. To make sure students gain that feeling, she gave particular attention to what she calls the *Three C's*—helping all students *feel Capable, Connect with others*, and *make Contributions* to the class.

To increase student sense of *Capability*, Albert encouraged teachers to do the following:

1. *Make mistakes okay.* The fear of making mistakes undermines students' sense of capability, and when they are fearful, many stop trying. Albert recommended that teachers minimize this fear by talking with students about what mistakes are, helping them understand that everyone makes mistakes, and showing them that mistakes are a natural part of learning.
2. *Build confidence.* In order to feel capable, students must have confidence that success is possible. To help students gain confidence, teachers should convey that learning is a process of improvement, not an end product.
3. *Make progress tangible.* Teachers should provide tangible evidence of student progress. Grades are ineffective because they tell little about specific accomplishments. Albert suggested that teachers use devices such as accomplishment albums and portfolios along with talks about specific progress students have made and ways to improve their work in the future.
4. *Recognize achievement.* Albert asserted that a student's sense of capability increases when the student receives attention for what he or she has accomplished. She suggested that teachers have class members acknowledge each other's accomplishments, recognize students at awards assemblies, set up exhibits, and make presentations for other classes and parents.

Albert also asserted that it is essential that all students *Connect*, meaning they establish and maintain positive relationships with peers and teachers. As students make these connections, they become more cooperative and helpful with each other and more receptive to teachers. Albert would have teachers facilitate making connections by practicing the *Five A's*—*Acceptance, Attention, Appreciation, Affirmation,* and *Affection.*

The third "C" refers to *Contributing.* Students who do not feel that they are accepted or needed may see school as purposeless. One of the best ways to help students feel they are needed, according to Albert, is to make it possible for them to contribute. Some of her suggestions are:

1. *Encourage student contributions in the class.* Ask students to state their opinions and preferences about class requirements, routines, and other matters. Students can also furnish ideas about improving the classroom environment.
2. *Encourage student contributions to the school.* Albert suggests creating *Three C Committees* whose purpose is to think of ways to help all students feel more capable, connected, and contributing. Teachers and administrators

can assign school service time, in which students perform such tasks as dusting shelves, beautifying classrooms, and cleaning the grounds, all of which help build a sense of pride in the school.

3. *Encourage student contributions to the community.* Albert suggests:
   - Adopting a healthcare center and providing services such as reading, singing, and running errands for residents of the center.
   - Contributing to community drives such as Meals on Wheels, Toys for Tots, and disaster relief funds.
   - Encouraging random acts of kindness, such as opening doors for people and providing help with their packages.

The Albert Model The key to good classroom behavior lies in close cooperation between teacher and students. Help students grow in the Three C's: personal *Capability, Connections* with others, and *Contributions* to school and society. Continually show students—and ask them to show each other—the Five A's of *Acceptance, Attention, Appreciation, Affirmation,* and *Affection.*

POSITIVITY AND HUMANENESS: HOW DO JANE NELSEN AND LYNN LOTT HELP TEACHERS BRING THOSE QUALITIES INTO THE CLASSROOM?

Jane Nelsen and Lynn Lott are educators who disseminate their views on classroom management through lectures, workshops, printed material, and video material. Their goal is to help adults and children learn to respect themselves and others, behave responsibly, and contribute to the betterment of the groups to which they belong. Nelson and Lott's book *Positive Discipline in the Classroom* (1993/2000/2013) explains how to establish a classroom climate that fosters responsibility, mutual respect, and cooperation. They believe such climates do away with most classroom management problems because they teach students to value respect and helpfulness. Nelsen and Lott have authored a number of books and teaching materials that can be previewed on the Positive Discipline website at www.positivediscipline.com and on the Empowering People website at www.empoweringpeople.com. Their work is based on the work of Dreikurs.

Nelsen and Lott assert that teachers foster positive discipline when they establish classroom climates of acceptance, encouragement, respectfulness, and support. Such classrooms enable students to behave with dignity, self-control, and concern for others. Nelsen and Lott contend that virtually all students can learn to behave in that manner.

The key lies in helping students see themselves as *capable, significant,* and *able to control their own lives.* These qualities are best promoted in classrooms where students are treated respectfully and taught the skills needed for working with others. In such classrooms, students (1) never experience humiliation when they fail, but instead learn how to turn mistakes into successes; (2) learn how to cooperate with teachers and fellow students to find joint solutions to problems; and (3) are provided an environment of firmness, kindness, and excitement for life and learning. Such environments reflect dignity and mutual respect, thereby replacing fear, discouragement, and feelings of inadequacy.

Nelsen and Lott especially emphasize the value of classroom meetings as venues for developing social skills of listening, taking turns, hearing different points of view, negotiating, communicating, helping one another, and taking responsibility for one's own behavior. When teachers involve themselves as partners in class meetings, a climate of mutual respect develops. Teachers and students listen to one another, take each other seriously, and work together to solve problems for the benefit of all. Antagonisms often seen in most classrooms tend to fade away.

Nelsen and Lott's Significant Seven

Nelsen and Lott identified three perceptions and four skills that contribute to the special benefits of *Positive Discipline in the Classroom*. They call these perceptions and skills the **Significant Seven**, which they describe as follows.

The Three Empowering Perceptions

Within a positive environment, students develop *three perceptions* about themselves that lead to success in life. Those three perceptions are:

1. Perception of *personal capability*. (I have ability; I can do this.)
2. Perception of *significance in primary relationships*. (I am needed; I belong.)
3. Perception of *personal power* to influence one's own life. (I have control over how I respond to what happens to me.)

The Four Essential Skills

In their approach, Nelsen and Lott strive to help students develop *four essential skills* that contribute significantly to success in life:

1. Intrapersonal skill. (I understand my emotions and can control myself.)
2. Interpersonal skill. (I can communicate, cooperate, and work well with others.)
3. Strategic skill. (I am flexible, adaptable, and responsible.)
4. Judgmental skill. (I can use my wisdom to evaluate situations.)

The Nelsen and Lott Model of Discipline Make sure the tone of your classroom is accepting, encouraging, respectful, and supportive. Discuss the Significant Seven with students and incorporate them into daily practice.

INNER DISCIPLINE: WHAT DOES BARBARA COLOROSO SAY ABOUT HELPING STUDENTS ACCEPT RESPONSIBILITY AND MAINTAIN SELF-CONTROL?

Barbara Coloroso believes that a major goal of education is to teach students to conduct themselves in a socially acceptable manner. She wants students to develop an inner sense of responsibility and self-control, and she thinks the school must help them to do so. Responsibility and self-control enable students to take positive charge of their lives while respecting the rights of those around them. This process can be made to occur when students are given responsibility for making decisions and for managing the outcomes of those decisions.

Classrooms are ideal places to learn this process, and teachers are in an ideal position to help. The paragraphs that follow present Coloroso's suggestions for helping students in this manner. Most of the material presented here comes from her book, *Kids Are Worth It: Giving Your Child the Gift of Inner Discipline* (1994/2002). To see more of Coloroso's contributions, consult her website at www.kidsareworthit.com.

Teachers help students learn self-control by taking the following steps when students misbehave:

1. Show students what they have done wrong.
2. Give students ownership of the problems involved.
3. When necessary, guide them to strategies that might solve the problems.
4. Make sure students' dignity remains intact.

These steps help students acquire integrity, wisdom, compassion, and mercy, all of which contribute to inner discipline.

Teachers must make sure they never speak hurtfully to students or provoke anger, resentment, or additional conflict. When misbehavior is sufficiently serious, Coloroso would have teachers quickly guide students through a process of *restitution*, *resolution*, and *reconciliation*. **Restitution** means doing what is necessary to repair whatever damage was done. **Resolution** means identifying and correcting whatever caused the misbehavior so it won't happen again. **Reconciliation** means healing relationships with people who were hurt or offended by the misbehavior. The offending student is asked to make decisions concerning future behavior, follow up accordingly, and then learn from the results of those decisions, even if they bring discomfort.

The teacher intervenes in student decisions only when they are physically dangerous, morally threatening, or unhealthy. Otherwise, students deal with matters on their own.

You give students ownership of classroom management problems when you ask them, "What do you intend to do about the situation?" That causes them to realize it is up to them to make matters better. Teachers are there to offer advice and support, but not to provide solutions. Inner discipline is acquired through learning how to think, not just what to think. The following are additional points that Coloroso emphasizes:

- Students have the right to be in school, but they also have the responsibility to respect the rights of those around them. Rights and responsibility go hand in hand.
- Teachers should never treat students in ways they, the teachers, would not want to be treated.
- Rather than rescuing students or lecturing them when they misbehave, give students opportunities to solve their problems in ways that everyone finds acceptable.
- Students who consistently experience realistic consequences for misbehavior learn that they themselves have positive control over their lives. In contrast, students who are bribed, rewarded, and punished become dependent on others for approval. They work to please the teacher and try to figure out how to avoid getting caught when they misbehave.

The Coloroso Model Strongly emphasize supporting students as they develop responsibility and self-control. When students misbehave, you should (1) have them state clearly what they have done wrong; (2) give them ownership of the problem by asking, "How will you fix the problem?"; (3) suggest options for resolution if the student needs them; (4) hold the student responsible for following through.

LEARNING COMMUNITIES: HOW DOES ALFIE KOHN SUGGEST WE INVOLVE STUDENTS MORE CLOSELY IN GENUINE LEARNING?

Alfie Kohn has been deeply troubled by teaching that tries to force students to behave compliantly. He often begins his workshops for teachers by asking, "What are your long-term goals for the students you work with? What would you like them to be—to be like—long after they've left you?" (Kohn, 1996/2001, p. 60).*

When you ask most teachers, they say they want their students to be caring, happy, responsible, curious, and creative. Unfortunately, says Kohn, there is a yawning chasm between what we teachers want and what we are doing to get it. We say we want children to continue reading and thinking after school has ended, yet we focus on testing and grading, which does little to make

*From *Beyond Discipline: From Compliance to Community*, by A. Kohn. © 2001 Published by Pearson.

students want to learn. We want students to be critical thinkers, yet we feed them predigested facts and conclusions—partly because of pressure from various constituencies to pump up standardized test scores. We act as though our goal is short-term retention of right answers rather than genuine understanding (Kohn, 1996/2001).

Kohn thinks traditional instruction—the type in which the teacher selects the curriculum; does the planning; delivers the lessons through lecture, demonstration, guided discussion, reading assignments, worksheets, and homework; and then uses tests to evaluate progress—is falling disastrously short of the expectations we hold for education. That kind of instruction is aimed at getting students to demonstrate behaviorally certain specific objectives, usually on tests. But it gives little attention to exploring ideas, seeking new solutions, looking for meaning or connections, or attempting to gain deeper understanding of the phenomena involved.

According to Kohn, in many instructional scenarios, students remain relatively passive most of the time. They listen, read assignments, answer questions when called on, and complete worksheets, all with little give and take. Instruction and learning are deemed successful in the extent to which students show on tests they have reached the stated objectives. But this approach, says Kohn, makes students focus on outcomes that are shallow, relatively insignificant, and of little interest or relevance to them. Students come to think of correct answers and good grades as the major goals of learning. They rarely experience the satisfaction of exploring interesting topics in depth and exchanging views and insights with others.

Kohn goes on to say that students taught in this way often develop poor attitudes toward learning. To them, learning is not an exciting exploration, but just a way of getting the work done. Once they have done the "stuff," they quickly forget much of it as they move on to learn more new stuff. They strive to get the right answers, and when they do not, or if they don't make top scores on the test, they experience a sense of failure that is out of place in genuine learning, where making mistakes is the rule. And even when students seem to be learning well, they may actually be doing poorly because they are not thinking widely and exploring ideas thoughtfully.

Kohn argues for instruction that is different from the traditional. He says, first, that students must be taken seriously, meaning teachers must honor them as individuals and seek to determine what they need and enjoy. Further, teachers must recognize that students construct their knowledge and skills from a basis of experience. When students explore, grapple with ideas, and try to make sense of them, they make many mistakes, but mistakes are always part of learning. Teachers in that approach facilitate learning by seeking out students' interests and finding what lies behind their questions and mistakes.

Kohn (1996/2006) says the kind of schooling he would like to see is best promoted by transforming schools and classrooms into *learning communities*, meaning places in which students feel cared about and are encouraged to care about each other. There they experience a sense of being valued and respected; they matter to one another and to the teacher. They come to think in the plural. They feel connected to each other; they are part of an "us." And, as a result of all this, they feel safe in their classes, not only physically but emotionally.

Kohn suggests the following as ways to develop a greater sense of community in schools and classrooms:

- *Show respect for students.* Students behave more respectfully when important adults in their lives behave respectfully toward them. They are more likely to care about others if they know they are cared about.
- *Help students connect with each other.* Connections among students are established and enhanced through activities that involve interdependence. Familiar activities for enhancing connections include cooperative learning, getting-to-know-you activities such as interviewing fellow students and introducing them to the class, and finding a partner to check opinions with on whatever is being discussed at the moment. Kohn also suggests using activities that promote perspective taking, in which students try to see situations from another person's point of view.
- *Use classroom meetings.* Kohn says the overall best activity for involving the entire group is the class meeting. He suggests holding class meetings at the beginning of the year to discuss matters such as, "What makes school awful sometimes? Try to remember an experience during a previous year when you hated school, when you felt bad about yourself, or about everyone else, and you couldn't wait for it to be over. What was going on when you were feeling that way? How was the class set up?" Kohn says not enough teachers use this practice, particularly in elementary schools.
- *Provide classwide and schoolwide activities.* To develop a sense of community, students need many opportunities for the whole class or the whole school to collaborate on group endeavors. This might involve producing a class mural, producing a class newsletter or magazine, staging a performance, taking care of the school grounds, or doing some community service.
- *Reflect on academic instruction.* In class meetings, talk about how the next unit in history might be approached, or what the students thought was best and worst about the math test. Academic study pursued in cooperative groups enables students to make connections while learning from each other, and units of study in language arts and literature can be organized to promote reflection on helpfulness, fairness, and compassion.

The Kohn Model Think of your students as serious learners who construct knowledge from a variety of experiences. Organize the class into a community of learners, interconnected and concerned with each other. Use classroom meetings to address concerns about instructional matters and personal behavior.

APPROACHING MANAGEMENT FROM A SCHOOLWIDE PERSPECTIVE: HOW DO STUDENTS BENEFIT FROM A PROGRAM OF POSITIVE BEHAVIORAL INTERVENTIONS AND SUPPORTS (PBIS)?

One of the most rapidly growing approaches to classroom management in American schools has its origins in legislation designed to ensure access and equity for people who face special challenges. When it was reauthorized in 1997, the Individuals with Disabilities Education Act (IDEA) included the stipulation that as schools worked with students who exhibited behavior disorders, they should use data about students' behavior to help them choose and implement effective interventions. Through grant funding, the Center on Positive Behavioral Interventions and Supports was established; the Center launched a partnership of researchers and education professionals from across the country who were focused on helping schools find effective ways to assist this challenging population (Sugai & Simonson, 2012).

In recent years, PBIS has been broadened in scope to include all students, not just those served under IDEA. In fact, you may also hear this approach referred to as School-Wide Positive Behavior Supports (SWPBS). The focus of PBIS/SWPBS is on applying evidence-based behavioral interventions to help students meet important academic, behavioral, and social outcomes (Lewis, Mitchell, Trussell, & Newcomer, 2015). In other words, schools should use all available data about student behavior as they select research-based interventions designed to move the student(s) toward one or more specified positive outcomes.

Part of PBIS's growing appeal is that it is not a curriculum or a packaged program; it is an "implementation framework" (Sugai & Simsonson, 2012, p. 1) that combines elements of behavior modification, social skills instruction, direct teaching of expectations, and individualized instruction. Each school develops its own plan within the framework, emphasizing the outcomes that are important and appropriate for its student population. More than 16,000 schools were using PBIS in 2012; that number is growing steadily, in part because research studies have demonstrated the effectiveness of the approach (Lewis, Mitchell, Trussell, & Newcomer, 2015).

PBIS is first and foremost designed to prevent inappropriate behavior throughout the school. Its focus is on guiding all students to specific academic, social, and behavioral outcomes specified by school staff members, generally a team of teachers and administrators. Its structure reflects three tiers of intervention:

1. Interventions appropriate for all students (otherwise known as *universal supports*). Actions at this level are designed to promote prosocial behavior and to address contextual factors in the school that contribute to problematic behavior (Sugai et al, 2000). The goal is to prevent new cases of misbehavior.

2. Interventions appropriate for some students (otherwise known as *targeted supports*). Actions at this level are implemented with students who present ongoing, low-level disruptions (often across multiple settings) that might develop into chronic patterns of inappropriate behavior. The goal at this level is to reduce problem behavior and move students toward schoolwide behavioral and academic expectations.

3. Interventions appropriate for a few students (otherwise known as *individual supports*). Actions at this level are undertaken with the 5% to 10% of the school population who require more intense, focused intervention. Students receiving these Tier 3 interventions are typically those who demonstrate chronic patterns of misbehavior and/or who are engaging in frequent and/or high-risk behaviors.

Students are served on the continuum on the basis of behavioral data and with the input of the highly trained site-based PBIS team. Interventions at each tier are carefully monitored for effectiveness, and systems are put in place to make sure that school personnel are using the interventions appropriately and with fidelity.

The PBIS Model Schools identify clearly defined academic and behavioral outcomes for students. They use behavioral data in decision making and problem solving with regard to student behavior. They consistently monitor the effectiveness of both the interventions themselves and the ways in which they are implemented. They directly teach appropriate behavior and self-management skills and use reinforcement as a means of increasing motivation and building a cooperative school community. Interventions are delivered in the form of tiered supports; tier placement is dependent on the particular needs of the student(s) in question.

PBIS will be covered in more detail in Chapter 12.

THEMES ACROSS TIME

As we said earlier in the chapter, studying the evolution of classroom management over time is helpful in that the themes that different authorities have addressed are still prevalent in today's schools and classrooms. The following table briefly summarizes (in no particular order) the themes we've identified within this chapter; can you identify which authority(ies) would be associated with each idea? (*Hint*: Many of the ideas have multiple supporters.)

As you observe in classrooms or work in your own, watch for instances of each theme. As you see teachers work to address these important ideas in their classrooms, remember that what you're observing (or doing, if you have your own class already) is built on a foundation laid for you by numerous educators, psychologists, psychiatrists, and other professionals.

Themes	
Meaningful, Successful Learning	Learning should be a meaningful, engaging, and cooperative activity. Classrooms work better when students experience success. All students (not just those who frequently misbehave) benefit from attention to their academic, social, and behavioral growth.
Effective Communication	Teachers' interpersonal skills and methods for communicating with students are critical to the class experience; teachers and students should interact in ways that are positive, civil, and humane.
Teaching Self-Management	Students benefit from learning how to manage themselves and their emotions. Teachers and students who view themselves as being on the same team are likely to have smoother relationships; teachers who run democratic classrooms (as opposed to autocratic or permissive ones) are more likely to be successful classroom managers.
Fostering Positive Interpersonal Relationships	Classrooms work better when teachers attend to group dynamics and cooperative, supportive interpersonal relationships.
Motivation, Rewards, and Punishment	Punishments and threats should be avoided, as they're ineffective; enhancing students' intrinsic motivation is critically important. Reinforcement can shape behavior, but should be carefully considered.
Making Appropriate Choices	Students grow in important ways when they realize that their behaviors are the results of choices they make and that they can make better choices when the situation calls for it.
Class Meetings	Class meetings are a useful way of building relationships and involving students in the problem-solving process. Reflection and problem solving are tools that not only help teachers and students change behavior, but also build community.
Normalizing Mistakes	Students benefit when teachers normalize error and help students understand the role mistakes play in the learning process.
Focus on Prevention	Effective managers focus on preventing, not just reacting to, misbehavior. Attending to management logistics when delivering instruction is critical to avoiding wasted time in classrooms.
Identifying Needs	Student needs impact their behavior. Students can learn to meet their needs without negatively affecting others.
Clarifying Expectations	Clarity of expectations supports good behavior. Helping students understand the relationship between behaviors and consequences is one aspect of clarity.
Using Data and Research	Behavioral intervention should be data-driven and should rely on evidence-based strategies.

Themes	
Establishing and Teaching Rules and Procedures	Effective managers spend a significant amount of time actively teaching rules and procedures.
Impact of Testing	Testing and accountability measures have strongly impacted teachers' approaches to curriculum, often to the detriment of student behavior and motivation.
Compliance	Students should be taught compliance as an automatic response to teacher directions.

THE FOUNDATIONS OF CLASSROOM MANAGEMENT: WHAT YOU HAVE LEARNED IN THIS CHAPTER

In this chapter, you have explored ideas about classroom management and the authorities who put those ideas forth. You've seen that even though some programs or recommendations are no longer in the spotlight, the themes they were designed to address are still relevant to today's teachers. You've read about some classroom management programs that are current and growing. You've begun to identify how management themes might be evident in today's classrooms, and you've got a firm foundation of ideas to include as you complete your planning guide, developing and refining your own belief system about what classroom management is going to look like for you.

MyLab Education Self-Check 4.1

MyLab Education Self-Check 4.2

MyLab Education Application Exercise 4.1 Simulation: Creating Classroom Behavioral Expectations

MyLab Education Application Exercise 4.2 Identifying Classroom Management Themes in Action

5

Insisting on Compliance: Ronald Morrish's *Real Discipline*

How Does Focusing on Student Compliance Move Students Toward More Responsible Behavior?

LEARNING OUTCOMES:

5-1 Identify the classroom management recommendations made by Ronald Morrish and the broad classroom management themes to which they relate.

5-2 Consider the strengths and weaknesses of Morrish's recommendations and evaluate their likely utility in various situational contexts.

Ronald Morrish says we have to teach students how to behave properly because many of them do not learn how to do so at home. Morrish asserts that while our ultimate goal is for students to develop self-control, that only happens over time, and almost never without the help of supportive adults. Unfortunately, supportive adults are missing from many students' lives today. We teachers are in an ideal position to offer that support, and, according to Morrish, it is our duty to do so.

Morrish's approach to discipline, which began growing in popularity in the 1990s, is a method he describes as straightforward, sensible, and easy to teach and learn. It consists of four main components: (1) rules of behavior; (2) compliance training, in which students are taught how to comply with expectations; (3) a few carefully chosen things you will do and say when students break rules; and (4) when students are old enough, a provision for allowing and helping them to make choices in a responsible manner.

As for rules of behavior, Morrish says teachers, not students, should make them. He believes it a major mistake for teachers to involve students in making rules before students have sufficient maturity and wisdom to do so.

Once teachers have established clear rules (about five will usually do), they should teach them carefully to students, emphasizing what the rules mean and why they are needed. After that, students must be taught why and how they are to comply with the rules. This is done over time and involves *compliance training*, in which you begin by helping students understand the difference between right and wrong behavior in general. From that point, you move to teaching the difference between right and wrong behavior in school. You teach these concepts through explanation, examples, demonstration, and guided practice. The compliance training process not only clarifies expectations, but also promotes students' acceptance of your authority. When those two understandings become established, students usually follow class rules consistently without hesitation.

Although rules and compliance training will prevent most problems, Morrish acknowledges that students will still misbehave at times. When that happens, you must be able to redirect student misbehavior in a positive direction, in a manner that leaves no residue of resentment. How is that best done? Simple, says Morrish. You make sure students understand that when they break a rule, you will ask them to *redo* the behavior in question, in a correct manner. Insist on that, he says, and you will get acceptable behavior from your students almost all of the time.

Finally, after compliance has been well established, you should teach students how to manage choice, provided they are sufficiently mature to do so. That final step will enable them to develop genuine self-discipline.

Components of Morrish's Approach (1) Teacher-made rules, (2) compliance training, (3) redo misbehavior correctly, and (4) later, make choices.

WHO IS RONALD MORRISH?

Ron Morrish, an independent consultant in discipline, was for many years a teacher and behavior specialist in Canada. He now writes, makes conference presentations, conducts professional development programs, presents courses for teachers, and works with parent groups and child care providers around the world. He has authored three books. The first, *Secrets of Discipline* (1997), was also produced as a video. In that work, Morrish discusses twelve keys for raising responsible children without engaging in deal making, argumentation, or confrontations. His second book, *With All Due Respect* (2000), focuses on improving teachers' discipline skills and building effective schoolwide discipline programs through a team approach. In 2003, he published *FlipTips*, a mini-book of discipline tips and maxims excerpted from his books and presentations. To see Morrish's own description of his program, called "Real Discipline," consult his 2005 article "What Is Real Discipline?" posted on his website at www.realdiscipline.com.

THE MORRISH MODEL

> **The Common Goal of All Approaches to Management** *Responsible, Civil Classroom Behavior That Becomes Habitual and Lasts over Time*
> Responsible means paying attention, making a strong effort, and doing what is proper without being told.
> Civil means respectful, polite, cordial, and well-mannered.

↑

Ron Morrish's Approach to Discipline

↓ ↑

Morrish's Overarching Strategy
Teach students how to behave properly and insist they comply with directions.

↓ ↑

Morrish's Principal Tactics
- Use class rules of behavior.
- Clearly affirm teacher authority.
- Establish student compliance.
- Teach more as a coach than as a boss.
- Correct misbehavior by having students redo the behavior properly.

↓ ↑

↓ ——————→ —————↑

IN MORRISH'S VIEW, HOW AND WHY HAS MODERN DISCIPLINE GONE WRONG?

Morrish (2005) fully agrees with other authorities that discipline continues to be a major problem in schools, with students frequently trying to manipulate teachers and refusing to cooperate fully. He assigns some of the blame to undesirable trends in society, such as "me-first" attitudes and a general disinclination to accept responsibility, but he also assigns much of it to what he considers bad advice teachers get in many popular systems of discipline.

All too often, he says, authorities urge teachers to involve students in decision making before the students are mature enough to do so responsibly. Consequently, teachers waste large amounts of time negotiating and haggling with students about behavior. Morrish says that for decades, experts have erroneously claimed that plentiful student choice leads to self-esteem, responsibility, and motivation to achieve. As those experts see it, the teacher's role is to encourage good choices and discourage poor ones.

That approach has failed, Morrish contends, for three reasons. First, it does not demand proper behavior from students, but instead allows them, if they don't mind the consequences, to choose to behave discourteously and irresponsibly. Systems based on fear of consequences, he explains, cannot be effective unless students truly find the consequences intolerable, which is virtually never the case today.

Second, many discipline approaches do not adequately teach students how they are to behave in school.

And third, many approaches leave teachers stuck with bargaining and negotiating endlessly, and often fruitlessly, to get students to cooperate.

Morrish contends that if discipline is to be effective, a different approach is required—one in which students are taught what is acceptable and what is unacceptable before they are given latitude to make choices. Otherwise, he says, they are likely to choose whatever appeals to them at the time, and teachers will find it difficult to live with many of those choices.

Although all of us want students to be successful, the discipline approaches we use often allow students to underachieve, behave discourteously, engage in high-risk behaviors, contribute little or nothing of value to the school environment, and use intimidation and violence in dealing with others. Clearly, says Morrish, such discipline is not producing the results we want.

WHAT IS THE "REAL DISCIPLINE" MORRISH ADVOCATES?

Morrish calls his approach *Real Discipline*. He explains that it is not a new theory, but an organized set of techniques that teachers and parents have used for generations in teaching children to be respectful, responsible, and cooperative. It emphasizes careful teacher guidance to ensure that children learn how to conduct themselves in an acceptable manner.

Morrish feels teachers have been sidetracked into focusing on what he calls "behavior management" rather than real discipline. Both management and discipline are needed, he says, but they are not one and the same. *Behavior management* is about making the learning environment functional, keeping students on task, and minimizing disruptions. It attempts to deal with whatever behavior students bring to school. Although important in teaching, behavior management is not very effective in helping students learn to behave responsibly.

Real Discipline, on the other hand, explicitly teaches students how to behave properly. It requires them to show courtesy and consideration. It helps them develop needed social skills and trains them to work within a structure of rules and limits. It does these things while protecting students from self-defeating mistakes they are otherwise likely to make. As Morrish (1997) puts it:

> Real Discipline is a lot more than simply giving choices to children and then dealing with the aftermath. We have to teach them right and wrong. We have to teach them to respect legitimate authority. We have to teach them the lessons that have been learned by others and by ourselves. Then, and only then, will we enjoy watching them develop into adults. (p. 33)

Morrish says these provisions are necessary because children, in their early years, are by no means wise and tolerant. They are frequently the opposite—impulsive and self-centered. If they are to develop into contributing members of society, they must learn to cooperate, behave responsibly, and show consideration for others.

Some young students are fortunate to have good caregivers and role models who teach them these things. But, Morrish asserts, many children are overly indulged and rarely called to account for their behavior. They remain self-centered and grow up concerned only with their own interests. They want things their way, they cooperate in school only when they feel like it, and they show little consideration for teachers and fellow students. For many, lack of effort, abusive language, and bullying are rules of the day.

Morrish says this condition has come about, at least in part, because the society in which we live stresses individual rights and freedom, but has lost sight of the personal responsibility that must accompany rights and freedom. Without responsibility, rights and freedom mean little. Personal responsibility is too important to leave to chance. Life requires us to live within certain constraints that limit individual freedom. We accept those constraints in exchange for life that is safer, more secure, and more orderly.

Morrish does believe students should be allowed to make choices and helped to make good ones, but only when they are sufficiently mature to do so intelligently. Students do not innately know how to do so, nor can they do so early in their lives. They first have to develop respect for, and a degree of compliance with, authority.

WHICH MAXIMS HELP US UNDERSTAND THE NATURE OF REAL DISCIPLINE?

As noted, Morrish also published a small book called *FlipTips* (2003), which contains comments and maxims from his various publications and presentations. They reflect the mindset that Morrish would like teachers to acquire. Here are a few of the tips that illustrate Morrish's ideas on discipline. How would you explain, in your own words, what each of them means or suggests?

- Discipline is a process, not an event.
- Discipline is about giving students the structure they need for proper behavior, not the consequences they seem to deserve for misbehavior.
- Discipline comes from the word *disciple*. It's about teaching and learning, not scolding and punishing.
- Discipline isn't what you do when students misbehave. It's what you do so they won't.
- Discipline isn't about letting students make their own choices. It's about preparing them properly for the choices they will be making later.
- Don't let students make choices that are not theirs to make.
- Train students to comply with your directions. Compliance precedes cooperation. If you bargain for compliance now, you'll have to beg for it later.
- Always work from more structure to less structure, not the other way around.
- To prevent major behavior problems, deal with all minor behavior problems when they occur.
- Students learn far more from being shown how to behave appropriately than from being punished.
- The best time to teach a behavior is when it isn't needed, so it will be there when it is needed. Today's practice is tomorrow's performance.
- If you teach students to be part of the solution, they're less likely to be part of the problem.
- When dealing with adolescents, act more like a coach and less like a boss.
- A single minute spent practicing courtesy has more impact than a 1-hour lecture on the importance of it.
- To stop fights, stop put-downs. Verbal hits usually precede physical hits.
- Discipline should end with the correct behavior, not with a punishment.
- Rapport is the magical ingredient that changes a student's reluctance to be controlled into a willingness to be guided.

WHAT ARE THE THREE PROGRESSIVE PHASES THROUGH WHICH WE SHOULD GUIDE STUDENTS?

Morrish explains that rather than approaching discipline from the perspective of choice, Real Discipline asks teachers to guide students through three progressive phases he calls *training for compliance, teaching students how to behave,* and *managing student choice.* Each of these three phases is aimed at a particular goal and involves the use of certain strategies, as explained in the following paragraphs.

Phase 1: Training for Compliance

In a September 2012 memo to the first author of this text, Mr. Morrish said some people react a bit negatively to the word "compliance." He wants teachers to think of compliance as meaning "following directions," which students must do if teaching is to be effective. When explaining this point to teachers, Morrish uses driver training as an illustration, where it is clear that the driving instructor will be giving directions that the learner must follow. In the same way, teachers teach routine behaviors that students are to follow. Doing so consistently results in a classroom that runs smoothly.

Morrish strongly urges teachers to train their students to comply with rules, limits, and authority. *Rules* are descriptions of how students are to behave. An example might be "Show courtesy and respect for others at all times." *Limits* specify behavior that will *not* be allowed. An example would be, "No name-calling in this room." *Authority* refers to power that has been assigned to certain individuals. By custom and law, teachers are given legitimate authority to control and direct students in school, and they should use that power to set and maintain standards of conduct.

Teachers' first task is to train their students to accept authority and comply with it automatically. Compliance should be taught as a *nonthinking activity*. Nonthinking activities are habits you don't have to reflect on or make choices about, such as stopping at red lights or saying "thank you" when a person does something nice for you.

Begin by telling your students straightforwardly that one of your most important jobs is to help each and every one of them be successful in school and life. Success comes from behaving in approved ways, with limits set on what people are allowed to do. He says he finds it astonishing that compliance receives virtually no attention in most approaches to discipline, even though compliance helps students learn to conduct themselves properly and at the same time provides the basis for later decision making.

Further explain to your students that in order to find success, they must learn to behave courteously, show self-control, and do what is expected of them to the best of their ability. Point out that as a professional teacher, you have been trained to help students accomplish those things, and that you have a clear plan for doing so that will bring success for everyone in the class. Indicate that you will begin by training your students to pay attention, follow directions, and speak and act respectfully to others. Those things will be practiced until they occur automatically, without anyone having to think about them.

As you proceed, use direct instruction and close supervision to teach students exactly how you want them to behave. For example, if you want students to raise their hands before speaking, tell them what you expect and show them how to do it. Then have them practice it until it becomes habitual. When students make mistakes, show them again how to do the act properly and, again, practice it. Morrish says to start small, and you will see a general attitude of compliance grow out of many small acts of compliance.

Because compliance is so important, you should address all instances of misbehavior. Do not overlook small misbehaviors, as suggested in many discipline programs. If you do, you will soon be overwhelmed with explaining, negotiating, and tending to consequences. This overload will cause you to "pick your battles" and not "sweat the small stuff." Thus, you might allow students to put their heads on their desks during opening routines, talk during announcements, throw their jackets in the corner instead of hanging them up, and wander around the room instead of getting ready to work.

Such minor misbehavior might seem unimportant, but it should never be overlooked. Poor habits easily expand into poor behavior overall. If you walk by students who are doing something wrong and you say nothing, they interpret that as meaning you don't care, and the next thing you know they are engaged in disruptive behavior.

Don't get the idea you can't manage such behavior, but do understand that you can't manage it by scolding and doling out consequences. Morrish repeats again and again that the most effective approach is to tell students what you want them to do and then insist they do it properly. When they do something wrong, have them do it right. That is how you establish good practices and habits in your classes. Students get the picture quickly.

What Role Do Rules Play in Training for Compliance?

Just as we need rules for structure and predictability in everyday living, so do we need rules for classroom behavior. Teachers should make the rules. There is no need to ask students if they agree with them. Students are supposed to learn rules, not determine them. Teach students why we have rules and why they are made by people in positions of authority. Explain your rules to students and take their opinions into account, but don't pretend they are helping decide what the class rules are to be.

Once you've established rules, you must commit to ensuring they are obeyed. Even after you've stated your rules, you really don't have them unless you can enforce them. Your enforcement should be consistent, even for misbehavior that seems incidental, such as carelessly dropping rubbish on the floor or talking during quiet study time. As noted earlier, small infractions have a way of growing into large infractions.

Morrish says *insistence* is the best strategy for enforcing rules. Punishment is rarely if ever needed. You must be absolutely determined that students will do what you want them to, and you must be willing to persist until they do. You should develop the mindset that once you give an instruction, there is no question about students doing what you say.

Morrish does not suggest you give up punishment altogether, even though he points out that punishment does not encourage cooperation or responsibility and that it sometimes produces unwanted side effects. However, he maintains that punishment can do two things well. First, it can teach that "no means no," a message that students need to learn quickly. Second, punishment can bring misbehavior to a stop when other tactics can't.

What Role Do Limits Play in Training for Compliance?

Morrish uses the term *rule* to refer to what students should do (e.g., "Raise your hand before speaking"). He uses the term *limit* to refer to what students should not do (e.g., "Absolutely no bullying allowed"). Rules and limits are set and enforced by teachers, in accordance with established standards. Teachers do not negotiate them with students. Morrish says the first secret of good discipline is: *Never give students a choice when it comes to limits.*

You set limits in many ways, formally and informally. For example, you may work with students so they know that when they arrive in the classroom, they are to hang up their jackets and get ready for work immediately (these are rules, according to Morrish). They also know they are not allowed to scuffle or swear (these are limits). You present the rules and limits and have your students practice the behaviors. Students do not have any say in them. If they have questions about limits, you should select a time to explain the reasons behind them, but in no case are students allowed to ignore your directions. Your word is final.

Morrish laments that limits in today's classrooms are so often compromised by bargaining between teacher and students. He says that the more teachers give special privileges in exchange for behaving properly, the more students are likely to misbehave. Bargaining simply does not produce the results teachers want.

Teachers expect that once the bargaining is done, students will assess the possible outcomes of their behavior choices and thus make good choices automatically. However, things don't work that way. The main result for students is not better choice making, but feeling that everything in the class is decided through bargaining. All that does is give students power in decisions they are ill-prepared to make.

Students usually enter Mrs. James's class casually, talking and joking among themselves. Mrs. James doesn't mind because she likes to use the first few minutes of class time to review her lesson plans and chat with individual students whose assignments have not been completed correctly.

What do you think Ron Morrish would say about her approach?
What do you think he would have her do differently, if anything?

What Role Does Teacher Authority Play in Training for Compliance?

Morrish insists we need to reestablish teacher authority in the classroom, and he reminds teachers that their authority is based in law, custom, and professionalism. The power of teacher authority comes from teachers' knowing their responsibilities, knowing why they are setting limits, and knowing what they expect students to learn. It is conveyed by tone of voice, choice of words, and the way teachers present themselves.

Teachers should clearly communicate what they expect of students and then accept nothing less. They should make clear that no negotiation is involved. They do this without threatening or raising their voices. They simply say, with confidence and authority, "This is what you must do. This is the job you are here for. Now let's get on with it" (Morrish, 1997, p. 65).

If, in this process, students question your authority, tell them, "It is my job." If they challenge your right to make demands, tell them, "It is my job." Morrish says not to worry if your students don't like some of the things you expect them to do. It is respect you need at this point, not appreciation. Appreciation will come later, provided respect comes first.

Morrish acknowledges that many teachers become uneasy when asked to train their students for compliance. They fear automatic compliance will make their students passive, submissive, and unable to think for themselves. But as you have seen, Morrish disagrees, insisting that today's discipline gives students too much freedom of choice, not too little. What we need, he says, is a balance, which is achieved through Real Discipline.

Phase 2: Teaching Students How to Behave

The second phase in Real Discipline involves teaching students the skills, attitudes, and knowledge they need for cooperating, behaving properly, and assuming responsibility. When beginning this phase, you will have already established class rules and limits, which you will have taught through explanation, demonstration, practice, corrective feedback, and repetition. Students understand the need for rules and limits, and they will comply with them if they accept your authority.

Consider what action steps might be involved in moving students toward each of these goals. What could you do, for instance, to help students learn to be courteous? What organizational skills might you help them develop as they learn and work in your classroom?

Now you begin to teach them how to be courteous, work and play together harmoniously, resolve conflicts, set personal goals, organize tasks, and manage time. Most teachers erroneously assume students will somehow learn those skills from experience. You can't wait for experience to produce this desired result, even if that were possible. If you are to have order and acceptable behavior in your classes, you will have to prepare your students. The best way to teach what they need to know is through direct instruction and supervised practice.

Again, here is the basic operating principle you should follow: When students fail to comply with expectations, don't scold or punish them. Simply have them redo the behavior in an acceptable manner. Do this as often as necessary. Morrish believes that you can expect them to show improvement very quickly.

Phase 3: Managing Student Choice

The third phase of Real Discipline is called *choice management*. It helps students move toward greater independence by gradually allowing them the opportunity to make more choices as they show they are able to handle them intelligently. At this point, a basic operating principle is that when students make choices, they must take into account the needs and rights of fellow students and school personnel. They also need to begin learning exactly who has the right, or duty, to make a particular choice. Teachers have to make certain choices. Students can be allowed to make others.

As a rule of thumb, if students don't care about the outcome of a particular concern, they should not be allowed to make choices about it. Many teachers think students who do poor class work should receive low marks, which will motivate them to do better in the future. This may work for some highly motivated students, but it does nothing for those who don't care and are perfectly willing to accept the low grades. If Alana indicates she doesn't care about her performance in school, then you don't let her make choices about it. You say to her, "That's okay, Alana. I do care how well you do, so I'll make the decisions for you. Someday, when you care how well you do, you can make your own choices" (Morrish, 1997, p. 101). If Alana turns in poor work, you say to her: "Alana, your work is disorganized and incomplete. I'm not accepting it. Take it back, please, and fix it up. I'll mark it when it is done properly" (Morrish, 1997, p. 105).

Note that Morrish does NOT rip up the paper and throw it away during the conversation. What do you think would change about the dynamic if he were to do so?

You should never suggest that Alana can choose to do poor work if she wants to. Morrish says this is one area where we truly need to get back to basics, meaning we should expect students to do quality work and accept nothing less. Remember that the goal of Real Discipline is to help students become self-disciplined. You don't promote self-discipline by allowing students to do whatever they please instead of what is right.

In his book *Secrets of Discipline: 12 Keys for Raising Responsible Children*, Morrish (1997, pp. 93–94)[*] relates a classroom incident that epitomizes self-discipline. Morrish was visiting a combination grade 2/3 class when the teacher told her students she would be leaving the classroom for a few minutes. The students were to continue working quietly. She asked them, "What does this mean you need?" Hands were raised. A student answered, "Self-discipline." The teacher continued, "What does self-discipline mean?" Another student answered, "It means we behave when you're not with us, exactly the same way we behave when you are standing right next to us."

The teacher and Morrish both left the room, but Morrish stopped in the hallway to watch the students from a distance. He observed that the students continued to work as if the teacher were in the room with them. Later he asked the teacher how she had accomplished that result. She said she had the class practice the skill from the first day. She would stand next to them and ask them to show their best behavior. Then she challenged them to continue behaving that way as

*Ronald G. Morrish, author of "With All Due Respect" copyright 2000 and "Secrets of Discipline" copyright 1997.

she moved farther and farther away. Before long, the students had learned how to maintain their behavior when the teacher left the room.

As students become older and move toward independence, Real Discipline will have already taught them three things about making independent choices: (1) independence requires balancing personal rights with personal responsibility; (2) the rights and needs of others must always be taken into account; and (3) students should look at every unsupervised situation as an opportunity to demonstrate personal responsibility. Morrish reiterates that independence isn't "doing your own thing"; it's doing what's right when you are on your own.

SPECIFICALLY, WHAT DOES MORRISH ADVISE IN REGARD TO PLANNING AND IMPLEMENTING A GOOD DISCIPLINE PROGRAM?

For discipline to be effective, teachers must plan proactively, meaning they anticipate problems, keep them from occurring, if possible, and prepare carefully for attending to problems that might occur. Morrish (2000) suggests that teachers follow these 11 steps when organizing their discipline system:

1. *Decide in advance how you want your students to behave.* Think through matters such as the following:
   - how students will demonstrate courtesy
   - the words and tone of voice they will use
   - how they will speak to you
   - what other signs of courtesy they will show
   - how they will treat visitors
   - how they will welcome new students to the class
   - how they will listen to you and other students
   - how they will contribute to class discussions
   - how they will help substitute teachers
   - what they will do when upset or when they disagree with you or others
   - how they will respond to other students who need assistance
   - how they will deal with losing
   - how they will comply when you tell them what to do
   - how they will respond when you correct them
   - how they will behave when you step out of the room.

2. *Design a supporting structure.* When you have in mind how you want students to behave, design a structure that will support your goals. This structure will consist mostly of procedures you teach students to follow, such as:
   - how students will enter and exit the room
   - what they will do if they arrive late

- how they will handle completed work
- how they will request assistance
- what they should do about missed assignments
- what they should do if they finish work early
- what they should do if the teacher does not appear on time
- how they will learn the class rules and enforcement procedures
- what the specific limits on behavior are.

3. *Establish a threshold for behavior at school.* You must not allow students to bring negative behaviors to the class from home and the community. You must create a clear separation between school and outside school. Say to students, "You're now at school. Remember how you behave when you are here." Then enforce the courtesy and work habits required in your class.

4. *Run a two-week training camp.* Effective teachers work hard the first two weeks in establishing class expectations and procedures. They give particular attention to behavior standards, clear limits, routines, and compliance. Morrish maintains that the investment you make in discipline during these first two weeks determines how the rest of the school year will unfold. This does not suggest you overlook academic work, but in the early stages, academic work is of lower priority than proper behavior. As students acclimate to Real Discipline, academic work moves to highest priority.

5. *Teach students how to behave appropriately.* Morrish believes students should be taught a number of skills necessary for school success, not only in the classroom but also in school assemblies, on school buses, and in the school cafeteria. They should practice courtesy and be taught how to treat new students and be good role models for younger students. They should be taught how to help substitute teachers. They should be taught to recognize and suppress incidents such as teasing and name-calling that escalate into conflicts in class. They should be taught always to take others into account, to help someone every day, and to acknowledge people who have helped them. And they should be taught to be good ambassadors for the class and school, displayed through behavior in public that brings credit to themselves, their school, and their families.

6. *Set the stage for quality instruction.* Discipline cannot succeed in an environment where students must be coerced to endure boring, tedious lessons and activities. You must make your classes interesting and worthwhile. Ask questions that force students to expand their thinking. Increase the use of hands-on activities. Make use of group learning activities. Include activities based on sports, music, drama, and crafts. Ask students to make presentations to the class and to younger students. These approaches keep students interested and less likely to behave disruptively.

7. *Provide active, assertive supervision.* Good discipline requires that you take certain steps to forestall misbehavior. Remind students of rules and

expectations ahead of time. Remind them of limits that might apply. Be specific and don't oververbalize. Govern and correct small misbehaviors. Reinforce good social skills when you see them. Move briskly around the classroom. Talk briefly with various students, provided it doesn't interrupt their work. Let everyone see your presence. Move with a sense of purpose. Let students know you see them.

8. *Enforce rules and expectations.* Most teachers believe they should make students aware of unpleasant consequences that will be applied when students misbehave. They use the consequences as warnings. But neither warnings nor consequences are very effective in getting students to conduct themselves properly. Success depends on the teacher's ability to *require* good behavior. You must be willing to establish your natural authority and take charge of students. There is no game playing involved. Don't allow them to decide whether or not to comply with rules. Don't allow them to call you by your first name, talk back, run around the room, or throw things at each other. Teachers worry that some students will confront them over expectations and rule enforcement they don't like. You can limit that concern by addressing all small infractions such as discourteous language or failure to clean up. Morrish asserts that when students learn to comply on small matters, they will continue to comply on larger matters. Meanwhile, connect with your students on a personal basis. Listen to them and take their concerns into account. Capitalize on their interests. Be understanding and supportive when a student is going through a hard time. Establish rapport, but combine it with insistence.

9. *Focus on prevention.* Real Discipline goes to some length to prevent misbehavior. Remember, discipline isn't as much what you do when students misbehave as it is what you do in advance so they won't misbehave. Use the suggestions presented earlier for making classes interesting and engaging. Emphasize civil behavior and do not allow verbal put-downs. Discuss potential behavior situations with students and devise ways of avoiding them.

10. *Set high standards.* Don't allow underachievement to be a student choice. You must make it clear you will not accept underachievement in any form, whether academic or social. When students do something inadequately or improperly, have them do it over again. Challenge your students and get them excited about improving everything they do in school.

11. *Treat caregivers as partners.* Keep caregivers informed about serious incidents and repetitive misbehavior involving their child, but don't worry them with minor matters—take care of those things yourself. When you need to communicate with caregivers, do so by email or by phone if possible. Don't send notes. Suggest ways they might help the student do better in school, but never suggest punishment. Talk *with* caregivers, not down to them. Reassure them that you and they both want success for their child and that you want to work together with them to make that happen.

Commentary From Anonymous Teacher 1

As I read Mr. Morrish's suggestions, I was aware I already do some of the things he recommends and find them effective. For example, I do deal with minor problems when they occur in order to keep them from escalating into bigger problems. I endeavor to provide a good model for students concerning helping others, speaking to them in a kindly way, and avoiding saying things they might find personally hurtful. I often have them repeat their behavior properly when they misbehave.

I also got some ideas from Mr. Morrish that I will begin using. My students are young (third grade) and I think I may have been involving them too much in giving input into the rules of behavior for the class. I think in reality my efforts have been more along the lines of leading them to suggest the kind of behavior I want to see from them in the first place. I think I might spend too much time on that. I like Morrish's suggestion about my making rules for the class and then talking with students to help them see how those rules will help them be successful in class, stay safe from harm, get along better with other members of the class, and better enjoy their experience in school.

I also became more aware of a few things I'd like to emphasize more with my students. For example, I will try spending more time teaching my students how to speak invitingly and encouragingly with each other during cooperative work activities. I think that might increase participation by all members of the group. I think I will also teach them to make positive comments about each other and avoid put-downs in other class activities. I think I sometimes just tell my students what is expected of them while not actually teaching them how to do things properly or efficiently. Usually I get good cooperation from my students. I treat them nicely and show them personal attention, and I get the feeling they want to please me—not always, but at least most of the time.

Source: Used courtesy of Timothy C. Charles.

HOW DOES ONE DEVELOP POSITIVE RELATIONSHIPS WITH STUDENTS?

No approach to discipline is going to accomplish what you hope unless you can establish and maintain good personal relations with your students. Building rapport with them is a good starting point. If students like you, they will want to please you and not disappoint you. They will be inclined to comply with your requests and will understand and accept that the rules you establish ensure security and proper treatment for everyone. Morrish offers a number of suggestions for strengthening relationships between you and your students:

- *Consistently focus on the positive.* Look for things students do right. If they make a mistake, help them improve. No need to criticize.

■ *Wipe the slate clean after students make behavior mistakes.* Deal with the mistake in a positive manner and move on. Don't hold grudges; they don't help in any way. The important thing is what the student does next.

■ *Don't back away from discipline.* Students sometimes don't like having to obey rules or practice appropriate behavior. That doesn't mean they don't want discipline. They understand it is important. They expect it and interpret the effort you expend on it as a sign of concern for them. Later, they will remember you with appreciation.

■ *Lead the way.* Students learn more from watching you than from hearing what you say they should do. Model civilized behaviors and attitudes. Listen to students. Speak kindly to them. Be helpful and give credit when it is due.

■ *Never humiliate students when correcting their misbehavior.* Morrish says teachers unintentionally humiliate students more than they imagine, as when they scold students in front of their friends or correct mistakes in an unpleasant manner. Whenever students need to be corrected, just make sure they know how to behave properly and then insist they do so.

■ *Don't accept mediocrity.* Some teachers fail to set standards of learning and behavior, believing they need only to befriend students in order to obtain their cooperation. Standards are essential if students are to recognize success and maintain their determination to improve. If you willingly accept mediocrity, that is what you will get. Reasonable standards tell students you believe they are bright and sensitive enough to learn and behave properly.

WHAT ABOUT CONSEQUENCES FOR MISBEHAVIOR?

Morrish believes students should face consequences when they misbehave. He maintains that consequences, when structured and applied correctly, are very helpful in discipline. But the consequences he advocates are not punishments. Instead, they involve teaching students to behave properly and then having them show they can do so. We have seen that Morrish's favorite consequence is to have the student repeat the behavior in a correct manner. But he uses other consequences as well, and would have you explain to students why they are applied and how they help students conduct themselves more responsibly. Here are some consequences he suggests you use when students push at boundaries or do something that hurts others:

■ *Make an improvement plan.* Have the student make a plan for handling the situation better in the future. Keep track to ensure the student follows through.

■ *Provide compensation.* Have the student do something positive to make up for negative behavior. This might include making the offended person feel better or the school or classroom look better.

- *Write a letter.* Have the offending student write a letter to the person who was offended, including a statement of commitment for better behavior in the future.
- *Teach younger children.* Have the offending student write and illustrate a story about the incident to read to younger children, emphasizing what was done wrong and what was learned from the experience. (Morrish, 2000, p. 66)

WHAT ABOUT MOTIVATION AND REWARDS?

Many experts in discipline assert that we can't *make* students do anything—that the best we can do is provide an environment and activities so appealing that students will naturally work and otherwise conduct themselves appropriately. Morrish doesn't entirely agree. He says we should certainly provide enticing learning opportunities, but it is ridiculous to believe we cannot make students do anything. The very purpose of discipline, he says, is to make students do what they don't want to do. He points out that students ordinarily do not want to obey rules, don't want to stay quiet, don't want to do homework, don't want to study for tests, and so forth. We use discipline to ensure that they set aside their natural desires and accept education as a tool that will help them succeed in life.

Morrish expresses a very strong philosophical argument here. What do you think of this assertion?

Morrish goes on to say that good discipline teaches students how to persevere and work through activities that are not especially appealing. To the extent you can make instructional activities interesting, do so, and everyone will enjoy school more, including you. But when that is not possible, don't shy away from teaching students what they need to know, even when lessons are tedious.

Morrish also advises teachers to forego praise and rewards when students merely do what is expected of them. He says occasional rewards are fine, because they give special recognition when it is needed. But overall, rewards are vastly overused and students often see them as ends in themselves. Teachers have two powerful natural rewards at their disposal, but they are not stickers, points, or special privileges. They are what you always have with you—your personal attention and your approval.

Morrish asserts that teachers typically dispense copious quantities of praise. Some of them really spread it on thick. But Morrish says we must be cautious about that, too. Beyond a certain point, praise actually reduces motivation and increases dependency. Students develop healthier attitudes if teachers praise student work and behavior only when they truly merit recognition.

Suppose Carmelo has defaced a bulletin board in the room.

What sort of consequence do you think Morrish would apply for that behavior? Suppose Carmelo helps Anthony resolve a personal problem with another student. What sort of reward, if any, would Morrish suggest for that behavior?

WHAT DOES MORRISH SAY ABOUT FOSTERING SELF-ESTEEM?

Morrish does not believe that low self-esteem is a root cause of student misbehavior. He acknowledges that students who do poorly in school and get into trouble sometimes (but not always) have low self-esteem, whereas those who do well tend to have higher self-esteem. But self-esteem does not determine success or failure. It is the other way around, he says—success in school or lack thereof influences self-esteem. If you are competent and successful, you usually think better about yourself than if you are incompetent and unsuccessful.

What role do you believe shame plays in classrooms? Would your response be different if, instead of the word "shame," Morrish used "personal responsibility"?

Morrish goes on to say that teachers who try to build student self-esteem directly may actually do more harm than good, especially if they never allow failure, never put pressure on students to excel, and permit students to express themselves freely without fear of rebuke. These things deprive students of the helpful criticism that normally follows misbehavior or lack of effort, and as a result, students become more self-indulgent. They gradually lose their sense of shame and begin to rationalize their misdeeds with explanations such as "I just felt like it" or "It made me feel good."

Genuine self-esteem comes from increased competence in academic and social matters and the ability to overcome obstacles. If we teach students academic and social skills, and if we help them achieve the high expectations we hold of them, we will see them come to think well of themselves. Competence is the goal; it comes first, then self-esteem follows.

WHAT SHOULD YOU DO WHEN STUDENTS FAIL TO COMPLY WITH YOUR DIRECTIONS?

Occasionally a student may fail to comply with your directions or may, in the heat of the moment, display other inappropriate behavior. Suppose one of your students has behaved discourteously toward you in class. Many teachers will send the offending student to time-out for an indefinite period before allowing him or her to rejoin the class. That does very little positive for the student. Instead of time-out or some other consequence, you should insist on a *do-over*. Have the student repeat the behavior in an acceptable manner. If a student speaks to you disrespectfully, tell him or her to start over and do it courteously this time.

The same procedure applies any time a student fails to follow directions or comply with class standards. Many teachers make the mistake of using *if–then statements*, such as, "If you speak to me in that manner again, then you will be going to the principal's office." Teachers should not use such statements with misbehaving students. They should give students no choice in the matter. They should say, "We don't speak that way in this class. Start over." Most of the time, that is all you need to do.

Remember, Morrish asserts, your most important and powerful tool is *insistence*. You must convey to students they have no choice in the matter, other than to do as you direct. Morrish says that students who are never required to act appropriately seldom will.

If a student still refuses to do as you direct, repeat your instruction in a serious tone of voice. If that doesn't work, use a mild punishment such as time-out to get across the message that you mean what you say. Then after a short time, bring the student back to do the task correctly. The discipline procedure does not end with the time-out. The student is still expected to show proper behavior, and only positive practice ensures that. As discussed previously, punishment is rarely necessary if you persistently help students behave properly.

Commentary From Anonymous Teacher 2

Some of Dr. Morrish's suggestions may sound like advice to parents, but the fact is I now usually have students in class who have not had the benefit of decent parenting. Sometimes I need to help students with a "reality check" of how things work in the real world. This past year, for example, I was challenged by the following students. I have changed their names:

✓ Venus, whose family had disintegrated, leaving her in foster care, uncertain and untrusting
✓ Tristan, the only child of older parents, who hadn't yet learned to take no for an answer
✓ Josh, treated as a peer by his parents, who felt entitled to question my every decision
✓ Sammy, an excellent student and charming to adults, who wielded her cell phone as a saber, slicing and dicing her classmates with rumor and innuendo on various social networking sites
✓ Dimitri, who studied me with the intensity of a profiler, figuring out my buttons and waiting for the optimal occasion to push them, purely for the sport of it

The truth is, students expect teachers to be in charge and keep order in the classroom, even though many don't act like it. With a strong structure in place and a strong teacher in authority, students feel safer, more confident, and more secure. At least that's what I believe. If you don't assume leadership of your students and of your classroom, some of your students will step up to fill the void. Personally, I found the following suggestions from Dr. Morrish to be right on target:

✓ Don't make rules you are not prepared to enforce.
✓ Plan interesting lessons and challenge students to achieve.
✓ Stay on your feet, stay on the move, and stay on top of things.
✓ Be patient, pleasant, persistent, and pragmatic.
✓ Cut down on the lecturing, preaching, and scolding, which students quickly tune out.
✓ Model your expectations and always try to show kindness, courtesy, respect, and appreciation in interactions with students.

Source: Used courtesy of Marilyn Charles.

Applying Morrish's Ideas: What Might They Look Like in Action?

CASE 1 Kristina Will Not Work

Kristina, a student in Mr. Jake's class, is quite docile. She socializes little with other students and never disrupts lessons. However, despite Mr. Jake's best efforts, Kristina will not do her work. She rarely completes an assignment. She is simply there, putting forth no effort at all. *What would Ronald Morrish suggest to help Kristina and Mr. Jake?*

Morrish would have Mr. Jake remind Kristina of the class rule about everyone doing their best to learn. He would insist that Kristina begin her work and follow through. Mr. Jake might need to stand beside her to help her get started. He would not punish her, but would continue to press her to comply with the assignment. He might ask questions such as, "Do you know what you are supposed to do in this activity?" "Do you understand why it needs to be done?" "Can I count on you to do your part?" As Kristina improves, Mr. Jake might make comments to her such as, "You made a good effort today. I can see you are trying. Thank you for that." If more intervention were required, Morrish would consider assigning Kristina to the school's study hall or keeping her in the classroom for additional time (a productive extension of her day, rather than a punitive detention). He might also have her create a daily plan for accomplishing her schoolwork, involve her caregivers in the process, or assign an older student to mentor her.

CASE 2 Sara Will Not Stop Talking

Sara is a pleasant girl who participates in class activities and does most, though not all, of her assigned work. She cannot seem to refrain from talking to classmates, however. Her teacher, Mr. Gonzales, has to speak to her repeatedly during lessons, to the point that he often becomes exasperated and loses his temper. *What suggestions would Ronald Morrish give Mr. Gonzales for dealing with Sara?*

CASE 3 Joshua Clowns and Intimidates

Joshua, larger and louder than his classmates, always wants to be the center of attention, which he accomplishes through a combination of clowning and intimidation. He makes wise remarks, talks back (smilingly) to the teacher, utters a variety of sound-effect noises such as automobile crashes and gunshots, and makes limitless sarcastic comments and put-downs of his classmates. Other students will not stand up to him, apparently fearing his size and verbal aggression. His teacher, Miss Pearl, has come to her wit's end. *Would Joshua's behavior be likely to improve if Ronald Morrish's techniques were used in Miss Pearl's classroom? Explain.*

Case 4 Tom Is Hostile and Defiant

Tom has appeared to be in his usual foul mood ever since arriving in class. On his way to sharpen his pencil, he bumps into Frank, who complains. Tom tells him loudly to shut up. Miss Baines, the teacher, says, "Tom, go back to your seat." Tom wheels around, swears loudly, and says heatedly, "I'll go when I'm *&$#^ good and ready!" *How would Ronald Morrish have Miss Baines deal with Tom?*

Having read these cases, what are your thoughts on which of Morrish's ideas, if any, would work well for you? What would you choose to avoid?

You Are the Teacher

HIGH SCHOOL BIOLOGY

You teach an advanced placement class in biology to students from middle- to upper-income families. Most of the students have already made plans for attending college. When the students enter the classroom, they know they are to go to their assigned seats and write out answers to the questions of the day that you have written on the board. After that, you conduct discussions on text material that you assigned students to read before coming to class. During the discussion, you call randomly on students to answer questions and require that they support their answers with reference to the assigned reading. Following that, students engage in lab activity for the remainder of the period.

A TYPICAL OCCURRENCE

You have just begun a discussion about the process of photosynthesis. You ask Sarolyn what the word *photosynthesis* means. She pushes her long hair aside and replies, "I don't get it." This is a comment you hear frequently from Sarolyn, even though she is an intelligent girl. "What is it you don't understand?" "None of it," she says. You say, "Be more specific! I've only asked for the definition!" Sarolyn is not intimidated. "I mean, I don't get any of it. I don't understand why plants are green. Why aren't they blue or some other color? Why don't they grow on Mercury? The book says plants make food. How? Do they make bread? That's ridiculous."

You gaze at Sarolyn for a while, and she back at you. You ask, "Are you finished?" Sarolyn shrugs. "I guess so." She hears some of the boys whistle under their breath; she obviously enjoys their attention. You say to her, "Sarolyn, I hope someday you will understand that this is not a place for you to show off." "I hope so, too," Sarolyn says. "I know I should be more serious." She stares out the window. For the remainder of the discussion, which you don't handle as well as usual, you call only on students you know will give proper answers. Now that the discussion is completed, you begin to give instructions for the lab activity. You notice that Nick is turning the valve of the gas jet on and off. You say to Nick, "Mr. Contreras, would you please repeat our rule about the use of lab equipment?" Nick drops his head and mumbles something about waiting for directions. Sarolyn says calmly, "Knock it off, Nick. This is serious business."

She smiles at you. After a moment, you complete your directions and tell the students to begin. You walk around the room, monitoring their work. You stand behind lab partners Mei and Teresa, who are having a difficult time. You do not offer them help, believing that advanced placement students should be able to work things out for themselves. But as they blunder through the activity, you find yourself shaking your head in disbelief.

CONCEPTUALIZING A STRATEGY

If you followed the suggestions of Ronald Morrish, what would you conclude or do with regard to the following?

- Pinpointing the problems in your class
- Preventing the problems from occurring in the first place
- Putting an immediate end to the misbehavior
- Maintaining student dignity and good personal relations
- Using the situation to help the students develop a sense of greater responsibility and self-control

REFLECTING ON MORRISH: WHAT YOU HAVE LEARNED IN THIS CHAPTER

Predominant Themes in Morrish's Work

Students should be taught compliance as an automatic response to teacher directions.

Effective managers focus on preventing, not just reacting to, misbehavior.

Clarity of expectations supports good behavior.

Learning should be a meaningful, engaging, and cooperative activity.

Effective managers spend a significant amount of time, particularly at the start of the school year, actively teaching rules, procedures, limits, and expectations.

One worthwhile exercise for anyone studying classroom management models is to consider how one theorist's ideas relate to those of other theorists in the discipline. It has probably occurred to you that while some of Morrish's ideas align with recommendations from other authorities covered in this text (e.g., Skinner), several assertions are in tension with those of other experts (Glasser, Ginott, and Kohn are a few). As we've said earlier in this text, thinking about the relationships among models is important for teachers interested in developing their own perspectives on classroom management.

Interestingly, there's little to no scholarly literature reviewing the effectiveness of Real Discipline, though the popularity of Morrish's ideas suggests that a number of teachers and parents find great value in the program. In the absence of scholarly review of the program, we've included Table 5.1, which highlights some potential positives of the Real Discipline model, and provides some questions that you should consider as you evaluate the appropriateness of his ideas for inclusion in your classroom management system. Remember to take notes in your planning guide as you reflect.

Table 5.1

Morrish's Ideas	Potential Positives	Questions to Consider
Teacher insistence and student compliance are key to successful classroom management. Student compliance should be taught as a *non-thinking* activity.	Students understand what is expected and learn to meet those expectations immediately	• How does a teacher avoid power struggles in this model? • Is there value in teaching students to think before they comply?
Students should not be involved in rule-making.	The teacher, as the authority figure in the classroom, knows what the climate should be like, and sets rules and consequences accordingly.	• How might involving students in rule-making increase their buy-in to following the rules?
Teachers lose when they bargain with students.	Students whose teachers don't compromise on management issues are more likely to be aware of the teacher's legitimate authority.	• What is the role of compromise in classrooms? • How does this idea sync with the idea of a democratic classroom? Is a democratic approach of value?
Students make choices only when sufficiently mature.	Some students may not be developmentally ready to understand the range of choices and/or the potential impact of a choice.	• What might a choice advocate like Glasser or Gossen say in response to this recommendation? • If you review Piaget's stages of development, how old would students have to be to engage in choice behaviors?

(continued)

Table 5.1 (continued)

Morrish's Ideas	Potential Positives	Questions to Consider
Teachers must teach students right and wrong.	Students benefit from having a structure for operating within the classroom; this structure may be carried into their out-of-school lives.	• How do teachers go about determining what values to teach students? • Are right and wrong always clear-cut?
Discipline involves teaching students how they are to behave in school and requires them to show courtesy and consideration.	Basic courtesy and consideration smooth the way for students in interpersonal relationships and in society.	• What shortcomings might be apparent when students demonstrate courtesy and consideration because they've been trained to do so, rather than because they value these traits?
Teachers should not overlook any instance of misbehavior.	Students will be aware that all facets of their behavior matter, and that they're not able to cut corners.	• Is every instance of misbehavior worth stopping for? Must students be 100% compliant to be well-functioning members of a class community?

MyLab Education **Self-Check 5.1**

MyLab Education **Self-Check 5.2**

MyLab Education **Application Exercise 5.1** Viewing a Lesson Through Morrish-Colored Lenses

MyLab Education **Application Exercise 5.2** Critique a Strategy: Involving Students in Establishing Rules

6

Taking Charge in the Classroom: Craig Seganti*

How Does Craig Seganti Establish Control, Especially When Students Are Hard to Manage?

LEARNING OUTCOMES:

6-1 Identify the classroom management recommendations made by Craig Seganti and the broad classroom management themes to which they relate.

6-2 Consider the strengths and weaknesses of Seganti's recommendations and evaluate their likely utility in various situational contexts.

Today, many teachers reluctantly accept that their students will misbehave much of the time. They are more or less resigned to it. But Craig Seganti insists you should not settle for that; he asserts that it's probably what you'll get if you don't immediately establish one understanding with your students—that you are in charge and are a professional who knows what you're doing.

WHO IS CRAIG SEGANTI?

For more than 20 years, Seganti was a teacher in inner-city Los Angeles schools, where he not only survived but flourished. He describes how he did so in his 2008 book *Classroom Discipline 101: How to Get Control of Any Classroom*. He believes the approach he developed will solve discipline issues for all teachers and will save the careers of many who've been beaten down by resistant, uncooperative students.

Mr. Seganti taught middle school and high school English and English as a second language (ESL) to students from many different backgrounds. He also taught juvenile offenders of both sexes in probation camps and interim schools for Los Angeles County. He now is devoted full time to disseminating his ideas on discipline. Seganti describes his approach as reality based rather than theory based, and says his tactics work with students in the real world. He invites you to examine his approach thoroughly. It will, he says, free you to teach, free your students to learn in a positive environment without disruptions and turmoil, and bring you the overall success you always hoped for.

*Used with permission from Craig Seganti.

In this chapter, we explore Seganti's main concepts and procedures. It is suggested that you also review the short articles he has posted at http://ezinearticles.com/?expert=Craig_Seganti (Seganti, 2008b). Those articles include the following:

- How to Get Any Student to Behave Well All of the Time
- How to Avoid Useless Arguments with Students
- Eliminating the Middle Man—the Myth of Giving Warnings
- The Role of Accountability in Classroom Management

THE SEGANTI MODEL

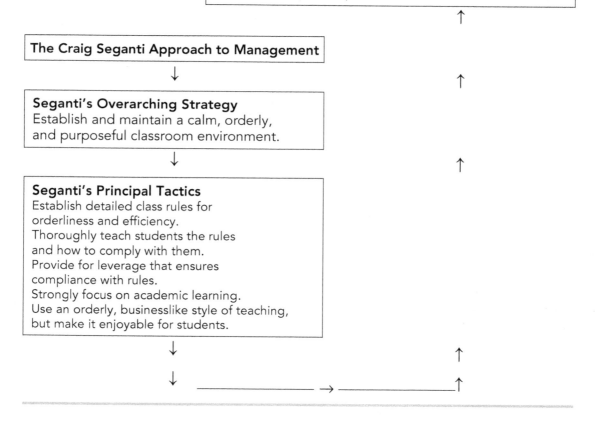

WHAT DOES SEGANTI SAY ABOUT DISCIPLINE?

Here is a preview of some of Seganti's main points of advice. We will examine them further throughout the chapter:

- Adopt and share with students the attitude that your class is, first and foremost, for academic learning.
- Emphasize that behavioral disruptions interfere with all students' right to a good education.
- Make it your first priority to teach all students to understand and comply with class rules of behavior. Then hold all students accountable for complying with those rules.
- Establish "leverage" that ensures you can enforce the rules. (Seganti recommends as very effective a 15-minute detention that misbehaving students must attend after school.)

In short, you can manage a productive class even for "difficult" students if you establish and clarify rules of behavior, teach the rules, and establish leverage that ensures student compliance with rules.

At first glance, Seganti's approach may appear a bit harsh. But he maintains that it works wonders in fostering respectful behavior and motivating effort to learn. He contends it is exactly what hard-to-manage students need, and that there is nothing better you can do for students than help them develop responsibility and gain a good education in a classroom that is focused on learning.

We now proceed to examine Seganti's core ideas and suggestions, organized around four elements featured in his approach: teacher attitude, class rules for student accountability, leverage for obtaining compliance, and management tactics that support desirable behavior. We will explore these elements in turn. If you wish to examine more deeply the nuances of Seganti's approach and see how he makes his points, you can view his video and obtain his e-book and other materials at www.classroomdiscipline101.com.

WHAT ATTITUDE DOES SEGANTI RECOMMEND FOR TEACHERS?

Seganti says it is the teacher's attitude toward discipline that ultimately affects how students behave, for better or worse. The attitude he recommends is conveyed to students via the following four messages, which are central and powerful and should be repeated as often as necessary:

- Any student who disrupts the class is interfering with other students' constitutional right to a good public education.

- We have separate roles in this class, which are equally important. My role: I am the expert, trained and experienced in how to teach and help you learn. I make the decisions about how to do those things. Your role: You are the students who are here to study under my guidance. Your job is to support our efforts and do your best to learn.
- The classroom is for academic learning. I'll make it as enjoyable as I can, but everything we do in class will be aimed at learning. Your duty is to focus and participate and learn. That is what I will always expect of you.
- I know you want to enjoy school and feel good about yourselves. I will help you do just that. But you need to understand that self-esteem doesn't come from messing around in the classroom. It comes from doing hard work to acquire the knowledge and skills that will enable you to enjoy a good life.

Seganti suggests many principles for greatly improving teacher effectiveness. For example:

- *Rely on Actions.* When dealing with students, make your points through actions, which speak far louder than words. It is worse than useless to spend time cajoling, arguing, and continually trying to justify your decisions to students. Just make good rules and enforce them without fail. No explanations are needed. If you don't enforce your rules, students will act as though your rules don't exist.
- *Don't Give Warnings.* Giving students warnings is self-defeating and it wastes time. Students beyond first or second grade know when they are misbehaving, so there is no need to warn them about it or say you are thinking of doing something about it. You can spend your day (week, month, career) giving warnings instead of teaching. If you don't want students to manipulate you, don't give warnings. (Seganti does give students one warning, on the first day of class only, as we will see when we review his rules.)
- *Don't Give Superfluous Rewards.* Don't spend time doling out rewards for learning. Learning is what students are supposed to do. Of course, you want your students to enjoy your classes and you will help them do so, but their reward for doing the assigned work lies in seeing their abilities expand as part of a good education. Emphasize that principle and help students keep track of what they have learned. Recognition of genuine progress is the only reward that truly counts. If you try to motivate students with gimmicks, pep talks, and tangible rewards, you send a poor message about education—that it is of so little value you need to bribe students to endure it. If students ask you what the reward will be for behaving properly, tell them the reward will be a good education, which is priceless.
- *Provide for Enjoyment.* All the while, you must do what you can to make the class enjoyable for students. Provide numerous fun activities. Treat students with kindness and consideration. Give them personal attention. Be helpful. Celebrate learning and show there can and should be some fun and enjoyment in the classroom.

■ *Speak Effectively*. Learn how to talk effectively with students. (The suggestions presented here have to do with teaching information and proper behavior. If you were counseling students or commiserating with them, you would speak in a different manner.) Look at the following exchange as an example of what *not* to do:

Teacher: Stop talking, Johnny.
Johnny: I wasn't talking.
Teacher: You were talking—I just saw you talking to Henry.
Johnny: Well, Jason was talking. He was doing it first.
(and so forth, on and on)

Seganti comments, "What's your strategy here? Are you going to stand there arguing with Johnny about whether or not he was talking? That only perpetuates the problem." The following shows how Seganti would interact with Johnny:

Teacher: There is no talking in my class, Johnny—stay after school 15 minutes today for detention.
Johnny: But I wasn't talking!
Teacher: Show up for detention. If you don't want another 15 minutes, stop disrupting now.

RULES: HOW DO THEY PROMOTE STUDENT ACCOUNTABILITY?

Seganti insists on holding students accountable for their behavior. There should be no getting around it. Class rules of behavior provide the specifics of accountability. You, the teacher, must establish effective rules and make sure students understand them clearly. Compose the rules yourself, before you see your students, and make copies to hand out. Every possible behavior that concerns your class, positive or negative, should be addressed somewhere in the rules. You are the professional and you know how students should behave. Don't waste time asking students to help you decide what the rules should be.

Right away when students arrive at your door for the first day of class, teach them the rules for your class and exactly what those rules mean. This is to be done so no misunderstanding is possible. The students' first assignment in class is to copy the rules neatly, sign their copy, and hand it in. From that point onward, students are held accountable for their actions in class. They can no longer claim they didn't know the rules. If they try that ploy, have them once again copy the rules, sign the copy, and give it to you.

Clearly, some of Seganti's methods are more easily used with older students. Students in the very early grades could not do this; what could an elementary teacher who uses Seganti's model do to accomplish the same purpose?

The following are rule topics Seganti advocates. The first two are given in Seganti's words. After that, additional topics for rules are presented with brief suggestions. In Seganti's book *Classroom Discipline 101* (Seganti, 2008a), you can find his exact wording for his 11 rules and the procedures he uses for teaching them to students.

Seganti's Rule 1 and Rule 2

Rule 1

You are to enter the classroom calmly and quietly and go immediately to your assigned seat. You are to sit at a 90-degree angle to your desk with your feet on the floor, showing good posture and a straight spine.

How to Teach Rule 1 to Students Stand in the doorway on the first day and teach this rule to each student in turn. This procedure is immediately established as a rule, not an option. A student who enters the room improperly has defied a rule and is subject to the consequence you have established for violating rules (Seganti's 15-minute detention consequence will be explained later). Once all students are seated, explain this rule again to the class as a whole.

Rule 2

Students are to show respect at all times and in all manners toward staff, others, and themselves. This includes all verbal and nonverbal forms of communication, including body language, facial expression, and tone of voice.

How to Teach Rule 2 to Students When all students are in the room, read this rule once. Even in the wildest schools there is usually a window of time the first day when students are curious and will listen. Now, read it again, piece by piece.

This can become a good lesson on nonverbal communication. Tell the students that most communication is nonverbal. Take your time here. Be a teacher—give examples and demonstrate. Tell the students, "If I give you a direction and you roll your eyes, it is just as disrespectful as if you insult me verbally, and you will get detention." Act it out—"Suppose I say: Jack, open your book to page 134." Pretend to be Jack and roll your eyes. Explain again that eye rolling and other disrespectful actions are just as unacceptable as saying something rude and will be met with the same consequences.

Additional Topics Seganti Suggests for Rules

Working on Task

This topic centers on clarifying when students should be on task, how they should be working, what they should do when they have completed their assigned work, and when and how they may talk.

Begin by clarifying exactly what *being on task* and *paying full attention* mean. Act out for students what these requirements look like and *do not* look like. Then, have selected students demonstrate behavior that complies with and violates the rule.

Seganti insists that you absolutely must train your students to get their materials out immediately and be quietly at work by the time the bell rings. You must insist on this, or else students will begin to dawdle more and more when entering the room. In addition, you must help students identify productive and respectful activities they can do when they have completed their work. This heads off the future manipulation technique in which students say, "I'm done with my work."

Eliminating Distractions

This topic centers on potential distractions, such as food, playthings, electronic media, and the like, that students might intentionally or inadvertently bring to class. Seganti provides a list of potential distractions and carefully explains exactly what he will do if any of those distractions appear in noncompliance with the class rule. He explains again to students that class time is devoted entirely to learning and strongly reiterates that nothing will be permitted to interfere with that time.

One of the distractions Seganti highlights is chewing gum. He says he is famous for his "no-chewing" rule, which helps make him manipulation-proof. Students sometimes appear to be chewing, but claim they are not, sticking their tongues out to prove it. Seganti says this act can earn two detentions—one for chewing gum and one for lying. As Seganti explains it, here is how this situation usually plays out:

> **Teacher:** Spit out the gum, Jane, and come after school for 15 minutes.
> **Jane:** I'm not chewing gum.
> **Teacher:** Well, there's no chewing in my class, even if you aren't chewing anything, so come to detention.
> **Jane:** But I'm not chewing anything!
> **Teacher:** I don't argue with students. You can either spit out the gum or get suspended for defiance.
> (Jane then either spits out the gum or the teacher suspends her from the class.)

Seganti says you won't have to do this often. Once or twice and everyone gets the idea you are manipulation-proof. Caregivers or administrators may complain if you suspend a student from class for merely chewing gum. If that happens, point out that the student has violated two rules—one for chewing gum and another for noncompliance with teacher directions. This point will be addressed again when we explore the roles of administrators, counselors, and caregivers.

Beginning the Period

This topic centers on what students must be doing when the bell rings at the beginning of class and what will happen to them if they violate the rule. Simply explain to students what the rule requires of them when the beginning bell rings. Although Seganti does not say so explicitly, it would be a good idea to have students practice moving into full compliance with the rule at least several seconds before you pretend to ring the tardy bell.

Being Ready for Work

This rule centers on how students should be prepared for class, which includes bringing any materials they need for immediate class participation. It also stipulates what students will not be allowed to do once the bell rings. This admonition covers several matters that might seem trivial, but are serious because they take away time for learning.

For example, your students may be accustomed to coming to class without having at hand all the materials they need for successful learning. They may have the feeling that missing an item or two is not very bad. Seganti would have you quickly correct that misconception. He says you should insist to students that they are old enough to take responsibility for this requirement. He advocates firm regulations regarding pencil sharpening in particular, because students often use sharpening as a distraction and manipulation tactic. Unless you are insistent on compliance with the readiness rule, your more disruptive students will be asking for various school-related materials all period long.

Attending to Miscellaneous Behavior

This topic centers on matters such as students calling out, leaving their seats, and dealing with the scrap paper and other trash that accumulates around desks and elsewhere in the room. Have students act out the behaviors associated with speaking out improperly, raising their hands, getting permission, and keeping the classroom environment neat. Show them the wrong way of doing things—such as raising their hands as they begin to speak—and the right way, such as raising their hands, waiting for permission, and then speaking. Have them practice everything you expect of them.

Remind them that you cannot get around to answering each and every question promptly—sometimes they will have to wait a minute when you are busy.

Regarding Procedures

This topic centers on procedures for various activities, including leaving the room when necessary. You might be surprised at what Seganti requires of students who request restroom passes, but he says his tactic has worked wonders in stopping the debates between teacher and students on whether or not the student really has to go. If a student begs and squirms to prove the need is real, do the following:

Teacher: Sure, here's the pass—but you have to make up 10 minutes after school.

Student: Huh? Why 10 minutes?

Teacher: (Don't say anything; just hold the hall pass and wait. The procedure has been stated and clarified. No need to repeat it.)

Regarding Teacher Requests and Directions

This topic centers on how students are to conduct themselves when the teacher asks them to do anything, such as change seats or pick up trash. Seganti has a steadfast way of interacting with students in these cases—he doesn't argue. Instead, he tells students that if they feel the direction is unreasonable, they may arrange to discuss it with the school counselor or vice principal, or in a conference involving student, parent, and teacher. He does not use class time for arguing with students, insisting the limited time for learning is too valuable to waste in that way.

As before, in teaching the rule, he advises you to read the rule aloud, then go back, explain, and have students practice complying in the manner expected. This rule must make it abundantly clear that you do not argue or debate discipline issues or directions with students. The focus is always on actions, not words.

End of Class

This topic centers on what students are to do when the bell rings at the end of class. Have students practice the procedure you require. Seganti suggests you make a bell noise and have students pack up their materials, then wait for you to say, "Okay, you are dismissed." Don't fall for the old "that's not my paper" retort when it's time to make sure the floor is clean. Students are accountable for their area.

Clarifying the System of Consequences

This topic centers on what will happen to students who violate any of the class rules. This system, once it is presented so students understand it, is the only warning Seganti gives. If students who have violated any of the prior rules do not abide by the indicated consequences, they are suspended from class and not allowed to reenter until they have fulfilled the requirement.

By this time, you have carefully gone through how you expect students to conduct themselves in class. You and your students will be tired of reading and talking about the rules, but rules must be stressed hard the first day so there is no room for doubt about what is expected. The time investment is very productive in making sure things go smoothly the rest of the year.

Leverage: How Do You Get Students to Follow the Rules?

The purpose of rules is to make sure your class operates responsibly and efficiently. But remember—rules are of no value unless you can enforce them and do so consistently. For that reason, you must create the mindset in all your students that breaking class rules is not going to get them what they want. To establish that mindset, you need some kind of *leverage* that makes students choose to follow the rules.

Seganti has determined that the most effective leverage for his classes is "Mr. Seganti's famous *15-minute detention* after school." This detention is only slightly inconvenient for students, but nevertheless they dislike it. And it works because they can't get out of it. Seganti calls this detention the "lever that can move boulders." It promotes psychological compliance while causing very little resentment. It doesn't punish teachers, either, because they usually have to stay after school for a while anyway.

A student who comes to your detention is tacitly agreeing that you are in a position of authority. Once you have established that understanding, behavior problems dwindle. But what if students simply don't appear at detention as directed? That rarely happens, Seganti says, but if it does, suspend the student from class, in accordance with the class rules. Don't let the student back into your class until (1) his or her parents or caregiver have been notified, (2) the student has once again copied all the class rules, and (3) the student has served the detention. Students quickly realize they simply cannot escape the detention.

In a 2008 personal communication with the first author of this book, Mr. Seganti made these further observations about students adjusting to the 15-minute detention:

> *Some students who are difficult to manage will not come to detention the first time you assign it unless they are convinced they cannot get out of complying with the consequence. Therefore, they all must learn very quickly that it is better to show up than not. The whole system depends on the idea that testing the rules will bring more discomfort than simply following them. You must make it clear that if students do not show up for detention when it is assigned, they will be suspended from your class and not allowed to attend until they do so. They must see that you will indeed follow through on this requirement. Once this is clear, you will seldom be tested.*

If you suspend a student from class, you will need to inform your administrator and the student's parent or caretaker. Preparations for doing so should be made in advance.

Figure 6.1 presents Seganti's protocol for calling caregivers.

Seganti maintains that detention of 10 to 15 minutes is the most effective leverage available to most teachers, but he recognizes that after-school detention is difficult or impossible in many schools because students have to catch buses. He advises teachers who encounter an obstacle to discuss with their administrator ways in which after-school detention can be managed. If no solution is evident, Seganti suggests three alternatives:

Figure 6.1 ■ Craig Seganti's Protocol for Calling Caregivers

"Hello, Mrs. Smith? I'm Mr. Jones, James's history teacher. James was disrupting my lesson today and I assigned him a 15-minute detention after school, but he didn't come. As he knows, that means he is suspended from my class until he does two things—copy the class rules and come to detention for 15 minutes. Can you make sure he copies the rules for me and comes to detention tomorrow so he can return to class?"

Sometimes the parent will take the student's side and say, "What exactly did he do?" Then you can say, "He was disrupting the lesson by talking," or "He defied instructions to change his seat," or whatever. Sometimes a parent will misunderstand and say, "You are suspending him for talking in class?" Answer like this: "No. I am suspending him for defiance of my rules and refusing to come to his 15-minute detention. As soon as he makes up his 15 minutes, he can return to class. Can you ensure that he does this and copies the rules for me?"

If you get the parent's assurance that James will come to detention the next day, you might delay the suspension until you see if he does. If James comes to class the next day, you should say in front of the class, "James, as you know I talked to your mother last night and she assured me you are coming to detention today—is that correct?" (James says, "Yes.")

"Okay, then I will hold off the suspension until tomorrow. But let's be clear that if you don't show today, you are suspended." This exchange lets the rest of the class know what will happen if they don't show up.

Source: Seganti, C. (2008). *Classroom discipline 101: How to get control of any classroom* (pp. 89–90), retrieved from http://www.classroomdiscipline101.com. Reproduced with permission.

- Arrange for students to serve detention during school time by going to a fellow teacher's room for 10 or 15 minutes to copy rules—this could be done as a favor or as an exchange.
- If most class members are misbehaving, stop and have everyone spend 15 minutes copying the rules. Seganti asserts that the well-behaved students seldom complain about this because they intuitively realize you are trying to help everyone.
- In cooperation with four fellow teachers, work out a detention schedule during lunch time. Each teacher can stay 20 minutes or so one day a week. This has the added advantage of establishing a consistent behavior code that involves other classes.

MANAGEMENT: WHAT SHOULD YOU DO TO SUPPORT DESIRABLE BEHAVIOR?

Seganti has identified several things teachers can do, both before and after they meet their students, to make this discipline approach more effective. Here are some of his suggestions:

Organize the room arrangement. The success of your program is affected by how you arrange your room physically. Have your desks in rows and, if you think students might deface the furniture, number each chair and desk so they remain together and students are accountable for them. Have everything in the room, including your materials, neat and organized—a sloppy room encourages sloppy behavior. Place one or two desks adjacent to your desk for students who are most likely to be disruptive. Put one desk in the back corner facing the wall, to use for in-class suspensions. If a student doesn't show up for detention, but is not usually disruptive, put him or her in the back of the room facing the wall to copy the rules. Then, if he or she comes to detention that afternoon, permission is given to rejoin class the next day.

Cultivate quiet. Cultivate a quiet classroom for a week or two with no group work and minimal talking—give a lot of reading and written work to acclimate the students to the idea that this classroom is quiet. The resultant habits are very powerful. When students get used to them, you can move into more vocal lessons.

Be at the ready. Have your referrals, detention logs, teaching props, and parent phone numbers at hand.

Dress professionally. In various walks of life, people who are leaders dress differently from those with whom they work. You see this, for example, in the military, religious institutions, and even the workaday world. Seganti believes the way you dress helps determine the impact you have on students by separating you from them psychologically, just as a priest looks different from the congregation or a general from a private. Seganti advises male teachers to wear ties and female teachers to dress in a professional manner. A professional appearance projects authority; but if you dress in a way that says, "I am one of you," then students will tend to treat you as one of them. When you establish a psychological separation from your students, they are less likely to challenge your authority.

Think about what you read in Chapter 2 regarding sociocultural influences on student behavior. What potential conflict do you see with Seganti's eye contact suggestion?

Make eye contact. Looking students in the eye and having them look you in the eye reinforces your authority. When you give a direction, and it looks as though your students are not committed to it, get their undivided attention. Say, "Look at me. Did you understand?" Remember, you are looking for full nonverbal and verbal compliance with your directions.

Give something back to students. Teach in a way of which you can be truly proud. Teach useful information in an engaging manner all period long. Students are not eager to cooperate with teachers who show little sparkle and assign meaningless tasks. If you teach as though you are just going through the motions, students will think you don't care about learning and are using rules as a power trip. But when you combine tight boundaries with teaching that is interesting and valuable, students see that you care enough about them to work hard for their benefit. They will be thankful there is an adult around who can take charge and help them become more competent.

Organize your procedures. Good organization is your best friend. Make sure you have procedures for everything. Clarify them for students—seating charts, labeled desks, referrals, detention, what you will do when students try to manipulate you, and so on. Everyone should know exactly what they should be doing from bell to bell and what you are likely to do.

Listen to students. Listen attentively to students. Don't listen merely to *what* students say. Listen for the *motivation* behind their words.

Speak in statements. When speaking with students about discipline matters, use statements, not questions—for example, "This is work time," rather than "Why aren't you working?"

Educate students. Recognize that your job is to educate students, not to counsel them or deal with emotional problems they may have. That's what counselors are for.

Hold students accountable for proper behavior. After a few years in school, your students know how to behave properly. Except for new procedures, you don't have to teach them how to behave. Your rules for the class are simply to make students accountable. Your main job is to educate. Every student can understand that message.

Prepare. Know in advance exactly what action you will take every time a student breaks a rule.

Hold the line. Do not settle for anything less than a quiet, respectful, focused classroom. Repeat all procedures as often as necessary to maintain that kind of classroom. Make sure students stay on task and complete their work. It is not enough just to be quiet.

Keep 'em busy. Keep your students busy from bell to bell. Don't have any downtime and don't leave any time for talking.

Review the rules. You can have a near-perfect classroom if you continue having students review the required rules and procedures. Do this every day, if necessary, until they get it. In a personal communication with the first author of this text, Mr. Seganti commented that feedback he has received from teachers confirms the powerful effect of teaching class rules two days in a row. You may say to your students, "Everybody got this yet? No?" (Laughingly) "Okay, we will go over the rules again tomorrow."

Assess yourself. Review your performance every day. Identify mistakes you have made and decide what you can do next time to get better results.

Take care of things. Don't count on administrative or parental support except to ensure that your established consequences are enforced.

Don't be manipulated. Students will invariably manipulate you if you allow them to do so. To students, it's a game. They will argue, waste time, cause you to become exasperated, and so forth. Seganti devotes much attention to this matter and shows teachers how to avoid being manipulated. The dialogs that follow indicate what you should do when students try to manipulate you. Notice that Seganti responds by stating a rule, rather than arguing with students. This tactic keeps attention on the teacher's agenda (in this case, following the rules) instead of moving attention to the student's agenda (such as wasting time, getting the better of the teacher, or trying to get out of detention).

Violation of Rule 1 Miguel is out of his seat during quiet study time.

> **You:** "Miguel, that's a 15-minute detention for getting out of your seat without permission."
> **Miguel:** "I was just getting my notebook!"
> **You:** "I don't argue with students."

Violation of Rule 2 Megan is chewing gum.

> **You:** "Megan, that's a 15-minute detention for chewing gum."
> **Megan:** "I'm not chewing gum."
> **You:** "Fine, but since giving the appearance of chewing gum is against the rules, you have detention anyway." Or you might say, "If you don't spit it out I will have to send you out for defiance."

Seganti provides more advice on answering manipulators in a piece called "Mr. Seganti's Big Kahuna Manipulation Destroyer" (Seganti, 2008a, p. 126). The manipulation destroyer he describes is *silence.* Seganti explains that when students make manipulative, irrelevant comments like those in the preceding dialogs, you just look at the students and say nothing. After all, there is no real answer to a manipulative question. A student is talking. You say, "Stop talking." They say, "I wasn't talking." What good can come of arguing back and forth in a silly exchange? So, try just saying nothing. Just look at the student, using a deadpan expression on your face, showing that you will not engage in the matter. Silence stops most manipulation in its tracks. The student may make a last feeble protestation such as, "Man, I wasn't even talking," but the matter will usually end there. If the student does continue talking, assign detention if you've not already done so.

HOW MIGHT I PUT SEGANTI'S IDEAS INTO EFFECT?

The following are suggestions from Mr. Seganti.

Use Effective Doorway Tactics

Seganti places great emphasis on *doorway tactics*, meaning what you do when students arrive at your classroom door. Before you let students through the door, make sure they are ready to get down to business. Do not wait inside the room for everyone to enter any way they like and then try to calm them down and get their attention afterward. When they approach your room, they may be noisy, rude, jumpy, eating, distracted, or doing other things that are not conducive to academics. Don't allow any of this. Make sure that as students walk through your doorway they are moving into a mindset for learning. Be attentive to students' body language, not just their words.

Here are details of his recommendations for interacting with students the *first* time they arrive for class (Seganti, 2008a, pp. 21–34):

- Stand in your doorway and stop *every* student briefly before they enter. You might have to block the entrance with your body.
- Hand each student a copy of the class rules and say, "I want you to go directly to the seat I have assigned you without talking and in an orderly manner. You are to sit down quietly, take out your materials and immediately copy these rules onto a separate sheet of paper. Do this without talking. Do you understand?" Point to the exact seat you want each student to sit in. Make an effort to repeat the part about "being quiet" and "not talking" three times before you let them in. Conveying these messages of "strictness" will help your classroom atmosphere enormously.
- If any students say they already know how to behave or if they ask why they need to copy the rules, or if they do or say anything disrespectful, say, "I gave you a direction. You need to follow it." Do not enter into a discussion or rationalize your requirements. Don't fool yourself by thinking that copying the rules is a small matter that can just be let go. From the beginning, get students to realize they have to comply with *all* your directions, great and small. Before long, that is what they will do.
- If students are disrespectful, or do not have their materials, or in any other way appear unprepared for class, do not let them through the door. They can borrow what they need from a friend, but they can't enter the room until they have all of their materials.
- If their nonverbal cues say they are not ready to study, have them stand to the side. Tell them what you expect and say honestly, "To me, you don't look ready to study." When they manage to meet your standards of a proper attitude for entry to the class, let them in. Otherwise just wait. There is no hurry.

■ If any students begin disrupting after entering, call them back to try again. You can say something like, "Now try again—go to your seat quietly, take out your materials without talking, and copy the rules." If the student interrupts while you are speaking, say, "Do not interrupt me again. This is not a conversation but a simple direction you can comply with, or else leave the room for defiance." Do this every day until students enter in a manner that meets your standards for entering and getting to work. Repeat this procedure for as long as necessary. Students do not resent it and they soon respond well. They will even start saying your entry rules before you do.

Watch for and Address Three Types of Behavior on the First Day

There are roughly three types of behavior you can expect to see among your students the first day of school. Seganti refers to them as Type A, Type B, and Type C. He comments on them as follows:

1. Type A behavior—these students are polite, prepared, and ready to enter class. Give them their instructions quickly and send them in.
2. Type B behavior—these students are basically respectful but appear a bit rowdy or distracted. Tell them to stop, take a deep breath, calm down, and then get ready to enter the class in an orderly manner. Make sure they look you in the eye and are clear about your directions—then send them in.
3. Type C behavior—these students appear disrespectful, arrogant, and/or rowdy. These are the students who are most likely to present problems. Show the class they are not going to be a problem for you. Establish right away that poor behavior in your presence will not go unchallenged. Have these students stand to the side while the rest of the class enters. Every small thing you do here helps or hurts your cause. You save many problems later on when students see that you are on top of everything from the start. Get compliance from all Type C students before you let them enter. Direct them to a specific seat right next to your desk, if possible. If they are noncompliant, argumentative, or rude, give them the simple choice of complying or being suspended for defiance. Do this as calmly as possible. You can say, "I don't argue with students. You can follow my directions or be sent out of the room for defiance." This is what sets your authority.

Assign Seats and Begin Learning Students' Names

Once students are all in the room and are busy copying the rules, get their attention and say the following: "I'm going to call roll now and assign new seats. When I tell you where to sit, get up immediately and move to that desk without questioning or complaining. There is no discussion about it, and if you try to engage me in a discussion about your assigned seat, you will be sent from the room. Just move to your seat right away. Does everyone understand?"

You should have a class roster with names in alphabetical order. As you call the names, assign the seats and tell students to return to the same seat the next day. When all students are seated and are again copying class rules, do the following: Silently to yourself say the names of the students in the first row. Repeat a few times. Then do the same with students in the next row. Review frequently. Remind yourself of the ones you forgot by checking the seating chart. Their names will come back to you quickly.

Explain Leverage for Rules and Exclusion From Class Procedures

As noted, Seganti's "leverage" consists of a 15-minute detention. As soon as students have finished copying the class rules, tell them you will enforce the rules through the 15-minute detention. Explain how you will do so. You might enlist two or three students to help you demonstrate enforcement.

In Seganti's approach, only three things call for students to get excluded from the room—defiance, repeated disruption, and gross disrespect. The following scenarios depict those reasons, as Seganti would explain them.

Reason 1: Defiance

I tell Judy to change her seat. She says, "Why?" I reply that I do not argue with students. She does not immediately change her seat and I assign her a 15-minute detention and tell her to change her seat. She continues to argue or just doesn't move. I write up a referral, whether or not she moves at this point, and send her from the class for defiance. She goes to the counselor. I have written on the referral that Judy is suspended for defiance until she comes to detention and copies the class rules.

Five minutes later Judy returns from the counselor's office with a note saying "Student counseled—please readmit student to class." If I readmit Judy now, I will be making a big mistake. I say to her, "No, you are suspended from my class. Come to detention after school today for 15 minutes, copy the rules, and you may reenter tomorrow."

At my first opportunity, I explain to the counselor once again how my system works, and that the only help I need from him or her is in enforcing my requirement that Judy comes to detention and copies the rules. If Judy does not meet my requirement, I will send her back again for defiance of my detention rule. I don't care if the counselor provides her counseling or not, so long as Judy comes to detention and copies the rules. Judy can copy rules in the counselor's office or she can be moved to somebody else's class, but will not be readmitted to my class until she copies the rules and does the 15-minute detention. The matter is simply about the necessity that Judy comply with my class rules.

Reason 2: Repeated Disruption

Disruption is anything that interferes with student concentration in class. It might be a little buzz of talk that I have to try to talk over. It might be a student tapping a pencil on the desk, or rumpling papers, or loudly sighing to show disinterest in the class, or turning away from me while I am talking. Those are all disruptions. They are specified in the class rules and are not allowed.

Let's say there is a lot of buzz in class, an undercurrent of noise I can't pinpoint. I'm not sure where to start—no one is being really bad, it seems, nothing that would normally call for detention. So, not knowing what else to do, I say "Quiet!" to the whole class. They get quiet for a minute, like boiling water does when you cut the heat.

But then it starts to boil again and you say, "Quiet! Okay, quiet down!" This vacillation can go on for awhile—in some cases for an entire teaching career. What do I do? I start with individuals. I pick one student.

"Brian, you are disrupting the class. Be quiet or come to detention."

Brian replies, "Everyone else is talking."

I ignore his comment, write down his name, and say, "Come for 15 minutes after school today. If you continue disrupting I will have to suspend you from the class."

I don't wait for the big disruptions. I make students adjust to the boundary being squeaky tight. My standard is no disruption during my lesson—not even a little. Follow this advice and, tomorrow, count the times you say "quiet" to your class. If it is more than once per class or five times per day, it is too much and likely to escalate. So, I have the counselor ensure that Brian will come to detention for 15 minutes that day and copy the rules in the meantime. If he doesn't, I won't readmit him.

Reason 3: Gross Disrespect

If a student swears at you or insults you or engages in any other highly offensive behavior, immediately suspend the student, send him or her from your class, and demand a parent conference as well as the detention and copying the rules or other consequence you use. Any of these things should include your basic consequence of detention because some students would rather have their caregivers called than have to serve detention. If it looks like a student is going to be a real problem, start a paper trail on them right away. You need to minimize the damage these students do to your teaching and other students' education.

OUTSIDE SUPPORT: WHAT DOES SEGANTI WANT OF ADMINISTRATORS, COUNSELORS, AND CAREGIVERS?

Seganti says to make sure you inform your administrator clearly about your discipline plan, including its logic, rules, and procedures. Administrators don't want to be caught off guard if a parent complains, and they need to know how they can help you make your program work. He says that they will usually be pleased to know you are handling discipline problems on your own and only need their help as backup when students are suspended from your class.

As for caregivers, Seganti doesn't believe they will be of much help to you in discipline matters. He says he cannot recall a single instance in his career when a parent conference had a significant long-term effect on a student's behavior. Parent conferences are simply not a consequence that students care about. However, they are useful in establishing a paper trail on students who chronically misbehave and defy the teacher. Seganti asserts that most administrators have no objection to your sending a student from your room for defiance, so it is helpful to document your calls to caregivers when you give detention for serious and repetitive breaches of the rules, especially those rules over which caregivers have some control, such as having class materials in hand.

When you talk with caregivers, most will listen to the problem and say something like, "Okay, I'll talk to her/him." Occasionally caregivers will take the student's side and express concern that you are not doing your job properly. When that happens, don't go on the defensive. Explain your rules and ask the parents if they see anything unfair in them (they won't). Explain that their child has not shown up for detention or continually violates the rules, which interferes with your teaching and the educational rights of other students.

A CLOSING COMMENT FROM MR. SEGANTI

The following comment was provided to the first author by Mr. Seganti:

> *Our schools are currently doing things out of sequence—trying to let students know all their rights and encouraging self-expression and independent thought, etc., before working to establish basic respect for others and the environment. Schools seem oblivious of the misery they cause students and teachers by emphasizing things in this order. In a more effective sequence, respect must be established first, as a fundamental principle of all classroom interactions.*

Commentary From Anonymous Teacher 1

Most of the time, my third-grade class is not very disruptive, and I would not need the detention leverage that Mr. Seganti describes. However, although his suggestions are new to me, I find I do use many that are similar. In teaching students how they are expected to behave, I make use of role-playing, in which I have them act out how they are to enter and exit the room, clean up after work, keep track of their materials, and so forth. The students actually enjoy acting these things out. Right from the beginning I explain how students are expected to behave. If they fail to do as directed, I have them show me they know the proper way of behaving. This takes a bit of time, but I only have to do it a few times before students get the idea I won't accept their behaving inappropriately. In addition to having them act out the desirable behaviors, I give them oral explanations and sometimes written explanations, too, that include what they are to do when they have completed assigned work earlier than expected. I add reminders now and then just to make sure they remember.

Mr. Seganti explains how he forbids students to bring various "distraction" objects into the room with them. I also have rules about those things—such as erasers, bracelets, hair clips, and so on—which I call "doo-dads." I explain that if they bring such things to class, I will take them and keep them until the end of the school year. I have a collection of doo-dads to prove I mean business. I have informed parents of this rule and that I will return the objects at the end of the year. Everybody knows my expectations, why they are used, and how they will be enforced. The students accept my policies and only rarely does a parent ask about them.

Source: Used courtesy of Timothy C. Charles.

Commentary From Anonymous Teacher 2

I think these suggestions and strategies have merit and reinforce ideas about good classroom management. I especially like the focus on academics, the notion of holding students accountable, the emphasis on teacher consistency in rule enforcement, and most of all the idea of teaching with energy and enthusiasm the entire class period. I think the keys to making this approach work are, as Mr. Seganti suggests, planning, organization, and determination from the teacher along with buy-in from administrators and parents.

One of the aspects of Mr. Seganti's approach that I find particularly valuable is the notion of the teacher taking care of the detentions, parent contacts, and record-keeping. I do think it is important to be seen by your students as being willing and able to manage your own students and their behavior, rather than passing them off to the assistant principal for disciplinary action. I'd just add the caution that a teacher who wants to implement leverage as Mr. Seganti suggests should be sure to consider carefully the requirements for enforcement. For example, in my district, it is necessary to give a parent or guardian 24 hours notice if you want to keep a child after school. We have forms available to use for this parent notification. In my state, a teacher can "suspend" a student for up to 3 days from his or her classroom. (If you have a

In this situation, a student's background may impact his or her ability to comply. What if a student comes from a low-income home? If you were going to implement Mr. Seganti's system, what would you do to prevent access to supplies from becoming an issue that eroded your plan?

student "hold-out" who refuses to serve detention, you will need to make a plan for that student. Office? Another teacher's room? Have the student sit out in the hallway? All of these solutions end up with the student missing out on class and basically becoming someone else's problem.)

One of my colleagues, Mr. Albert, had very exacting standards for student classroom behavior. He also had stringent requirements for supplies that students were to bring to class daily. If students did not have the required supplies or did not complete a homework assignment, he would write out referrals and send the students to the AP's office for the period. In short order, some students figured out that an easy way to get out of class and spend time with friends in the AP office was to not comply with Mr. Albert's requirements. This practice put a burden on the school administration, office staff, and other personnel. Ultimately, Mr. Albert backed down and gave up. He wouldn't have had to do that if he had used the ideas as presented by Mr. Seganti.

Source: Used courtesy of Marilyn Charles.

Applying Seganti's Ideas: What Might They Look Like in Action?

CASE 1 Kristina Will Not Work

Kristina, a student in Mr. Jake's class, is quite docile. She socializes little with other students and never disrupts lessons. However, despite Mr. Jake's best efforts, Kristina will not do her work. She rarely completes an assignment. She is simply there, putting forth no effort at all. *How would Craig Seganti deal with Kristina?*

Mr. Seganti provided the following commentary on this particular case: Kristina is required by the rules to be on task at all times. Therefore, she will be assigned a 15-minute detention if she does not stay on task. At the detention, I will try to determine the root of the problem: It is almost always that the work is too challenging, so in this case I might help her with the work after school a bit and/or contact her caregivers to see if they can help her at home.

CASE 2 Sara Will Not Stop Talking

Sara is a pleasant girl who participates in class activities and does most, though not all, of her assigned work. She cannot seem to refrain from talking to classmates, however. Her teacher, Mr. Gonzales, speaks to her repeatedly during lessons, to the point that he often becomes exasperated and loses his temper. *What suggestions would Craig Seganti give Mr. Gonzales for dealing with Sara?*

CASE 3 Joshua Clowns and Intimidates

Joshua, larger and louder than his classmates, always wants to be the center of attention, which he accomplishes through a combination of clowning and intimidation. He makes wisecrack remarks, talks back (smilingly) to the teacher, utters a variety of sound-effect noises such as automobile crashes and gunshots, and makes limitless sarcastic comments and put-downs of his classmates. Other students will not stand up to him, apparently fearing his size and verbal aggression. His teacher, Miss Pearl, cannot control his disruptive behavior. *Would Joshua's behavior be likely to improve if Miss Pearl implemented Seganti's approach in her class? Explain.*

CASE 4 Tom Is Hostile and Defiant

Tom has appeared to be in his usual foul mood ever since arriving in class. On his way to sharpen his pencil, he bumps into Frank, who complains. Tom tells him loudly to shut up. Miss Baines, the teacher, says, "Tom, go back to your seat." Tom wheels around, swears loudly, and says heatedly, "I'll go when I'm *&$#^ good and ready!" *How would Craig Seganti have Miss Baines deal with Tom?*

You Are the Teacher

Class Clowns

Your new fifth-grade class consists of students from a small, stable community. Because the transiency rate is low, many of your students have been together since first grade, and during those years they have developed certain patterns of interacting and assuming various roles such as clowns and instigators. Unfortunately, their behavior often interferes with teaching and learning. During the first week of school you notice that four or five students enjoy making smart-aleck remarks about most things you want them to do. When such remarks are made, the other students laugh and sometimes join in. Even when you attempt to hold class discussions about serious issues, many of the students make light of the topics and refuse to enter genuinely into an exploration of the issues. Instead of the productive discussion you have hoped for, you find that class behavior often degenerates into flippancy and horseplay.

A Typical Occurrence

You have begun a history lesson that contains a reference to Julius Caesar. You ask if anyone has ever heard of Julius Caesar. Ben shouts out, "Yeah, they named a salad after him!" The class laughs and calls out encouraging remarks such as "Good one, Ben!" You wait for some semblance of order, then say, "Let us go on." From the back of the classroom, Jeremy cries, "Lettuce and cabbage!" The class bursts into laughter and chatter. You ask for their cooperation and no more students call out or make remarks, but you see several continue to smirk and whisper, with a good deal of barely suppressed giggling. You try to ignore it, but because of the disruptions you are not able to complete the lesson on time or to get the results you hoped for.

Conceptualizing a Strategy

If you followed Seganti's suggestions, what would you do with regard to the following?

- Preventing the problem from occurring in the first place
- Putting an immediate end to the misbehavior now
- Maintaining student dignity and good personal relations
- Using follow-up procedures that would prevent the recurrence of the misbehavior

REFLECTING ON SEGANTI: WHAT YOU HAVE LEARNED IN THIS CHAPTER

Predominant Themes in Seganti's Work

Students should be taught compliance as an automatic response to teacher directions.

Learning should be a meaningful, engaging, and cooperative activity.

Clarity of expectations supports good behavior.

Effective managers spend a significant amount of time actively teaching rules and procedures.

Effective managers focus on preventing, not just reacting to, misbehavior.

Craig Seganti's model of discipline is, in many ways, aligned with that of Ron Morrish; students are expected to comply with teacher expectations at all times, without questioning, explaining, or arguing. As you read in his bio, Seganti worked with urban youth who were very diverse and whose backgrounds and behaviors often led them to display inappropriate behavior in school; thus, he developed this very structured approach to managing classroom behavior. It's possible that you'll end up teaching (or are already teaching!) in a similar situation. It's also possible that your school setting and the students with whom you work would not mesh well with Seganti's methods; your own school setting and mission will, without doubt, have an effect on the classroom management system you employ. Even if your situation does not parallel Seganti's, you might still be able to identify some facets of his plan that would help you shape your classroom management system and support your students.

As is the case with Morrish, little scholarly evidence is available to support Seganti's recommended procedures, but as you can see by the commentaries from anonymous teachers in this chapter, his ideas do resonate strongly with some educators. Anecdotal evidence can be powerful, but it's important for you to consider contextual factors as you evaluate any model of management. As we did in the chapter on Morrish, we're including Table 6.1 to get you thinking of the potential positives of Seganti's model, and to provide you with some reflective questions to guide you as you evaluate whether there is a place for his strategies in your classroom management system. Remember to take notes in your planning guide as you reflect.

Table 6.1

Seganti's Ideas	Potential Positives	Questions to Consider
Teachers must establish themselves as authority figures with students, and students should accept this authority without question or comment.	Students see the teacher as a committed leader who insists that they behave in ways that facilitate academic learning.	• Do you believe teachers should demand respect from their students, or work to earn it? • Are teachers infallible? Should students have some right to ask questions or make explanations?
Teachers can effectively use punishment to decrease instances of misbehavior.	Students may adjust their behavior as a means of avoiding punishment.	• What effects might punishment have on interpersonal relationships in the classroom? • What happens if the punishment is not significant enough to motivate a behavior change?
Teachers should not engage in bargaining with students; any failure to comply results in the escalation of consequences.	Time may be saved because teachers and students do not spend time negotiating.	• What happens when a situation escalates through several consequences quickly? • What benefit is there to listening to students and considering their motivations for misbehavior?

Seganti's Ideas	Potential Positives	Questions to Consider
Students who are noncompliant should be excluded from the classroom.	Student disruption may be diminished if the catalysts for it are not in the classroom.	• What are the shortcomings of exclusion, suspension, and expulsion as disciplinary measures?
Punishing students who were not actually misbehaving can be a powerful tool in shaping class behavior.	Peer pressure can be a strong motivator for students.	• How does one justify the time lost for learning when a well-behaved student is punished for the actions of others? • What ethical concerns exist in using peer pressure as a tool in a system of discipline?
Class rules are extremely specific and cover many procedural issues.	Students receive a clear message about what they are expected to do and when and how they are expected to do it.	• When rules are extremely specific, and when they reflect procedures rather than statements of general behavior, what problems may arise for the teacher?

MyLab Education **Self-Check 6.1**

MyLab Education **Self-Check 6.2**

MyLab Education **Application Exercise 6.1** Simulation: What Would Seganti Do?

MyLab Education **Application Exercise 6.2** What Would Seganti Say?

Getting Off to a Good Start: Harry and Rosemary Wong on Preventing Management Problems*

What Do Harry and Rosemary Wong Say About How to Navigate the First Minutes and Days of a New Class?

LEARNING OUTCOMES:

7-1 Identify the classroom management recommendations made by Harry and Rosemary Wong and the broad classroom management themes to which they relate.

7-2 Consider the strengths and weaknesses of the Wongs' recommendations and evaluate their likely utility in various situational contexts.

In 2009, Harry Wong and Rosemary Wong, two of the most highly acclaimed educators in America, interviewed four administrators of schools where students were showing unusually high levels of achievement. The Wongs wanted to know what those leaders did to promote such strong learning and outstanding behavior. What they discovered was rather simple—it was just that everyone—students, teachers, and administrators—knew exactly *what they were supposed to do* at all times and *how to do it*. Consequently, they did those things as expected, more or less automatically.

As the Wongs put it, there was no hocus-pocus, bag of tricks, special program, or funding from multimillion-dollar endowments. There was simply a schoolwide mindset of success, where teachers continually sought to become more effective. Those teachers began by teaching students very thoroughly, schoolwide, the roles, procedures, processes, and routines they were expected to follow. Once students understood those requirements and procedures, teachers were left free to focus almost entirely on promoting learning.

That simple process, say the Wongs, opens the royal road to success in teaching. Their view is that the main trouble in classrooms is not discipline, as most people think, but rather teachers' failure to teach students very clearly the roles, responsibilities, and procedures that make classrooms run like clockwork. They point out that virtually everything teachers ask students to do involves a procedure. When students learn to follow procedures automatically, they behave better, learn more, and are far easier to teach.

*Used courtesy of Harry and Rosemary Wong.

The beginning of a new class or term is an especially important time. That is when the teacher sets the structure and expectations for the class. The first few days should be devoted to two matters: (1) clarifying the proper roles and responsibilities of students and teacher, and (2) teaching students exactly how to follow the various procedures expected of them. The results that follow will be good learning, good behavior, and a thoroughly successful school year.

THE WONGS' MODEL

The Common Goal of All Approaches to Classroom Management: *Responsible, Productive Classroom Behavior That Becomes Habitual and Lasts over Time*
Responsible means paying attention, making a strong effort, and doing what is proper without being told. Civil means respectful, polite, cordial, and well mannered.

↑

Harry and Rosemary Wong's Approach to Classroom Management

↓   ↑

The Wong's Overarching Strategy
Ensure that all students understand their duties and learn to follow all class procedures automatically.

↓   ↑

The Wongs' Principal Tactics
Clarify roles: what you expect students to do and what you will do.
Carefully script what you will do and say for the first 10 days of school.
Write out procedures for students to follow in all class activities.
Have students practice the procedures until they can follow them automatically.

↓   ↑

↓ ——————————→————————— ↑

WHO ARE HARRY AND ROSEMARY WONG?

Harry and Rosemary Wong are widely acclaimed authorities in teaching and classroom management. Harry Wong, an educational speaker and consultant, previously taught science at the middle school and high school levels. He received numerous awards for outstanding teaching and high student achievement, including the Horace Mann Outstanding Educator Award and the National Teachers Hall-of-Fame Lifetime Achievement Award. *Instructor* magazine named him one of the 20 most admired people in education.

Rosemary Wong taught grades 1 to 8 and served as media coordinator and student activity director. She was selected as one of California's first mentor teachers and has received numerous awards for her contributions to the profession.

The Wongs' book *The First Days of School* (2009b) has sold millions of copies, making it one of the best-selling education books of all time. It has been translated into five languages. They have also produced a video series entitled *The Effective Teacher*, which won the Gold Award in the International Film and Video Festival and the Telly Award as the best educational staff development video. For years, Harry and Rosemary wrote a monthly column for www.teachers.net/wong; the entries provide easy access to how their ideas have been implemented in classrooms, schools, and school districts. We highly recommend that you view the site, as it is a tremendous resource for classroom teachers.

A QUICK READ OF THE WONGS' PRINCIPAL SUGGESTIONS

The Wongs' ideas you see here are gleaned from the following sources: Starr (1999); Wong and Wong (2004b, 2007, 2009b); Glavac (2005); Wong, Wong, Rogers, and Brooks (2012); and numerous articles by Wong and Wong currently posted on www.teachers.net.

About Roles and Responsibilities

Help students understand *your* responsibilities and *their* responsibilities in the classroom. The following example, appropriate for secondary classes, appears on the cover of *The First Days of School* (Wong and Wong, 2004b):

My Responsibilities as Your Teacher

- to treat you with respect and care as an individual
- to provide you an orderly classroom environment
- to provide the necessary guidance for success

- to provide the appropriate motivation
- to teach you the required content

Your Responsibilities as My Students

- to treat me with respect and care as an individual
- to attend classes regularly
- to be cooperative and not disruptive
- to study and do your work well
- to learn and master the required content

About Classrooms and Procedures

- The single most important factor affecting student learning is not discipline; it is how a teacher manages a classroom.
- Your classroom need not be chaotic; it can be a smoothly functioning learning environment.
- A well-managed classroom is task-oriented and predictable.
- *Ineffective teachers* begin the first day of school attempting to teach a subject. They then spend the rest of the school year running after students.
- *Effective teachers* spend most of the first two weeks of school teaching students to follow classroom **procedures** that help them become responsible learners.
- What is done on the first day of school or a class—even in the first few minutes—can make or break a teacher.
- The very first day, the very first minute, the very first second of school, teachers should begin to establish a structure of procedures and routines for the class.

About School

- School is where students go to learn how to be productive citizens and reach their potential as human beings.
- School should be challenging, exciting, engrossing, and thought-provoking, but its program must have structure to ensure success.
- You cannot give students self-esteem, which has no validity in education, but you can ensure they find success in school.

About Teaching

- Teaching is a craft—a highly skilled craft that can be learned.
- By far the most important factor affecting school learning is the ability of the teacher. The more capable the teacher, the more successful the student.

- Good teachers enhance the lives and spirits of the students they teach.
- When students arrive, start class immediately. Do not take roll until later.
- Learning is often most effective when it takes place in a supportive community of learners.
- The more students work together responsibly, the more they learn.
- Shorter assignments produce higher student achievement.
- Intersperse questions throughout a lesson. Ask a question after you have spoken a few sentences rather than many. By doing so, you significantly increase student learning and retention.
- Students usually learn more from an activity–question approach than from a textbook–lecture approach.
- Teachers go through four stages of development—fantasy, survival, mastery, and impact. Good management moves you quickly from fantasy to mastery.
- Those who teach well never cease to learn.

About Testing and Evaluation

- Use criterion-referenced tests rather than norm-referenced tests to evaluate student performance. Grade students according to how close they are to mastering the desired content and skills, not on how their performance compares to another's performance.
- Within reason, the more frequent the assessments, the higher the achievement.

About Student Behavior

- Classroom rules indicate the behavior you expect from students. In order to provide a safe and effective learning environment, establish and enforce appropriate rules.
- Rules of behavior set limits, just as do rules in games. They create a work-oriented atmosphere in the classroom.
- Behavior associated with rules must be taught through discussion, demonstration, and practice.
- Consequences should be attached to rules—positive consequences for compliance and negative consequences (but not punishment) for noncompliance.

About the First Day of Class

- Have your classroom ready for instruction and make it inviting.
- Organize your class by preparing a written script that covers precisely what you will say and do.
- Plan for more than you can get around to, so there will be no dead time with a chance of losing the students' involvement in the class.
- Stand at the doorway and greet students as they enter.

- Give each student a seating assignment and a seating chart.
- Position yourself in the room near the students. Problems are proportional to the distance between you and your students.
- Post an assignment in a consistent location so students can begin when they enter the room.
- Display your diploma and credentials with pride.
- Dress in a professional manner that models success and suggests you expect achievement.

About the First Week of Teaching

- The two most important things you must teach the first week of school are procedures and rules.
- Explain your management plan to students and put it into effect immediately.
- State your procedures and have students rehearse until they follow them automatically.

More About Management Plans

Although the Wongs focus mainly on the *management* of procedures, they remind us that in addition to good management, teachers need an approach that specifies and *teaches* procedures. This approach helps students know how to be successful in the class. The Wongs have found that most teachers want to begin teaching lessons before procedures are addressed. Then, when misbehavior occurs, those teachers apply harsh measures that are counterproductive. Without an effective classroom management plan that begins the first day, you are setting yourself up for failure.

The Wongs do say that you need a management plan, but they are not particular about the plan you use, other than to say that you should (1) develop one that is suited to your requirements and your students' needs, and (2) make sure it includes rules of behavior, steps for teaching those rules, and actions that are applied when students comply with or break rules.

As for class rules, the Wongs (2004b) suggest you think carefully about what your students need to do in order to be successful and, when necessary, write those expectations as rules, post them in the class, and go over them with students on the first day. You will have firm confidence in your ability to manage the class if you and your students understand clearly what is expected.

The Wongs suggest you limit the number of rules to a maximum of five, stated in a positive fashion (although in some cases it is more effective to state them in a negative manner, such as "No fighting"). Here are five universal rules the Wongs (2004b, p. 146) provide as examples:

- Follow directions the first time they are given.
- Raise your hand and wait for permission to speak.
- Stay in your seat unless you have permission to do otherwise.

■ Keep hands, feet, and objects to yourself.
■ No cursing or teasing.

Introduce the rules on the first day of class and post them in a prominent place. The Wongs suggest introducing them approximately as follows, using your own language and explanations:

Rationale for rules. The rules are to help you learn in a classroom that is safe and effective. They help make sure nothing keeps you from being successful in this class.

Working together comfortably. We will be working together closely. We need to keep this classroom a place where you will never have fear of being ridiculed or threatened. I care about all of you, and I will not allow anyone to do anything that interferes with someone trying to learn.

My job. My job is to teach you and help you be successful, so I will not allow you to do anything that interferes with my teaching and our group success and enjoyment.

Our class rules. So I can teach and all of us can learn in the best possible conditions, I have prepared a set of rules that help make this classroom safe, orderly, and productive. I'll explain those rules to you now so you understand clearly what they mean, how you are to follow them, and how I will enforce them.

About Planning and Organizing

Begin by acknowledging and accepting the overriding importance of organization. It enables you to keep on schedule, know where things are, and make your time and space work for you. It eliminates chaos, lets you get things done, and allows you some time to enjoy life.

Procedures and What They Entail

Think of procedures as involving what you want students to do in the classroom and precisely how they will do those things. Student behavior and learning will be determined in large part by how well you establish good, workable classroom procedures, beginning the very first day.

Students accept and appreciate procedures that provide security while minimizing confusion. If you don't put those procedures in place, students will likely behave undesirably and develop poor work habits that are difficult to correct later.

To establish good procedures, do three things: First, decide what *routines* are necessary in the activities you intend to conduct; second, list the steps students must follow in order to participate in and benefit from the activities; and third, teach students through explanation, demonstration, and practice in how to follow the procedures.

You will find you end up with a very large number of procedures for students to learn. Don't worry; students can learn them. Just keep in mind that every time you want students to do something, they need to know the procedure to follow—for example, how to enter and exit the classroom; how to begin the period or day; how to come to attention; how to begin and finish work; what to do on returning after being absent; how to ask for help from the teacher or others; how to move about the classroom; how papers, materials, and supplies are to be distributed and collected; how everyone is to listen to and respond to questions; how directions are given for each assignment, and how to find the directions. And the list goes on.

The Wongs give specific attention to these matters and many more. Good procedures allow a variety of activities to occur without confusion, often several at the same time. But you have to teach students the procedures, not just talk about them. The Wongs suggest a three-step method for teaching procedures:

1. *Teach.* You state, explain, and demonstrate the procedure.
2. *Rehearse.* The students practice the procedure under your supervision.
3. *Reinforce.* You reteach the procedure, have students rehearse it, and keep repeating it until students follow it automatically.

Here is an example of how a teacher might introduce a procedure for how third-grade students turn in work:

First, explain and provide a rationale for the procedure: "Math class is coming to an end, and I want to show you something. We're going to use a routine for turning in math work. This routine will help us all; you'll know just what to do with an assignment when math class is over, and I will know with just a quick glance whether you got finished or whether you need more time."

Second, explain the procedure: "Each of you has an orange folder in your desk. Please take those out now so we can look at them. You'll see that I've labeled your folders for you. The outside of the folder says, 'Math Work.' Inside, I've labeled the left pocket 'My Finished Math Work,' and I've labeled the right pocket 'Math Assignments I'm Still Working On.'

"When I say that math class is over, you're going to get your orange folder out of your desk. If you are *finished* with your math work, and it's ready to be checked, you're going to put it in the left pocket of your folder. (Demonstrates.) If you haven't finished the assignment, you'll put it on the right side of your folder—the one that says 'Math Assignments I'm Still Working On.' Then one of our classroom helpers will come around and collect all the math folders and put them in this basket near my desk . . . see how it's labeled 'Math Folders'? In this way, I'll be sure to get an assignment from every student, and you will know exactly where your math work is so that you don't lose it.

"Each afternoon while you're at PE or art or music, I'll look through your math folders. I'll check your work and put your math folders back in your desks. If you weren't finished, you can finish your assignment the next morning for morning work, and then put it in the 'finished' pocket in the folder. And at the end of the week, we'll put your graded math work into your Take Home folder so your families can review it."

Third, rehearse with the students. "Since it's the end of math class, let's do this procedure using the math puzzle you were just doing.

"Math class is over. Get out your orange folders. Please put your work on the left side of your folder if you're finished, and on the right side of your folder if you still have some work to do. Do that now." (Teacher circulates to observe and answer questions.)

"Raise your hand if you have put your math puzzle into your orange folder. (Looks around, checking with any student whose hand isn't raised.) Now, turn your folders around and show them to me." (Teacher checks, saying, "Looks like Brittany and Quentin have finished their work; is that right? And it looks like Eduardo and Felix still have some work to do. Is that right? Remember, if your work is finished, you put it in the finished pocket, and if you still have work to do, you put it in the other pocket.")

Then ask, "Who remembers what happens next? That's right . . . our helper for today is Malinda, and she is going to go around and pick up the folders. Malinda, when you have all the folders, please put them in the Math Folder basket.

"When will you get your folders back? That's right, they'll be in your desks this afternoon when you come back from P.E. What do you do if you didn't finish your work yet? That's right, you'll do it for morning work, and then when you're done, you'll move it to the left pocket in your folder. I'll check it tomorrow while you're at music."

You can set up your procedures in any way that makes sense to you. Some teachers would have a different idea about how they wanted to collect math work; they should develop, teach, and rehearse the procedure that works best for them and their students.

Examples of Procedures in a Fourth-Grade Classroom

The Wongs provide the following guidelines and procedures for structuring successful classes, which the Wongs credit to teacher Nathan Gibbs. The following recommendations show how one teacher has structured his fourth-grade class for success, using procedures to create a safe and caring learning environment. You may teach kindergarten or high school physical education and feel these procedures do not apply to you. But the Wongs remind us that this scheme reflects realities that exist in all classrooms. As you read these procedures, consider how they can assist you in creating procedures for your own classroom.

Make your classroom a place where students feel genuinely cared for. Provide personalized instruction within a warm, relaxed, refined learning environment. On the first day of school give your students a written list of all the classroom procedures, with a cover page that says, "Follow these procedures to reward yourself with complete success."

Spend the first two weeks of class teaching the procedures, and expect students to follow them to the letter. The number of procedures may seem overwhelming, but the students soon learn and appreciate them. Here are some of the things you might emphasize (Wong & Wong, 2004a): "You will be safe in this class. I will do my best for you, and I want you to do your best for yourself. Be ready to begin learning very well."

Morning Entry Procedures

✓ Enter the classroom in a quiet and orderly manner.

✓ Greet your teacher as you enter and say "hi" to your classmates.

✓ Turn in homework or keep it at your desk if it is to be graded in class.

✓ Begin your seat work.

Desk Procedures

✓ Only your notebook, assignment book, textbooks, reading book, and supply box belong in your desk. Toys, food, and loose paper do not belong in your desk.

✓ Keep hands, feet, paper, books, and pencils off your neighbors' desks.

✓ Push in your chair every time you get up.

✓ Clean your desk and the area around it before you leave.

Line-Up Procedures

✓ When dismissed, stand in two equal lines and wait quietly.

✓ First excused line goes out of room, and then the second line follows.

✓ Walk quietly in the hallway.

Lunch Procedures

✓ When excused for lunch, get your lunch if you brought it.

✓ Lunch Leaders stand in front with lunch buckets.

✓ Follow the line-up procedures.

✓ When dismissed by teacher, walk to the cafeteria.

✓ If you have brought your lunch, go and sit at the correct table.

✓ If you are buying lunch, get your card from the slot and wait quietly in line.

✓ Talk with a low voice.

✓ Clean up your area and raise your hand when you want to be dismissed.

✓ Put all leftover food and trash in the trashcans.

✓ Place your lunchbox in the bucket when you leave.

Bus Pick-Up Procedures

✓ Walk quickly to bus area.
✓ Quietly wait behind the line for the bus.
✓ Show respect for the teacher on duty.
✓ Show respect for the bus driver.

Car Pick-Up Procedures

✓ Walk to car pick-up area.
✓ Don't walk onto the blacktop where cars park or drive.
✓ Show respect for the teacher on duty.
✓ Quietly wait for your ride.
✓ If your ride is more than 10 minutes late, go sit quietly in the office and wait.

Bicycle Rider Procedures

✓ Walk your bike on campus before and after school.
✓ Lock your bike to the bike rack and leave other bikes alone.
✓ Wear your helmet while riding your bike.
✓ Obey all traffic laws.
✓ Come straight to school and go straight home.

Walker Procedures

✓ Walk straight to school.
✓ Walk straight home.
✓ Obey all traffic laws.

Basic Assembly Procedures

✓ Line up inside or outside our classroom first.
✓ Follow the student council representatives to the correct area.
✓ Pay attention and sit where you are instructed to.
✓ Show respect for the presentation.
✓ Be patient if you have a question for the presenter.
✓ Return to the classroom in a quiet, orderly manner.

End-of-Day Procedures

✓ Copy down the homework assignment in your notebook.
✓ Clean around your desk.

✓ Pack your assignment book and what you need for homework.

✓ Leave only when dismissed.

✓ Remember to tell your family about your day at school.

Restroom Procedures

✓ Only one person at a time may go.

✓ Quietly hold up three fingers and shake your fingers if it is an emergency.

✓ Wash your hands afterward.

✓ Come right back and enter quietly.

Drinking Fountain Procedures

✓ Do not line up at the drinking fountain outside or inside the classroom after the recess bell has rung.

✓ No more than three people at the sink area at any time.

✓ Wipe the sink after you drink.

Computer Procedures

✓ Wash your hands before using the computer.

✓ No more than two people at a computer.

✓ Refer your questions to the technology assistant.

✓ Log out of all programs you have been using.

✓ Shut off the computer at the end of the day if you are the last to use it.

When You Have a Substitute Teacher

✓ Respect and follow the substitute's directions and rules, even if they are not exactly the same as ours.

✓ Remember the substitute is taking my place and is an equal of mine.

✓ Be as helpful as possible. The substitute has a copy of all our class procedures.

✓ Assist the substitute in finding supplies.

Group Work

✓ Be prepared with the necessary tools and resources to be successful.

✓ All members participate, share, learn from, and help one another. Collaboration is the key to being a successful learning club.

✓ Use the same procedures for speaking as you do during class.

✓ Practice active listening.

✓ Cooperate.

✓ Do your best.

To view these procedures and more in detail, access http://teachers.net/wong/ MAR04.

WHAT DO THE WONGS SUGGEST FOR BEGINNING A CLASS SUCCESSFULLY?

As we have seen, the Wongs place great emphasis on what teachers should do to begin the term effectively (for review, see Wong & Wong, 2005a). New teachers, the Wongs say with a note of irony, often have bags brimming with lesson plans, boxes of activities, the state performance appraisal instrument, five interpretations of educational foundations, nine theories of child development, conflicting advice from a plethora of educational specialists, and a collection of buzzwords and current educational fads. But they have little idea about exactly what to do in the first days and weeks of school.

To help new teachers overcome this problem, the Wongs (2007) present a First Day of School Action Plan, which they credit to teacher Sarah Jondahl. Ms. Jondahl developed a plan of step-by-step procedures having to do with preparing the classroom before students arrive, academic expectations, time frames, lesson plans and activities for first days of school, steps in establishing working relations with students and caregivers, class schedules, maintaining a good learning environment, and procedures for documenting and evaluating student progress. *Note:* If you're working with older students, Ms. Jondahl's plan may seem too elementary for you, but as you read it, think about how you could accomplish the same basic goals in ways that are appropriate for older students.

In preparing the classroom before the first day of school, Ms. Jondahl lists the following matters that require her attention:

✓ "Be Prepared" sheet

✓ Preparation checklist

✓ Getting organized

✓ "Cooperative Classroom" dry-erase board

✓ Student contract for classroom materials

✓ "Our Class Fits Like a Puzzle" bulletin board

✓ Classroom door decoration

✓ "Brag About Me" bulletin board

✓ "All About Me" bulletin board

✓ Room arrangement

In the section on establishing relationships with students and caregivers, she included the following:

✓ Letter to students

✓ Open house activities

✓ Substitute teacher handbook

✓ New student folder

✓ Parent letter

✓ Homework policy

✓ Homework tip list

✓ Transportation checklist

✓ Rules, consequences, and rewards

✓ Volunteer sheet

✓ "Welcoming phone call" planning sheet for caregivers of potential problem students

✓ "Positive phone call" form

✓ Parent conferences outline

For the section on maintaining a good learning climate, she detailed what she would do concerning the following:

✓ Reasons for the behavior management plan

✓ Rules, consequences, and rewards

✓ Procedures in behavior management

✓ First morning greeting and seating arrangement

✓ Housekeeping ideas

✓ "Duty wheel" for student jobs

✓ Intervention plan packet

✓ Socio-gram

✓ Form used to create a socio-gram

✓ Notes of encouragement

✓ Student postcard

✓ "Special News about a Very Special Student" certificate

✓ "Super Job/Way to Go/Great Day" letter form

In summary: The Wongs stress that teachers should set high expectations on the first day, plan the entire day right down to the minute, and make sure to give attention to establishing routines and learning students' names. They also emphasize that during the first week, the most important thing you can do is to provide the security of consistency.

They add that if the furniture is movable, you do best to align all the desks facing the teacher during the first day of school. Keep them that way until there is a purpose for changing the arrangement. Make sure to provide a well-organized, uncluttered, attractive classroom. Have the room ready and inviting when students arrive on the first day.

On a bulletin board or elsewhere, post schedules, rules, procedures, and a preview of what is to come. Also post information about yourself, including a picture and a sign that welcomes students to the class. Wear neat clothing—first perceptions affect how students relate to you. Stand when you speak and use short, clear sentences or phrases. Use a firm but soft voice. When emphasizing something, do not point your finger, as that behavior may seem adversarial to students.

If you have very young students, place their name on their coat hooks, desks, and cubbyholes and tell them to use that particular coat hook, desk, or cubbyhole every day. Set up a seating plan beforehand, as this helps you to get to know your students quickly. Begin addressing your students by name as quickly as you can.

On the first day, go to school early and take time to double-check everything. Have your first bell-work assignment ready (a short assignment that students begin working on when they first arrive in the room). Make it interesting but fairly easy so students will have an initial sense of accomplishment. Students who fail early tend to create problems in the classroom. Before class begins, tell yourself the following:

- I will establish classroom management procedures from the beginning.
- I will convey that this class will be work-oriented, with a competent and caring teacher.
- I will establish work habits in my students first before teaching content.

As the students arrive, position yourself in the doorway to greet them. This action establishes rapport and shows you consider the students important. If students are to line up before entering, insist on an orderly line. If you pick up your class from another area, don't say: "Follow me" or "Come on." Rather, greet the students, introduce yourself, and then teach the procedure you want students to follow as they walk to your room.

WHAT DO THE WONGS SAY ABOUT THE FIRST FIVE MINUTES OF CLASS?

The Wongs say you should always have an assignment posted for the students to begin working on the second they walk into the room (Wong & Wong, 2000a). They say if you establish that procedure, you eliminate 90% of the management problems that otherwise arise. Engaging students in learning keeps them involved and less prone to off-task behavior. If free time happens for students, then a list of choices should be available; students should be responsible for selecting something to do in the classroom while waiting for others. It is far better to have too much planned for the class period than too little.

The first few minutes with your students are crucial to maintaining a productive tone in your class. Students must know what they are expected to do. When they come in, explain what you want to have happen at the start of the day or period. For instance, let them know what materials they need that day and that they should have pencils sharpened and paper ready. Explain where the warm-up activity will be located each day and make clear that they are to start on it even before the official start of class.

As students work, take roll while you walk around and observe. Check homework, if needed, and assure yourself that your students are ready for learning.

WHAT ELSE DO THE WONGS SAY ABOUT THE FIRST DAY OF SCHOOL?

As you have seen, the Wongs suggest you carefully plan your first day of class or school in detail. They describe how art teacher Melissa Pantoja attends to this task (see Wong & Wong, 2000b). They liken Mrs. Pantoja to a football coach who scripts the first several plays of a game. They say a teacher should not "wing it" in a classroom any more than a coach would wing it on a football field or a pilot would wing it on a flight from Baltimore to Kansas City. The effective teacher goes in with a plan and modifies that plan as needed. Each teacher's plan will be different. Here is Mrs. Pantoja's plan for the first day:

Greeting Each Student at the Door

✓ Hand each student a classroom rules sheet (goes in notebook).
✓ Direct the student to his or her assigned seat (alphabetical).
✓ Tell the student to read and follow the instructions that are written on the board.

Welcoming Students to Class and Introducing Myself

✓ My name
✓ My family (spouse, kids)
✓ Where I'm from and where I live
✓ Why I wanted to teach

Establishing Rules and Procedures

✓ Explain and teach the rules, which are posted at the front of the room.
✓ Introduce the daily procedures for arrival and dismissal of class.

Assigning Numbers to Students

✓ Explain that each person will have a number that represents him or her.
✓ The numbers will be on all of their art papers and on their art folders to help all of us keep the papers straight.

Respecting the Classroom and the Art Supplies

✓ Teach students how to be responsible for the art supplies and room.
✓ Teach the procedures for obtaining, using, and replacing art supplies.

Clarifying Teacher's Things and Students' Things

✓ Explain with examples that some things are only for me, while other things are for students to use as needed.

Using the Art Centers

✓ Everyone will get the opportunity to go to all the centers.
✓ The art center board will have names (numbers) that tell us who does what that day.

Keeping Portfolios and Notebooks

✓ Each student will receive a portfolio he or she can take home.
✓ Each student will keep a notebook for recording grades and vocabulary words and for writing a weekly entry about what he or she liked most in the week's work.

WHAT DO THE WONGS SAY ABOUT THE FIRST 10 DAYS OF SCHOOL?

The Wongs (2005a) further provide detailed suggestions for procedures to be followed in the first 10 days of school. In that regard, they present a guide they credit to Jane Slovenske, a National Board-Certified Teacher. Ms. Slovenske's class uses a *self-manager plan* in which students are taught to manage their own behavior in a responsible manner.

Standards are established through class discussions about responsible behavior, treatment of others, and working promptly to the best of one's ability. Once a list of behaviors is agreed on, the students are presented a *self-manager application* to use as a self-evaluation of their behaviors and standards. When students are able to manage all of the items on the application, they fill in the form and take it home for parental review. When the adults are in agreement with the student's self-evaluation, they sign the form and have the student return it to school.

Ms. Slovenske must then see if she agrees with the student's self-evaluation. She discusses with students any differences of opinion. She reports that most students, with input from the adults at home, are honest about self-evaluating their performance. Here, space limitations preclude the inclusion of Ms. Slovenske's plan in detail. If you wish to examine it you can find it on the Internet at http://teachers.net/wong/JAN05.

WHAT DO THE WONGS SAY ABOUT PROCEDURES FOR COOPERATIVE WORK GROUPS?

The Wongs maintain that, generally speaking, most students do better in school when allowed to work in cooperative learning groups. The Wongs suggest you call your cooperative groups *support groups*, with each member of the group known as a *support buddy*. Instead of isolating children with seat work, consider surrounding them with support buddies and teaching them how to support each other. Group procedures must be taught clearly, and it is important that each student in the group has a specific job to do. *Ineffective* teachers divide students into groups and simply expect the students to work together. *Effective* teachers directly teach the group procedures and social skills needed for functioning in a group. Before you begin your first group activity, teach students how to do the following:

- Be responsible for your own work and behavior.
- Ask a support buddy for help if you have a question.
- Help any support buddy who asks for help.
- Ask for help from the teacher only when support buddies cannot supply it.

As you can see, the Wongs identify a multitude of procedures that come into play every day in the classroom. For further detailed information on how to work with groups, consult Chapter 20 in *The First Days of School* (Wong & Wong, 2009).

DO THE WONGS' IDEAS WORK FOR SECONDARY TEACHERS?

Secondary teachers sometimes comment that the Wongs' suggestions appear to be too elementary for use in high school, but the Wongs emphasize that their approach works equally well at the high school level. Their website includes testimonials from secondary teachers, many of whom assert that the Wongs' suggestions actually saved their professional careers.

For example, Chelonnda Seroyer (see http://teachers.net/wong/FEB05), a first-year teacher, used the Wongs' ideas as the basis for managing her class and had a very successful year academically. In addition, she was senior class sponsor, homecoming parade assistant, and a member of the support team for the school's efforts related to her school's accountability program. In recognition of her contributions she received her school's "First Year Patriot Award," which is given to the first-year teacher who is recognized for outstanding accomplishments and achievements in academics, athletics, or cocurricular pursuits.

Jeff Smith (see http://teachers.net/wong/MAY04), a teacher of welding at a Career Tech Center in Pryor, Oklahoma, reports he was almost fired during his first year because of his poor classroom management. But he happened to hear one of the Wongs' tapes and later wrote the Wongs to say, "You saved my job, and someday I want to help other beginning teachers just like you helped me." Jeff went on to set the state record for the most Career Tech students certified under the industry standard welding certification. He reports that his former students have the highest pay average for high school graduates in the state. He goes on to say that he always knew his subject matter, but had no clue about classroom management until he encountered the Wongs' ideas.

Ed Lucero (see http://teachers.net/wong/MAR05), a high school teacher of business, marketing, and finance in Albuquerque, New Mexico, wrote, "Last year was my eleventh year of teaching. I was miserable! Students weren't paying attention. I constantly repeated myself. Students would ignore my instructions and at times talk back. Some students would attempt to call me 'bro' instead of Mr. Lucero."

Ed decided if things did not improve, he would leave teaching and return to public accounting. His wife suggested he read the Wongs' *The First Days of School: How to Be an Effective Teacher*. He spent the summer studying their suggestions and when the next school year began, he was able to implement them. He reported that very quickly he began enjoying the pleasures of teaching.

Commentary From Anonymous Teacher 1

Now with many years of teaching under my belt, I have my opening-of-class instructions well memorized, so I don't need to script the first day of school. But I could certainly have used that information (but didn't have it) when I first began teaching. Back then, I sort of began the year with trial and error, plenty of both. I really didn't know quite what to convey to my students or how to do so.

Even now, although I have most things under control, I learn a lot from the Wongs. It is no wonder they have such a large following. I especially like what they suggest we tell students about rules—that rules ensure a calm, respectful classroom where everybody will be safe and successful. I also like their ideas about teaching procedures to the point that students have a complete understanding of what they are to do. That suggestion alone really cuts down on confusion and disorder.

Source: Used courtesy of Timothy C. Charles.

Commentary From Anonymous Teacher 2

Rosemary and Harry Wong are great champions of teachers and of the teaching profession. The suggestions they provide for managing a classroom are uplifting and empowering. The collective wisdom of their experiences and of the many teachers who have used their ideas is readily accessible and inspires pride and self-confidence. Their ideas are not just pretty words; they are practical, classroom-tested solutions to some of the most annoying situations in a classroom. Here are situations I often encounter that are easily controlled with the Wongs' suggestions:

> *Problem:* Students come in very chatty and rambunctious from previous period, recess, lunch.
> *Solution:* Bell work. I, and almost every teacher I know, use this tried-and-true method to achieve a calm and orderly start to the class.
> *Problem:* Students bombard you with the same questions (totally unrelated to subject matter), over and over, the sheer volume of which is exhausting and exasperating.
> *Solution:* Create and teach procedures for all of these common situations:
>> "May I use the restroom? I really need to pee. Ms. Forsythe wouldn't let me go!"
>> "Can I go call my mom? I forgot my PE clothes/homework/project at home!"
>> "I need to go take my project/model/essay/book to _____. Can I please, please go, really fast?"
>> "Where do I turn in my late work?"
>> "I'm done. What do I do with this and what do I do now?"
>> "I've been absent for 3 days. Did I miss anything important?"

The Wongs' advice does help us make things easier for ourselves and our students. I use PowerPoint presentations to teach my students the processes of creating group posters, murals, role-plays, and skits. Sometimes we make a Jeopardy-style game for reviewing and reinforcing what has been learned. I like the visuals to reinforce the words and also keep everything more interesting for the kids. Also, PowerPoint presentations keep me on track so I don't forget something I intended to say. PowerPoint slides are easy to move around or replace as needed without redoing an entire presentation. As follow-up, I have students make charts and other displays and sometimes let groups act out what we should be doing when we go out to fire drills or other activities.

Source: Used courtesy of Marilyn Charles.

Applying the Wongs' Ideas: What Might They Look Like in Action?

CASE 1 Kristina Will Not Work

Kristina, a student in Mr. Jake's class, is quite docile. She socializes little with other students and never disrupts lessons. However, despite Mr. Jake's best efforts, Kristina will not do her work. She rarely completes an assignment. She is simply there, putting forth no effort at all. *What would Harry and Rosemary Wong suggest to help Kristina and Mr. Jake?*

The Wongs would advise Mr. Jake to carefully teach Kristina the procedures associated with completing assignments and other work activities. He should ask her to show him that she understands the procedures. He might consider having Kristina work with a support buddy with whom she feels comfortable. He would supply positive consequences for all improvements Kristina shows. If Kristina does not improve, Mr. Jake should talk further with her privately, and in a positive, supportive tone reiterate that he cares about her, wants her to succeed, will let nothing interfere with her progress if he can help it, and will help correct anything that might be standing in the way of her completing her work.

If Kristina still doesn't improve, Mr. Jake should seek help from school personnel who are trained to assess Kristina and help provide conditions that improve her likelihood of success.

CASE 2 Sara Will Not Stop Talking

Sara is a pleasant girl who participates in class activities and does most, though not all, of her assigned work. She cannot seem to refrain from talking to classmates, however. Her teacher, Mr. Gonzales, has to speak to her repeatedly during lessons, to the point that he often becomes exasperated and loses his temper. *What suggestions might Harry and Rosemary Wong give Mr. Gonzales for dealing with Sara?*

CASE 3 Joshua Clowns and Intimidates

Joshua, larger and louder than his classmates, always wants to be the center of attention, which he accomplishes through a combination of clowning and intimidation. He makes wise remarks, talks back (smilingly) to the teacher, utters a variety of sound-effect noises such as automobile crashes and gunshots, and makes limitless sarcastic comments and put-downs of his classmates. Other students will not stand up to him, apparently fearing his size and verbal aggression. His teacher, Miss Pearl, has come to her wit's end. *Do Harry and Rosemary Wong provide suggestions that might improve Joshua's behavior? Explain.*

CASE 4 Tom Is Hostile and Defiant

Tom has appeared to be in his usual foul mood ever since arriving in class. On his way to sharpen his pencil, he bumps into Frank, who complains. Tom tells him loudly to shut up. Miss Baines, the teacher, says, "Tom, go back to your seat." Tom wheels around, swears loudly, and says heatedly, "I'll go when I'm *&$#^ good and ready!" *What suggestions might Harry and Rosemary Wong offer to help improve Tom's behavior?*

You Are the Teacher

MIDDLE SCHOOL MEDIA CENTER

You are the specialist in charge of the middle school media center. You see your job as serving as a resource person to students who are seeking information, and you are always eager to give help to those who request it. Each period of the day brings different students to your center. Usually, small groups come to do cooperative research. In addition, unexpected students frequently appear who have been excused from their regular classes for a variety of reasons, but often have no particular purpose for visiting the center.

A TYPICAL OCCURRENCE

You have succeeded in getting students settled and working when Tara appears at your side, needing a book to read as makeup work for missing class. You ask Tara what kinds of books interest her. She resignedly shrugs her shoulders. You take her to a shelf of newly published books. "I read this one last night," you tell her. "I think you might like it. It's a good story and fast reading." Tara only glances at it. "That looks stupid," she says. "Don't you have any good books?" She glances down the shelf. "These are all stupid!"

Another student, Jaime, is tugging at your elbow. He is trying to deliver a note to you from his history teacher. You ask Tara to look at the books for a moment while you keep Jaime at your side. At that moment you notice that a group of students, supposedly doing research, are watching Walter and Teo have a friendly pencil fight, hitting pencils together until one of them breaks. You address your comments to Walter, who appears to be the more eager participant. Walter answers hotly, "Teo started it! It wasn't me!" "Well," you say, "if you boys can't behave yourself, just go back to your class." Teo smiles and Walter feels he is being treated unjustly. He sits down and pouts.

Meanwhile, Tara has gone to the large globe and is twirling it. You start to speak to her but realize that Jaime is still waiting at your side with the note from his teacher. Somehow, before the period ends, Tara leaves with a book she doesn't want and Jaime takes a citation back to his teacher. The research groups have been too noisy. You know they have done little work and wonder if you should speak to their teacher about their manners and courtesy. After the period is over, you notice that profane remarks have been written on the table where Walter was sitting.

CONCEPTUALIZING A STRATEGY

If you followed the suggestions of the Wongs, what would you conclude or do with regard to the following?

- Pinpointing the problems in your class
- Preventing the problems from occurring in the first place
- Putting an immediate end to the misbehavior
- Maintaining student dignity and good personal relations
- Using the situation to help the students develop a sense of greater responsibility and self-control

REFLECTING ON THE WONGS' IDEAS: WHAT YOU HAVE LEARNED IN THIS CHAPTER

Predominant Themes in the Wongs' Work

Effective managers spend a significant amount of time, particularly at the start of the school year, actively teaching rules, procedures, limits, and expectations.

Clarity of expectations supports good behavior.

Effective managers focus on preventing, not just reacting to, misbehavior.

Classrooms work better when students experience success.

Classrooms work better when teachers attend to group dynamics and cooperative, supportive interpersonal relationships.

For years, Harry and Rosemary Wong have helped teachers navigate the first days of the school year, and in doing so have equipped thousands of teachers to better manage their classrooms. These management gurus recommend that teachers think carefully about everything that needs to be accomplished in the classroom and develop specific procedures for how those things will get done. They then advocate teaching the expectations directly to students, spending a significant portion of the first two weeks of school firmly establishing classroom procedures for everything from starting the day to ending it (and all actions in between!).

The Wongs' recommendations are in keeping with many research studies about what effective classroom managers know and do, both at the elementary and secondary levels. The Wongs' work builds upon the initial studies undertaken by Kounin, Evertson, Emmer, and others; these researchers found that effective managers give special attention to procedures and routines, ensuring that they teach, model, and provide feedback systematically. Better managers maximize available time for learning and hold students accountable for operating within the established classroom system. They are clear about their expectations and in making sure students know what to do and how to do it. And as the Wongs recommend, effective managers are organized and provide students with a meaningful framework in which to operate (Brophy, 2006).

Table 7.1 presents the basic tenets of the Wongs' work along with potential positives and questions for your consideration. Remember to take notes in your planning guide as you reflect.

Table 7.1

The Wongs' Ideas	Potential Positives	Questions to Consider
Effective teachers develop and teach classroom rules.	Students know what is expected of them and are thus more likely to comply.	• What are the behaviors that you want to see covered by your classroom rules? • What are the consequences that you'll apply when students don't comply with your rules?
Effective teachers develop and teach classroom procedures for virtually all aspects of the school day.	Students know what is expected of them and are thus more likely to comply. Further, procedures become routine for students, thus saving the teacher time over the course of the school year.	• What procedures can and should be taught from the first day of school? What procedures can be introduced later? • Under what circumstances might you need to revise or re-teach procedures?
At the start of the school year, better teachers spend significant amounts of time teaching rules and procedures and less significant amounts of time teaching curricular content.	Once rules and procedures are well established, teachers will be freer to focus on teaching content and skills.	• How does the amount of time invested in teaching rules and procedures likely vary with students' ages and developmental levels? • What do teachers do to keep students engaged when the first two weeks are more about teaching procedures than content?

The Wongs' Ideas	Potential Positives	Questions to Consider
Teachers should carefully plan (and overplan!) everything they'll say and do for the first days of school.	Teachers who have carefully planned (or even scripted) the first days of school are less likely to forget to cover important information. Classroom management problems tend to occur during "dead" time when students don't know what to do and/or how to do it; teachers who are "overplanned" will avoid some management problems.	• How do teachers deal with the potential fallout of overplanning: the feeling that they have started off the school year "behind" because they can't get to everything that was included in their plans? • How does one balance the need to plan small details with the limited time available to teachers?
Teachers who are extremely organized eliminate many management problems by reducing chaos.	Teachers who have systems in place for remaining organized are likely to reduce time lost to making last-minute decisions and to scrambling to find materials and resources.	• What if a teacher is not naturally adept at organization? How do more fluid, global thinkers move toward a more organized system of operation when it doesn't come naturally to them?
Teachers of older students can still benefit from teaching rules and procedures early on in the school year, and from clarifying expectations for students.	Regardless of their age or level of development, students typically benefit from knowing what is expected from them.	• In what ways can the Wongs' recommendations be adapted to respect older students' experience and maturity? • How much can teachers assume that older students already know about why classroom structure benefits all members of the classroom community?

MyLab Education **Self-Check 7.1**

MyLab Education **Self-Check 7.2**

MyLab Education **Application Exercise 7.1** Finding Commonalities With the Wongs' Work in Actual Classroom Settings

MyLab Education **Application Exercise 7.2** Considering Procedures to Reduce Issues During Class Transitions

Time Use in Classrooms: How Fred Jones Helps Students Stay Focused and On-Task*

How Does Fred Jones Keep Students Willingly Engaged in Learning?

LEARNING OUTCOMES:

8-1 Identify the classroom management recommendations made by Fred Jones and the broad classroom management themes to which they relate.

8-2 Consider the strengths and weaknesses of Jones's recommendations and evaluate their likely utility in various situational contexts

Some years ago, psychologist Fred Jones conducted large-scale studies of outstanding teachers who were identified as "naturals" by their administrators and colleagues. He hoped to discover what those teachers did that made teaching and classroom management seem so effortless. The answer, he found, was that those teachers kept students fully engaged in learning while teaching them to be self-disciplined. Jones decoded what these teachers did and translated the techniques into coachable skills. He then taught a set of struggling teachers in the same school to use these skills. The results showed that disruptions decreased by 87%. To validate that the intervention was what changed the behavior, he did a reversal study wherein the teachers stopped using their new skills. The students' behavior reverted, indicating that the new skills were the critical factor. In this chapter, we examine Jones's findings and conclusions and see how they are applied in the classroom.

WHO IS FRED JONES?

Dr. Jones, an independent consultant in teaching and classroom management, is the author of *Tools for Teaching* (2012, 2007a), in which he explains tactics for motivating students, instructing them effectively, and helping them develop self-discipline. He first became interested in the nature of better teaching while on the faculties of the UCLA Medical Center and the University of Rochester School of Medicine and Dentistry. He now devotes himself to making presentations and

*Used with permission of Fredric H. Jones and Associates, Inc.

developing materials for educators. In addition to *Tools for Teaching*, Jones is author of *Positive Classroom Discipline* (1987a) and *Positive Classroom Instruction* (1987b). Jones has also developed a video course of study called *The Video Toolbox* (2007b) and has published a number of articles on effective teaching in *Education World*. The manual for *The Video Toolbox* is authored by Patrick T. Jones. Descriptions of these materials, programs, and available presentations are posted on Dr. Jones's website at www.fredjones.com.

THE JONES MODEL

The Common Goal of All Approaches to Management
Responsible, Civil Classroom Behavior That Becomes Habitual and Lasts over Time
Responsible means paying attention, making a strong effort, and doing what is proper without being told. Civil means respectful, polite, cordial, and well-mannered.

↑

Fred Jones's Approach to Management

↓　　　　　　　　　　　↑

Jones's Overarching Strategy

Keep students actively and purposefully involved in lessons and enable them to follow directions on their own.

↓　　　　　　　　　　　↑

Jones's Principal Tactics

Use Say, See, Do Teaching

Work the Crowd (interact with students)

Use Body Language Effectively

Provide Help Efficiently

Use Visual Instructional Plans

Use Preferred Activity Time to Motivate

↓

↓————————→———————— ↑

WHAT FIVE MANAGEMENT PROBLEMS DID JONES BRING TO LIGHT?

Jones and his associates spent thousands of hours observing and recording in hundreds of elementary and secondary classrooms. Their analyses of those recordings pinpointed the misbehaviors that most often occurred in classrooms and located the points in lessons where they usually appeared. The information also revealed many tactics that highly effective teachers used to prevent and deal with misbehavior.

Jones concluded that five major conditions are usually evident in less effective classrooms. They are massive time wasting, student passivity, student aimlessness, "helpless handraising," and ineffective nagging by teachers. His research showed that by using the skill set he developed, you can reduce misbehavior, increase learning, make schooling enjoyable for you and your students, and promote positive attitudes for everyone concerned.

Massive Time Wasting

Jones found that the main problem in less productive classes was simply *massive time wasting*. Even though many of the classrooms he studied were in inner-city schools and alternative schools for students with behavior problems, Jones found relatively little student hostility and defiance—the behavior teachers fear and that many people believe predominates in schools. Instead, students wasted huge amounts of time by talking, goofing off, daydreaming, and moving about. He found they were doing one or more of those things in about 95% of the classroom disruptions that affected teaching and learning.

Jones also determined how frequently disruptions occurred. In well-managed classrooms, one disruption occurred about every two minutes. In louder, more unruly classes, the disruptions averaged about 2.5 *per minute*. He found that the typical class did not get down to business until 5 to 7 minutes after the bell rang, while in-class transitions from one activity to another normally took 5 minutes. The resultant inefficiency contributed to teachers losing almost 50% of the time that could have been devoted to teaching and learning (Jones, 1987a).

Jones described students in the less effective classes as "expert time wasters" who had no vested interest in "hustle" and took every opportunity to dawdle. Jones consequently set out to determine how this time wasting could be reduced. He concluded it could best be remedied by: (1) clearly communicating class requirements to students and following through with class rules, (2) establishing and practicing class routines, (3) increasing students' initial inclination to participate, (4) using tactics and activities that keep students involved in lessons, and (5) efficiently providing help to students who need it. Presently we will see Jones's suggestions for making those improvements.

Student Passivity

Jones found that students in typical classes were passive most of the time, rather than active. Passivity tends to reduce attention, and so students would disengage from lessons and daydream, look out the window, or talk with others. (Though it wasn't true at the time of Jones's initial research, cell phone use certainly contributes to passivity in classes today.)

Jones concluded that this passivity was fostered by the teaching methods being used, which only infrequently asked students to participate or show accountability, especially in the early phases of lessons. Students mainly sat and (supposedly) listened while teachers explained and demonstrated.

Jones hastens to add that the teachers who encountered problems were working hard at their jobs—he described their efforts as "bop 'til you drop" and likened their activities to actors performing five matinees a day. Yet, despite all their effort, when the lesson transitioned from teacher input to independent student seat work, waving hands would shoot into the air because students simply didn't know what to do. The hands, Jones noted, usually belonged to the same *"helpless handraisers"* every day. When hands went up, the teachers would begin chasing from student to student, repeating over and over the same information they had tried so hard to impart earlier in the lesson.

Aimlessness

Another problem Jones found was that students either had scant knowledge of the procedures they were to follow or else chose not to follow them. This lack of knowledge, or disregard, resulted in apathetic inaction. Jones believes students usually know, generally if not specifically, what is expected of them, yet many disregard those expectations.

The students Jones observed did not behave the same in all their classes. They adjusted their behavior to match the standards that each teacher was able to uphold. As Jones put it, if your second-period teacher let you talk and fool around while your third-period teacher did not, you talked in second period and cooled it in third period. The standards in any classroom, he says, are defined by whatever students can get away with. If teachers do not take the time to teach expectations and procedures carefully—and if they fail to ensure compliance with those expectations—they will invariably get whatever the students feel like giving them, which usually is not much. Jones's views correspond with those of Harry and Rosemary Wong (discussed in Chapter 7) that teaching and enforcing classroom procedures is probably the most neglected aspect of classroom management.

Helpless Handraising

Jones found that when teachers were working hard in the first parts of lessons, students seemed to pay attention and understand well enough. But when students were directed to continue work on their own, hands went up, talking began, students rummaged around or stared out the window, and some got out of their seats. As Jones (1987b) put it, "that was when the chickens came home to roost" (p. 14), meaning the natural results of incomplete student understanding became painfully evident.

Often, teachers did not know what to do at that time other than admonish, nag, or reteach the lesson to the handraisers. That scene, said Jones (1987b), reflected "another day in the life of a typical classroom" (p. 14). Teachers everywhere can relate to that scenario and the frustration it brings. Later we will examine Jones's solution to that problem.

Ineffective Nagging

Jones's observations revealed that many teachers spend a great deal of time nagging students—telling them over and over what they ought to be doing and admonishing them when they don't comply. Jones calls that the *nag-nag-nag syndrome*, which many teachers use even though experience has repeatedly shown them it doesn't work. Jones says instead of nagging, teachers should calmly show they mean business. As we will see later, Jones believes they can do this more effectively through body language than through verbal language.

HOW WOULD JONES HELP TEACHERS BECOME MORE EFFECTIVE?

Jones says that all the highly touted efforts to improve education—all those policies, mandates, and well-intentioned "solutions"—don't mean a thing until they are translated into workable practices in the classroom. Most teachers try their best not only to maintain reasonable behavior in the room, but also to implement the latest and best teaching practices. And what does that get them? Usually, little more than an increasingly heavy workload that over time becomes more and more difficult to manage.

But, says Jones, there is a much easier way to get things done, and done well. By using a better approach, teachers can raise their effectiveness without working themselves to exhaustion, as many do today. Here we review some of Jones's suggestions for promoting active involvement, purposeful behavior, and responsibility.

Conserve Time and Don't Allow Students to Waste It

The most effective teachers make maximum use of the time available for instruction. They do this by establishing a classroom structure of rules, routines, and responsibility training that uses time efficiently. The structure puts students on task when the bell rings and allows 30-second transitions from one activity to another. These two tactics alone can save 10 minutes of learning time that is wasted in a 50-minute class period.

Arrange Class Seating to Facilitate Active Teaching and Close Proximity to Students

Jones would have you maintain close proximity and eye contact with students and move among them, both during direct instruction and while students are engaged in seat work or cooperative learning. To allow you to move easily among students, classroom seating must provide generous walkways. Jones advocates an *interior loop* arrangement, where desks or tables are set with two wide aisles from front to back, with enough distance between side-to-side rows for you to walk comfortably among the students. Your path of circulation would be along the dark gray loop, as shown in Figure 8.1.

This seating arrangement not only allows you to maintain close proximity to all students, but is especially helpful when you *work the crowd*, as Jones says, meaning you monitor and interact with students who are doing independent or group work. It also allows you to bring body language more effectively into play, as will be described later in this chapter. These conditions keep students attentive and actively involved.

Teach Your Students the Meaning and Purpose of Your Management System

Jones wants you to make it plain to your students that the purpose of classroom management is to help them learn, be successful in school, and have an enjoyable

Figure 8.1 ■ Jones's Interior Loop Seating Arrangement

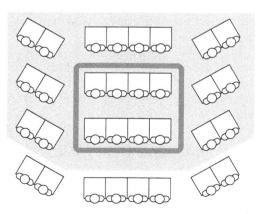

Source: Jones, F. (2007a). *Tools for teaching*. Santa Cruz, CA: Fredric H. Jones & Associates.

time doing so. Think of your management plan in that way—a means of helping students rather than clashing with them. Help students see it that way, too. Jones suggests a number of positive, *unobtrusive tactics* that provide good results. Here are three examples:

- Prevent the occurrence of misbehavior. Jones stresses that the best way to manage behavior problems is to prevent their occurrence, and that the best preventive strategy involves setting limits, specifying class rules, giving students class responsibilities, organizing an effective seating arrangement, and establishing a routine for beginning the class.
- Set limits on behavior. In *setting limits*, you clearly establish the boundaries that separate acceptable behavior from unacceptable behavior. Those boundaries are then verbalized as class rules, which you must enforce. Jones urges you to begin this process when you first meet your students. At that time, discuss with them the class rules and explain how rules ensure behavior that allows everyone to learn and feel safe.
- Use workable class rules. Jones describes two types of class rules—general and specific. *General rules*, fairly few in number, define your broad guidelines, standards, and expectations for work and behavior. Examples of general rules:
  - Do quality work every time; don't settle for anything else.
  - Treat every member of the class as you would like them to treat you.
  - General rules should be posted, referred to regularly, and reviewed periodically.

Specific rules refer to procedures and routines. They detail exactly what students are to do in various learning activities. Examples:
- When you enter the room, sit down and begin bell work immediately.
- When you wish to speak, raise your hand and wait to be called on.

There will be many specific rules. The behaviors they set out must be taught and rehearsed until they are learned, just like any academic skill. Jones advocates spending the first two weeks making sure students understand them thoroughly. (Do you see the relationship between Jones's general and specific rules and the Wongs' rules and procedures? The terminology may differ, but the ideas are quite similar.)

Introduce rules by involving your students in identifying examples of desirable and undesirable classroom behavior. This process helps students recognize the need for rules. You will have formalized your rules in advance, but you should go through them with students until students clearly understand their purpose and the behavior they require. Then you should have students practice complying with rules until doing so becomes second nature.

In your discussions about rules, be sure to explain what you will do to help students abide by the rules. Indicate how you will teach the required behavior when necessary. Explain how you will show your approval and appreciation when students follow rules properly, and also explain what you will do when students break rules.

Assign Your Students Specific Responsibilities in Caring for the Classroom

Jones believes in assigning a classroom chore to every student, if possible. This practice helps students develop a sense of personal responsibility and ownership in the class program. The number and type of classroom jobs you assign depends upon your grade level, teaching assignment, and personal preferences. Here are some examples of jobs that many teachers use: teacher assistants, classroom librarians, paper distributors, assignment collectors, zoologists/animal handlers, computer technicians, materials managers, room inspectors, and mail carriers. You can check the Internet to learn how other teachers have organized their systems for classroom jobs. You will find teachers are very generous in sharing their systems and ideas with fellow educators.

Begin Every Class with Bell Work

Class sessions in many schools begin in a fragmented way, with announcements, taking attendance, handling tardies, and the like. According to Jones, this fragmentation causes the loss of 5 to 8 minutes at the beginning of most classes.

You can avoid losing this time simply by beginning lessons promptly. Jones would have you teach students to sit down and begin doing *bell work* immediately upon entering the room. Bell work engages students and focuses their attention. No active instruction from you is required. Examples of bell work are answering review questions, doing warm-up problems, solving brain teasers, doing silent reading, and writing in journals.

Keep Your Students Actively Engaged in Learning

To help teachers maintain student involvement, Jones emphasizes a teaching approach he calls *Say, See, Do teaching*. In that approach, the teacher *says* the task, the students *see* the teacher perform the task, and then the students *do* it. This process is used frequently through the lesson.

You can see that Say, See, Do teaching is preferable to the traditional approach in which teachers tell about, explain, and demonstrate a quantity of information before students do anything active. Jones (2007a) graphically depicts the old-fashioned approach as follows:

Teacher input, input, input, input, input → Student output

This traditional approach contains some built-in faults, such as:

- The large amount of teacher input produces cognitive overload in students, which makes them want to disengage from the lesson.
- The students sit passively for too long and the urge to do something builds up.
- The teacher does not adequately work the crowd, that is, interact with individual students, particularly in the back of the classroom.

Say, See, Do teaching is different. Teachers present smaller bits of information and then quickly have students do something with it. This approach is *doing oriented*, with activities occurring often and at short intervals. Jones depicts it as follows:

Teacher input → Student output → Teacher input →
Student output → Teacher input → Student output

Use Visual Instructional Plans

Say, See, Do teaching becomes even more effective when augmented with *visual instructional plans (VIPs)*. VIPs are graphics or picture prompts that students use as guides in completing processes or activities. They come into play during the second part of the lesson, when students are asked to work on their own. VIPs are displayed in the room, and students are taught to consult them for guidance instead of raising their hands and waiting for the teacher when they get stuck. To illustrate, Jones (2007a) asks you to imagine you are teaching a class how to divide 495 by 6. Typically, you would explain and demonstrate the calculation one step at a time, and, when finished, your work on the chalkboard might look like that in Figure 8.2.

Now, Jones says, imagine the helpless handraiser during independent work, stuck on step four. What does the student do? Step four is not evident in the summary graphic in Figure 8.2. Our typical technique of laying one step over another produces only a single *summary graphic*. The helpless handraiser will now call for help and do nothing until the teacher arrives to provide yet another tutoring session.

Figure 8.2 ■ Summary Graphic.

$$
\begin{array}{r}
82\ r\ 3 \\
6\ \overline{|\ 495} \\
-48 \\
\hline
15 \\
-12 \\
\hline
3
\end{array}
$$

Source: Jones, F. (2007a). *Tools for teaching*. Santa Cruz, CA: Fredric H. Jones & Associates.

Figure 8.3 ▪ **Portion of a Step-by-Step Graphic.**

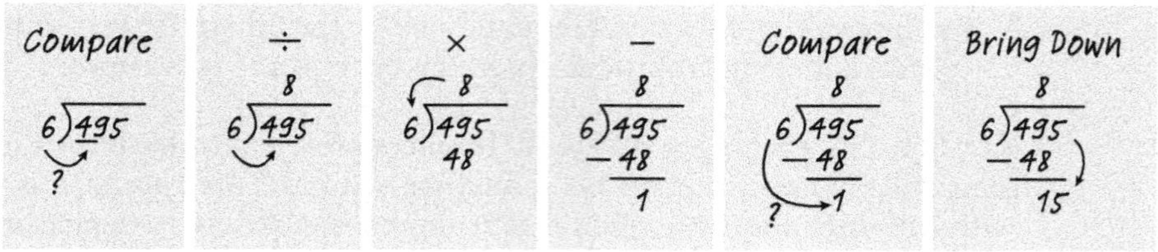

Source: Jones, F. (2007a). *Tools for teaching*. Santa Cruz, CA: Fredric H. Jones & Associates.

Jones's remedy is to display a graphic plan that shows one step at a time and a picture for every step. Such plans are easy to consult and follow, allowing students to continue working on their own. Figure 8.3 shows a guide to helping students who forget the steps in long division. This VIP, with the first six steps shown along the top, offers guidance that is simple, clear, and permanent. A student can refer to it at any time to answer the question, "What do I do next?"

Keep in mind that VIPs for different subject areas may look quite different; nevertheless, if you make clear the order in which a task is accomplished, you can significantly reduce your students' reliance on you to help them get back on track when they get stuck.

Use Body Language to Communicate Pleasantly and Clearly That You Mean Business

It is essential that your students understand that their job is to acquire important learning, while your job is to help them do so in pleasant circumstances. You need to convince them that you will not permit any behavior that interferes with those basic jobs. But, says Jones, you have to show them you mean business, and many teachers don't know how to do so convincingly. If students don't believe that you mean what you say, they will push back at you and you will find yourself nagging and cajoling for compliance—you'd do better to save your breath.

Here is Jones's main suggestion for showing you mean business: Say what you mean and use *body language* to reinforce your words. Body language works nonverbally through body carriage, eye contact, and tone of voice. When used properly, it is low key and nonadversarial, and it eliminates most student backtalk and argumentation. Better yet, it increases learning for those who need it most—the low achievers who typically spend vast amounts of class time goofing off. Jones claims that simply by using body language, you can increase achievement for the bottom half of your class by as much as 50% while eliminating the majority of classroom disruptions—and you hardly have to open your mouth.

Bring body language to students' attention right away. When discussing rules, demonstrate examples of body language you will use to help students stay on task. Include eye contact, facial expressions, gestures, and *physical proximity*. Jones says teachers are most effective in setting limits when they use their bodies correctly but say nothing and take no other action. He emphatically reminds us that we cannot manage with our mouths—that if we could, nagging would have fixed every kid long ago. He warns that when you open your mouth, you often do more harm than good. Jones does not leave to chance the interpretation of what constitutes effective body language. He coaches teachers in every detail. The prompts used for coaching are available in the study Group Activity explained later in this chapter. Following are further suggestions Jones makes about body language.

Body Carriage

Posture and *body carriage* are both very effective in communicating authority. Good posture and confident carriage suggest strong leadership, whereas drooping posture and lethargic movements suggest resignation or fearfulness. Students read body language and are able to tell whether you are feeling in charge or are tired, disinterested, or intimidated. Even when you are tired or troubled, remember to stand tall and move confidently.

Regarding Calm and Proper Breathing

Teachers do well to remain calm in all situations. Calm conveys strength and can contribute to the de-escalation of classroom events. In part, calm is attained and conveyed through proper breathing. The way teachers breathe when under pressure signals how they feel and what they are likely to do next. Teach yourself through practice to breathe slowly and deliberately before responding to annoying situations. Jones noted that some teachers take two deep breaths before turning to a misbehaving student. In doing so, they project an aura of self-control.

Eye Contact

Suppose you are explaining how one develops a thesis statement. You see that Jacob has stopped paying attention. You pause. The sudden quiet causes everyone to look at you. Jacob sees you are looking directly at him. He straightens up and waits attentively. Jones says few physical acts are more effective than eye contact for conveying the impression of being in control. He adds that turning and pointing the eyes and the feet toward misbehaving students shows your commitment to classroom management.

Physical Proximity

Suppose you have explained a process and have directed students to complete some exercises on their own. After a time, you notice that Jacob has stopped working and has begun talking to Jerry. You move toward Jacob. When he becomes aware of you, he immediately gets back to work. Jones maintains that teachers who use physical proximity rarely need to say anything to get offending students back on task.

Facial Expressions

Your facial expressions communicate a great deal. They can show enthusiasm, seriousness, enjoyment, and appreciation, all of which encourage good behavior; or they can reveal boredom, annoyance, and resignation, which may promote student lethargy and inattention. Facial expressions such as winks, smiles, and raised eyebrows demonstrate a sense of humor and personal connection, traits students appreciate in teachers. Teachers can also cultivate "the look"—a facial expression that clearly says, "I'm aware of what you're doing, and I suggest you refocus on the task at hand."

Increase Motivation and Responsibility Through Wise Use of Incentives

An *incentive* is a desired reinforcement that prompts an individual to act. For instance, you may tell students that those who do their work and behave appropriately will have time at the conclusion of the work period to engage in an activity they enjoy. This offer is not a bribe; the incentive is not awarded until the behavior occurs acceptably. Examples of incentives include the opportunity to work with a group to present a report or play an instructional game that reviews material pertinent to the subject. Jones features such incentives prominently as a means of motivating students and teaching them to be responsible. He found that some of the most effective teachers use incentives systematically, whereas less effective teachers use them improperly or not at all.

As for effective incentives, Jones says you should discuss with students the kinds you will make available and how you will manage them. He says the incentives should be provided in the form of *Preferred Activity Time (PAT)*, meaning instructional activities students especially enjoy. To obtain them, students must work steadily rather than fool around. The time they save in doing so is then returned to them in the form of the incentive—the activity they enjoy. Jones says those activities must all have instructional value. Avoid the temptation to use time for activities that don't move you and your students toward their learning goals.

In elaborating further on PAT, Jones provides comments and reminders related to (1) Grandma's rule, (2) student responsibility, (3) genuine incentives, (4) preferred activities, (5) educational value, (6) group concern and management, (7) omission training, and (8) backup systems. Let us see what is involved in each.

Grandma's Rule

Grandma's rule states: "First eat your vegetables, and then you can have your dessert." Applied to the classroom, this rule requires that students first do their assigned work, and then they can enjoy a preferred activity. It is a fact of life that children—and we adults, too—prefer to dive into the dessert, promising to eat our vegetables afterward. But, as we all know, even the best intentions fade away once the motivation behind them is gone. Incentives are of no value unless they are delivered after, and only after, students have done their work in an acceptable manner.

Student Responsibility

Jones contends that properly used incentives help foster *student responsibility*, by which students learn to take responsibility for their decisions and actions. For example, one way that students can show responsibility is through cooperating with others. However, because cooperation is voluntary, it is difficult to force it on anyone. When asked to cooperate, students who enjoy goofing off and daydreaming can ask themselves, "Why should I? What's in it for me?" Jones argues that when incentives are provided for cooperation, students see they have something to gain by it. At first, they may cooperate primarily to obtain the incentive bonus, but over time, cooperation becomes natural and enjoyable in itself.

Genuine Incentives

There is a wide difference between what many teachers might consider to be incentives (e.g., "Let's all work in such a way that we will later be proud of what we do") and what students consider *genuine incentives* (e.g., "If you complete your work on time, you can have 5 minutes of preferred activity time"). Certainly, students are more motivated by specific outcomes they like than by vague outcomes that mean little to them. Jones comments on the different effects promoted by a promise of "free time" versus a promise of "preferred activity time." He says students won't work for long to earn free time, but they will work hard to gain time for an activity they enjoy. Teachers simply have to be sure the incentive is genuine in students' eyes. The following, for example, are *not* incentives for most students:

- "The first person to complete a perfect paper will receive two bonus points."
- "If you really work hard, you can be the best class I have ever had."

The first may motivate a few of the most able students, but all the others know they have little chance to win so they see no point in trying. The second statement sounds good to the teacher but means very little to the students and is not sufficient to get them to make extra effort.

On the other hand, students respond well to the anticipation of activities such as art, games for learning or review, viewing an instructional video, or having time to pursue interesting topics with friends. Such group activities are effective because almost all students desire them sufficiently to make extra effort to obtain them *and* they are available to all students, not just a few.

Jones suggests that tangible objects, awards, and certificates should not be used as incentives. Although teachers often find extrinsic rewards to be motivating to students, their use may undermine their intended consequences; you may want to read some of the extensive research that has studied the use of external motivators and its impact on motivation (Reeve, 2006).

Earning Preferred Activity Time

PAT may be earned in a number of different ways. Mr. Jorgensen gives his fourth graders three minutes to put away their language arts materials and prepare for science. Any time left over from the three minutes goes later to PAT. In Mrs. Nguyen's English class, if everyone is seated and ready when the bell rings, the class earns two minutes of PAT. However, if some or all of the class continues to be noisy, the class loses PAT commensurate with the amount of time they have wasted. Some teachers opt to have their students use PAT on the day it is earned, whereas others allow PAT to accumulate for a future activity.

Educational Value

It has been emphasized that to the extent feasible, class time, including PAT, should be devoted to activities that have educational value. Work that keeps students occupied but teaches them nothing of value can seldom be justified, particularly in today's high-accountability classrooms. Although most educators are comfortable in allowing occasional frivolity in the class, holding regular parties or watching noninstructional movies as incentives is difficult to condone. What, then, should one use as PAT?

Jones maintains that when teachers introduce PAT to their students, they must make sure of three things: (1) the activity has educational value, (2) students want to participate in the activity, and (3) students understand they earn the activity by conducting themselves responsibly. There are many activities with educational value that students enjoy greatly, both individually and in groups. Among the best activities are learning games and enrichment activities, which are both fun and educational. Examples of such activities are playing games with new vocabulary words, completing art projects, or reading for pleasure.

In PAT, students are never left to do just anything, nor do they proceed without guidance. The freedom they enjoy lies in being able to choose from a variety of approved activities. Activities can be chosen by vote, with all students engaging in the same activity during the time allotted. Elementary school students often select physical education, art, music, drama, or construction activities; they also frequently enjoy having the teacher read to them. Secondary students often choose to hold class discussions on special topics, participate in performances by class members, or work together on a project such as a class magazine. Posted on the Jones website (Jones, n.d.), you can find suggestions from teachers for a large number of educationally sound activities that are effective as preferred activities; see www.fredjones.com/PAT/-index.html.

Group Concern and PAT Management

Jones also emphasizes the importance of making sure every student has a stake in earning the PAT incentive for the entire class. This *group concern* motivates all students to keep on task, behave well, and complete assigned work. PAT can be managed thus: The teacher agrees to set aside a period of time in which students might be allowed to engage in a preferred activity. The PAT can be at the end of the school day for self-contained classes—perhaps 15 to 20 minutes. For departmentalized classes, the time can be set aside at the end of the week—perhaps 30 minutes on Friday. The students can decide on the activity for their "dessert" time, and to earn it, they have only to work and behave in accordance with class standards.

The teacher keeps track of the time that students earn. Of course, it is possible that a single student, by misbehaving, can prevent the class from earning full PAT. Teachers often think it unfair to penalize the entire class when only a few have transgressed. In practice, this is rarely a problem, because the class quickly understands that this is a group effort, not an individual one. The group is rewarded together and punished together regardless of who misbehaves. A strength of this approach is that it engenders peer pressure in favor of proper behavior.

In ordinary circumstances, a misbehaving student obtains reinforcement from the group in the form of attention or laughter. With proper PAT, the opposite is true. The class is likely to discourage individual misbehavior because it takes away something the class members want. Nevertheless, some students do occasionally misbehave to the detriment of responsible students. When this occurs, the teacher may decide to work with the offending student individually.

Omission Training

Generally speaking, incentives and PAT bonuses are earned by the entire class. Teachers cannot possibly monitor incentives for all students individually. The exception lies in the occasional student whose misbehavior repeatedly ruins PAT for the rest of the class. The following case shows how *omission training* is useful in earning PAT for the entire class:

Kevin is a student in Ms. VanEtten's class. He disregards the requirements of PAT and is continually late, loud, and unprepared, thus ruining PAT for the others. Ms. VanEtten privately explains to Kevin that he doesn't have to participate in PAT because he doesn't care about it, but she does want him to be successful with his own work and behavior. She explains that she will use a timer, and when Kevin behaves in accordance with class rules, he will earn time for himself individually, and also extra time for the class. When he misbehaves, he will lose time for himself but not for the class. Kevin soon learns he can gain status in the class by earning PAT for other members of the class.

Backup Systems for Misbehavior

As a last option for students who subvert PAT, Jones suggests *backup systems*, which are hierarchical arrangements of sanctions for putting a stop to unacceptable student behavior. Jones identifies three levels of backup:

1. Small backup responses, conveyed privately or semiprivately to the student: "I expect you to stop talking so we can get on with our work." With such low-key messages, the student knows the teacher means business.
2. Medium backup responses, delivered publicly in the classroom: "Emily, sit in the thinking chair for three minutes and think about what you have done that caused me to send you there." Or, "Brian, because you are late again, you will have detention with me tomorrow after school." Other medium backup responses include warnings, reprimands, loss of privileges, and parent conferences.
3. Large backup responses are used to deal with repeated disruptions or other intolerable behavior. They require the involvement of at least two professionals, usually the teacher and an administrator. These responses include trips to the office and in-school or out-of-school suspension.

Provide Help Efficiently During Independent Work

As noted earlier, Jones puts particular emphasis on how teachers should provide help to students who get stuck during seat work. Suppose Mrs. James is teaching a lesson in determining percentages. She illustrates at the board by showing how to calculate 4% of three different amounts, asks a couple of questions to verify that students are understanding, and then assigns independent exercises for students to calculate a number of percentages ranging from 5% to 120%.

Almost immediately, Arnell raises his hand for help. If he were the only one to do so, there would be little problem. But Mrs. James sees other hands begin to wave, as well. She knows most of those students will sit and do nothing productive while waiting for her.

In his research, Jones asked teachers how much time they thought they spent, on average, when providing help to individuals who raised their hands. The teachers felt that they spent from one to two minutes with each student, but when Jones's researchers timed the episodes, they found that teachers actually spent around four minutes with each student. The total amount of time consumed made it impossible for the teacher to attend to more than a few students during the work period. Even if the teacher spent only one minute per contact, several minutes would pass while some students sat and waited.

Jones's research led him to conclude that independent seat work is especially susceptible to four problems: (1) wasted time, (2) insufficient time for teachers to answer all requests for help, (3) high potential for misbehavior, and (4) perpetuation of student dependency on the teacher. Jones determined that all four could be resolved if teachers learned to provide help efficiently, using the following tactics we have examined previously.

First, organize the classroom seating so that all students can be reached quickly. The interior loop seating arrangement previously described is suggested because it allows quick and easy access to all students in the room.

Second, use visual instructional plans, which, as noted, are graphic reminders displayed in the room that provide clear examples and step-by-step instructions for students to consult. The reminders are posted where students can see them and thus continue on their own without needing to call for the teacher.

Third, minimize the time used for giving help to students. To see how this can be accomplished, consider that teachers normally give help through an inefficient questioning tutorial, in which the teacher poses questions and makes comments similar to the following:

"What's the problem?"

"All right, what did we say was the first thing to do?" [Waits; repeats question.]

"No, that was the second. You are forgetting the first step. What was it? Think again." [Waits until student finally makes a guess.]

"No, let me help you with another example. Suppose . . ."

In this manner, the teacher often reteaches the concept or process to each student who requests help. Four minutes can be spent very easily in each interaction. In place of these tutorials, Jones trains teachers to give help in 20 seconds or less, with an optimal goal of 10 seconds. If the VIP does not help a student know what to do next, Jones would have teachers do the following when arriving beside the student:

1. (Optional for initial contact.) Quickly find anything that the student has done correctly and mention it favorably: "Your work is very neat." or "Good job up to here."
2. Give a straightforward prompt that will get the student going: "Follow step 2 on the graphic," or "Regroup here." Jones also recommends that, instead of tutoring students through the whole exercise, teachers should prompt students to ask themselves, "What do I do next?"
3. Leave immediately. Don't stay to see if students follow the prompt you have given.

Help provided in this way solves the time problem that plagues teachers during independent work. Students who need help receive it quickly, with little lost time. Rapid circulation also permits the teacher to monitor the work of students who do not raise their hands. When errors are noted in those students' work, the teacher should provide help just as for students who have raised their hands.

Have Stronger Backup Systems Ready for Use If and When Needed

As noted earlier, you will need to organize backup systems for use when students refuse to comply with rules or directives. Discuss and explain them to students. Ordinarily you can limit misbehavior by using benign tactics such as proximity, eye contact, or showing personal interest. But there will be times when those tactics come up short. In those cases, Jones suggests that you tell the offending student, "If you are not going to do your work, sit there quietly and don't bother others. I'll speak with you later." And for yet more serious defiance or aggression, you need to plan for stronger backup systems—such as isolating the student or calling for help, if needed. You should explain and demonstrate to students these stronger tactics, which you should clear in advance with your administrator.

Commentary From Anonymous Teacher 1

I said "ouch" when reading Dr. Jones's comments on nagging because, honestly, I do that quite a bit, way more than necessary, I know. It seems I feel it is my teacherly duty to add a lot of verbiage to what I have already accomplished through body language. I realize it sometimes makes students want to answer back, and then I have another problem to deal with. Aside from that, I don't think I waste a lot of time in my classes, except for trying to teach students during seat work what I already taught (I thought). I have my share of helpless handraisers, and spending lots of time with them probably does more harm than good. I'm going to make myself learn to provide adequate help in under 15 seconds. We'll see if I can do it.

Source: Used courtesy of Timothy C. Charles.

WHAT IS JONES'S STUDY GROUP ACTIVITY?

Jones makes available a free Study Group Activity Guide that can be downloaded from his website. It is associated and aligned with *The Video Toolbox* and is for use by small groups of teachers or student teachers who meet regularly to discuss and practice the skills Jones advocates. The Study Group Activity Guide and *The Video Toolbox* also present class activities that you can use immediately to enhance your management skills.

Jones highly recommends meeting and working with colleagues. He suggests the ideal group size is three to eight people. The structure he provides includes focus questions, study-group questions, and performance checklists, with 12 meetings titled as follows:

- Working the Crowd and Room Arrangement
- Praise, Prompt, and Leave

- Visual Instructional Plans
- Say, See, Do Teaching
- Rules, Routines, and Standards
- Understanding Brat Behavior
- Calm Is Strength
- The Body Language of Meaning Business
- Eliminating Backtalk
- Responsibility Training
- Omission Training and Preferred Activity Time
- Dealing with Typical Classroom Crises

IN REVIEW, HOW MIGHT I IMPLEMENT JONES'S APPROACH IN MY CLASSROOM?

Jones (1987a, p. 321) suggests you organize a five-tiered system that gives careful attention to: (1) physical classroom organization; (2) limit setting; (3) Say, See, Do teaching; (4) incentives; and (5) backup systems. The system should be planned in advance and introduced as a whole. In the planning phase, you might wish to keep the following in mind:

- Do what you can to preserve and make wise use of instructional time that is so often wasted. A few simple management techniques will conserve this time.
- Present instruction in a way that maximizes attention, active involvement, and student responsibility.
- Use an effective seating arrangement, establish clear routines, and assign individual chores to students.
- Use Say, See, Do teaching to increase student alertness, involvement, and learning.
- Actively "work the crowd," moving about and interacting frequently with individual students as you teach and monitor their work.
- Use visual instruction plans (VIPs) and other graphic reminders to help students follow procedures.
- Learn to give individual help to students in 20 seconds or preferably less, a tactic that eliminates student dependence on your presence and enables you to provide help as needed to all students quickly.
- Use class incentives, including PAT, to foster student involvement and increase responsibility.
- Use body language and personal-relations skills more than verbal messages to limit misbehavior and help students stay on track.

Commentary From Anonymous Teacher 2

When it comes to Fred Jones's ideas for better teaching, seeing is believing. I, along with the rest of our staff, was encouraged by my principal to read Dr. Jones's *Tools for Teaching*. She was impressed with the research behind his ideas as well as with the practicality of his suggestions. I started by taking small steps and then building on those. First, I changed the furniture arrangement to create an interior loop. I really liked the idea of being able to move around the room easily and quickly. I appreciated the notion of being no more than a few steps away from any student. I had a perfect layout in place before classes began, which I then had to modify slightly once actual students were sitting in those chairs. I found I needed a little more room in the aisles so I could walk without getting my feet tangled up in backpacks or tripping over outstretched legs. It was easy to fix that and the students and I both liked the seating arrangement. The principal had already indicated she believed teachers should be on their feet, "moving continuously, like a shark," 80% of the time. She firmly believed in the concept of proximity in maintaining acceptable student behavior.

I improved my lessons with more frequent guided practice and independent practice, as suggested in Say, See, Do teaching. It really did work better for my students and was less frustrating for me. Using graphic organizers and/or picture prompts and reminders became part of my standard operating procedures. I found that I learned better with a visual representation of concepts and steps in a process, and so did many of my students. I even created a few reminders on sticky notes (such as taking two deep breaths before responding to a negative event, and a reminder not to nag!) and placed them on my desk. What I found very useful for the students was to provide them with blank graphic organizers and let them fill in and illustrate their own VIPs as they learned.

For PAT, I just assigned each activity a certain amount of time for successful completion. I would subtract a given amount for noncompliance. I usually had the minutes add up over the course of a week so there would be a reward on Fridays, and then we could start over again the following Monday. I regulated their activities by the choices I offered. Some students liked learning a poem or dialog in French, some loved written games or board games (like Scrabble) where they could use their new vocabulary, and so forth. Everyone's favorite activity, though, was something I offered once each trimester—croissants and hot chocolate for everyone as we practiced French conversation. I admit, that was my favorite PAT as well.

Source: Used courtesy of Marilyn Charles.

Applying Jones's Ideas: What Might They Look Like in Action?

CASE 1 Kristina Will Not Work

Kristina, a student in Mr. Jake's class, is quite docile. She socializes little with other students and never disrupts lessons. However, despite Mr. Jake's best efforts, Kristina will not do her work. She rarely completes an assignment. She is simply there, putting forth no effort at all. *What would Fred Jones suggest to help Kristina and Mr. Jake?*

Jones would probably suggest that Mr. Jake take the following steps to improve Kristina's behavior:

- Make frequent eye contact with her. Even when she looks down, Mr. Jake should make sure to look directly at her. She will be aware of it, and it may be enough to encourage her to begin work.
- Move close to Kristina. Stand beside her while presenting the lesson.
- Give Kristina frequent help during seat work. Check on her progress several times during the lesson. Give specific suggestions and then move quickly on.
- Increase the amount of Say, See, Do teaching so Kristina has less information to deal with and is called on to respond frequently.
- Set up a personal incentive system with Kristina, such as doing a certain amount of work to earn an activity she especially enjoys.
- Set up a system in which Kristina can earn rewards for the entire class. This brings attention and support from her peers.

CASE 2 Sara Will Not Stop Talking

Sara is a pleasant girl who participates in class activities and does most, though not all, of her assigned work. She cannot seem to refrain from talking to classmates, however. Her teacher, Mr. Gonzales, has to speak to her repeatedly during lessons, to the point that he often becomes exasperated and loses his temper. *What suggestions would Fred Jones give Mr. Gonzales for dealing with Sara?*

CASE 3 Joshua Clowns and Intimidates

Joshua, larger and louder than his classmates, always wants to be the center of attention, which he accomplishes through a combination of clowning and intimidation. He makes wise remarks, talks back (smilingly) to the teacher, utters a variety of sound-effect noises such as automobile crashes and gunshots, and makes limitless sarcastic comments and put-downs of his classmates. Other students will not stand up to him, apparently fearing his size and verbal aggression. His teacher, Miss Pearl, has come to her wit's end. *What specifically do you find in Fred Jones's suggestions that would help Miss Pearl with Joshua?*

CASE 4 Tom Is Hostile and Defiant

Tom has appeared to be in his usual foul mood ever since arriving in class. On his way to sharpen his pencil, he bumps into Frank, who complains. Tom tells him loudly to shut up. Miss Baines, the teacher, says, "Tom, go back to your seat." Tom wheels around, swears loudly, and says heatedly, "I'll go when I'm *&$#^ good and ready!" *How effective do you believe Fred Jones's suggestions would be in dealing with Tom?*

You Are the Teacher

MRS. WARDE'S SCHEME OF DISCIPLINE

You are a student teacher in an inner-city magnet school that emphasizes academics. Half of your students are African American. The other half, of various cultural groups, have been bused in to take advantage of the instructional program and resources. All are academically talented and none has what would be called a bad attitude toward school. Mrs. Warde, the regular teacher of the class, does not seem to rely on any particular scheme of discipline, at least not any that is obvious to you. She simply tells the students what to do and they comply. For the first few lessons you have taught, Mrs. Warde has remained in the room, serving as your aide. The students worked well, and you felt pleased and successful.

WHEN MRS. WARDE LEAVES THE ROOM

Mrs. Warde tells you that she will leave the room during the math lesson so that you can begin to get the feel of directing the class on your own. Mrs. Warde warns you that the class might test you with a bit of naughtiness, although nothing serious is likely to occur. "Just be in charge," Mrs. Warde counsels. The math lesson begins well, without incident. The lesson has to do with beginning algebra concepts, which you approach through a discovery mode. You tell the class, "I want you to work independently on this. Think your way through the following equations and decide if they are true for all numbers."

$$a + 0 = a$$
$$a + b = b + a$$
$$a(b + c) = ab + c$$
$$a + 1 = 1$$
$$a \times 0 = a$$

The students begin work, but within two minutes hands are shooting up. You go to help Alicia, who is stuck on the third equation.

"What's the matter?" you whisper.

"I don't understand what this means."

"It was like what I showed you on the board. The same."

"Those were numbers. I don't understand it with these letters."

"They are the same as the numbers. They take the place of the numbers. I showed you how they were interchangeable, remember? Go ahead, let me see. Tell me what you are doing, step by step."

You do not realize it, but you spend almost five minutes with Alicia. Meanwhile, a few of the students have finished and are waiting, but most are holding tired arms limply in the air. You rush to the next student and repeat your questioning tutorial. Meanwhile, Matt and Alonzo have dropped their hands and are looking at each other's papers. They begin to talk, then laugh. Others follow, and soon all work has stopped and the classroom has become quite noisy. You repeatedly say, "Shhh, shhh!" but with little effect. Finally, you sternly tell the class how disappointed you are in their rude behavior.

CONCEPTUALIZING A STRATEGY

If you followed Jones's suggestions, what would you do with regard to the following?

- Preventing the problem from occurring in the first place
- Putting an immediate end to the misbehavior now
- Maintaining student dignity and good personal relations
- Use follow-up procedures to prevent the recurrence of the misbehavior

REFLECTING ON JONES'S RECOMMENDATIONS: WHAT YOU HAVE LEARNED IN THIS CHAPTER

Predominant Themes in Jones's Work

Effective managers spend a significant amount of time, particularly at the start of the school year, actively teaching rules, procedures, limits, and expectations.

Effective managers focus on preventing, not just reacting to, misbehavior.

Attending to management logistics when delivering instruction is critical to avoiding wasted time in classrooms.

Punishments and threats should be avoided, as they're ineffective; enhancing students' intrinsic motivation is critically important. Reinforcement can shape behavior, but should be carefully considered.

Learning should be a meaningful, engaging, and cooperative activity.

Fred Jones's work parallels that of many other well-regarded classroom management theorists and is based in research that he himself conducted about how classroom management affects the way time is used in classrooms. Jones wants teachers to battle against the time that is lost when classrooms are not well managed; he also addresses how to make instruction more motivating to students and how to use low-intrusion strategies to facilitate appropriate student behavior. His work focuses more on prevention than on intervention, relying on the identification and teaching of general and specific classroom rules. He suggests that teachers pay attention to their body language and nonverbal communication, as these can be powerful tools in the classroom management toolbox; he also encourages teachers to actively and efficiently monitor students, providing them with visual assists to get them "unstuck" and to reduce the time spent in answering individual questions.

Jones's work is applicable with both young students and with older ones; his methods can be adapted for use with any age group. He encourages teachers to make sure that they are providing interesting lessons divided into short segments and involving high levels of student interaction; his plan reflects the notion that keeping students engaged is a matter of careful planning and instructional delivery.

Table 8.1 presents the basic tenets of Jones's work along with potential positives and questions for your consideration. Remember to take notes in your planning guide as you reflect.

Table 8.1

Jones's Ideas	Potential Positives	Questions to Consider
Pay careful attention to how time is used in class; avoid time wasted on inefficient rules/procedures, disengaged students, and students who are too reliant on the teacher for help.	Time is likely to be used effectively and student learning is likely to increase. Students are likely to be more responsible and more able to get themselves "unstuck" when working independently.	• What class rules (general and specific) would contribute to efficient class functioning? • To what extent would you encourage student collaboration when students need assistance? • Might giving a quick answer and moving on seem dismissive?
Reduce student passivity by restructuring lessons to include more student involvement.	Students have less time in which to be off task if the teacher is involving them more frequently in lesson tasks and discussions.	• How might you use See, Say, Do teaching in various curricular areas? Would some areas be more easily adapted to this format than others? • How will you engage students who are shy/reluctant or who are culturally inclined to be less participatory during class lessons?
Structure your class in such a way that students clearly know your expectations and be consistent in helping students meet them. Use explicit teaching and VIPs.	Making sure that students not only know what to do but also that they're going to be held accountable for doing it is likely to reduce aimlessness, often a cause of inappropriate behavior and wasted time.	• What consequences will you use when students don't comply with your general and specific rules? Which back-up systems will you match with which problem behaviors? • What will you do with students who are habitually uncompliant?

Jones's Ideas	Potential Positives	Questions to Consider
Develop a system for students in need of assistance in class and an incentive system for encouraging students to work productively.	Students will likely spend more time on task if an assistance system is in place. Students may be more productive when working toward a desirable activity.	• How will you manage the time demands associated with creating VIPs and managing PAT? • What negative outcomes might you experience if you deprive an entire class of PAT because of the behavior of one student?
Use body language, eye contact, and other nonverbals to encourage students to behave appropriately.	These strategies can often be implemented with no lesson break; the fact that they are unobtrusive can both save time and reduce negative/unproductive conversations about behavior.	• What will you do if your students aren't responsive to your nonverbals or if they react badly to your proximity or eye contact? • What will you do if you have a student who does not pick up on nonverbal cues or whose home culture discourages eye contact with persons in authority?
Use your room arrangement to facilitate access to students during instruction and monitoring.	Having easy pathways to students can save time by allowing you to get to students readily; use of proximity can also reduce the number of times you have to issue verbal desists to students.	• How do you arrange your room so you can easily get to students if the room itself is not conducive to an inner-loop setup? • How can you set up your classroom if you're more interested in having students work in small cooperative groups? What about if you prefer having students in a more traditional setup like rows?

MyLab Education **Self-Check 8.1**

MyLab Education **Self-Check 8.2**

MyLab Education **Application Exercise 8.1** Assigning Roles in the Classroom

MyLab Education **Application Exercise 8.2** Ideas for Enhancing Motivation
and Appropriate Behavior

The Power of Positive Choice: William Glasser on Quality Learning

How Did William Glasser Use Noncoercive Choice to Promote Quality Learning and Student Self-Control?

LEARNING OUTCOMES:

9-1 Identify the classroom management recommendations made by William Glasser and the broad classroom management themes to which they relate.

9-2 Consider the strengths and weaknesses of Glasser's recommendations and evaluate their likely utility in various situational contexts

Everybody wants students to behave responsibly in school, but sometimes educators are unsuccessful at getting them to do so. William Glasser believes that the problem is the approach teachers use, one that ultimately relies on force. We face a losing battle, Glasser says, when we try to *force* students to do anything. We get far better results when, instead of using force, we use *positive influence* to get students to behave more effectively. We do this by employing *noncoercive tactics* in working with students—strategies such as relating personally with students, providing a curriculum that is genuinely attractive to students, and helping students understand how responsible choices lead to personal success. Glasser urges us to emphasize quality in all aspects of teaching and learning.

WHO IS WILLIAM GLASSER?

Psychiatrist William Glasser was one of the great educational thinkers of our time. He made a number of important contributions to classroom management through his work with Quality Schools. He is well known for introducing two major strategies that are still popular in education circles.

The first strategy focuses on helping students learn to choose more effective conduct, rather than trying to force it on them. This idea grew out of a psychiatric approach Glasser developed called *reality therapy*, in which clients are helped to deal with present-day reality instead of addressing matters that went wrong for them in the past.

Glasser's second strategy promotes the idea of eliminating failure from students' school experience. He believes that a sense of failure is highly damaging to students' motivation to work and learn. His remedy? Structure school learning so that it leads to a genuine sense of accomplishment among students.

Glasser set forth those ideas and others in his 1969 book *Schools Without Failure*, in which he asserted that all students choose to behave as they do—that they are not victims of circumstances that force them to do one thing or another. When given proper guidance, students can learn to make more effective choices and, in so doing, improve their lives.

Glasser continued to make major contributions to the field of education until his death in 2013. In 1986, he published *Control Theory in the Classroom*, in which he provided insights into how we can influence students to make more effective behavioral choices. In that work, he made two important assertions. The first was that the use of noncoercive influence, not teacher forcefulness, helps students succeed in school. The second assertion was that we simply cannot expect students to work and behave appropriately unless they believe that doing so will help them meet their needs. Glasser insisted that teachers have the power to make school interesting and fulfilling for students, and that the key to doing so is to help students satisfy their needs for *security, love and belonging, power, fun,* and *freedom*. Choices and behaviors reflect attempts to satisfy one or more of these basic needs. Teachers, Glasser says, must interact with students in ways that influence them to make more effective choices.

In 1996, Glasser changed the name of this approach from control theory to **Choice Theory** in order to emphasize that student behavior is not controlled from the outside, but is the result of choices students make internally.

In 1998, Glasser published a succession of three books that greatly expanded his views about teaching and learning. Those books included the second edition of *The Quality School: Managing Students Without Coercion* (1998b), *Choice Theory in the Classroom* (1998a), and *The Quality School Teacher* (1998c). In 2001, he published *Every Student Can Succeed*, which he said wrapped up his conclusions about teaching and would be his last book in education.

In these later works, Glasser expressed his strong conviction that students will engage willingly in schoolwork if it offers interesting information that is accessed through activities that help students meet their needs. All of us, he says, continually make choices in trying to meet our needs, which are genetically encoded and cannot be denied. Some of our choices lead to success, whereas others lead to trouble or failure. A teacher's main obligation is to teach students how to make choices that lead to high-quality learning and socially acceptable behavior—and hence, success.

But what, exactly, can and should schools do? Glasser would have us (1) provide a genuinely engaging curriculum, (2) emphasize quality in teaching and learning, and (3) influence students—in a noncoercive manner—to make choices that bring academic and social success.

Glasser asserts that teachers remain frustrated, and their students shortchanged, when teachers use the traditional teaching style he calls *boss management*. He described boss management as follows: Teachers and schools select the curriculum. Teachers deliver the curriculum to the students. Teachers attempt to make the students learn the curriculum while also trying to make the students behave acceptably in class. Results typically fall well short of expectations.

Teachers are much more effective, Glasser says, when they use a style he calls *lead management*. He described lead management in education as follows: Students are helped to explore topics they find interesting or useful. Teachers help students pose questions they would like to answer and then help students locate and use helpful resources. Teachers help students learn to do high-quality work.

Glasser focuses on how teachers effectively relate with and to students. He identified what he considered to be some serious mistakes teachers make in interactions with students. He called the mistakes *seven deadly habits*. He said teachers are far more effective when they replace the deadly habits with *seven connecting habits*. You learned a bit about these habits in Chapter 1; later in this chapter, we'll do a quick review of what Glasser meant by "deadly habits" and "connecting habits."

THE GLASSER MODEL

> **The Common Goal of All Approaches to Noncoercive Classroom Management** *Responsible, Civil Classroom Behavior That Becomes Habitual and Lasts over Time*
> Responsible means paying attention, making a strong effort, and doing what is proper without being told. Civil means respectful, polite, cordial, and well mannered.

↑

> **William Glasser's Approach to Classroom Management**

↓   ↑

> **Glasser's Overarching Strategy**
> Provide positive conditions that help students meet their needs and influence students, without coercion, to conduct themselves responsibly and do high-quality work.

↓   ↑

> **Glasser's Principal Strategies**
> Use noncoercive influence strategies to help students make responsible behavior choices.
> Conscientiously use connecting habits in your interactions with students.
> Provide quality teaching and help students strive for quality learning.
> Address discipline issues as "incidents" by looking for resolutions rather than using punishment.
> Engage students in problem solving.

↓

↓ ————————— → ————————— ↑

WHAT WERE GLASSER'S MAJOR ASSERTIONS ABOUT NONCOERCIVE CLASSROOM MANAGEMENT?

Noncoercive classroom management relies on the use of *positive influence* rather than forceful tactics to motivate student effort. Research in classroom management has long shown that demands and other types of force seldom motivate students to want to learn or behave responsibly (Brophy, 2006). Glasser joined others in asserting that motivation comes from within the individual; accordingly, the teacher's role is to influence students, without coercion, to voluntarily make choices that bring success combined with pleasure so they'll begin to view positive feelings as the natural payoff of learning.

Here are some of Glasser's basic concepts:

- *All human behavior is purposeful.* Our behavior is never aimless or accidental. For the most part, it reflects our attempts to satisfy specific needs.
- *We are naturally disposed to be in charge of our own behavior.* Because our behavior is purposeful and self-chosen, we cannot ascribe it to circumstances, fate, or other people. Any credit for proper behavior, or blame for improper behavior, goes right back to us.
- *Our behavior can be thought of as our best attempts to meet our basic needs, five of which are for survival, love and belonging, power, fun, and freedom.* The school experience should be refined so that it helps students meet these five needs.
- *Many students will not commit themselves to learning if they find their school experience boring, frustrating, or otherwise dissatisfying.* There is no way teachers can "make" students commit to learning, although they can usually force behavioral compliance temporarily.
- *Many students do not do their best work.* Unfortunately, large numbers of students are apathetic about schoolwork. Some do no schoolwork at all.
- *If schools are to be successful, they must maintain quality conditions that ensure psychological comfort and reduce frustration for both students and teachers.* To be at their best, everyone must feel safe, feel they belong, have a degree of power, find fun in learning and teaching, and experience a degree of freedom in the process.

High levels of accountability and extensive high-stakes testing can make it challenging for teachers to engage students in lessons. How will you balance the need to prepare students for testing with their need for interesting, active, and meaningful learning?

- *Schools and teachers should commit to the idea of quality education—meaning education that promotes competence and behaviors that lead to success.* Quality education occurs naturally when the curriculum is made attractive to students and students are encouraged, supported, and helped to learn.
- *In order to be adequately attractive, the school curriculum must be comprised of learnings that are engaging, useful, or otherwise relevant to students' lives.* Usefulness and relevance are hallmarks of a quality curriculum, which should be delivered through activities that attract student interest, involve students actively, provide enjoyment, and lead to meaningful accomplishments.

- *Students should be helped to acquire in-depth information about topics they consider useful or interesting.* Doing so increases the likelihood of quality learning.

- *Quality learning is evident when students become able to demonstrate or explain how, why, and where their learnings are valuable.* Opportunity and practice in making such explanations should be incorporated into the daily classroom activities.

Befriending students doesn't mean you give up your authority. What boundaries might need to be in place to keep students from misunderstanding a teacher's friendliness?

- *Instead of scolding, coercing, or punishing, teachers should endeavor to befriend their students, build strong supportive relationships with them, provide encouragement and stimulation, and show consistent willingness to help.*

- *Teachers who dictate procedures, order students to work, and berate them when they do not comply are increasingly less effective with students.* Glasser calls teachers who function in this way *boss managers*.

- *Teachers who provide a stimulating learning environment, encourage students, and help them as much as possible are most effective with today's learners.* Glasser calls teachers who function in this way *lead managers*.

- *Motivation is the single most important factor in learning.* Students are motivated by what they find pleasurable at any given time. It is up to teachers to ensure that the learning activities are pleasurable and/or worthwhile for students. When that's the case, learning difficulties and behavior problems are less likely to be evident.

WHY IS BOSS MANAGEMENT CONSIDERED FUTILE?

Glasser repeatedly points to the futility of attempting to force students to behave in ways that are contrary to their natural inclinations. For example, when a student is not paying attention because the lesson is boring, it is a losing battle to try to force the student's attention. Conversely, when lessons are interesting, students pay attention naturally and don't have to be continually cajoled and persuaded to engage in the class. This fact is fundamental in Glasser's focus on what he calls *quality education*, in which students are seen to engage willingly in work that they perceive to be worthwhile.

Glasser observed that many students are content to do low-quality schoolwork, and that some do no work at all. Glasser's solution is to offer instruction in a form that influences students to do at least some high-quality schoolwork. To his way of thinking, meeting this goal would require only modest changes in curricula, materials, and physical facilities, but a significant change in the way teachers work with students. Glasser acknowledged that teaching is difficult, and he expressed sympathy for beleaguered teachers who yearn to work with dedicated, high-achieving students but are continually frustrated by students' lack of effort. Glasser wrote that those teachers repeatedly told him that the main behavior problems they encountered did not involve defiance or disruption, but students' overwhelming apathy.

Students, for their part, told Glasser that they disliked schoolwork not because it was too difficult, but because it was too boring. In Glasser's mind, that meant that students didn't see schoolwork as helping them meet their needs. If schooling is to be effective, Glasser wrote, students' needs must be recognized and the curriculum organized in ways that enable students to have their needs met.

Teachers, for their part, must move toward quality teaching and the implementation of Choice Theory, which holds that our actions are not determined by external causes, but by what goes on inside us. When we teach others, we cannot "make" them learn. All we can do is open possibilities, provide information, and expose them to the influence of good models (such as ourselves); in doing so, we will influence them (we hope!) to make more effective choices about what they do in school.

HOW CAN SCHOOLS HELP STUDENTS MEET THEIR BASIC NEEDS?

Teachers can use particular strategies to manage the classroom and help students meet the needs Glasser identified. Students' *survival (safety)* needs are met when the school environment is kept safe and free from personal threat, both physical and emotional. Students' senses of *belonging* are addressed when they receive attention from the teacher and others and are enabled to take part in class matters.

Students' senses of *power* are met when they are encouraged to participate in making decisions about topics to be studied and procedures for working in class, and also when they are given responsibility for classroom chores such as caring for class plants and animals, distributing and taking care of materials, keeping the classroom neat, and so forth.

Students experience *fun* when they are able to work and talk with others, engage in interesting activities, and share their accomplishments. And students sense *freedom* when the teacher encourages them to make responsible choices concerning what they will study, how they will learn the material, and how they will demonstrate their accomplishments.

WHAT DOES GLASSER MEAN BY THE TERM "QUALITY WORLD"?

As you have read, Glasser describes basic needs that students hope to satisfy. These needs are universal. Glasser further asserts, however, that each individual adopts a unique *Quality World*. People's Quality Worlds reflect the people, things, experiences, ideas, and values that they associate with happy, meaningful lives. In other words, a Quality World captures an individual's mental image of what they want life to be like.

Though the various facets of our Quality Worlds are changeable and can vary in intensity and attainability, each of us is motivated by our current Quality World picture. Our behaviors reflect our attempts to make reality match our Quality World pictures.

Teachers who reflect on their own Quality World pictures as well as those of their students can often figure out how to facilitate positive student learning and behavioral outcomes. If students' current realities coincide with their Quality World images, they are likely to feel content and fulfilled and to continue their current patterns of behavior. However, if their current realities do not align with their Quality World pictures, they may feel dissatisfied and frustrated. Their classroom behavior may be affected by this mismatch.

So, what happens when reality and a Quality World picture don't match up? Basically, we can either change our reality or we can alter our Quality World picture. Effective teachers evaluate the match between their students' realities and their Quality World images and work to bring them into closer alignment. Sometimes the teacher can facilitate change for a student—for instance, by making sure information and activities are engaging and relevant—and sometimes the teacher can lead the student to make changes. Attending to students' needs and their Quality World views is a key way to relate to and motivate students and to develop meaningful interpersonal relationships with them.

HOW DID GLASSER CHARACTERIZE A QUALITY CURRICULUM?

If Glasser were alive today, what do you believe he would say about high-stakes testing and the ways in which it has affected the curriculum?

Glasser asserted that if schools are to be effective, they must provide a *quality curriculum* that helps students learn useful information and learn it well. He believed that in many cases, the curriculum focuses far too much on memorizing facts that are irrelevant to students' lives, while quality of teaching is judged by how many fragments of information students can retain long enough to be measured on written tests. Glasser (1992) advised that any part of the school curriculum that doesn't help students learn useful information and learn it well should be discarded as "nonsense."

Glasser says if students are old enough, you can ask for their input concerning what they would like to explore in depth. Once the topics have been selected, adequate time should be allocated for students to explore the topics thoroughly. Learning about a smaller number of topics in depth is always preferable to covering many superficially. Quality learning requires depth of understanding combined with clear awareness of its value. To ensure students recognize that value, they should always seek to explain why the material they are learning is valuable and how and where it can be used or make their lives better.

HOW DOES GLASSER CHARACTERIZE QUALITY TEACHING?

Glasser (1993, 1998c) stresses the importance of *quality teaching* and says it is reasonably easy to accomplish, although it requires a change in approach for many teachers. He recognizes that it can be challenging for teachers to change their teaching style, but he nevertheless urges them to work toward the following:

1. *Provide a warm, supportive classroom climate.* This is done by helping students know and like you. Use natural occasions over time to tell students who you are, what you stand for, what you will ask them to do, what you will not ask them to do, what you will do for them, and what you will not do for them. Show them you are willing to help and that you believe they can be successful.

2. *Use lead management rather than boss management.* This means using methods that encourage students and draw them out, rather than trying to force information into them. Leader teachers work *alongside* students; boss teachers expect students to work *for* them.

3. *Ask students only to do work that is useful.* **Useful work** consists of knowledge and skills that are relevant to students' lives. At times, teachers may have to point out the value of new learnings, but if that value doesn't become quickly evident to students, they will not make a sustained effort to learn. Information to be taught and learned should meet one or more of the following criteria:
   - The information is directly related to an important skill.
   - The information is something that students express a desire to learn about.
   - The information is something the teacher believes to be especially useful.
   - The information is required for college entrance exams.

4. *Always ask students to do the best work they can.* The process of doing quality work occurs slowly and must be nurtured. Glasser suggests that a focus on quality can be initiated as follows:
   - First, discuss quality work so that students understand what it means.
   - Next, begin with an assignment that is clearly important enough for students to want do well.
   - Then ask students to do their best work on the assignment. Do not grade the work at this point because grades suggest to students that the work is finished.

5. *Ask students to evaluate work they have done and improve it.* Quality usually comes from modifications made through continued effort. Glasser suggests that when students feel they have completed work on an important topic, you should help them make **value judgments** about their work through the process of self-evaluation, as follows:
   - Ask students to explain why they think their work is of high quality.
   - Ask students how they think they might improve their work still further. As students see the value of improving their work, higher quality will result naturally.

- Progressively help students learn to use self-evaluation, improvement, and repetition (*SIR*) until high quality is achieved.
6. *Help students recognize that they feel good when doing quality work.* Help students to capitalize on the fulfilling feeling that comes from doing something worthwhile, believing it is the very best work they can do, and finding that others agree. As students begin to sense this feeling, they will want more of it (Glasser, 1993).
7. *Help students see that quality work must never be destructive to oneself, others, or the environment.* Teachers should help students realize that it is not possible to achieve the good feeling of quality work if their efforts harm people, property, the environment, or other creatures.

WHAT ELSE DOES GLASSER SAY ABOUT BOSS MANAGEMENT AND LEAD MANAGEMENT?

We have seen Glasser's strong recommendation that teachers give up boss management and replace it with lead management. He asks teachers to recognize that they cannot force motivation into students and, in the long run, can seldom do high-quality teaching when using the boss approach. The following scenario depicting boss management illustrates Glasser's point:

Mr. Márquez (a boss teacher) introduces his unit of study on South American geography as follows:
"Class, today we are going to begin our study of the geography of South America. You will be expected to do the following things:

1. Learn the names of the South American countries.
2. Locate those countries on a blank map.
3. Describe the types of terrain typical of each country.
4. Name two products associated with each country.
5. Describe the population of each country as to ethnic makeup and wealth.
6. Name and locate the most important river in each country.

You will learn this information from our textbooks and reference books. You will have two tests over the material."

Given these requirements, it is unlikely that many students will pursue the work eagerly. Most will do only enough, and only well enough, to get by.

Lead managers proceed differently. They attempt to activate the genuine motivation that resides within students. Therefore, they spend most of their time organizing interesting activities and providing assistance to students. They follow a regimen similar to the following:

- They lead the class into the discussion of several topics of interest.
- They encourage students to identify topics they would like to explore in depth.
- They discuss with students the nature of the schoolwork that might ensue, asking students what they would do to show evidence of quality learning.
- They explore with students the resources that might be needed for quality work and anticipate the amount of time such work might require.
- They review ways in which the work can be done and, if possible, show or describe examples of finished work that reflect quality.
- They emphasize the importance of students continually self-evaluating their effort and progress.
- They clearly affirm that students will be provided good tools and a safe workplace.

To illustrate how lead teaching might proceed, consider this example of Mr. Garcia's introduction to a unit of study on the geography of South America.

Keep in mind that Mr. Garcia is not expecting Samuel to speak for or represent the entire population of Perú. It's fine to invite students to share their experiences with the class, but please be careful not to make any person the full authority on any subject because of their experiences.

"Class, have any of you ever lived in South America? You did, Samuel? Which country? Perú? Fantastic! What an interesting country! I lived for a while in Brazil. I traveled in the Amazon quite a bit and spent some time with jungle Indians. Supposedly they were head hunters at one time. But not now. At least so they say. Tomorrow I'll show you a bow and arrow I brought from that tribe. Samuel, did you ever eat monkey when you were in Perú? I think Perú and Brazil are very alike in some ways but very different in others. What was Perú like compared to here? Did you get up into the Andes? They have fabulous ruins all over Perú, I hear, and those fantastic 'Chariots of the Gods' lines and drawings on the landscape. Do you have any photographs or videos you could bring for us to see? What a resource you could be for us! You could teach us a lot!"

"Class, Samuel lived in Perú and traveled in the Andes. If we could get him to teach us about that country, what do you think you would most like to learn?" (The class discusses this option and identifies topics.)

"We have the opportunity in our class to learn a great deal about South America, its mountains and grasslands, its dense rain forests and huge rivers, and its interesting people and strange animals. Did you know there are groups of people originally from England, Wales, Italy, and Germany now living in many parts of South America, especially in Argentina? Did you know there are still thought to be tribes of Indians in the jungles that have had no contact with the outside world? Did you know that almost half of all the river water in the world is in the Amazon Basin, and that in some places the Amazon River is so wide that from the middle you can't see either shore?

"Speaking of the Amazon jungle, I swam in a lake there that contained piranhas, and look, I still have my legs and arms. Surprised about that? If you wanted to learn more about living in the Amazon jungle, what would you be interested in knowing?" (Discussion ensues.)

"How about people of the high Andes? Those Incas, for example, and their ancestors who in some unknown way cut and placed enormous boulders to make gigantic, perfectly fitting fortress walls? Samuel might have seen them. The Incas were highly civilized and powerful, with an empire that stretched for three thousand miles. Yet they were conquered by a few Spaniards on horseback. How in the world could that have happened? If you could learn more about those amazing Incas and the area in which they lived, what would you like to know?"

(Discussion continues in this manner. Students identify topics about which they would be willing to make an effort to learn.)

"Now let me see what you think of this idea: I have written down the topics you said you were interested in, and I can help you with resources and materials. I have lots I can share with you, including photographs, South American music, and many cultural objects I have collected. I know people who lived in Argentina and Colombia that we could invite to talk with us. We can concentrate on what you have said you would like to learn about. But if we decide to work in that manner, I want to see if we can make this deal: We explore what interests you and I will help you all I can. For your part, you agree to explore some information I think you should know, and all along you agree to do the very best work you are capable of. We would need to discuss what you'd like to learn about and some things I want you to learn, and from that we could decide what you might do to show the quality of your learning. In addition, I hope I can count on each of you to regularly evaluate yourselves as to how well you believe you are doing. Understand, this would not be my evaluation, it would be yours—not for a grade but so you can see what you are doing very well and what you think you might be able to do better. What do you think? Want to give it a try?"

HOW IS CHOICE THEORY APPLIED IN THE CLASSROOM?

Given a high level of motivation, students can learn almost anything taught in school, and when fully engrossed in learning, they seldom misbehave. This chapter has emphasized Glasser's contentions that educators too often assume that student motivation comes from teacher encouragement. You know Glasser's counterargument—that students are highly likely to do whatever is most satisfying to them at any point in time, if they can. That being the case, most students work hard and comply with expectations only when they get satisfaction from doing so. If natural satisfaction does not occur, they may work to please you, but usually not for long. To persevere, they must find satisfaction in the activity itself.

Glasser says one way to improve behavior in your class is to involve students in specifying what a quality existence in the classroom would be like—in other words, exploring students' Quality World pictures. Then, you plan for allowing the choices that would help bring about the realization or attainment of those pictures. You can do the same with your manner of teaching. Try it: Begin by identifying one thing you could easily choose to change or add in your lessons that would make your classes more enjoyable for everyone—perhaps role-playing, enacting skits that verify learning, holding debates, working in small groups, things of that sort. What would you have to do to put the change into practice? Exchange ideas with fellow professionals if possible.

HOW DOES QUALITY TEACHING AFFECT CLASSROOM MANAGEMENT?

Glasser acknowledges that no instructional approach can eliminate all less desirable or less effective behavior, but he maintains that such behavior can be reduced greatly if teachers do the following:

- Know your students and begin to build and maintain strong supportive relationships with them.
- Work with students to establish standards of conduct in the classroom.
- Begin with a discussion of the importance of quality work (to be given priority in the class) and explain that you will do everything possible to help students learn and enjoy themselves without trying to force them into it.
- Lead the discussion on quality work by asking students about class behavior they believe will help them get their work done and truly help them learn. Glasser says that if teachers can get students to see the importance of courtesy, no other rules may be necessary.
- Solicit student input on what should happen when behavior agreements are broken. Glasser says students usually suggest punishment, even though they know punishment is not effective. If asked further, they will agree that behavior problems are best solved by looking for ways to remedy whatever is causing the rule to be broken.
- Once agreements and consequences are established, they should be put in writing and all students should sign the document, attesting that they understand the agreements and that, if they break them, they will endeavor—with the teacher's help—to correct the underlying problem. Agreements established and dealt with in this way, says Glasser, show that the teacher's main concern lies in quality, not power, and that the teacher recognizes that power struggles usually damage the quality of learning.
- Show interest in students and, when appropriate, ask them, "What might I do to help?"
- Avoid adversarial encounters with students. Adversity dampens enthusiasm, damages cooperation, and reduces people's inclination to do quality work. When you have disagreements with students, look for solutions without getting angry. It's very hard to expect students to move toward you (or forward with you) when your words and actions are putting them on the defensive.

■ Hold classroom meetings to explore what students like and dislike about the class. Show them you are willing to change what they dislike if you can.

> You may recall that other authorities—such as Ron Morrish in Chapter 5 and Craig Seganti in Chapter 6—do not agree with Glasser on involving students in making class rules of behavior. They consider rule making to be the teacher's job, although they would have you explain to students why the rules exist and what they are intended to accomplish. At this point in time, which would be your preferred approach—making and explaining the rules yourself, or involving students in a total class effort to establish the rules? What is your rationale?

WHAT WOULD GLASSER HAVE ME DO WHEN STUDENTS BREAK CLASS RULES?

Glasser says you must intervene when a student breaks rules or class agreements in order to help the student choose a more effective behavior and direct the student's mind back to productive class work. Suppose Jonathan comes into the room obviously upset. As the lesson begins, he turns heatedly and throws something at Michael. Glasser suggests you say the following:

> "It looks like something is bothering you, Jonathan. How can I help you with it?"
>
> [Jonathan frowns, still obviously upset, and says nothing.]
>
> "How about taking a few deep breaths? Then, when you're feeling calmer, we can discuss it. I'll bet we can figure something out."

Glasser says that you should make it clear to Jonathan that you are unable to help him until he calms down. You should say this without emotion in your voice, recognizing that anger on your part will only put Jonathan on the defensive. If Jonathan doesn't calm down, there is no good way to deal with the problem. Glasser (1990) says to allow him 20 seconds, and if he isn't calm by then, admit that there is no way to solve the problem at that time. Give Jonathan a time-out from the lesson, but don't threaten or warn him. Say something like the following:

> "Jonathan, I want to help you work this out. I am not interested in punishing you. Whatever the problem is, we can solve it. But for now, you can go sit at the table and work on feeling more settled. When you feel calm, come back to your seat."

Later, at an opportune time, discuss the situation with Jonathan, perhaps as follows:

"What were you doing when the problem started? What can we do to keep it from happening again?"

If the problem involves hostilities between Jonathan and Michael, the discussion should involve both boys and proceed along these lines:

"I'd like to hear from each of you about what you were doing, and then I want us to turn our thoughts to how the three of us can work things out so this won't happen anymore."

It is important to note that no time is spent trying to find out whose fault it was, and no blame is assigned to either Jonathan or Michael. You make clear to the boys that all you are looking for is a solution so that the problem won't occur again. Glasser says if you treat Jonathan and Michael with respect and courtesy, if you show you don't want to punish them or throw your weight around, and if you talk to them as a problem solver, their classroom behavior and the quality of their work will both improve. Glasser brings a third entity into the discussion with the boys, that of the relationship. He will encourage the boys to engage in behavior that helps them build or rebuild a friendly relationship and avoid behavior that might damage or break that relationship.

WHAT DOES GLASSER MEAN BY "QUALITY CLASSROOMS," AND HOW DO WE GET THEM?

Many educators avidly support Glasser's ideas concerning teaching and education. Numerous teachers have met the stringent requirements for earning the Choice Theory/Reality Therapy (CT/RTC) certification given by The William Glasser Institute. Several entire schools have done so as well, and when they meet the requirements, they declare themselves a Glasser Quality School and are officially recognized by The William Glasser Institute as such. Glasser (2001) describes Quality Schools as those that display the following characteristics (as updated on the Glasser website, http://www.wglasser.com/the-glasser-approach/quality-schools):

Criteria for a Glasser Quality School (2015)

- A GQS creates and maintains a joyful, positive, supportive learning and working environment.
- Total Learning Competency is expected of all students and students are instructionally supported until competency* is achieved. (*Dr. Glasser identified "B" as competency.)
- All students do competent work as well as some quality* work each year. (*A Quality School rubric is available at www.wglasser.com.)

- All students, staff, and members of the school community have participated in the study of Choice Theory and/or the Glasser Quality School Model.
- Students do well on measurements of learning and school performance.
- Read the revised 2015 Rubric for Measuring Glasser Quality School Progress (pdf).

In 2006, Therese Hinder conducted an independent review of seven Glasser Quality Schools in various states in the United States with enrollments that reflected a cross section of the American school population. She found that all of the schools she reviewed adhered closely to Glasser's teachings and that student achievement in all of them ranked in the top category on their statewide student testing program.

WHAT ARE THE SEVEN DEADLY HABITS IN TEACHING, AND HOW DO I AVOID THEM?

A fundamental operating principle in Glasser's approach is that teachers and administrators must make school a happy place for students. Glasser asserts that if you are having trouble with a student, you can be sure the student is unhappy in your class and very likely unhappy in school. Glasser believes most problems between teachers and students are caused by unsatisfactory relationships; he therefore maintains that good relationships are of fundamental importance.

You can immediately improve relationships with and among students simply by avoiding what Glasser refers to as the *seven deadly habits* and replacing them with the *seven connecting habits*. You'll remember these from a brief introduction in Chapter 1; we'll review them here.

The *seven deadly habits* are actions or behaviors that prevent the establishment of caring relationships, specifically: *criticizing, blaming, complaining, nagging, threatening, punishing,* and *rewarding others to control them.* (These same deadly habits are equally detrimental to relationships with others outside of school.) If you wish to establish good relationships with students and gain their willing cooperation, you'll want to work to eliminate any of these habits immediately and help students do so as well.

In place of the deadly habits, find ways of promoting connections with others, as epitomized in the *seven connecting habits* Glasser identifies as *caring, listening, supporting, respecting, encouraging, trusting,* and *negotiating differences.* Glasser believes—and results at his Quality Schools support his contentions—that all students who come to school can do competent work. You make this possible when you strongly connect with your students on a personal level and show them how to maintain good connections as well. Glasser makes his point by describing how we relate with friends: We do not criticize, blame, or speak harshly to them. Instead, we build and maintain strong relationships and use the connecting habits Glasser has identified. Teachers who build strong relationships with their students discover that they have been added to their students' Quality World pictures, meaning that the teachers are important people in students' lives.

Deadly Habit	What It Might "Look" Like	Connecting Habit	What It Might "Look" Like
Criticizing	*That work is sloppy.*	Caring	*I want to make sure you're successful and that your work shows your best effort.*
Blaming	*You failed this test because you didn't get your homework done.*	Listening	*What might have made this test easier for you?*
Complaining	*It drives me crazy when you don't listen . . . it means you make a lot of mistakes.*	Supporting	*I can tell you're trying hard. It's normal to make mistakes; that's when we learn the most.*
Nagging	*Everybody in the group should be participating, remember? One person can't do it all.*	Respecting	*It can be tricky to work together with other people, but it's a skill we can all learn to do well.*
Threatening	*If you don't finish this work before the period is up, you're going to fail the assignment.*	Encouraging	*You're getting the hang of this! I know you can do it. Just three more examples to do and you'll be finished.*
Punishing	*Since you can't seem to comply with class expectations, I'm sending you to the principal's office.*	Trusting	*I believe you can figure out a way to keep this problem from happening again.*
Rewarding Others to Control Them	*If you'll sit and listen quietly, I will give you a no-homework pass.*	Negotiating Differences	*How about if, instead of working by yourself on this assignment, you work with a classmate? That might make it easier and more fun.*

Commentary From Anonymous Teacher 1

As a classroom teacher with 20 years of experience in a low-income neighborhood, I find myself in close agreement with Dr. Glasser's commentaries on the "seven deadly habits" and the "seven connecting habits." I try very hard to maintain a good personal relationship with my students, in the belief it helps them feel all right about school, want to be there, and in turn want to do good work to please me. I know for sure the younger students don't perform nearly as well when they are overly criticized. They seem to have a strong need for positive comments from me. That's human nature, I think. I tell my students that, and I try to exemplify it in how I treat my students. I also tell them it is difficult for me to teach well and it also makes me feel bad when my students misbehave and don't show any interest in school.

Realistically, no teacher is going to have perfectly behaving students 100% of the time, no matter what they do. And some classes are definitely more difficult than others. However, I find that Glasser's connecting habits win over most students' cooperation and loyalty before long and the result is a more pleasant classroom environment, fewer behavior problems, and a higher level of student engagement and competent work. I just try to treat my students as good friends. It's rather easy, actually.

Source: Used courtesy of Timothy C. Charles.

IN SUMMARY, HOW CAN I MOVE TOWARD BUILDING A QUALITY CLASSROOM?

Here is a review of Glasser's main suggestions:

- *Replace deadly habits with connecting habits.* Determine that beginning today, you will assiduously avoid the seven deadly habits when working with your students, replace them with the seven connecting habits, and help your students do the same.
- *Make plain to students how you will work with them.* The message you want to get across to students is the following: "We are in this class together. I want to help you to become highly competent. My job is to teach you and help you learn, not to find out what you don't know and punish you for not knowing it. If you have a question, ask me. If you need more time, I'll give it to you. If you have an idea how to do what we are trying to do better, tell me. I'll listen" (Glasser, 2001, p. 113). (Authors' note: It may not be possible to give students more time in every instance, but successful teachers do try to identify and meet individual student needs.)
- *Build strong relationships with your students.* Instead of telling students what they must do and not do, endeavor to befriend all of them. To begin, say something like, "I think an important part of my job is to do all I can to make sure you have a good time learning. You have to come to school and no one's going to pay you for doing schoolwork. So the least I can do is make this class fun for both you and me. I think we can learn a lot and still have a very good time" (Glasser, 2001, p. 54). Then implement a quality curriculum and steadfastly use the seven connecting habits.

■ *Establish reasonable rules of class behavior.* Rely on one fundamental rule of behavior—the Golden Rule. Discuss the Golden Rule with students. A few other rules may occasionally be necessary, but the Golden Rule is fundamental to all.

■ *Take the energy out of impending less-effective behavior.* Replace traditional discipline (external control) with talking and listening to students as soon as you sense that undesirable behavior is likely to occur. Listen carefully. Inject humor into the situation if you can, but do not make light of students' concerns.

■ *Teach things that make a real difference in students' lives.* It is very important that students be able to make good use of what they learn in school. Therefore, ensure that your curriculum focuses on skills and information that interest students and make them more knowledgeable and competent. Go for deep learning; avoid having students memorize information just so they can repeat it back on tests. Explain to students that you will not ask them to learn anything that is not useful to them, and when there might be doubt, you will explain clearly how the new learning will benefit them.

Does the underlined sentence make you raise your eyebrows? How do you think the practice of making sure no student ever fails would play out in your classroom setting?

■ *Help students learn to strive for quality.* Glasser recommends telling students that you will use a way of teaching that makes sure everyone can do competent work and that everyone will make good grades (meaning a grade of B or better). Explain that you will ask students to work at any given assignment until they have achieved an acceptably high level of competence. <u>Nobody will fail or receive a low grade.</u> Does the underlined sentence make you raise your eyebrows? They can use any resources available to help them, including textbooks, caregivers, and other students. The primary objective is to do competent work. Beyond that, encourage students to work for even higher quality to help them learn what it feels like to do A-level work.

■ *Test students frequently, but productively.* Teach students using your best techniques, help them self-evaluate their work, and then test them regularly. Explain that the tests are for learning only and promise that no one will fail or receive a poor grade on them. When they have completed a test, have them go back over it and correct any incorrect or incomplete answers. Ask them to explain why each correction is better. Give them the time and help needed to achieve success.

■ *Emphasize understanding and making use of new learning.* Ask students always to focus on understanding and using the information and skills being taught. Ask them to share and discuss the learnings with caregivers.

■ *Provide options for students after competence is achieved.* Students who complete their work competently can then have the option of helping other students or moving ahead to doing something of yet higher quality or challenge. To experience the full sense of Glasser's ideas, consult his 2001 book entitled *Every Student Can Succeed* and/or visit his websites at www.wglasser.com and www.wglasserbooks.com.

Commentary From Anonymous Teacher 2

I cringed when I read Glasser's list of deadly habits, because I am guilty of all of them. I would like to believe I have been a positive model for my students, but am ashamed to admit I have criticized, blamed, complained, nagged, threatened, punished, and rewarded students with the intent of shaping their behavior and work habits. I can, of course, see the downside to blaming, complaining about, nagging, and threatening students or anyone else. I am a little confused about criticizing, though. Isn't it part of a teacher's function to offer a critique on student work in an effort to improve it? Most students have not had enough academic or life experience to know if their work is quality, and must depend upon the teacher for guidance. Feedback can be given gently.

I am conflicted (or possibly just lack complete understanding) about viewing punishing and rewarding as deadly habits. Every school in which I have taught has had a schoolwide discipline plan, and this plan has invariably included rewards (special activities, events, treats, recognition for good grades, awards, privileges) and punishment (exclusion from reward activities). I think most kids (and parents) expect this, and I am not sure what would take its place in individual classrooms or in schoolwide plans if the notion were abandoned.

I felt a little better about myself as a teacher when I reflected on the connecting habits. I have exhibited all of those behaviors at one time or another, as have most teachers. But before I pat myself on the back too vigorously I must add the caveat: with some students. And there's the rub, for it is easy to connect with students who are bright, cheerful, good-natured, respectful, and seem to like me and the subject. I have not always done everything possible to befriend the more difficult students. This is my own failing, and maybe I can rectify it.

I very much like Dr. Glasser's suggestions on creating interesting lessons and being friends with students as means of creating a joyful classroom where students achieve and don't misbehave. I like the notion of ditching the "boring" parts of the curriculum, because, frankly, those parts are harder to teach. But I'm struggling a bit with visualizing how it would all look in practice, with real teachers and real students.

Source: Used courtesy of Marilyn Charles.

What is the relationship between criticism and feedback?

You've been reading about several other theorists' ideas regarding the use of rewards and punishment. Given what you've learned, what would you say if you were in a conversation with this teacher?

HOW CAN I GO ABOUT IMPLEMENTING GLASSER'S IDEAS IN MY CLASSES?

Glasser's ideas for increasing quality in teaching and learning need not be implemented all at once. They can be introduced gradually, allowing you to evaluate each suggestion in terms of class climate and morale. Here are some of Glasser's suggestions:

- Remember that your students' behavior is internally motivated and purposeful, directed at attaining their Quality World pictures.
- Remember that most of your students will not commit themselves to class activities they find boring, frustrating, or otherwise dissatisfying. Therefore, do what you can to eliminate those topics and replace them with alternatives that students like and find beneficial; when you can't alter the curriculum, seek novel and engaging ways to present the required material.
- Hold a discussion with your class on how school could be made more interesting and enjoyable. Identify a topic in which they show interest and brainstorm ways to explore the topic, procedures for reporting or demonstrating accomplishment, personal conduct that would make the class function better, and how disruptions might be handled positively and effectively. The process is mainly for student input, but you might offer some of your opinions as well.
- Following that, indicate that you will try to organize a few activities as students have suggested and that you will do all you can to help them learn and succeed. Meanwhile, give yourself a crash course on functioning as a lead teacher, eliminating the seven deadly habits and establishing the seven connecting habits in your relations with students.
- As you get things under way, hold meetings with your class to discuss the new efforts and any results you see in effort and behavior. The meetings should focus only on improving learning and never be allowed to degenerate into fault finding, blaming, or criticizing.
- Instead of coercing, scolding, and punishing your students to get them to learn and behave properly, build supportive relationships with them, provide encouragement and stimulation, and show consistent willingness to help.
- Ask students what kinds of class behavior will help them acquire quality learning. Ask them to reach class agreements that promote such behavior. Ask them what should happen when anyone breaks a behavior agreement. Ensure that their suggestions are positive rather than negative.
- When students choose a less effective behavior, discuss this behavior and why it was not appropriate for the class. Refer to the agreement or class contract. Ask students what they can do differently in the future. A student can replace a behavior that may be less effective with one that is more effective *only* if the more effective behavior is at least as need-satisfying as the original behavior, the one that teachers often call not appropriate or undesirable. So, just saying, "Stop it!" may work immediately as an external measure, but it does not help students develop new ways of dealing with situations that are not satisfying their needs. If the behavior is serious or chronic, make time to talk with those students privately. Some schools have set up a *Connecting Place* where students are taught Choice Theory and begin to understand why they behave the way they do, giving them more control over their own lives.

Applying Glasser's Ideas: What Might They Look Like in Action?

CASE 1 Kristina Will Not Work

Kristina, a student in Mr. Jake's class, is quite docile. She socializes little with other students and never disrupts lessons. However, despite Mr. Jake's best efforts, Kristina will not do her work. She rarely completes an assignment. She is simply there, putting forth no effort at all. *What would William Glasser suggest to help Kristina and Mr. Jake?*

Glasser would first suggest that Mr. Jake think carefully about the classroom and the program to try to determine whether they contain obstacles to Kristina's meeting her basic needs. He would then have Mr. Jake discuss the matter with Kristina, not blaming her but noting the problem of nonproductivity and asking what is at the root of the problem and what he might be able to do to help. In that discussion, Mr. Jake might ask Kristina questions such as the following:

- It appears that you may have a problem with this work. I believe the work is important and will help you in the future, but only you can decide whether or not to do it. Is there anything I can do to help you get started?
- Is there anything I could do to make the work more interesting for you?
- Is there anything in this class that you especially enjoy doing? Is there anything we have discussed in class that you would like to learn very, very well? How could I help you do that?

Glasser would not want Mr. Jake to use a disapproving tone of voice with Kristina, but every day make a point of talking with her in a friendly and courteous way about nonschool matters such as trips, pets, and movies. He would do this casually, showing he is interested in her and willing to be her friend. Glasser would remind Mr. Jake that there is no magic formula for success with all students. Mr. Jake can only encourage and support Kristina. As Mr. Jake continues to build a relationship with Kristina, she is likely to begin to do more work of better quality. Glasser would also recommend that Mr. Jake reflect on the material he is teaching and the approach he is using to see if he can make the material more engaging and meaningful to Kristina and the other students in his class.

CASE 2 Sara Will Not Stop Talking

Sara is a pleasant girl who participates in class activities and does most, though not all, of her assigned work. She cannot seem to refrain from talking to classmates, however. Her teacher, Mr. Gonzales, has to speak to her repeatedly during lessons, to the point that he often becomes exasperated and loses his temper. *What suggestions would Glasser give Mr. Gonzales for dealing with Sara?*

CASE 3 Joshua Clowns and Intimidates

Joshua, larger and louder than his classmates, always wants to be the center of attention, which he accomplishes through a combination of clowning and intimidation. He makes wise remarks, talks back (smilingly) to the teacher, utters a variety of sound-effect noises such as automobile crashes and gunshots, and makes limitless sarcastic comments and put-downs of his classmates. Other students will not stand up to him, apparently fearing his size and verbal aggression. His teacher, Miss Pearl, has come to her wit's end. *How do you think Glasser would have Miss Pearl deal with Joshua?*

CASE 4 Tom Is Hostile and Defiant

Tom has appeared to be in his usual foul mood ever since arriving in class. On his way to sharpen his pencil, he bumps into Frank, who complains. Tom tells him loudly to shut up. Miss Baines, the teacher, says, "Tom, go back to your seat." Tom wheels around, swears loudly, and says heatedly, "I'll go when I'm *&$#^ good and ready!" *What would Glasser advise?*

You Are the Teacher

MIDDLE SCHOOL WORLD HISTORY

Your third-period world history class is comprised of students whose achievement levels vary from high to well below average. You pace their work accordingly, ask them to work cooperatively, and make sure everyone understands what they are supposed to do. For the most part you enjoy the class, finding the students interesting and refreshing. Your lessons follow a consistent pattern. First, you ask the students to read in groups from the textbook, then you call on students at random to answer selected questions about the material. If a student who is called on is unable to answer a question, the group he or she represents loses a point. If able to answer correctly, the group gains a point. For partially correct answers, the group neither receives nor loses a point. For the second part of the period, the class groups do something productive or creative connected with the material they have read, such as making posters, writing a story, doing a skit, or the like. As appropriate, these efforts are shared with members of the class.

A TYPICAL OCCURRENCE

You call on Hillary to answer a question. Although she has been participating, she shakes her head. This has happened several times before. Not wanting to hurt Hillary's feelings, you simply say, "That costs the group a point," and you call on someone else. Unfortunately, Hillary's group gets upset with her. The other students make comments under their breath. Later, Clarisse also refuses to answer. When you speak with her about it, she says, "You didn't make Hillary do it."

You answer, "Look, we are talking about you, not Hillary." However, you let the matter lie and say no more. Just then, Deonne comes into the class late, appearing very angry. He slams his pack down on his desk and sits without opening his textbook. Although you want to talk with Deonne, you don't know how to approach him at that time.

Will is in the opposite mood. Throughout the oral reading portion of the class, he continually giggles at every mispronounced word and at every reply students give to your questions. Will sits at the front of the class and turns around to laugh, seeing if he can get anyone else to laugh with him. He makes some *oooh* and *aaaah* sounds when Hillary and Clarisse decline to respond. Although most students either ignore him or give him disgusted looks, he keeps laughing. You finally ask him what is so funny.

He replies, "Nothing in particular," and looks back at the class and laughs. At the end of the period, there is time for sharing three posters students have made. Will makes comments and giggles about each of them. Clarisse, who has not participated, says, "Will, how about shutting up!" As the students leave the room, you take Deonne aside. "Is something wrong, Deonne?" you ask. "No," Deonne replies. His jaw is clenched as he strides past you.

CONCEPTUALIZING A STRATEGY

If you followed Glasser's suggestions, what would you do with regard to the following?

- Preventing the problems from occurring in the first place
- Putting an immediate end to the less-effective behavior
- Involving other or all students in addressing the situation
- Maintaining student dignity and good personal relations
- Using follow-up procedures that would prevent the recurrence of the misbehavior

REFLECTING ON GLASSER'S RECOMMENDATIONS: WHAT YOU HAVE LEARNED IN THIS CHAPTER

Predominant Themes in Glasser's Work

Learning should be a meaningful, engaging, and cooperative activity.
Classrooms work better when students experience success.
Teachers' interpersonal skills and methods for communicating with students are critical to the class experience; teachers and students should interact in ways that are positive, civil, and humane.
Student needs impact their behavior.

Class meetings are a useful way of building relationships and involving students in the problem-solving process.

Effective managers focus on preventing, not just reacting to, misbehavior.

Students grow in important ways when they realize that their behaviors are the results of choices they make and that they can make better choices when the situation calls for it.

Glasser is one of the preeminent influences in classroom management; his writings and experiences have been integrated into the classroom management ideas of many other educators and classroom management theorists. He focuses on interpersonal relationships as fundamental to successfully managed classrooms; he also emphasizes meaningful curriculum and student choice. He encourages the use of class meetings as a means of furthering not only interpersonal relationships, but also class community and commitment to quality learning goals.

You can read about the effectiveness of Glasser's work by visiting his website (http://www.wglasser.com/research/ctrtc-evidence-based).

Table 9.1 outlines Glasser's work, identifies potential positive effects, and offers questions for your consideration. Remember to take notes in your planning guide as you reflect.

Table 9.1

Glasser's Ideas	Potential Positives	Questions to Consider
Teachers should eliminate failure from students' school experiences.	Positive relationships and motivation are likely to be heightened when the focus is not on grades, but on learning.	• How do teachers find the time to ensure that every student is learning at an A or B level? • How do expectations for frequent assessment and high-stakes testing fit into a "no-failure" model?
Classroom management is more successful when teachers exert positive influence and when they manage the students by leading rather than serving as the "boss" of the classroom. Teachers should lead their students through problem-solving activities to address behavior problems.	Student dignity is preserved; students likely respond well when teachers demonstrate attention to students' needs, interests, and feelings.	• How does a teacher "befriend" students while still retaining legitimate authority as the classroom leader? • How might time use in the classroom be impacted if each interaction with students is a problem-solving activity? Is there ever a time when a teacher should just give a directive and expect it to be followed?

Glasser's Ideas	Potential Positives	Questions to Consider
Teachers should make school interesting and avoid teaching information that isn't meaningful and interesting.	Student engagement will likely be higher if the material under study is of interest to students; classroom behavior problems will likely be reduced because students will be more motivated to learn.	• How do teachers who are required to cover certain curricular material "sell" students on the idea that it is interesting and meaningful? • How do teachers find time to make each lesson engaging and interesting when their responsibilities are so broad and time-consuming?
Students' behavior results from their attempts to meet their needs for security, belonging, power, fun, and freedom; teachers should be aware of these needs and attempt to help students meet them.	Students whose needs are met are less likely to display inappropriate behavior.	• Are there needs other than the ones that Glasser has articulated that impact student and teacher behavior? What happens when a student's most basic needs (food, shelter, safety) aren't being met?
Motivation is the single most important factor in learning.	Students who are motivated to engage with material are less likely to misbehave.	• What should a teacher do when a student is seemingly not motivated by any ideas or materials? How do we motivate the apathetic student, or the student who, despite our best efforts, can't or won't see the benefit of engaging in quality learning?

MyLab Education **Self-Check 9.1**

MyLab Education **Self-Check 9.2**

MyLab Education **Application Exercise 9.1** Unlocking Student Motivation: Making Lessons Engaging

MyLab Education **Application Exercise 9.2** Facilitating Positive Relationships in School

Fostering Responsible Behavior: Marvin Marshall on Motivation and Student Choice*

How Does Marvin Marshall Help Students Learn to Make Good Choices and Take Responsibility for Their Behavior?

LEARNING OUTCOMES:

10-1 Identify the classroom management recommendations made by Marvin Marshall and the broad classroom management themes to which they relate.

10-2 Consider the strengths and weaknesses of Marshall's recommendations and evaluate their likely utility in various situational contexts.

As Glasser did, Marvin Marshall believes that students happily engage in class activities when they find school satisfying, and that they come to behave more responsibly when they are taught how to make responsible decisions and choices. Some teachers seem naturally able to promote satisfaction and responsibility, but many are not, and so they unwittingly teach in ways that leave students disaffected with school and inclined to do as little work as possible. This chapter reviews Marvin Marshall's suggestions for helping students be more successful in school and helping teachers maximize the pleasure in teaching. He identifies the ineffective practices that many teachers use and then outlines positive alternatives that produce the results all teachers want.

WHO IS MARVIN MARSHALL?

Dr. Marshall is an experienced teacher, counselor, and administrator who has served at all levels of public education. Currently, he devotes himself to writing, helping with staff development in schools, and speaking nationally and internationally. His views on classroom discipline and how it can be improved are set forth in his book *Discipline without Stress, Punishments, or Rewards: How Teachers and Caregivers Promote Responsibility & Learning* (2001, 2007, 2012) and his monthly electronic newsletter entitled *Promoting Responsibility &*

*Used with permission from Marvin Marshall & Associates, Inc.

Learning, which is available free of charge at www.marvinmarshall.com. From his foundation, *Discipline without Stress, Inc.*, any U.S. school that would like to be thoroughly noncoercive—but not permissive—can receive free books and materials (www.disciplinewithoutstress.org).

Marshall believes classroom management improves significantly when students are helped to increase their personal level of responsibility, which occurs naturally when internal motivation is activated. Teachers can activate internal motivation, he says, by consistently working with students as follows: (1) Teach and practice *procedures*, (2) Infuse *positivity* into communications, (3) *Empower* students by giving *choices*, and (4) Learn to ask *reflective questions* to influence students rather than trying to force obedience. In this chapter, you will see how these four processes improve both teaching and learning.

THE MARSHALL MODEL

> **The Common Goal of All Approaches to Management**
> *Responsible, Civil Classroom Behavior That Becomes Habitual and Lasts over Time*
> Responsible means paying attention, making a strong effort, and doing what is proper without being told.
> Civil means respectful, polite, cordial, and well mannered.

↑

> **Marvin Marshall's Approach to Management**

↓   ↑

> **Marshall's Overarching Strategy**
> Help students analyze, reflect on, and adopt personal behavior that brings them success in school.

↓

> **Marshall's Principal Tactics**
> Rely on teaching procedures rather than rules.
> Teach the Hierarchy of Social Development.
> When students misbehave, ask them to identify the level of development they are choosing.
> If disruptions continue, elicit a procedure or consequence, rather than imposing one.
> Become aware of the 10 common practices that damage teaching.
> Show positivity in all dealings with students.

↑

↓

↓_____→_____↑

LET'S BEGIN WITH WHAT *NOT* TO DO

Marshall says virtually all teachers would like to organize meaningful, challenging lessons for their students, and they would like for students to control themselves and make reasonable efforts to learn. But in many classes, the outcomes fall short of the goal. Why? One reason, says Marshall (2008a), is that many teachers unknowingly engage in 10 practices that are counterproductive to success. He insists you can greatly improve your effectiveness if you avoid those damaging practices and replace them with alternatives that bring out the best in students. Here are the 10 damaging practices. Later we will see Marshall's suggestions for better approaches.

Damaging Practice 1: Being reactive rather than proactive. Reactive teachers are those who wait for misbehavior to occur and then react to it. They have not anticipated misbehavior or made plans for dealing with it. Consequently, their reactions are too often inappropriate and even counterproductive, especially when they are under stress.

Damaging Practice 2: Relying on rules of behavior. Rules are meant to control; they do not inspire. Rules are necessary in games, but when used between people, enforcement of rules automatically creates adversarial relationships. Instead of rules, *teach procedures.*

Damaging Practice 3: Aiming for obedience rather than responsibility. Obedience does not create desire. Successful teaching and learning require inspiration rather than obedience.

Damaging Practice 4: Creating negative images. You create the wrong image when you tell students what they should *not* do instead of what they *should* do. When people tell others what not to do, what follows the "don't" is what the brain visualizes, because the brain thinks in pictures, not words. To illustrate, if you say, "Don't run," you create an image of running. Instead when you say, "We walk in the hallway," the person visualizes walking.

Damaging Practice 5: Unknowingly alienating students. Even the poorest salesperson knows that alienating a customer is counterproductive, but teachers often criticize students or talk to them in ways that prompt negative feelings. That dampens students' desire to cooperate with the teacher.

Marshall defines the term *discipline* differently than several other theorists. How does his use of the word differ from the way others use it?

Damaging Practice 6: Confusing classroom management with discipline. Management has to do with *making instruction efficient* by classroom organization, procedures, and the efficient use of materials. It is the *teacher's* responsibility. Discipline has to do with self-control and appropriate behavior. It is the *student's* responsibility.

Damaging Practice 7: Assuming that students know what is expected of them. Too often, teachers assume students know what to do and how to do it. Avoid assuming that students know. Teach them *how* to do what you would like them to do.

Damaging Practice 8: Employing coercion rather than influence. Although teachers can use coercion to control students temporarily, this approach, which aims only at obedience, does little to increase cooperation or motivate students to learn.

Damaging Practice 9: Imposing consequences rather than eliciting procedures or consequences. When you impose a consequence, you take away students' ownership of the problem and their desire for changing themselves. Anything imposed is weak or transitory. Involving students in problem solving is a much more reliable way to increase the possibility of meaningful change.

Damaging Practice 10: Relying on external influences rather than internal processes. We make a serious mistake when we use reward and punishment to manipulate and coerce young people. Rewards and punishments come from outside the individual, rather than from inside. Behavior may change temporarily when external influences are applied, but the new behavior usually disappears when the teacher is not there to watch. Using *external* agents to foster *internal* responsibility is counterproductive.

SO WHAT SHOULD WE DO INSTEAD?

Marshall urges you to abandon the 10 negative practices just listed and replace them with the following productive practices. We'll introduce them here, and then go into more detail later in the chapter.

Inspire responsible behavior. You will enjoy much better results if, instead of waiting for and reacting to misbehavior, you proactively inspire students at the outset to want to behave responsibly. Marshall advocates teaching students the difference between internal and external motivation.

As you read, look for parallels between Marshall's work and Glasser's work.

Emphasize the importance of procedures. Rather than relying on rules, which prompt an enforcement mentality, teach students classroom procedures and have students practice them so they know what is expected.

Promote responsibility rather than obedience. Rather than aiming at obedience, focus on promoting responsibility. Obedience then follows as a natural by-product.

Create positive images in students' minds. To help students behave responsibly, have them create mental pictures of what you want—images that depict what they should do rather than what they should not do. For example, instead of saying, "No talking," it is more effective to say, "This is quiet time."

Cultivate a tone of positivity. People perform better when interactions are pleasant and positive. If you speak with students in a friendly and supportive manner, they are more likely to make an effort and cooperate with you willingly.

Clarify your expectations. Explain that you will provide a safe and supportive classroom in which students can learn comfortably. It is the students' responsibility to conduct themselves in an acceptable manner. Let your students know you do not believe punishment is effective. When they are not mature enough to act responsibly, you will show them how to control their inappropriate impulses.

Clarify the reasons for responsible behavior. After teaching procedures (the key to good classroom management) and expected standards of behavior, assure students that the positive feelings they receive for acting responsibly are more satisfying than any token given them.

Teach and inspire, rather than coerce. Recognize that people change themselves and will do so willingly when inspired and taught. Most students resist to some degree when "made" to do anything; in fact, most people in general would much prefer to be asked to do something rather than told they must do it. Focus on inspiring and influencing students rather than trying to coerce them.

Elicit responsible ideas from students. When students misbehave or fail to meet expectations, elicit from the student involved a consequence or a procedure that he or she feels will improve the likelihood of responsible behavior. When you elicit, rather than impose, the student has ownership of the decision. People do not generally argue with their own decisions.

Help students build desirable behavior from within. Long-lasting change comes from self-satisfaction gained by one's own efforts, not from threats that induce fear or from prizes that reinforce the need for external sources of motivation. Therefore, do what you can to help students find pleasure in making personal improvements in learning and behavior.

WHAT IS INTERNAL MOTIVATION, AND WHY IS IT SO POWERFUL?

Marshall emphasizes that although humans are influenced by many external factors, all motivation emanates from *within* the person. Motivation can be stimulated from the outside, but the action emanates from within. Successful teachers tap into **internal motivation** so students *want* to become responsible. One step on this pathway is to get out of the habit of thinking that students should automatically do what teachers want. Instead, we should create curiosity, interest, enjoyment, and challenge with activities that will have students *want* to put forth effort in their learning.

In working with students, teachers have traditionally relied on urging, directing, cajoling, admonishing, criticizing, rewarding, and punishing. These external motivators are unlikely to enhance a student's desire to engage authentically and behave responsibly. Rewards and punishments, which are two sides of the same coin, are both external motivators. Rewards encourage students to ask, "What will I get if I do what you want?" and punishments encourage them to ask, "What will you do to me if I don't?"

WHAT ARE MOTIVATIONAL THEORIES X AND Y?

Marshall says if we are to get the best results in our classes, we must inspire students to achieve; we must also ensure they find enjoyment in learning. He describes two opposite approaches to managing people, set forth by Douglas McGregor in 1960. McGregor called the approaches *Theory X* and *Theory Y*.

Which of these theories is most reflective of your experiences as a student? Can you identify teachers who were more "Theory X" teachers? Did you have any "Theory Y" teachers?

Theory X holds that people usually dislike their work, try to avoid it, and must be directed, coerced, controlled, or threatened with punishment before they will work as expected. *Theory Y* holds that people work gladly if their jobs bring satisfaction and allow them to exercise self-direction, self-control, and personal responsibility.

Marshall's approach to discipline is aligned with Theory Y. He says that even though students are generally inclined to behave responsibly, they often don't—either because they don't know how, or because of peer pressure, or because lack of self-control overrides their better judgment. In keeping with Theory Y, Marshall (2005e) advises you to teach in ways that promote positive attitudes and good relationships that make school enjoyable for students and for you too. He suggests that using the three practices of *positivity*, *choice*, and *reflection* in your daily interactions with students produces these desired results.

Positivity leads to feelings of optimism. Being around optimistic people makes us feel better, whereas being around negative people has the opposite effect. Students will be more likely to respond well to you and be pleased to be in your class if they see you as positive in outlook and in your dealings with others, rather than being negative and demanding.

Unfortunately, students often perceive their teachers and schools in a negative light. That is because teachers unwittingly set themselves up as enforcers of rules rather than encouragers, mentors, and role models. They aim at promoting obedience, without realizing that obedience has no energizing effect on students, but instead promotes reluctance, resistance, resentment, and, in extreme cases, rebellion and retaliation.

Choice empowers students by offering them options. Marshall (2005b) reports the following comments about the *empowerment of choice* he received from a school administrator:

I began to experiment with giving choices to students. When speaking to students about their behavior at recess, in the lunchroom, or on the bus, I would try to elicit from them what choices they had and how they could make better choices. If a consequence were needed, we would talk together about some of the choices. I would usually start with, "What do you think we should do about the situation?" When I was satisfied with the student's choice, I would say, "I can live with that." The process worked every time and I would wonder at its simplicity.

Reflection is a process of thinking about and evaluating one's choices. It is the most successful approach to having people change and improve. It is exemplified in what every super salesperson knows: *The art of influence is to induce people to influence themselves.* We can control students by aiming at obedience, making demands, or imposing consequences, but we cannot change anyone but ourselves. We cannot force change in how students think, want to behave, or will behave once our presence is no longer felt. Coercion is not long-lasting and pride cannot be mandated.

What we *can* do is establish expectations and empower students to attain them. This is done in a noncoercive manner by asking **reflective questions** that prompt students to think about their choices. Reflection often sets in motion a positive change in behavior. The way to jumpstart reflection is to prompt students to ask themselves questions such as, "If I wanted to be successful in this class right now, what would I be doing?" In most cases, the answer will be apparent and students will begin behaving accordingly.

WHAT IS MARSHALL'S HIERARCHY OF SOCIAL DEVELOPMENT, AND HOW IS IT USED?

Marshall created the **Hierarchy of Social Development** that many teachers use in promoting responsible behavior in their classrooms. When students are taught the four levels of social development, they naturally begin moving upward on the hierarchy toward more responsible behavior. If students should slip and behave irresponsibly, teachers seldom have to do more than ask students to identify their chosen levels. This reflection prompts students to self-correct. Here is Marshall's hierarchy:

Marshall's Hierarchy of Social Development

- *Level A—Anarchy (an unacceptable level of behavior).* This is the lowest level of social development. When students are functioning at this level, they are narcissistic, think only of themselves, and have little concern for others.
- *Level B—Bossing/bullying/bothering (also an unacceptable level of behavior).* When functioning at this level, students are bossing, bullying, or bothering others without regard for the harm they are doing. They only obey the teacher when authority is used. In effect, they are saying to the teacher, "We are unable to control ourselves. We need you to boss us." Marshall says sharing this concept with students has a profound effect on how they behave.
- *Level C—Cooperation/conformity (an acceptable level of motivation).* When functioning at this level, students conform, comply, and cooperate. The key to understanding, though, is that, at this level, behavior comes from external

influences: Behavior occurs either to please others, in order to receive a reward, or to avoid negative consequences. Discussing and thinking about the nature and effects of external motivation helps students understand how and why many people are motivated.

- *Level D—Democracy and taking the initiative to do the right thing (the highest and most desirable level of motivation).* When functioning at Level D, students take the initiative to do what is right and proper—they behave responsibly without having to be told to do so. Marshall advises that teachers explain to students that democracy and responsibility are inseparable. At this motivational level, people do the right thing because they understand it is best for themselves and for the people around them.

Marshall says that although Level C behavior is acceptable in school, teachers should have students aim for Level D, where they are motivated to make good decisions about their personal behavior regardless of circumstances, personal urges, or influence from others.

To illustrate how the Hierarchy of Social Development is used to help students reflect on their behavior, suppose two boys are talking audibly while another student is making a class report. The teacher quietly asks the disruptive boys, "At what level is that behavior?" They think for a moment and answer, "Level B." Their misbehavior typically ceases at that point and they return to behavior at a higher level.

How Does the Hierarchy Help Students Develop Self-Control?

Marshall says that once students understand the hierarchy, their attention turns away from compliance and toward self-control and social responsibility. This process is greatly helpful not only to teachers but to administrators as well (Marshall, 2005b). According to Marshall, the hierarchy:

- enables teachers (and administrators) to separate the act from the actor, the deed from the doer. Without that separation, students become defensive when asked to change their behavior.
- helps students realize they are constantly making choices, both consciously and unconsciously.
- helps students understand and deal with negative or inappropriate peer pressure.
- fosters internal motivation to behave responsibly and put forth effort in learning.
- promotes good character development without calling attention to personal values, ethics, or morals.
- serves as a vehicle for communication that uses the same conceptual vocabulary for youths and adults.

- encourages students to keep their classroom conducive to learning, rather than relying solely on the teacher to do so.
- raises awareness of individual responsibility.
- empowers students by helping them analyze and correct their own behavior.
- serves as an inspiration to improve.
- encourages mature decision making.
- fosters understanding about internal and external motivation.
- promotes self-management and interest in doing the right thing, even when no adult is around or when no one else is watching.

Commentary From Anonymous Teacher 1

I've become a convert to Dr. Marshall's approach. My third-graders can understand the levels and are showing the ability to take personal responsibility for their behavior. Previously I had been using a "card system" of three different colors, based on Canter's assertive discipline. That system worked all right, but I think my students responded to it more out of fear than anything else. The Marshall approach provides a number of additional benefits that help me and my students keep everything more positive and productive.

Source: Used courtesy of Timothy C. Charles.

How Should I Teach the Hierarchy to My Students?

Marshall (2007) suggests a number of activities that are useful in teaching students the names and characteristics of the four levels in the hierarchy. Examples include visualizing each level and then drawing a picture of it, describing it in writing, describing it orally to others, and listening to others' examples of applying the levels to what goes on in school. Marshall explains that these various modalities help turn the levels into pictures students hold in their minds. He argues that it is the pictures in our minds that drive behavior—toward those activities we believe will bring satisfaction and away from those we believe will bring displeasure.

Marshall urges teachers to explain to students that the major difference between the acceptable levels of C and D is the nature of the motivation and where it comes from. Level C is motivation for behaving responsibly because of adult directions and may involve rewards and punishments. At that level, students are not really taking charge of themselves, and they remain overly susceptible to inappropriate peer influence. At Level D, students take the initiative to do the right thing because they consider it best for the class, the school, and themselves.

You might wonder how well students can understand these levels and relate them to real life. The brief excerpts (see Figure 10.1) from "A Letter Worth

Figure 10.1 ▪ A Letter Worth Reading

Just this week we had a discussion with our students about how they could use their understanding of the four levels of development to help themselves become better readers. We talked about our 30-minute "Whole School Read" time that we participate in each morning. We had the children come up with scenarios of what it would look like if someone were operating at each of the four levels. Students were able to clearly describe conduct at each level.

At Level D, the students described that a person would be using reading time each morning to really practice reading. They wouldn't have to have an adult directly with them at all times; they would keep on task simply because they know what is expected of them. They would read and re-read sections of their book because they know that by doing so they will become better readers. The motivation would be INTERNAL. They wouldn't be wasting any time watching the teacher in hopes of being specially noticed as "someone who was reading," and they wouldn't rely on an adult to keep them on task. Instead they would be reading in an effort to become the best reader that they could be.

The children discussed further that Level D is where people take the initiative to do things that are truly going to pay off for them—what is right or appropriate. People at this level *motivate themselves* to work and achieve. The results are long lasting and powerful. These people put in the necessary effort to become good readers and therefore can get a lot of enjoyment from reading. Because they get enjoyment, they keep reading and therefore become even better readers. People behaving at this level feel good about themselves because they experience improvement and are aware that it is a result of choices that they have consciously made.

It is amazing to see the results of discussions such as these. That night, without any suggestion or prompting on my part, our poorest reader in the class went home and read his reader over and over again. Although his parents are kind people, they haven't understood the importance of nightly reading for their child despite many conversations with us. That night they watched as their little boy independently read and re-read his reader. Both the parents and little boy could see the dramatic improvement in his ability to read. They experienced the powerful impact that internal desire, coupled with one night of true effort, could have on someone's skill at reading. He came back to school the next day bursting with pride and determination to practice more and more so that he could move on to a new, more difficult reader. It only took one more night of practice, and he was able to do that.

Source: Marshall, M. (2005a). Letter worth reading, retrieved from http://www.marvinmarshall.com/discipline/responsibility-system-letters/a-letter-worth-reading/.

Reading" (Marshall, 2005a) presented provide commentary on that question. The letter, sent to Dr. Marshall by a teacher using his system, is presented here with Dr. Marshall's permission.

The Butterfly Analogy: Another Way to Teach the Hierarchy to Students

In a post from 2008, Marshall explains how he conveys the idea of the hierarchy to students in a way that is both helpful and understandable. Here's what he says about using a butterfly analogy to make the idea of the hierarchy accessible to students:

Dr. Marshall gives permission to download and reproduce anything from his websites as long as www .MarvinMarshall.com is included.

I began by reminding the students of their study in third grade of the life cycle of a butterfly. They recalled that there are four stages of development in the life cycle of a butterfly: egg, caterpillar, pupa, and butterfly. We talked about how all butterflies are in some stage of this process, but they have no control over their movement through this process.

*We then moved on to comparing the butterfly's life cycle to that of humans. We decided that humans go through four basic stages as well. We called them: **baby/infant**, **child/youth**, **adolescence/teen**, and **adult/grown-up**. Again we agreed that humans had little control over the stage of physical development in which they found themselves.*

*Then we began to look at the four **stages of social development** in which one human and/or a society could operate. We talked about what a human and a society in **anarchy** would look like and how such a situation was so hopeless.*

*Then we talked about what would likely occur to remedy the problems of an anarchy-based society. We decided that someone would **rise up and take control of the situation** (thereby becoming a **boss**) and that this may or may not be a good thing. We looked at countries around the world where we thought this might have happened.*

*Next we moved on to looking at the level of control or power in a group of friends. We decided that a **group of friends works together** to share control based on what they agree is their mission and that oftentimes this mission and the group control is not ever discussed; it is more or less just understood among the group members. From here a **discussion of blind conformity** developed and how this type of cooperation is not necessarily good. We went on to look at how being **considerate** of others and **cooperating** for the right reasons resulted in a **democratic society** like the United States.*

*We decided that **doing what is right because we know it is the best thing to do is a much higher level of development** than doing what is right as a result of peer pressure.*

*Finally, we talked about how we had more control over our stage of social development than we did over our stage of physical development. The thought of being in control over something about themselves heightened their interest in the **Raise Responsibility System**.*

*The important part of the hierarchy is having students reflect on their motiva-tion—**Level C, external motivation**, or **Level D, internal motivation**. The more students reflect on their level of motivation, the more they want to get to the highest level.*

For additional information on how the hierarchy promotes learning in read-ing, mathematics, spelling, physical education, and other areas, see "Samples of Hierarchies for Promoting Learning" (Marshall, 2005g).

WHAT OTHER TACTICS DOES MARSHALL SUGGEST FOR STIMULATING STUDENTS TO BEHAVE RESPONSIBLY?

Marshall suggests six groups of tactics that stimulate responsibility in students and help them increase their reliance on internal motivation.

General Tactics

Think and speak with positivity. If we approach students and situations in a posi-tive manner, we enjoy ourselves more and bring greater pleasure to our students. Students are often put off if they perceive a negative tone in our communications with them. By helping students think in positive terms, we reduce stress, improve relationships, and help them become more successful.

Use the power of choice. We all have the power to choose our responses to and atti-tudes toward situations, events, impulses, and urges. The optimists among us per-ceive that choices are available; the pessimists perceive a lack of choice. Optimistic thinking engenders responsibility and helps students move away from seeing them-selves as victims of life events. All of us like to feel we have control over our lives; when we are encouraged to make choices, we become more aware of that control. Consider offering your students choices in school activities, including homework, if you give it. Doing so promotes optimism and desire to do what you ask.

Emphasize the reflective process. Reflection increases positivity and choice and, when applied to one's own behavior, can lead to self-evaluation, correction, and gratitude (a major key to happiness). Ask students reflective questions and encour-age them to ask themselves questions, especially about behavior they have chosen. The questioning process activates the thinking process.

Establish trust. Relationships with others are extremely important to students, especially students at risk. Students who do not value school are often motivated to put forward effort only for a teacher they trust and who they believe cares about them. Trust inside the classroom requires removing any sense of coercion and providing emotional and psychological safety. To promote trust, employ the three principles of positivity, choice, and reflection. Be impeccable with your word and with follow-through, and encourage the same behaviors among students.

Tactics for Interacting With Students

Use acknowledgment and recognition more than praise. Providing acknowledgment and recognition of students' efforts helps them feel affirmed and validated. Such a simple comment as, "I see you picked up the trash," fosters reflection and feelings of competence. In contrast, praise too often implies that the action was done to please someone else, as "I'm so pleased that you picked up the trash."

Encourage students. One of the most effective techniques for stimulating students is to let them know you believe they can accomplish the assigned task. For many students, a word of encouragement following a mistake is worth more than a great deal of praise after a success. Emphasize that learning is a process and no one can learn and be perfect at the same time. Not being successful at a task is a valuable way of learning. It should be seen as a learning experience, not as failure (see Marshall, 2005f).

Foster interpersonal relationships in the class. Connecting with your students one on one is extremely valuable, but helping them connect with each other one on one is also valuable. Relationships are extremely important to young people. At the end of a lesson, consider having students participate in *think*, *pair*, and *share*, in which students think about an idea individually, discuss their thoughts with a peer, and then share their thoughts with the class as a whole.

Control the conversation by asking questions. One way for teachers to remain in control of conversations is to ask questions. When you ask people questions, they have a natural inclination to answer them. If, in a discussion or argument, you find yourself in a reactive mode and want to move into a proactive mode, ask a question of your own. For example, a student asks you, "Why do we have to do this assignment?" Instead of answering, redirect the conversation by simply asking, "Why do you think this lesson is in the curriculum?"

Tactics for Motivating and Teaching

Get yourself excited. You can't expect others to get excited about what you are teaching if you are not excited about it yourself. Relate a story or elicit one from students. When lecturing, use a little more animation than when you are conversing, facilitating, or reviewing.

Raise your likeability level. Most teachers want students to like them. Many believe they can make that happen by trying to be friends with students and may

We've read about a couple of theorists who suggest that teachers "befriend" their students. What does "befriending" your students mean to you? What will that look like in practice?

decide, for example, to let students call them by their given name. There is much to be said for friendliness, but personal friendship is not what students need or even want from teachers. If you provide encouragement and empowerment through positivity, choice, and reflection, your students will like you.

Create curiosity. Marshall says curiosity may be the greatest of all motivators for learning. He suggests presenting a problem or a challenge to students and allowing them to grapple with it at the beginning of a lesson.

Create desire to know. Allow some time at the beginning of each lesson to talk about what the lesson offers. Students like to know what's in it for them. Point out how new knowledge, skills, and insights can help them solve problems, make better decisions, get along better with others, and live life more effectively and enjoyably. A simple way to start is to ask yourself, "Why am I teaching this lesson?" and share your responses with your students.

Use collaboration. Generally speaking, allowing students to work together cooperatively promotes better learning than does competition. Competing with others is not effective for youngsters who never reach the winner's circle. Students who never feel successful would rather drop out or misbehave than compete and never win. Instead of competing, allow students to work together, preferably in pairs. Even a very shy student will usually participate with one other person (see Marshall, 2005d).

Use variety. Variety spices up topics that students might otherwise find tedious. A myriad of visual, auditory, and manipulative techniques can be employed in teaching, such as charts, cartoons, models, videos, and PowerPoint creations. Students often also enjoy listening to music, recording music, creating verse, creating rhythms, enacting the roles of characters in stories or events, participating in large-group discussions, exploring case studies, and working with small groups or buddies.

Tutor a few students every day. Tutoring students one on one is the easiest, quickest, and most effective way of establishing personal rapport with students.

Tactics for Influencing Positive Behavior

See situations as challenges, not problems. If we help students take a positive approach and view situations as *challenges*, rather than as problems, we help students feel they have more control. Emphasize to students that they can use adversity as a catalyst to becoming better, stronger, wiser, and more capable of dealing with life's challenges.

Use responsibility rather than rules. Consider calling behaviors you expect in class *responsibilities* rather than *rules*. You will discover that rules are either procedures, in which case they should be taught, or they are expectations. Responsibilities should always be stated in positive terms, telling students what you want rather than what you do not want.

Use listening to influence others. It is surprising how strongly we can influence students simply by listening to them. The more students open up to us, the greater our influence. Asking reflective and evaluative questions accomplishes this.

Be careful when challenging students' ideas. People generally dislike being put on the defensive. Instead of disagreeing with a student's idea, aim at clarification by probing, as in, "Tell me more." Even if you have to point out that a student's idea is flawed, there are ways to do it that make it apparent to the students that you're not putting them down; one recommendation we have for you is to think through/rehearse how you'll address a difficult subject with students. Saying, "You're wrong, and here's why" is going to be less successful than saying, "Let's hold that thought for a minute, because I'd like you to consider some other information." The old adage "It's not what you say, it's how you say it" is extremely relevant to Marshall's work.

Think in terms of sharing, rather than telling. When we tell someone to do something, the message is often perceived as criticism or an attempt to control, regardless of our intentions. Rather than telling, phrase your idea as a suggestion, such as, "You may want to consider doing that later and focusing on the current lesson now." Or use a reflective question stated as if you were curious, such as, "What would be the long-term effect of doing that?" Three more questions you will find useful are: "Is there any other way this could be handled?" "What would a responsible action look like?" and "What do you think a highly responsible person would do in this situation?"

Tactics for Empowering Students

Empower by building on successes. Great teachers know that learning is based on motivation, and students are best motivated when they can build on existing interests and strengths. That doesn't mean we should ignore the negative or disregard what needs improvement. But students are more likely to achieve success through their assets than through their shortcomings. The more they are successful, the more they are willing to put effort into areas that need improvement. This is especially true for students at risk who have negative perceptions of their success in school.

Nurture students' brains. Marshall refers often to Marian Diamond, an internationally known neuroscientist who has studied mammalian brains for decades and who, with Janet Hopson, co-authors *Magic Trees of the Mind: How to Nurture Your Child's Intelligence, Creativity, and Healthy Emotions from Birth Through Adolescence*. In that book, Diamond and Hopson (1998) present some excellent advice on teaching, such as: Provide a steady source of positive emotional support for students, stimulate all the senses (though not necessarily all at the same time), maintain an atmosphere free of undue pressure and stress but suffused with a degree of pleasurable intensity, present a series of novel challenges that are neither too easy nor too difficult for the students, and allow students to select many of their own instructional activities. Further, they suggest that you offer opportunities for students to assess the results of their learning and modify it as they think best, provide an enjoyable learning atmosphere that promotes exploration and fun, and allow time for students to reflect and let their brains assimilate new information.

Emphasize the four classical virtues. The four classical virtues are prudence, temperance, justice, and fortitude. *Prudence* is making proper choices without doing anything rash. *Temperance* is remaining moderate in all things, including passions and emotions. *Justice* refers to ensuring fair outcomes based on honesty. *Fortitude* is showing courage, strength, and conviction in pursuit of the right path. Through the ages, philosophers have contended that these four virtues help people meet challenges effectively and find greater satisfaction in life.

Tactics for Addressing Problems (or Meeting Challenges)

Hold frequent classroom meetings. Classroom meetings provide excellent opportunities for all members of the class to think together. These meetings are valuable for resolving challenges that confront the whole class and for helping individual students deal with certain problems (see Marshall, 2005c).

Resolve conflict in a constructive manner. When people are involved in conflict, ask each of them what they are willing to do to resolve the situation. Get across the notion that we can't force other people to change, but we can *influence* them through our actions, including the changes we are willing to make in ourselves. This is a critically important understanding.

HOW SHOULD TEACHERS INTERVENE WHEN STUDENTS MISBEHAVE?

When considering any classroom management plan, teachers always want to know the procedures for stopping misbehavior. You have seen how Marshall's Hierarchy of Social Development is used to empower students to move toward more responsible behavior. Let's suppose one of your students behaves inappropriately and you need to intervene. Here's how Marshall would have you proceed. (It is assumed that the hierarchy has been taught and students understand how it applies in the classroom.)

Step 1: Use an Unobtrusive Tactic. Suppose Syong is annoying Neri. Before saying anything to Syong, you would prompt her to stop by using an unobtrusive technique, such as facial expression, eye contact, a hand signal, moving near Syong, changing your voice tone, recognizing other students for working, or saying,

Consider: When you tell, who does the thinking? When you ask, who does the thinking? Consistently asking students to reflect is the key for actuating change.

"Excuse me." Marshall (2001) lists 22 unobtrusive visual, verbal, and kinetic techniques that are useful at this juncture.

Step 2: Check for Understanding. If the unobtrusive tactic doesn't work, have the student identify the level of the hierarchy their behavior represents. (Note that you're not asking the student to identify the inappropriate behavior, and thus you eliminate the natural desire to deny or self-defend.) For example, if moving close to Syong in the classroom doesn't stop her misbehavior, check to see if she understands the level her behavior reflects. Using a neutral, unemotional tone of voice, say, "Syong, which level are you choosing?" or "Syong, reflect on the level you have chosen." Without the hierarchy—which separates the student from the student's inappropriate behavior—a teacher may ask, "What are you doing?" This question often leads to a confrontational situation, especially if Syong responds, "Nothing." However, asking, "On what level is that behavior?" prompts not only acknowledgment but also self-evaluation. You are not attacking Syong; you are *separating* her as a person from the inappropriate behavior, something educators often talk about but find difficult to do.

Step 3: Use Guided Choice. This final strategy is used for students who have already acknowledged irresponsible behavior but continue to behave on an unacceptable level. Guided choices stop the disruption by using authority without being coercive or punitive. Rather than imposing punishment, Marshall *elicits* a procedure or consequence to help the student prevent repetition of Level A/B behaviors. (When something is imposed, the student feels like a victim and relationships between the teacher and student become adversarial. In contrast, *eliciting* allows for ownership because people do not argue with their own decisions.) Marshall says this tactic allows you to use **authority without punishment**.

In the case of Syong's misbehavior, Marshall would suggest you say, "What can you think of that will help us move your behavior to a higher level?" which is eliciting a procedure—the student helps come up with a solution to raise the behavior to a higher level. In a case where a student's behavior has been more seriously problematic, you can ask questions to elicit a consequence, like, "What do you think should happen now, given that you haven't raised the level of your behavior?"

Another option is to use a variety of forms with upper grade students. If Syong continues to bother Neri, you can place an essay form on Syong's desk while quietly offering her three choices such as, "Do you prefer to fill out this form in your seat, in the rear of the room, or in the office?" The form, prepared in advance, contains the following headings Syong is to write about:

What did I do? (Acknowledgment)
What can I do to prevent it from happening again? (Choice)
What will I do? (Commitment)

Guided Choice should be adjusted in accordance with the grade level, the individual student, and the class. Before leaving class, the student is asked two questions: (1) "Do you know the reason the form was given to you?" and (2) "Do you think it is personal?" Students understand that the form was given because when the student behaves on an unacceptable level, the teacher needs to quickly resolve the disruption and return to the lesson. The second question is asked to assure the student that the teacher is only interested in the student's accepting responsibility and has no ill feelings against the student.

After the student responds to the second question, the teacher (of grades 4 and above) asks, "What would you like me to do with the form?" Students generally respond, "Throw it away." Although some teachers might wish to keep the forms, Marshall's approach is to tear up the form and place it in the wastepaper basket right then in front of the student, thus allowing the student to leave the class without negative feelings.

Guided Choice effectively stops the disruption, provides the student a responsibility-producing activity to encourage self-reflection, and allows the teacher to return promptly to the lesson. It is crucial to understand that when providing guided choices, the teacher does so by *asking* the student, not *telling*. This reduces confrontation, minimizes stress, and helps preserve student dignity.

It is unlikely that Syong, having completed the essay form, will continue to bother others; however, it could happen. If the teacher uses the forms, rather than eliciting a procedure or consequence, Marshall suggests using a *Self-Diagnostic Referral* as the next step.

Before moving to this more in-depth reflective form of using authority without punishment, Syong is given the essay form to complete a second time. If this procedure is not effective, then a **self-diagnostic referral** form is given. This form contains items such as the following:

- Describe the problem that led to writing this.
- Identify the level of behavior.
- Explain why this level of behavior is not acceptable.
- On what level should a person act in order to be socially responsible?
- If you had acted on an acceptable level, what would have happened?
- List three solutions that would help you act more responsibly.

Marshall advises keeping the completed referrals on file for the entire year, as they might be used in discussions with caregivers or administrators.

If Syong continues to bother other students, assign an additional referral to complete, in the same manner as the first. Then send a copy of the first and second referrals to Syong's caregiver, together with a brief note explaining the problem.

If Syong continues to behave on an unacceptable level, assign a third and final self-diagnostic referral. Mail a copy to her caregivers, along with copies of the first two referrals and both notes. The final note indicates to the caregivers that you have exhausted all positive means of fostering social responsibility and will refer future disruptions to the administration. Marshall points out that in all of these cases, it is the *student who has identified the problem and proposed positive solutions*. All the teacher does is write brief notes to caregivers and mail them copies of the student's self-diagnostic referrals. The student has done most of the thinking and planning, which gives ownership to the student—a necessary ingredient for lasting change. Marshall says the last few steps rarely, if ever, need to be used.

Marshall (2008a) goes on to emphasize that *having a system to rely on is superior to having a talent for teaching*. Even teachers with natural talent are challenged by student behaviors that teachers in former generations did not have to deal with. To retain the joy that the teaching profession offers and to reduce your stress, be proactive by teaching the *Hierarchy of Social Development* at the outset. Marshall advises explaining the system to caregivers when implementing the system. A form letter for this purpose is shown in Figure 10.2.

Figure 10.2 ■ Sample Letter to Caregivers

Dear Parent(s) or Caretaker(s): Our classroom houses a small society. Each student is a citizen who acts in accordance with expected standards of behavior. With this in mind, rewards are not given for expected behavior—just as society does not give rewards for behaving properly. Also, irresponsible behavior is seen as an opportunity for growth, rather than for punishment. Our approach encourages students to exercise self-discipline through reflection and self-evaluation. Students learn to control their own behavior, rather than always relying on the teacher for control. We want our classroom to be encouraging and conducive to learning at all times. In this way, young people develop positive attitudes and behavioral skills that are so necessary for successful lives.

Sincerely, (teacher)

Source: Courtesy of Marvin Marshall.

HOW DOES MARSHALL SUGGEST TEACHERS EVALUATE THEMSELVES?

If you wish to move in the direction Marshall advocates, the following questions will help you evaluate your progress:

- Are you teaching students the procedures you expect them to follow?
- Are you communicating with your students in a positive manner?
- Do you give your students choices (preferably three)?
- Do you ask questions that prompt reflection?

PERTINENT COMMENTS IN DR. MARSHALL'S WORDS

These statements are excerpted from a response Dr. Marshall (2010) made to a teacher who wrote to him. The original material is posted in *Promoting Responsibility & Learning*, Dr. Marshall's monthly newsletter, Vol. 10, No. 9, September 2010, available at www.MarvinMarshall.com.

- The difference between Level C (external motivation) and Level D (internal motivation) is not in the behavior; it is in the motivation. Level C is expected; Level D is voluntary.
- It is virtually impossible to know someone's motivation. And many kids have no idea how to articulate their motivation. (This is one reason that asking "Why?" leads to problems.)
- Someone behaving at Level B only understands a greater authority. So, the students are saying to the teacher, "We are not mature enough to be responsible, so you need to boss us." The message to students is that they decide on the type of teacher they have. If they act on Level B, the teacher also needs to act on that level because the students will only behave responsibly when authority is used. (Notice the paradoxical approach: No one wants to be bossed.)
- *Discipline without Stress* (the official name of Marshall's total system) emphasizes that everyone always has a response to any situation, stimulation, or urge. He maintains that the only way to change an emotion is to change thought because an emotion always follows cognition. For example, if a student gets angry with you, simply ask this question: "Are you angry at me or at the situation?" Reflection is engendered, the student is prompted to think, and the negative emotion typically dissipates.

- Empower students by having them reflect on their motivational level—Level C or Level D—rather than on unacceptable behavior levels of A or B.
- The sooner you get in the habit of asking reflective questions, the more effective and easier it will be for you—and the better for your students.

Commentary From Anonymous Teacher 2

When considering Dr. Marshall's ideas, I immediately thought of Mrs. Mack, a colleague with whom I have taught for many years. Students love her, including those who have a hard time and seldom care much for their teachers. As I heard one boy say, "She doesn't hold it against us that we're just kids." Her classes are always packed, partly because of her reputation and partly because the school counselor recommends her classes as places where "challenging" students can fit in.

What Mrs. Mack seems to do naturally, I now realize, is quite similar to what Dr. Marshall suggests. I don't believe she knows about his hierarchy of social development, which I think can bring many "natural teacher" qualities easily within reach of all of us. Dr. Marshall's suggestions definitely prompt me to think in terms of positive messages and promoting student self-reflection. And they appear to help us teachers break away from ingrained habits of making rules, looking for mistakes, offering unbounded criticism, and all the while expecting student compliance. His procedures also show students that school need not be something that is done to them, but rather something that helps them increase self-control and assume responsibility for more enlightened behavior. In my opinion, students are always seeking those capabilities but often have the wrong idea about how to get them.

I very much like Dr. Marshall's approach to intervening when students misbehave. It relieves me from the frequent "policing" I do to make sure students don't get away with wantonly breaking rules. Guiding the student to pause and reflect on his or her own behavior and then describe solutions in writing seems to me more effective than repeatedly telling students how to behave and threatening punishment if they don't. I think students appreciate the opportunity to manage their behavior and, at the same time, understand how their behavior affects the way they are treated by others, including adults.

Source: Used courtesy of Marilyn Charles.

SUMMARY OF THE MARVIN MARSHALL TEACHING MODEL

A summary of Marshall's teaching model is provided in Figure 10.3.

Figure 10.3 ■ The Marvin Marshall Teaching Model

I. Classroom Management Versus Discipline

The key to effective classroom management is teaching and practicing pro-cedures. This is the teacher's responsibility. Discipline, on the other hand, has to do with behavior and *is the student's responsibility.*

II. Three Principles to Practice

1) *Positivity.* Communicate in positive terms. This may often require changing negatives into positives. "No running!" becomes "We walk in the hallways." "Stop talking!" becomes "This is quiet time."

2) *Choice.* Give options whenever possible. Teach choice-response thinking—that regardless of the stimulation, situation, or urge, people always have a choice as to the response. Also, teach choice-response thinking and impulse control in order to redirect impulsive behavior.

3) *Reflection.* Although you can control someone, you cannot change anyone but yourself. The key to effectiveness is to hone the *skill of asking reflective questions* to prompt change.

III. The Raise Responsibility System

1) *Teaching the Hierarchy (Teaching).*

The hierarchy, by its very nature, engenders a desire to behave responsibly and put forth effort to learn. Students differentiate between internal and external motivation—and learn to rise above inappropriate peer influence.

2) *Checking for Understanding (Asking).*

When students act on an inappropriate level, they are prompted to re-flect on their chosen level. This approach separates the person from the behavior, thereby negating the usual tendency toward self-defense that leads to confrontations between student and teacher.

3) *Guided Choices (Eliciting).*

If disruptions continue, a consequence or procedure is elicited to redi-rect the inappropriate behavior so it will not be repeated. This approach contrasts with the usual coercive approach of imposing consequences.

IV. Using the System to Increase Academic Performance

Using the hierarchy for review *before* a lesson and for reflecting *after a les-son* increases effort and raises academic achievement.

Source: Courtesy of Marvin Marshall.

WHAT GUIDANCE DOES MARSHALL PROVIDE FOR APPLYING HIS SYSTEM IN THE CLASSROOM?

Marshall provides the following guidance for implementing his system:

■ Carefully review the 10 practices that damage teaching.

- Clarify and differentiate Theory X and Theory Y and which mindset you will use.
- Understand the nature and power of internal motivation. Teach the difference between internal and external motivation.
- Evaluate yourself in terms of:

✓ Have I carefully taught, and have my students adequately learned, the unacceptable behavior levels of A and B and the motivational levels of C and D of the *Hierarchy of Social Development*?

✓ Do I use the hierarchy to promote a desire in students to put forth effort in learning?

✓ When disruptions occur, do I ask questions in a noncoercive, nonthreatening manner that prompts student reflection and self-evaluation?

✓ If disruptive behavior continues, do I elicit a procedure or consequence from the student for redirecting future impulsive behavior?

- Place a card on your desk with the following three reminders: *positivity, choice, reflection.*
- Keep a list of reflective questions, even considering posting them around the room to help when an immediate response is called for. Remember that the person who asks the question controls the situation. Learn to respond by asking, rather than telling.

Applying Marshall's Ideas: What Might They Look Like in Action?

CASE 1 Kristina Will Not Work

Kristina, a student in Mr. Jake's class, is quite docile. She socializes little with other students and never disrupts lessons. However, despite Mr. Jake's best efforts, Kristina will not do her work. She rarely completes an assignment. She is simply there, putting forth no effort at all. *What would Marvin Marshall suggest to help Kristina and Mr. Jake?*

Marshall would classify this as a *learning challenge*, not as a *behavior problem*. He would tell Mr. Jake not to attempt to force Kristina to learn. Mr. Jake could not force her even if he wanted to: To learn or not to learn is Kristina's choice. Mr. Jake has seen that Kristina is capable of learning and would reassure her of this fact. If she chooses to put forward the effort to learn, she will feel more competent, enjoy herself more, and be happier. But this is her choice.

Accordingly, Mr. Jake would attempt to establish a positive relationship by sharing with her his belief in her competency. He would then find out what Kristina likes to do and weave into the assignments some activities that would capitalize on her interests. He would continually check with her to see how she is doing, and thereby communicate his interest in her. He would suggest that what she chooses to do or not do affects her more than anyone else and that she will not gain any satisfaction if no effort is put forth. Marshall also would encourage Mr. Jake to employ the hierarchy of social development as follows:

1. Ask Kristina to identify the level she is choosing.
2. Elicit from Kristina a few guided choices.
3. Ask her to start on one and see how it feels.
4. Reiterate the belief that Kristina is capable.
5. Ask her to reflect about her future decisions.

CASE 2 Sara Will Not Stop Talking

Sara is a pleasant girl who participates in class activities and does most, though not all, of her assigned work. She cannot seem to refrain from talking to classmates, however. Her teacher, Mr. Gonzales, speaks to her repeatedly during lessons, to the point that he often becomes exasperated and loses his temper. *What suggestions would Marvin Marshall give Mr. Gonzales for dealing with Sara?*

CASE 3 Joshua Clowns and Intimidates

Joshua, larger and louder than his classmates, always wants to be the center of attention, which he accomplishes through a combination of clowning and intimidation. He makes wisecrack remarks, talks back (smilingly) to the teacher, utters a variety of sound-effect noises such as automobile crashes and gunshots, and makes limitless sarcastic comments and put-downs of his classmates. Other students will not stand up to him, apparently fearing his size and verbal aggression. His teacher, Miss Pearl, has come to her wit's end. *Would Joshua's behavior be likely to improve if Marvin Marshall's noncoercive—but not permissive—approach were used in Miss Pearl's classroom? Explain.*

CASE 4 Tom Is Hostile and Defiant

Tom has appeared to be in his usual foul mood ever since arriving in class. On his way to sharpen his pencil, he bumps into Frank, who complains. Tom tells him loudly to shut up. Miss Baines, the teacher, says, "Tom, go back to your seat." Tom wheels around, swears loudly, and says heatedly, "I'll go when I'm *&$#^ good and ready!" *How would Marvin Marshall have Miss Baines deal with Tom?*

You Are the Teacher

STOP! JUST STOP!

You are an eighth-grade teacher at a medium-size suburban middle school. Your students are a pretty homogeneous group—some are from wealthier homes; some from poorer ones. Some have very involved caregivers; others are basically raising themselves. They come from a variety of cultural and linguistic backgrounds; most have grown up in the area and speak English well, even those whose family members speak another language in the home. Your students reflect a fairly broad range of abilities, with some performing slightly below grade-level expectations, some performing as expected, and others achieving at very high levels. You find them to be a typical group of adolescents, displaying the sorts of behavior standard for their age.

A TYPICAL OCCURRENCE

Your students are working in small groups. Jonah, Finn, Isobel, and Octavia are to read a short article about a recent current event; in the allocated 15 minutes, they are to read the article, discuss the event, and be prepared to share their summary and reactions with the whole class.

As you circulate through the classroom checking on groups, you realize that there is some tension in this particular group. As you watch, you realize that now that the students have finished reading the article and started discussing it, Finn has taken it upon himself to mimic everything that Isobel says, quietly repeating her words verbatim in a sing-song voice. He and Octavia are laughing together, and it's obvious that Isobel is getting more and more upset. You hear her ask Finn to please stop, then, when he continues, to say "Stop" more forcefully. Finn says, "STOOOOP!" in a whiny, sing-song voice. Octavia giggles. Jonah looks uncomfortable.

CONCEPTUALIZING A STRATEGY

If you followed Marvin Marshall's suggestions, what would you conclude or do with regard to:

- Preventing the problem from occurring in the first place.
- Maintaining student dignity and good personal relations.
- Addressing the behavior in the moment.

REFLECTING ON MARVIN MARSHALL'S DISCIPLINE WITHOUT STRESS: WHAT HAVE YOU LEARNED IN THIS CHAPTER?

Predominant Themes in Marshall's Work

Learning should be a meaningful, engaging, and cooperative activity.
Teachers' interpersonal skills and methods for communicating with students are critical to the class experience.
Students benefit from learning how to manage themselves and their emotions.

Students grow in important ways when they realize that their behaviors are the results of choices they make and that they can make better choices when the situation calls for it.

Effective managers focus on preventing, not just reacting to, misbehavior.

Punishments and threats should be avoided, as they're ineffective; enhancing students' intrinsic motivation is critically important. Reinforcement can shape behavior.

Class meetings are a useful way of building relationships and involving students in the problem-solving process.

Marshall's work draws heavily on the work done by William Glasser, with a particular focus on the role that student choice plays in classroom management. Marshall originated the Hierarchy of Social Development, which distinguishes levels of behavior (A and B) from levels of motivation (C and D). He recommends helping students evaluate their own actions in terms of the framework, and encouraging them to move toward the highest level, at which people behave appropriately because doing so is motivating and intrinsically rewarding. Marshall advocates that teachers use tactics that are positive and noncoercive, pointing out that most people generally respond better when others use this approach. Marshall's *Discipline without Stress* resources are available to any teacher for free at http://www.marvinmarshall.com.

Table 10.1 explores Marshall's foundational principles, along with potential positives associated with them. It also gives you questions to consider about his recommendations. Remember to take notes in your planning guide as you reflect.

Table 10.1

Marshall's Ideas	Potential Positives	Questions to Consider
Teachers should articulate clear behavioral expectations and then empower students to reach them.	When students know what is expected and feel that they're empowered to meet expectations (as opposed to being coerced into it), behavior is likely to be better.	• Marshall talks about expectations and procedures rather than rules. How do you think rules differ from expectations? • What do teachers do when students reject the chance to make choices and assert control over their own behavior?

Marshall's Ideas	Potential Positives	Questions to Consider
Teachers can increase their influence by approaching situations from a positive stance and from promoting students' desire to do the right thing. Teachers should work to increase their own likeability levels.	The tone of the classroom is likely to be more comfortable and supportive when teachers adopt a positive, collaborative, optimistic approach; students are likely to respond better than in a classroom where the focus is on obedience.	• How do teachers retain a positive tone in the face of the sometimes relentless petty irritations and annoyances that are part of typical classroom operations? • Are there times when students should be expected to obey teacher authority without question? • What boundaries will you use when developing relationships with your students?
Students can reflect on their own motivation and behavior and can choose to enhance their own level of functioning.	Students who understand and are allowed to make choices about their own motivation are more likely to behave appropriately than are those whose teachers emphasize compliance and obedience.	• What sorts of reflective questions might help move a student from a lower-level position on the hierarchy to a higher one? • What would a teacher do to address the needs of a student whose disability(ies) might affect how well they understand and can use the Hierarchy of Social Development?
When students misbehave, having them reflect on their level of motivation/behavior is often enough to effect meaningful change.	Teachers can't change students, but they can facilitate students' willingness to modify/moderate their behavior. When students have genuine reasons to behave appropriately, they're more likely to do so.	• What if a student is oppositional in the face of needed/requested change? How would you proceed if he or she is in the middle of an emotional outburst or temper tantrum? • How can teachers change their own behaviors as a catalyst for encouraging students to change theirs?

(continued)

Table 10.1 (*continued*)

Marshall's Ideas	Potential Positives	Questions to Consider
Teaching in ways that are engaging and that incite curiosity will increase students' desires to invest in learning and behave appropriately.	When students are interested in the curriculum and in the ways lessons are presented, they are less likely to misbehave.	• How do you help students who, perhaps as a means of exerting control, refuse to be engaged by any teaching or learning situation? • How do you keep students on track to cover the curriculum when they are deeply interested in a topic you don't have time to cover?

MyLab Education **Self-Check 10.1**

MyLab Education **Self-Check 10.2**

MyLab Education **Application Exercise 10.1** Listening for Elements of Marshall's Philosophy

MyLab Education **Application Exercise 10.2** Empowering Students to Resolve Conflict

Working on the Same Side With Students: Spencer Kagan's Win-Win Discipline*

How Does Spencer Kagan Foster Good Behavior by Working in Tandem With Students?

LEARNING OUTCOMES:

11-1 Identify the classroom management recommendations made by Spencer Kagan and the broad classroom management themes to which they relate.

11-2 Consider the strengths and weaknesses of Kagan's recommendations and evaluate their likely utility in various situational contexts.

Here's an abridged version of a little story told by Spencer Kagan:

> *Two women are standing on a bank of a swift river. In the strong current, flailing about and desperately struggling to stay afloat, is a man being carried downstream toward them. The women both jump in and pull the man to safety. While the brave rescuers are tending to the victim, a second man, also desperate and screaming for help, is carried toward them by the current. Again the women jump to the rescue. As they are pulling out this second victim, they spot a third man flailing about as he is carried downstream toward them. One woman quickly jumps in to save him. As she does, she turns and sees the other woman resolutely walking upstream. "Why aren't you helping?" she cries. "I am," states the other. "I am going to see who is pushing them in!"* (Kagan, 2001)

How does Kagan's story relate to the idea of classroom management?

*Used with permission of Spencer Kagan.

WHO IS SPENCER KAGAN?

Spencer Kagan, originator and principal disseminator of Win-Win Discipline, is a professor of psychology and head of Kagan Publishing and Professional Development. For several years, Dr. Kagan has been investigating how teachers can best establish harmonious classrooms, promote responsible behavior, and improve students' social skills, character qualities, and academic achievement. Kagan believes discipline is not something you do to a student, but rather something you help a student achieve. All disruptive behavior is an immature attempt to meet a need associated with a student position. Let's say, for example, that a student disrupts the class by acting like a clown. The student's position is attention-seeking. The job of the teacher, rather than disciplining the student, is to help the student learn responsible ways to meet the need for attention. When a student has responsible ways to meet his or her individual needs, the student is no longer disruptive.

What is the relationship between Kagan's thinking and that of Glasser and Marshall?

The focus in Win-Win Discipline is to help teachers recognize the seven positions from which disruptive behaviors spring, and to provide ways the teacher can help students learn responsible alternatives to their disruptive behaviors. Kagan believes that when classes are managed in this way, everyone can win. Disruptive students learn responsible ways to meet their needs. The class and the teacher have to deal with fewer disruptive behaviors.

To help teachers teach students responsible behaviors, Kagan and his colleagues have developed many structures—step-by-step procedures that are used to prevent disruptive behaviors, to deal with disruptive behaviors in the moment of disruption, and to help students learn responsible behaviors following a disruption. Thus, Win-Win is a *before*, *during*, and *after* approach to discipline.

Kagan is extremely enthusiastic about the value of structures in various aspects of teaching. To see what he has to say about them, you might take a few minutes to read his online article, "A Brief History of Kagan Structures," *Kagan Online Magazine*, Spring 2003, at www.kaganonline.com. You will find several other Kagan articles also available at that site.

WHAT IS THE KAGAN MODEL OF MANAGEMENT?

> **The Common Goal of All Approaches to Management** *Responsible, Civil Classroom Behavior That Becomes Habitual and Lasts over Time.*
>
> Responsible means paying attention, making a strong effort, and doing what is proper without being told. Civil means respectful, polite, cordial, and well mannered.

↑

Spencer Kagan's Approach to Management

↓ ↑

Kagan's Overarching Strategy

Establish same-side cooperation with students and use "structures" to prevent and address student misbehavior.

↓ ↑

Kagan's Principal Tactics

- Foster a same-side relationship with students.
- Recognize four categories of irresponsible behavior.
- Recognize seven "positions" that might exist within students when they misbehave.
- Develop and/or apply "structures" for short- and long-term effect when addressing various combinations of irresponsible behavior and positions.

↓

↓——————— → ———————↑

WHAT IS THE FUNDAMENTAL PROPOSITION IN KAGAN'S APPROACH?

Classroom management works best, Kagan maintains, when teachers do two things: (1) work on the same side with students to establish mutual agreements (rules) concerning acceptable and unacceptable behavior in the classroom, and (2) continue thereafter to work collaboratively with students by using "structures" to help them make good decisions that lead to responsible behavior.

Irresponsible Behavior

Kagan uses the term "irresponsible behavior" to mean disruptive student behavior (i.e., misbehavior), which Kagan assigns to four categories: aggression, breaking rules, confrontations, and disengagement. He refers to the four categories as the *ABCD of disruptive behavior.*

Aggression. Student aggression can be shown physically, verbally, and sometimes passively. Physical aggression includes hitting, kicking, biting, pinching, pulling, and slapping. Verbal aggression includes put-downs, swearing, ridiculing, and name-calling. Passive aggression involves stubbornly refusing to comply with reasonable requests.

Breaking Rules. When unable to meet certain needs satisfactorily, students often try to do so through behavior that violates class rules. Common examples of rule-breaking behavior are talking without permission, making weird noises, chewing gum, passing notes, being out of seat, and not turning in work. Sometimes students break rules just to see what it feels like or to see what happens when they do.

Confrontation. Confrontations occur among students or between student and teacher when the parties involved try to get their way, vie for control, or attempt to show dominance. Examples of confrontational behavior are refusing to comply, complaining, arguing, calling names, and giving myriad reasons why things are no good or should be done differently. When students don't get their way in confrontations, they often sulk or make disparaging remarks about the task, teacher, or fellow students.

Disengagement. Students may disengage from lessons for a variety of reasons. They may have something more interesting on their minds, feel incapable of performing the task, or find the task to be meaningless. Passive disengagement includes inattention, being off task, not finishing work, and pretending to be incapable. Active disengagement includes put-downs, excessive requests for help, and comments such as, "This stuff is stupid."

Student Positions

Kagan uses the term *student positions* to refer to the physical and emotional states students are experiencing at the time they make ineffective behavior choices. In Kagan's terminology, misbehaving students are said to be "coming from" one or more of seven positions; these positions reflect the state of mind the student is experiencing at the time of misbehavior. The seven positions that Kagan identifies are:

How do these student positions relate to the student needs identified by Glasser, Dreikurs, and others?

- ■ Attention-seeking
- ■ Avoiding failure
- ■ Angry
- ■ Control-seeking

- Energetic
- Bored
- Uninformed

When addressing misbehavior, the teacher acknowledges and accepts the student's emotional state (e.g., "I can see you are angry") but explicitly *does not* accept the inappropriate behavior (e.g., "But it is not all right to push anyone"). Indicating to students that you recognize their positions can increase the likelihood that they will then shift their behavior in a more appropriate direction.

Kagan says all misbehavior is linked to one or more of the seven student positions. One example of a misbehavior-position combination is a student behaving aggressively (the misbehavior) while being angry (the position). Another example is a student breaking a rule (the misbehavior) because he or she is attempting to avoid a sense of failure (the position).

> Think about the seven positions. What sorts of ineffective behavior would most likely occur as a result of each? For instance, it makes sense that aggressive behavior would stem from a position of anger; it makes sense that a student who refuses to work might be coming from either a position of boredom or a position of being uninformed (not knowing what to do/ how to do it). What other misebehavior-position combinations can you anticipate?

Structures

According to Kagan, *structures* are specific plans of action that teachers use for two purposes—to teach the curriculum and to address misbehavior. For our purposes, we are going to focus mainly on structures for addressing misbehavior, but we recommend you review Kagan's instructional structures as well.

Kagan says teachers who are more effective classroom managers learn to select and apply a structure that deals effectively with a particular combination of misbehavior and student position. Kagan has developed a large number of structures, which he presents in *Win-Win Discipline* (Kagan, Kyle, & Scott, 2004/2007) and in some of his website articles. Kagan shows teachers how to identify the category of misbehavior, identify the position the student is "coming from," and apply an appropriate structure to help the student contend with the situation in a positive manner. You can visualize the process as follows:

Teacher Identifies *Misbehavior* → Teacher Identifies *Student Position* → Teacher Selects and Applies a *Structure that Addresses the Particular Combination of Misbehavior and Position*

Kagan, Kyle, and Scott (2004/2007) explain that teachers continually use structures without recognizing them as such. They explain that structures are simply plans of action and ways of reacting. For example, one of the most frequently used (and least effective) structures in discipline is posing the *why* question, which proceeds as follows:

[Teacher hears and sees Anthony talking abusively to Jason during silent work time.]

Teacher asks: "Anthony, why are you talking?"
Anthony replies: "Just answering a question for Jason."
Teacher replies: "Well it didn't sound like it. You both know better than that."

In *Win-Win Discipline* (2004/2007) Kagan, Kyle, and Scott describe in detail a large number of structures for dealing with types of disruption and student positions. These structures are similar, but not identical, to the "procedures" emphasized by Harry and Rosemary Wong and others, indicating steps and the order in which they occur. Some of Kagan's structures are designed to prevent disruptions. Examples of such preventive structures are reviewing class rules, having students practice complying with rules, and having students familiarize themselves with class routines.

Other structures are designed for responding to disruptions when they occur. These responsive structures are applied at three different points in time: (1) at *the moment of disruption*, to stop the behavior and re-direct it toward responsible behavior; (2) during *follow-up*, when students require further assistance in moving beyond a particular disruptive behavior; and (3) repeatedly over the *long term*, to help students develop and maintain effective life skills such as positive self-direction and getting along with others.

Kagan asserts that once the Win-Win philosophy of same-side collaboration has been internalized, students who disrupt usually need only a reminder to get back on track. Teachers can refer to the chart of rules posted in the room and ask,

How does this idea relate to Glasser's concept of Quality Worlds?

"Are we living up to the way we want our class to be?" If more is required, the teacher might use a structure such as *Picture It Right*, which asks students to picture how they would like the class to be and verbalize what they need to do to make it that way.

Structures for the Moment of Disruption

At the moment of disruption, you should intervene in a way that ends the disruption and quickly refocuses attention on the lesson. You might acknowledge the student's position, communicate that the disruptive behavior is not acceptable, request cooperation, or involve the student in specifying a satisfactory alternative. Here are three examples of structures designed for use at the moment of disruption:

- *Picture It Right.* "If we were at our very best right now, how would we look?"
- *Make a Better Choice.* "Try to think of a better choice to make right now."
- *To You . . . To Me.* "To you, this lesson may be boring; to me, it is important because . . ."

Structures for Follow-Up

Follow-up structures are used when students need additional assistance in behaving responsibly. They are applied when moment-of-disruption structures do not bring about a complete or lasting result. Here are some sample follow-up structures:

- Establish a new preventive procedure or reestablish an existing preventive procedure.
- Select a new moment-of-disruption procedure for use the next time the student disrupts.
- Provide training in a life skill such as self-control or relating well with others.

Follow-up structures often involve highly prescriptive activities such as directly practicing appropriate behavior. They may even call on students to make apologies and restitution, or experience time away from the lesson. If still stronger measures are needed, students may be required to develop a *personal improvement plan* that specifies behavior changes the student intends to make and how those changes will be accomplished.

If it is necessary to administer consequences to control disruptive behavior, Kagan suggests that they should be applied in the following sequence:

1. The student is given a warning.
2. If that doesn't work, the student is given reflection time to sit alone and think about the disruptive behavior and how to improve it.
3. If that doesn't work, a personal improvement plan is formulated by the disruptive student to help develop responsible ways of meeting needs in the classroom.
4. If that doesn't work, the student's parent or guardian is contacted.
5. If that doesn't work, the student is assigned to make a visit to the principal's office.

Structures for Long-Term Success

Long-term structures are intended to help students get along with others, become more self-directing, and control their volatile emotions. They fortify proper behavior after preventive and moment-of-disruption structures have begun producing their desired results. Keep in mind that the major goal of Win-Win Discipline is to help students learn to control themselves responsibly over time in various situations. Thus, when opportunities present themselves, teachers should allow students to try to resolve problems on their own and display responsible behavior. Different long-term goals come into play for various student positions. For example:

- Students who continually seek attention need help with self-validation.
- Students who avoid failure or embarrassment need help with self-confidence.
- Students who are often angry need help with self-control.
- Students who seek control need help with recognizing others' capabilities.
- Students who are overly energetic need help with self-direction.
- Students who are frequently bored need help with self-motivation.
- Students who are frequently uninformed need help in obtaining information for themselves or from others.

Win-Win Discipline offers a progression of follow-up structures to help students move toward these long-term goals. Here are a few such structures, ranging from less directive to more directive:

Same-Side Chat. Teacher and student talk together in a friendly manner. In so doing, they get to know each other better and come to see themselves as working on the same side toward better conditions for all.

Responsible Thinking. Discussions are used to prompt students to reflect on three considerations: (1) their own and others' needs, (2) how they treat others, and (3) how they conduct themselves. When this sort of structure is applied to a specific misbehavior, students can be asked to consider the following three prompts in relation to their own behavior:

- What if everyone in our class acted that way?
- How would I like to be treated? Did I treat others the way I would like to be treated?
- What would be a win-win solution? What would meet everyone's needs?

Reestablishing Expectations. Discuss and, if necessary, reteach expectations concerning rules, procedures, and routines.

Identifying Replacement Behavior. Guide students to generate, accept, and practice responsible behavior they can use in place of disruptive behavior.

Agreeing on Contracts. Make written contracts in which the teacher and individual students clarify and formalize agreements they have reached. Contracts sometimes increase the likelihood that the student will remember, identify with, and honor the agreement.

Establishing Consequences. Agree on actions the teacher will take when students chronically disrupt. These consequences are held as a last resort and are used only when all other follow-up efforts have failed. Consequences should be aligned with the three pillars of Win-Win Discipline—they begin with same-side orientation, are established through teacher–student collaboration, and are instructive and aimed at helping students learn to conduct themselves with greater personal responsibility.

When disruptions harm others and responsible thinking is not enough, students may need to *apologize* to those they have offended or make *restitution* of some sort. Genuine apologies have three parts: a statement of regret, a statement of appropriate future behavior, and the request for acceptance of the apology. (Here's an example of a genuine apology: "Luis, I'm sorry that I made fun of you when you made a mistake. I will remember that it hurt your feelings, and I won't do that anymore. Instead, I'll remember that mistakes are part of learning. Would you please accept my apology?") *Restitution* means making amends for emotional damage that was done or repairing or replacing physical damage or damaged materials. Restitution is a tangible way of taking responsibility and dealing with the consequences of inappropriate choices. It also has the potential to "heal the violator." An example of restitution might be that since Joretta scribbled on Natasha's new folder, she keeps the scribbled-on folder and gives Natasha her clean one.

Structures for Promoting Life Skills

One of the major goals of Win-Win Discipline is to promote the progressive development of a number of *life skills* that help students live more successfully. Examples of life skills are self-control, anger management, good judgment, impulse control, perseverance, and empathy. Teachers are urged to teach these skills as part of the curriculum and exhibit them at all times, especially when responding to misbehavior. Kagan says that when teachers foster life skills, they move beyond interventions that simply end disruptions but leave students likely to disrupt again. He illustrates his points in this manner (2007):

> *A student puts down another student. The recipient of the put-down, having been publicly belittled, has the impulse to retaliate by giving back a put-down or even initiating a fight. If the recipient has developed adequate self-control and/or anger management, he might smile and rise above the affront.*
>
> *A student is finding an assignment difficult. She is tempted to avoid a sense of failure by saying to herself and others, "This assignment is stupid." But if she has acquired adequate self-motivation and pride in her work, she may decide to persevere.*
>
> *A student is placed on a team with another student he does not like. He is tempted to mutter, "Oh no! Look who we're stuck with!" If the student has developed sufficient empathy and kindness, he might dispose himself to working with the other student.*

HOW DO I MATCH INTERVENTION STRUCTURES TO VARIOUS TYPES OF DISRUPTION?

Interventions are the actions teachers take to deal with disruptions. They usually involve a structure the teacher applies to stop the disruption and help students return to appropriate behavior that lasts over time. Following are some examples provided by Kagan.

Interventions for Attention-Seeking Behavior

Most individuals have a strong need for attention. They want to know others care about them or at least take notice of them. When they feel left out or not cared for, they often behave undesirably in trying to get the attention they crave. They may interrupt, show off, annoy others, work more slowly than others, ask for extra help, or simply goof off. These acts seldom bring the results students would like—in fact, they are likely to lead to further disruption and increased teacher annoyance.

What You Can Do

For the moment of disruption, you can use physical proximity and hand or facial signals to stop the disruption, or provide additional personal attention, appreciation, and affirmation. If attention seeking becomes chronic, ask students to identify other positive ways they can get attention, such as helping others or doing exemplary work. You can follow up by meeting with disruptive students and discussing the need for attention and how it can often be obtained in a positive manner. Strategies for long-term solutions include helping students strengthen their self-concepts and acquire the skills involved in self-validation.

Interventions for Attempts to Avoid Failure or Embarrassment

We have all been in situations where we rationalize our inadequacies in order to soften the embarrassment of failure. No one likes to appear inept. The student who says, "I don't care about the stupid math quiz" knows it is more painful to fail, especially in front of others, than not to try at all, and therefore will rationalize failure as lack of caring.

What You Can Do

Win-win teachers help students find ways to persist and continue to perform without feeling bad if they aren't first or best. For the moment of disruption, you can encourage students to try to complete the task, assign partners or helpers, or reorganize the task into smaller pieces. For follow-up and long-term strategies, ask students how they think responsible people might deal with fear of failure. You can also provide for peer support, review the fact that mistakes are always part of the learning process as people move toward excellence, and use "team–pair–solo," a structure in which students practice first as a team and then in pairs before doing the assigned activities by themselves.

Interventions for Anger

Anger is a natural reaction many students have to situations that involve frustration, humiliation, loss, or pain. Angry students may act out in unacceptable ways because they do not know how to deal effectively with the emotions they are experiencing.

What You Can Do

Teachers don't enjoy interacting with angry students. They sometimes experience hurt or indignation. Often, because they feel personally attacked, their immediate reaction is to retaliate against the students, which does little to help students manage their anger. Win-Win Discipline provides several structures to help you respond positively to angry disruptions. Three of those structures are teaching responsible ways of handling anger, allowing students to cool down and have time to think, and tabling the matter for attention at a later time. Long-term interventions include having students practice the skills of self-control and teaching them how to resolve conflicts in a positive manner.

Interventions for Control-Seeking Behavior

All of us want to feel we are at least partly in charge of ourselves and able to make our own decisions. In our efforts to exercise self-direction, we sometimes try to control others as well. At times, students display this take-charge attitude by disregarding or defying directions from the teacher. Doing so often leads to power struggles between student and teacher. Teachers don't take kindly to noncompliance, arguing, or making excuses, and they often counter in ways that show their dominance, which does little to help the student.

What You Can Do

At the moment of disruption, acknowledge the student's power, use language of choice (a structure in which the teacher provides students with a choice such as, "You may either . . . or . . ."), or provide options for how and when work is to be done. For follow-up, you might schedule a conference or class meeting at a later time to discuss the situation, ask the class why they think students often struggle against the teacher, and consider how such struggles can be avoided. Long-term strategies include involving students in the decision-making process and requesting their help in establishing class agreements about showing respect for the teacher and fellow students.

Interventions for the Overly Energetic

At times, humans experience periods of high energy, so strong they cannot sit still or concentrate. Some students are in this state a good deal of the time, moving and talking incessantly.

What You Can Do

If overly energetic behavior becomes troublesome, at the moment of disruption take a brief class break or switch to another activity that allows energy to dissipate. You might also provide time for progressive relaxation, remove distracting elements and objects, and channel energy productively. Follow-up strategies include teaching a variety of calming strategies and providing activities that allow students to work off energy in positive ways. Long-term solutions include managing energy levels during instruction and helping students learn how to channel their energy in ways that bring positive results.

Interventions for Boredom

To say that students are bored is to say they are no longer enjoying particular activities enough to continue them willingly. Their boredom will be evident in their body language, disengagement, and disinclination to participate.

What You Can Do

To help bored students at the moment of disruption, you can restructure the learning task, involve students more actively, and inject short activities that energize the students. As follow-up, you might talk privately with the students and assign them helping roles such as caretakers for the classroom, materials assistants, or coaches to assist other students. For long-term solutions, you can provide a rich, relevant, and developmentally appropriate curriculum that actively involves students in the learning process, emphasizes cooperative learning, and calls on students to use different skill sets.

Interventions for the Uninformed

Sometimes students respond or react disruptively because they simply don't know what to do or how to behave responsibly. Disruptions stemming from being uninformed do not occur because of strong emotions, but because of lack of information, skill, or appropriate habit. Even when these disruptions are not emotionally volatile, they are nonetheless frustrating to teachers.

What You Can Do

To determine whether students know what is expected of them, at the moment of disruption gently ask students to say or do what is expected of them. If they are unable to do so, you can reteach them at that time. If they only need support, let them work with a buddy. Follow-up strategies include more careful attention to giving directions, modeling desired responses, and providing practice in responsible behavior. Long-term solutions include encouragement and focusing on student strengths.

WHAT ELSE SHOULD WE KNOW ABOUT WIN-WIN DISCIPLINE?

Here is further information that will help you conceptualize Win-Win Discipline and how it is used:

1. *The goal of Win-Win Discipline.* The name—Win-Win Discipline—indicates that teachers and students both win, or benefit from using the approach. The goal is to help students develop *lifelong responsible behavior.* In order

to be fully effective, the Win-Win process requires a classroom environment that consistently emphasizes and supports a "we" approach that gives teachers and students a joint interest in maintaining responsible behavior. Kagan refers to the "we approach" as *teacher–student same-side collaboration*.

2. *Three pillars of Win-Win Discipline.* **Three pillars** form the philosophical structure of Win-Win Discipline. They are (1) *same side*, meaning students, teachers, and sometimes others all work together on the same side to enhance the school experience for students; (2) *collaborative solutions*, meaning students and teachers cooperate in formulating workable solutions to discipline problems; and (3) *learned responsibility*, meaning students acquire the desire to behave appropriately as they practice self-management and the skills of getting along with others.

3. *Class rules.* Win-Win Discipline makes use of **class rules**, which are agreements worked out cooperatively by teacher and students. You can have the class begin by discussing what they believe to be responsible behavior— you might call the result "The Way We Want Our Class to Be." Rules (agreements) are then derived from statements about responsible behavior. They should be worded simply, limited to about five in number, posted in the room for easy reference, and reviewed periodically. Students are guided in practicing the behavior associated with each rule. All the while, teachers and other adults conduct themselves in a manner that is consistent with the class rules.

   This process builds student involvement and cooperation. Students begin to behave responsibly without feeling that rules are being imposed on them. Although rules may vary somewhat from class to class, they usually turn out to be quite similar overall. Kagan suggests that the following rules are likely to emerge:

   Ready rule: Come to class ready to learn.

   Respect rule: Respect the rights and property of others.

   Request rule: Ask for help when needed.

   Offer rule: Offer help to others.

   Responsibility rule: Strive to act responsibly at all times.

   Kagan says that some teachers prefer to condense rules into only one, such as: *In our class, we agree to foster our own learning, help others learn, and allow the teacher to teach.*

4. *Attention to needs.* Kagan asks us to think of disruptions as students' ineffective efforts to meet their needs. We saw in Chapter 9 that William Glasser lists five predominant needs of students in school: survival (safety), belonging, power, fun, and freedom. Students grow noticeably uncomfortable when any of those needs is not being met. Win-Win Discipline helps students meet their needs in acceptable ways that do not disrupt teaching or learning.

WHAT DOES KAGAN SAY ABOUT PARENT AND COMMUNITY ALLIANCES AND SCHOOLWIDE PROGRAMS?

Kagan, more than most other authorities in discipline, urges teachers to establish partnerships with caregivers and the wider community to assist students in making responsible behavior choices. Caregivers and community citizens usually appreciate and support teachers who handle disruptive behavior in a positive manner. Input, support, follow-through, and backup from caregivers and other adults strengthen the likelihood of success. Teacher–parent–community cooperation depends largely on teachers reaching out to make contacts. Kagan urges you not to give up when caregivers or community members seem reluctant to participate. Continue inviting them to become actively involved.

Win-Win Discipline provides many helpful suggestions for teacher–parent–community communication and interaction. Contact with potential participants should be made during the first week of school. Phone calls, letters, class newsletters, class websites, and emails are efficient ways to connect with caregivers. Parent nights and open houses offer opportunities for person-to-person communication, showing caregivers and others they are valued as allies and possibly mentors and tutors. The broader community can become involved through field trips, guest speakers, apprenticeships, and having students work with day-care and senior centers. Schoolwide efforts in this endeavor usually bring good results.

Keep in mind that just because caregivers don't participate, there's no reason to believe that they don't care about your students. Some caregivers' schedules won't allow them to participate in activities during the school day; some won't be able to be involved in after-school experiences. Some caregivers probably had experiences when they themselves were in school that make them reluctant to get involved in their children's education, and some may just feel that they have little to contribute. Some may be reluctant to get involved because of language differences or because they are afraid a commitment will tax their financial resources. Some may not have access to the information you disseminate, especially if you do so via the Internet. Personal contact and careful consideration of each family's situation may allow you to increase involvement; even if caregivers never engage in school-related activities, keep in mind that 99 times out of 100, they love their children dearly and want what's best for them.

Commentary From Anonymous Teacher 1

Several of the principles Dr. Kagan teaches have worked effectively for me over the years, although I tweak some of them so they are better suited to my students (third grade, lower performing). For example, I regularly review class rules and expectations when it seems students are not complying with them. This is helpful not only in the beginning weeks of school, but throughout the year. At the time I am writing this, there are only 3 weeks left in our school year. Yet, only last week, as a class we reviewed our expectations and rules, not only for the classroom but for the playground, as well, helping students remember that expectations last right up through the last day of school.

One of our expectations has to do with "responsible thinking," which many of my students do not learn at home very well. For this reminder, I use role-playing (a favorite activity of my students) to help get the meaning across.

My students also respond very well to same-side chats, in which I often ask students privately if they have ideas on how we might cut down on interruptions during learning time. If no one overhears them, students usually tell me honestly what they can do to help. But if peers can hear, their responses are not so honest or helpful. I also find the "to you . . . to me" structure effective with individuals, groups, and the class as a whole. When more serious misbehavior occurs, such as name-calling or hitting, I sometimes ask students to write apology notes to the person or persons they have offended. Just last week, I asked a student to write such a note for continually teasing a girl about liking a certain boy. The unwanted behavior stopped and everyone seemed to feel okay. In that case, I kept the matter private to the persons involved.

Source: Used courtesy of Timothy C. Charles.

HOW DO I IMPLEMENT WIN-WIN DISCIPLINE IN MY CLASSROOM?

The Three Essentials

In order to implement Win-Win Discipline as intended, you must do three things. The first is to commit yourself to complying with what Kagan calls teaching's **Big Three**:

- Establish an interesting and challenging *curriculum*.
- Provide *cooperative activities* that allow students to work together meaningfully.
- Be an *interesting, stimulating teacher* who adapts the curriculum to student interests and needs.

The second is to familiarize yourself with the seven student positions and relate them to the types of misbehavior you are likely to encounter. Remember, you are to accept and validate the seven positions, but not accept the disruptive behavior associated with them.

The third is to select or design structures that help disruptive students return to responsible conduct. You will put some of these structures in place as preventive measures before classes begin; you will use others to help redirect misbehavior; and you will use still others to help students develop long-term responsibility.

Introducing Win-Win Discipline

When you introduce Win-Win Discipline, begin by setting the tone for the class. Let the students know that the class will be built on the three pillars of Win-Win Discipline—same side, collaborative solutions, and learned responsibility. You might say something like the following:

> This is our class, and with all of us working together we will create a place where each person feels comfortable and all of us can enjoy the process of learning. As your teacher, I have a responsibility to create an environment where this can happen, but I need your help to make it work. I want each of you to realize you are an important member of this class, with important responsibilities, and that you can help make the class a pleasant place for all of us. One of your main responsibilities is to help create and maintain a positive learning atmosphere where everybody's needs are met. To accomplish this, we all must work together. I suggest that we begin by creating an agreement about how we will treat each other in this class.

Next, consider creating class agreements as follows: Begin by constructing a chart with the headings *Disruptive Behavior* and *Responsible Behavior*. Under each heading write two subheadings, *Say* and *Do*. Ask the students to name some of the disruptive things people say and do when they want attention. Record their responses under *Disruptive Behavior*. Then ask the class to name some of the responsible things people say and do for attention. Record their responses under *Responsible Behavior*. Continue this process for each of the seven positions.

When you have reasonable lists, ask students, "How do you feel about these lists? Would you be willing to adopt the responsible behaviors as our class agreement? Can we agree to avoid the disruptive behaviors?" It is essential that students believe their opinions and cooperation are valued. Tell them,

> You and I need to be on the same side and work together to create a classroom we all enjoy and where everyone can learn. You will be included in the decision-making process. You will be able to have your say. We will learn and practice skills that are important for being citizens in a democratic society. Choosing responsible behavior will be one of the most important things you will learn.

During the first weeks, use activities that strengthen the concept of the three pillars. This reassures students that discipline will not be done *to* them, but will happen *with* them. In collaboration with the class, you might discuss discipline structures and their purposes, develop logical consequences and follow-ups, and solicit student input on some curriculum decisions.

You can also show students how you will help them turn disruptive behavior into positive learning situations, where reflection, follow-up, and long-term structures come into play. You can do these things in a series of class meetings. Kagan adds that very early in the school year, you should begin establishing alliances with caregivers and interested members of the community.

REMINDERS AND SUGGESTIONS

Review with your class the four types of disruptive behavior and the seven student positions associated with them. Explain that (1) disruptive behavior (which is unacceptable) consists of inappropriate actions people take in trying to meet their needs; (2) when students disrupt, they are "coming from" a particular emotional state that is natural and identifiable; and (3) for the various emotional states, there are procedures for helping students meet their needs and return to acceptable behavior.

Continuing to stress collaboration, ask students to think along with you about what could be done to help them behave more appropriately, should they misbehave. You might discuss an example such as the following:

> During a cooperative group situation, Samuel, a new boy in class, disrupts the class by standing up and calling over to Duwahn in another group. Samuel may or may not know that this behavior is inappropriate, but his action violates one of the class rules that class members have agreed on. What should be done?

In accordance with advice from Kagan, Kyle, and Scott (2004/2007), you might describe the following approach and ask for your students' reactions to it:

- Identify the category of disruption. Using Kagan's ABCD categories, we see Samuel's behavior is category B (breaking rules).
- Look beyond the behavior to identify the position Samuel is coming from. (Let's suppose you determine that Samuel's position is "being uninformed.")
- Apply a structure for the moment of disruption that is consistent with Samuel's position. You might say, "Samuel, because you are a new member of our class, you may not know, or may not remember, our rule against calling out in class. Do you remember that rule? No? Let's take just a moment to review it so you will remember it in the future."
- It is not likely you will need to say more, but if necessary you could use a follow-up structure to help Samuel make better decisions in the future. For example, you and Samuel might, in private, have a friendly same-side chat to help Samuel understand the rule against calling out and help him identify an alternative behavior that would be acceptable.

Ideally, implementation of Win-Win Discipline should begin before the school year starts, with advance preparation for procedures, routines, and materials associated with each of the seven student positions. But teachers who want to try the approach after the year has begun will find they can put Win-Win

Discipline in place at any time. You will need to teach the fundamental concepts and procedures thoroughly, but once your students are comfortable with them, the program is relatively easy to maintain.

Commentary From Anonymous Teacher 2

My first student-teaching assignment was with an eighth-grade class taught by a cool, calm, and collected master teacher. She made everything look so easy. I was young and very green and really thought if I were kind to the students they would behave nicely. As luck would have it, most of them did, but not Stevie and Nickie, twin sisters who wanted to rule the world, or at least the class. They did whatever they could to mess up my lessons and my composure, and they were very successful at both. My master teacher invited me over for dinner and gently let me know that my students didn't need another friend, they needed a Teacher, and it was up to me to become one. I learned there must be a system in place to define the "society" of the classroom. I wish I had had the insight of Win-Win to help me and the students.

In staff lounges and workrooms, or anywhere teachers congregate, you will hear some lamenting, "In addition to teaching, we have to civilize them, too!" It is true; many students come to us not really knowing how to work respectfully with others or how to be responsible for their own behavior. What I like about Kagan's plan is it doesn't overlook the power that we teachers do have: the power to create interesting lessons; the power to organize meaningful cooperative activities; the power to be a dynamic teacher. But in addition, he gives us "handles" to help us grasp how disruptions and emotions can get in the way of a peaceful and productive classroom. For me, personally, Win-Win provides a way that I can be more objective about misbehavior, more understanding of students and their emotions, and best of all, have access to a plan to help them. I really wish I could have a second chance to work with Stevie and Nickie. I know I could do better now.

Source: Used courtesy of Marilyn Charles.

Applying Kagan's Ideas: What Might They Look Like in Action?

CASE 1 Kristina Will Not Work

Kristina, a student in Mr. Jake's class, is quite docile. She socializes little with other students and never disrupts lessons. However, despite Mr. Jake's best efforts, Kristina will not do her work. She rarely completes an assignment. She is simply there, putting forth no effort at all. *What would Spencer Kagan suggest to help Kristina and Mr. Jake?*

Kagan would advise Mr. Jake to do the following: Mr. Jake would identify Kristina's problematic behavior and ask behavior-specific questions. He also would identify and help Kristina acknowledge her position. Mr. Jake might ask Kristina how she feels about the work, determining if it is too difficult for her (leading to avoidance of failure) or not interesting (leading to boredom). If the work is too difficult for Kristina, and her position is avoiding, or if she doesn't know how to do the work, he might say quietly, "I really want to help you be successful, Kristina. I see this work is not getting finished. None of us wants to tackle something we know will be too hard for us. The best thing to do if something is too hard is to break it into smaller pieces, mastering a part at a time. Another good strategy is to work on the difficult pieces with someone else. What suggestions do you have that will help you be successful?"

Together they come up with possible solutions and then, if they agree that Kristina could benefit by working with a partner on smaller pieces, Mr. Jake may ask, "Would you like to work on this section with Danielle before moving on?" Throughout the interaction, Mr. Jake is attempting to help Kristina find a nondisruptive way to meet her needs. But more importantly, Mr. Jake is helping Kristina internalize a process of validating her own needs and seeking responsible rather than disruptive ways to fulfill them. As follow-up, Mr. Jake might focus on her success by saying something like "Kristina, I knew you could do this. We made the pieces smaller. That's a strategy you can use with other assignments going forward." His long-term solutions will include further encouragement and individual attention to Kristina's strengths.

CASE 2 Sara Will Not Stop Talking

Sara is a pleasant girl who participates in class activities and does most, though not all, of her assigned work. She cannot seem to refrain from talking to classmates, however. Her teacher, Mr. Gonzales, has to speak to her repeatedly during lessons, to the point that he often becomes exasperated and loses his temper. *What suggestions would Spencer Kagan give Mr. Gonzales for dealing with Sara?*

CASE 3 Joshua Clowns and Intimidates

Joshua, larger and louder than his classmates, always wants to be the center of attention, which he accomplishes through a combination of clowning and intimidation. He makes wise remarks, talks back (smilingly) to the teacher, utters a variety of sound-effect noises such as automobile crashes and gunshots, and makes limitless sarcastic comments and put-downs of his classmates. Other students will not stand up to him, apparently fearing his size and verbal aggression. His teacher, Miss Pearl, has come to her wit's end. *Would Joshua's behavior be likely to improve if Win-Win Discipline were used in Miss Pearl's classroom? Explain.*

CASE 4 Tom Is Hostile and Defiant

Tom has appeared to be in his usual foul mood ever since arriving in class. On his way to sharpen his pencil, he bumps into Frank, who complains. Tom tells him loudly to shut up. Miss Baines, the teacher, says, "Tom, go back to your seat." Tom wheels around, swears loudly, and says heatedly, "I'll go when I'm *&$#^ good and ready!" *How would Tom's behavior be handled in a Win-Win classroom?*

You Are the Teacher

SEVENTH-GRADE SCIENCE

Your seventh-grade science students have been working on group projects together for several days. Each group selected a topic related to the structure and function of living organisms. Some topics chosen by students included plant cells; animal cells; the organization of multi-cellular organisms from cells to tissues to organs to systems to organisms; and the general functions of the major systems of the human body (digestion, reproduction, respiration, circulation, and excretion). Student assignments consisted of a variety of parts, including the creation of a visual aid to help others understand the presented material. Students generally work pretty well in groups in your class, but you have a couple of students whose behavior in collaborative situations is challenging.

A TYPICAL OCCURRENCE

On the final day of the unit, students are asked to post their visual aids in assigned spaces around the classroom. Most groups have created posters or other two-dimensional visuals that you have them hang up on the walls; one group, however, created a 3-D clay model of a cell. You direct them to display it on a table at the back of the room in preparation for a "gallery walk," where students circulate through the room looking at one another's projects. As they move through the exhibits, students are supposed to complete a short evaluation sheet about their peers' projects; they are to provide feedback on visual appeal, clarity of content, and other aspects of the work.

You ask each group to stand in front of another group's project in preparation for beginning the gallery walk. While you're making sure that the students are in the right places and have their evaluation sheets and pencils, Toby, whose group is standing by the soft clay model of the cell, reaches out and presses down on it a little, laughing as he does so. The other students call your attention to the situation. You realize that the model is not significantly damaged.

CONCEPTUALIZING A STRATEGY

If you followed Kagan's suggestions, what would you do with regard to the following?
- Categorizing the behavior according to Kagan's ABCD model
- Identifying the position(s) from which Toby might have been operating
- Choosing a structure for the moment of disruption
- Maintaining student dignity and good personal relations
- Using follow-up procedures to prevent the recurrence of the misbehavior
- Helping the students involved develop increased responsibility and self-control

REFLECTING ON KAGAN'S RECOMMENDATIONS: WHAT YOU HAVE LEARNED IN THIS CHAPTER

Predominant Themes in Kagan's Work

Learning should be a meaningful, engaging, and cooperative activity. Teachers' interpersonal skills and methods for communicating with students are critical to the class experience; preserving student dignity should always be a consideration, as should interacting in ways that are positive, civil, and humane.

Effective managers focus on preventing, not just reacting to, misbehavior.

Students benefit from learning how to manage themselves and their emotions. Teachers and students who view themselves as being on the same team are likely to have smoother relationships.

Student needs impact their behavior.

Class meetings are a useful way of building relationships and involving students in the problem-solving process.

Students grow in important ways when they realize that their behaviors are the results of choices they make and that they can make better choices when the situation calls for it.

Kagan's approach to classroom management incorporates many of the themes we identified in Chapter 4. The collaborative, supportive framework of his approach helps teachers maintain a focus on positive, productive classroom relationships. The structures Kagan uses to categorize and respond to student behaviors help teachers operationalize the problem-solving process.

Table 11.1 explores Kagan's foundational principles, along with potential positives associated with them. It also gives you questions to consider about his recommendations. Remember to take notes in your planning guide as you reflect.

Table 11.1

Kagan's Ideas	Potential Positives	Questions to Consider
Classroom management works best when teachers and students approach situations from the same side and look for solutions where no one "loses."	Adversarial relationships are less likely to develop, and a cooperative class spirit is likely to evolve.	• Are there aspects of the school/classroom experience that couldn't be approached from a same-side stance? If so, how does a teacher explain those to students? • What happens when a teacher has an off-day and slips back into a more authoritarian win-lose system? • How is time use in classes likely affected by the use of win-win approaches?

(continued)

Table 11.1 (continued)

Kagan's Ideas	Potential Positives	Questions to Consider
Students behave inappropriately because of their emotional position—often related to an attempt to meet needs.	When teachers identify the reason behind misbehavior, it is more likely that they will be able to help the student toward long-term change.	• What happens when students aren't self-aware enough to be able to identify their position and its impact on their behavior? • What is the role of student development (think Piaget) in the implementation of this model? Could this model be used with primary-grade students?
Teachers should apply structures for intervening in instances of ineffective behavior.	Knowing what structure matches well with which behavior and position gives teachers a certain degree of automaticity in responding to concerns, both in the moment of disruption and over the longer term.	• How does the use of structures promote the prevention of misbehavior? • What do teachers do when confronted with behaviors for which they don't have an existing structure ready?
Teachers should present an engaging, interesting curriculum.	When students are interested in the material under study, they are less likely to misbehave.	• How do teachers, especially beginning teachers, attend to all aspects of management and the logistics of teaching and still find time to develop lessons that are engaging and high impact? • What strategies can a teacher use when the curriculum that must be taught contains elements that are dry or seemingly less relevant to students?

MyLab Education Self-Check 11.1
MyLab Education Self-Check 11.2
MyLab Education Application Exercise 11.1 Identifying Categories of Behavior and Student Positions
MyLab Education Application Exercise 11.2 Win-Win Discipline in Action

12

Positive Behavior Interventions and Supports: A Data-Driven, Evidence-Based Approach to Whole-School Behavioral Management

What Happens When Schools Develop a Universally Applicable Set of Behavioral Expectations and Responses?

LEARNING OUTCOMES:

12-1 Describe the PBIS framework and the broad classroom management themes to which it corresponds.

12-2 Consider the strengths and weaknesses of the PBIS framework and evaluate its likely utility in various situational contexts.

As you've read about the classroom management programs and strategies put forth, you may have thought to yourself, "Well, what happens if, in *my* classroom, I adopt and use a certain set of expectations, but other teachers in my grade level or school approach classroom management from a completely different angle?" This situation, as you might imagine, can cause some confusion for students, who have to navigate different expectations in different school settings. What if, during first period, Daquan has Mr. Mendoza, who has adopted a student-centered, democratic approach to classroom management, but for second period has Ms. Michaelson, who prides herself on running a "tight ship" and expects students to comply with no questions asked? While many students can and do adapt to behaving differently according to teachers' different expectations, some students will really struggle with meeting one set of expectations for one teacher and a different set of expectations for another.

A growing management trend in schools is called Positive Behavioral Intervention and Supports (PBIS); you may also hear this management model referred to as School-Wide Positive Behavior Support (SWPBS). PBIS is currently in use in over 23,000 schools, including urban, rural, and suburban settings; it has even been used successfully within the juvenile justice system (pbis.org).

PBIS can be described as a systematic, team-based structure that focuses on prevention and early intervention rather than on remediating problem behaviors or using punishment in response to inappropriate behavior. Schools that adopt the PBIS framework do so because they want to establish and maintain a positive school climate, reduce disciplinary referrals, and increase time available for instruction.

According to the pbis.org website, which is maintained by the U.S. Department of Education's Office of Special Education Programs Technical Assistance Center, all PBIS schools share seven components:

> *a) an agreed upon and common approach to discipline, b) a positive statement of purpose, c) a small number of positively stated expectations for all students and staff, d) procedures for teaching these expectations to students, e) a continuum of procedures for encouraging displays and maintenance of these expectations, f) a continuum of procedures for discouraging displays of rule-violating behavior, and g) procedures for monitoring and evaluating the effectiveness of the discipline system on a regular and frequent basis.* (U.S. Department of Education, Tier 1 FAQs, n.d.)

Schools that adopt the PBIS model develop a schoolwide framework that sets out how all students are expected to behave in all school settings as well as how all school personnel will respond to both appropriate and inappropriate behavior. Students in PBIS schools understand that behavioral expectations will be consistent across all their classes; furthermore, they know that behavioral expectations will be the same in non-classroom settings like the cafeteria, the auditorium, and the hallways.

Commentary From Anonymous Teacher 1

I have been using PBIS in my current school for three years. Our theme is BEARS. We have a poster-sized matrix of behaviors that students are expected to follow at locations all around the school. I even created a song called "BEARS Hunt" that incorporates our positive behaviors in the format of the "Going on a Bear Hunt" song. So instead of looking for the bear in the swamp, lake, and forest, we follow the BEARS rules all around the school. It is catchy for students to learn and a fun way to teach schoolwide behaviors.

Figure 12.1 shows you the Behavior Matrix used in this teacher's school.

Figure 12.1

Expectations	Classroom	Bus	Hallway	Cafeteria	Bathroom
B= Best Effort	Do your best. Be on task. Begin with the end in mind.	Bottom to bottom, back to back	Walk and move carefully.	Practice good manners.	Wash hands and throw away trash.
E= Encourage Others	Use kind words. Share. Help others. Be a leader.	Be a good example to others. Be in charge of yourself.	Smile and wave. Be an example to others	Use kind words.	Make good choices in front of other students.
A=Act Responsibly	Be in charge of yourself. Fix your mistakes. Ask for help. Be proactive.	Keep hands, feet and objects to yourself. Listen.	Stay in control even when no one is watching	Clean up after yourself Keep hands, feet, and objects to yourself.	Wash hands and throw away trash. Leave the bathroom nicer than you found it.
R= Respect	Look at and listen to the speaker.	Listen to the bus driver and the bus assistant.	Walk quietly.	Talk in quiet voices. Clean up after yourself.	Flush the toilet, wash your hands, and clean up after yourself.
S= Safety	Follow directions. Keep hands, feet, and objects to yourself.	Stay seated. Keep hands and feet to yourself.	Walk. Stay to the right and use handrails.	Wait patiently. Walk in the correct direction.	Lock your door. Keep feet on the floor. Wash your hands.

WHAT IS PBIS?

The notion of PBIS has been around since 1997, when the Individuals with Disabilities Education Act (IDEA) was reauthorized. PBIS was originally intended for use with students with behavioral disorders who were served under IDEA, but by 2000, the focus had shifted to providing behavioral support for all students, regardless of ability or disability.

It's important for you to know that PBIS is not a fixed program of school-wide behavior management; it is not a prepackaged management program. Instead, it is described as

> an implementation framework that is designed to enhance academic and social behavior outcomes for all students by (a) emphasizing the use of data for informing decisions about the selection, implementation, and progress

monitoring of evidence-based behavioral practices; and (b) organizing resources and systems to improve durable implementation fidelity. (Sugai & Simonsen, 2012, p. 1; U.S. Department of Education)

Let's see if we can deconstruct that definition to make it more comprehensible.

Definition point 1: designed to enhance academic and social behavior outcomes for all students

Schools that adopt the PBIS framework are focusing not just on students' academic progress, but also on enhancing their prosocial behaviors, because when students hone their social skills, their academic progress is likely to be positively affected. Because PBIS is a framework, not a fixed program, each school can identify the prosocial skills on which they'll focus; they identify the particular skills and behaviors that match their institution's mission, vision, and values. For instance, some schools may focus on helping their students grow in the areas of responsibility and respect, while others may focus on making sure their students are safe and demonstrating integrity. In general, schools identify three to five target behaviors that serve as the basis for their model.

Definition Point 2: emphasizing the use of data for informing decisions about the selection, implementation, and progress monitoring of evidence-based behavioral practices

As they develop their model, representatives from a PBIS school (teachers, administrators, school staff, parents, and sometimes even students) look at the nature and scope of the school's behavioral challenges. They look to see not only how many problem behaviors are occurring (typically determined by the number of students receiving disciplinary referrals), but also what sort of problems are occurring. (Are many students late to school or class? Are there frequent instances of disrespect? Are students behaving aggressively?) The school also investigates when behavioral problems are occurring (mornings? afternoons? during transitions?), where they're occurring (in the classroom? in the cafeteria? in the hallways?), and who is involved (do many students misbehave infrequently, or is there a core group of regular "offenders"?). You'll see examples of the data schools might collect later in this chapter.

Once they've identified a baseline of school behavior, the PBIS team members figure out what areas of concern they want to address, which strategies they will use to acknowledge and encourage positive behavior, and which methods they'll use to intervene in cases of inappropriate behavior. The strategies they use aren't just pulled out of the air, but are based on evidence of appropriateness and usefulness in improving student behavior. PBIS schools work to avoid using exclusionary consequences like suspension and dismissal; instead, they directly teach appropriate behaviors.

Definition Point 3: organizing resources and systems to improve durable implementation fidelity

In a PBIS school, systems are put into place to ensure that all staff members are on the same page about what is expected and how they'll implement the system. As you can imagine, this outcome requires a great deal of planning, professional development, monitoring, and communication; getting everybody in a school to use the same approach is a significant (but worthwhile) undertaking.

PBIS: Core Principles

There are seven core principles of PBIS (pbis.org, Tier 1 Supports, n.d; U.S. Department of Education). They are paraphrased here:

1. *All children can behave appropriately, and appropriate behavior can be taught.* A staff member at a PBIS school might say, "If students don't know how to write a paragraph, we teach them. If students don't know how to balance an equation, we teach them. And if a student doesn't know how to interact appropriately in the classroom, we have to teach them that, too; using punishments to change behavior is simply not effective."

2. *Early intervention works best.* Prevention is the key, not only to effective management, but to students' continued social and academic growth and development. All members of the school community should work to prevent misbehavior, and to monitor and then act in instances where misbehavior is occurring or seems likely to occur.

3. *Deliver support and intervention at the minimal level required to promote acceptable behavior.* PBIS identifies tiers of support and intervention; students receive supports at the level appropriate to their needs. Some students just need to know what the expectations are; others need more direct intervention to help them replace inappropriate behaviors with acceptable ones. You'll read more about these levels of support later in the chapter.

4. *When intervening, use strategies and methods that have been shown to be effective.* To the extent possible, all members of the staff in a PBIS school use interventions that are research based and scientifically validated; they typically opt for positive, instructional strategies as opposed to punishments and exclusionary strategies. Many, many resources exist to help teachers and their colleagues identify appropriate interventions; keep in mind, however, that not all interventions that are identified as being PBIS-appropriate are necessarily research based. If you're in a PBIS school, you'll work with a behavior team to help match needed supports to student behavior challenges.

5. *Use frequent monitoring as a way of determining what's working and what needs to be changed.* A strategy is only working if the desired outcome is achieved. Once an intervention is underway, teachers need to evaluate how well it is working. If the desired outcome is not achieved, school personnel must modify the intervention until it does work, or they must change to a different form of support. In most cases, PBIS behavior teams recommend that an intervention be tried for a specific period of time (e.g., 4 weeks)

before any decision is made about its effectiveness. It's important that any intervention be applied with *fidelity*; in other words, a given intervention should be delivered in the same manner by any member of the school community and in any location within the school.

6. *Data should drive decision making.* Teachers and other school staff members collect and use data to determine how well interventions are working. While professional judgment does play a role in these determinations, it must be supported by evidence regarding behavior. PBIS schools don't leave teachers to flounder, though; trained team members provide support and guidance as teachers work to enhance student behavior.

7. *Assessment serves three different purposes.* As we mentioned earlier, PBIS schools first collect disciplinary referral data. Further, PBIS leadership and behavior team members review data to determine the scope and nature of behavior problems. And finally, team members assess data about the effectiveness of supports and interventions, using what they find to help school personnel refine or revise their strategies.

The Collaborative Nature of PBIS

If you were teaching in a PBIS school, you would not be on your own in terms of figuring out how to set up your classroom management system. Nor would you be alone in trying to determine what strategies to use to address inappropriate behavior when it occurs. As you might expect, given its schoolwide nature, PBIS implementation relies on the "hive mind." PBIS schools typically form a team made up of members of the school community—regular teachers, special education teachers, administrators, parents, and others—who meet to help match interventions to student needs. This behavior support team often serves not only as leadership for the school's PBIS implementation in general, but also meets regularly to consider what interventions might be best for students who are in need of Tier 2 or Tier 3 support.

Why Is PBIS Growing in Popularity?

You've heard many times as you've worked through this text that classroom management is a high-level concern for teachers, and of course, that's true. But perhaps you haven't stopped to consider that when students are exhibiting what might seem to be minor misbehaviors, they can be on a fast track to exhibiting more serious ones.

Lewis, Mitchell, Trussell, and Newcomer (2015) report on studies that indicate a correlation between the sorts of low-level, nonviolent offenses that occur at schools (e.g., defiance, disrespect) and later emergence of more significant or violent behaviors. Research has shown that, while teachers in general are concerned about an increase in violence, particularly at the middle and high school levels, they are also seriously concerned that "minor offenses such as verbal intimidation, threats, shoving, and harassment were escalating at a far greater rate than more serious violations" (p. 41). The PBIS model is designed to break this cycle.

Further, Lewis, Mitchell, Trussell, and Newcomer (2015) report on studies that show that teachers in non-PBIS schools spend more time on reactive and punitive measures than they do on prevention and positivity. The PBIS framework is designed upon the core belief that when schools focus on preventing minor misbehaviors and on establishing and maintaining a positive school climate, there is likely to be less escalation of problem behaviors. In addition, each member of the school community is more likely to feel that school is an emotionally safe and enjoyable place to be. PBIS schools embrace the idea that the best way to provide this sort of environment is to use a whole-school approach, sustain a positive school climate, and teach students needed skills for managing their emotions and behavior.

The 3-Tiered Structure of PBIS

PBIS is designed primarily to help teachers anticipate and prevent behavior problems. However, as we know, all students are likely to misbehave at some time, and some students are likely to misbehave frequently. The PBIS structure is designed in such a way that it helps teachers and school staff members prevent as much misbehavior as possible, and then to respond consistently when misbehavior does occur.

In terms of implementation, PBIS can be thought of as a 3-tiered system (see Figure 12.2 for a visual representation of the structure).

The bottom part of the pyramid, Tier 1, reflects *universal supports*. Universal supports are designed and implemented primarily as a means of encouraging positive behavior and preventing misbehavior; they're used with all students in the school. Some examples of Tier 1 supports include clear expectations (rules and procedures), schoolwide recognition of positive behaviors, and direct teaching of prosocial behaviors. Though precise numbers vary, schools implementing the PBIS framework generally expect about 80% of students to need no more support or intervention than what is given at this level.

Figure 12.2

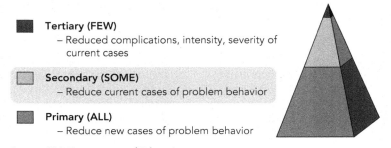

Tertiary (FEW)
– Reduced complications, intensity, severity of current cases

Secondary (SOME)
– Reduce current cases of problem behavior

Primary (ALL)
– Reduce new cases of problem behavior

Source: U.S. Department of Education

The middle section of the pyramid, Tier 2, reflects the fact that some students, generally about 15% in most schools, will need more than just preventive strategies to manage their behavior. Tier 2 supports reflect high-efficiency, rapid response small-group or individual interventions for these students; these interventions reflect evidence-based practices that have been shown to lead to positive student outcomes. Tier 2 supports might include supplementary social skills training, daily check-ins with an adult, and evidence-based classroom behavioral interventions such as self-monitoring, completion of daily behavior forms, and behavior contracting. When a PBIS school develops its implementation plan, a standard is set for when Tier 2 supports would be used with students; for instance, a school might decide that when a student has been referred to the office for disciplinary reasons three to five times, initiating Tier 2 supports is appropriate.

The top section of the pyramid, Tier 3, represents the sort of individualized, intensive intervention that is needed by students who don't respond to Tier 2 strategies. These supports are generally used with about 5% of a school's student population, often those who have had more than five disciplinary referrals (though, of course, each school can set its own standards for when Tier 3 intervention kicks in).

Tier 3 interventions are generally used when inappropriate behavior is dangerous, highly disruptive, or an impediment to learning for the student and/or classmates. The goal is to diminish the problem behaviors and move the student toward more appropriate behavioral choices. Interventions at this level include functional behavioral assessment ("In what context(s) does the behavior occur? What purpose is this inappropriate behavior serving for the student, and how can we find an alternative that meets that same need/function?") and a support plan designed to move the student's behavior forward. A support plan might include identifying new skills that the student could use to replace the inappropriate behavior; these skills are then taught directly to the student, and school personnel provide guidance about moving toward them, instead of relying on the inappropriate behavior.

To make sure you have a firm grasp on the kind of thinking that goes into a PBIS plan and how behaviors are differentiated among the three tiers, we're including the following Discipline Flowchart (Figure 12.3). It shows the thought processes and strategies a teacher follows when using PBIS to manage behavior.

Tier 1 in Depth

Universal supports are those that are, well, universal. They're provided for and used with all students in the school, in all settings, and at all times of day throughout the school year. Tier 1 supports can be thought of as the foundation of the PBIS framework; although they may vary from school to school, they generally include certain expectations and experiences designed to anticipate and prevent inappropriate behavior, such as these described by Sugai and colleagues (2010):

Figure 12.3

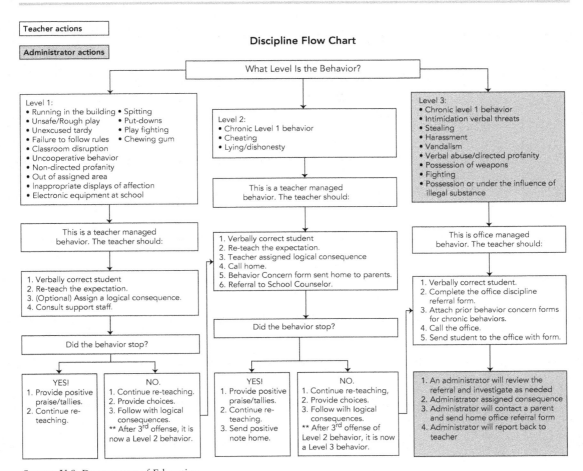

Discipline Flow Chart

Teacher actions

Administrator actions

What Level Is the Behavior?

Level 1:
- Running in the building
- Unsafe/Rough play
- Unexcused tardy
- Failure to follow rules
- Classroom disruption
- Uncooperative behavior
- Non-directed profanity
- Out of assigned area
- Inappropriate displays of affection
- Electronic equipment at school
- Spitting
- Put-downs
- Play fighting
- Chewing gum

This is a teacher managed behavior. The teacher should:

1. Verbally correct student
2. Re-teach the expectation.
3. (Optional) Assign a logical consequence.
4. Consult support staff.

Did the behavior stop?

YES!
1. Provide positive praise/tallies.
2. Continue re-teaching.

NO.
1. Continue re-teaching.
2. Provide choices.
3. Follow with logical consequences.
** After 3rd offense, it is now a Level 2 behavior.

Level 2:
- Chronic Level 1 behavior
- Cheating
- Lying/dishonesty

This is a teacher managed behavior. The teacher should:

1. Verbally correct student
2. Re-teach the expectation.
3. Teacher assigned logical consequence
4. Call home.
5. Behavior Concern form sent home to parents.
6. Referral to School Counselor.

Did the behavior stop?

YES!
1. Provide positive praise/tallies.
2. Continue re-teaching.
3. Send positive note home.

NO.
1. Continue re-teaching,
2. Provide choices.
3. Follow with logical consequences.
** After 3rd offense of Level 2 behavior, it is now a Level 3 behavior.

Level 3:
- Chronic level 1 behavior
- Intimidation verbal threats
- Stealing
- Harassment
- Vandalism
- Verbal abuse/directed profanity
- Possession of weapons
- Fighting
- Possession or under the influence of illegal substance

This is office managed behavior. The teacher should:

1. Verbally correct student.
2. Complete the office discipline referral form.
3. Attach prior behavior concern forms for chronic behaviors.
4. Call the office.
5. Send student to the office with form.

1. An administrator will review the referral and investigate as needed
2. Administrator assigned consequence
3. Administrator will contact a parent and send home office referral form
4. Administrator will report back to teacher

Source: U.S. Department of Education

- ■ *a statement of purpose that includes desired behavioral and academic outcomes for students.* All members of the school community agree to work toward a particular set of behavioral and academic outcomes, and to use the PBIS framework to move students toward these outcomes. Remember that the main goal of universal supports is to anticipate and prevent misbehavior.
- ■ *a clear definition of the behaviors that are expected of students.* The school identifies the constructive behaviors students are expected to exhibit; these are few in number and stated positively. For instance, one expectation might be "We are respectful" (as opposed to "No arguing or backtalk"). The focus is on what the students *should* do, not what they *shouldn't* do.

■ *procedures for teaching the expected behaviors, and reinforcing them with students.* As with other models we've discussed, teachers in PBIS schools actively teach students the expected behaviors. For instance, if one behavioral expectation for students is to "Be safe," the teachers might take them through exercises designed to explore what behaviors are and are not safe across a variety of classroom and non-classroom settings. What does it look like to be safe in the art classroom? What sorts of behaviors would be unsafe in the restroom? In PBIS schools, the desired prosocial behaviors are taught directly and reinforced consistently.

■ *procedures for discouraging inappropriate behaviors.* Although expected behaviors are identified and taught to students, PBIS schools still have to have plans in place for addressing inappropriate behavior. In a PBIS school, there might be a standard low-level response to students who use inappropriate language ("Mattias, that language is not respectful. Please don't use it anymore; if you do, you'll need to complete a Think Sheet to help you come up with a better choice."). For students who do not respond to the low-level (universal) response, there might need to be a more focused intervention. A Tier 2 response might be, "Let's talk about what words you could use in place of those inappropriate ones." The teacher might provide a Social Skills lesson to a small group of students who struggle with appropriate word choices. If Tier 2 responses do not produce the desired result (note that any intervention has to be given time to work; it's not expected to be a "once and done" thing), other Tier 2 interventions might be tried and data collected about their effectiveness. If, after a set time period, Mattias is still exhibiting inappropriate language, he might be moved toward Tier 3 (targeted individual) interventions.

■ *procedures for record keeping and decision making.* In PBIS schools, the leadership team examines data to establish baselines and to gauge the impact of interventions at all three levels.

Data Collection in Depth

You might be curious about the sort of data that schools use as they begin to flesh out their PBIS plans. Figures 12.4–12.10 give examples of the sorts of data that might drive a school's decisions. As you view these figures, what conclusions can you draw about what this school's focus might be?

As you can see, schools collect and utilize a great deal of data when figuring out their approach to a schoolwide management system.

Tier 2 in Depth

You're probably curious about what happens when students in a PBIS school need more intervention than what is given as part of Tier 1. Tier 2 interventions are typically used with small groups of students, or are used with individual students

Figure 12.4

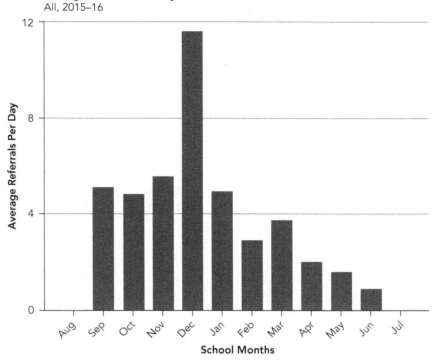

Average Referrals Per Day Per Month
All, 2015–16

What are some plausible reasons that might explain the large spike in referrals in December? Can you use this data to "tell the story" of what behavior looked like in this school in the 2015–2016 school year?

Source: U.S. Department of Education

when a relatively simple intervention is likely to effect change. Tier 2 interventions are usually entered into with the guidance of the school's behavior support team (pbis.org, Tier 2 FAQ section, n.d.).

There are many, many interventions that can occur at the Tier 2 level, but we'll give you a couple of examples here so you get the idea of how Tier 2 interventions might look.

One Tier 2 intervention is called Check In, Check Out, also known as CICO (Crone, Hawken, & Horner, 2010). Research has shown that Check In, Check Out is effective in improving student behavior. CICO can be used in any number of situations, but is especially appropriate when a student has been disrespectful, has not completed work, and/or creates low-level disruptions in school.

When a student uses CICO, she is set up with an adult mentor in the school community; each morning when the student arrives, she checks in with her adult mentor/guide. During check-in, the adult and the student check the student's preparation for the day and talk about the student's attitude and how she's feeling. The mentor reminds the student of the behavioral expectations for the day,

Figure 12.5

Given what you see in this graph, can you identify some areas a PBIS leadership team might identify for universal expectations (rules/goals) for all students?

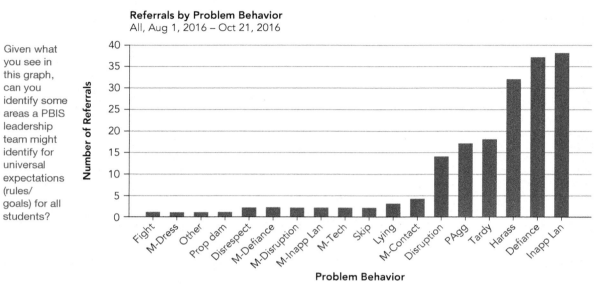

Referrals by Problem Behavior
All, Aug 1, 2016 – Oct 21, 2016

Note: PAgg means Physical Aggression. When you see the letter M before a behavior category, it means "Minor."

Source: U.S. Department of Education

Figure 12.6

It's probably not surprising that most referrals originate in classes, because that's where most students spend most of their school days. But if you look at the other places where disciplinary referrals are originating, what patterns do you see? Might you be able to make any recommendation to a school's PBIS leadership team about which non-classroom settings need attention?

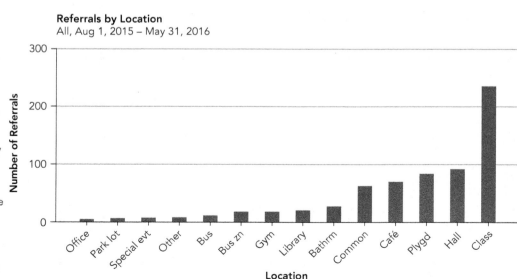

Referrals by Location
All, Aug 1, 2015 – May 31, 2016

Source: U.S. Department of Education

Figure 12.7

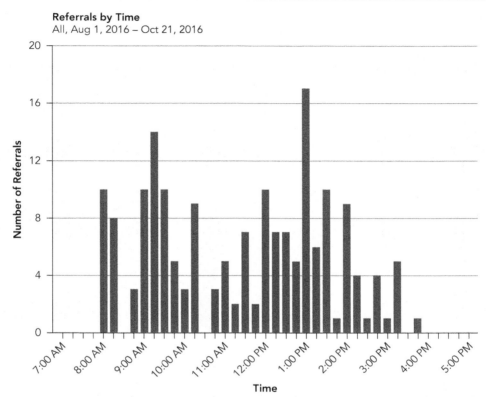

Referrals by Time
All, Aug 1, 2016 – Oct 21, 2016

What possible explanations can you think of that would explain the spikes in referrals at 9:15 and 1:00?

Source: U.S. Department of Education

and gives the student a goal card that the student will share with her teachers and others in the school community throughout the day. Those adults give the student feedback about how well she is meeting the goals. (Sample goals on the card generally align with the school's identified prosocial behaviors, such as being respectful, being responsible, and being safe.)

During the day, in both classroom and non-classroom settings, the student takes the goal card to the teacher or adult in charge; the adult thanks the student for checking in, then rates the student's performance (on a scale of 0 to 2, for instance) and gives the student feedback on what was done well and what additional changes would improve things. Criticism is not part of these conversations; an adult who gave the student 1 point for behavior in the hallway would not say, "Your behavior in the hall today was pretty bad. I'm surprised you didn't keep it together better than that." Instead, that adult might say, "Today after Period 1 you earned one point for keeping your hands to yourself in the hallway, because I saw you touching Elise when she was at her locker. When

Figure 12.8

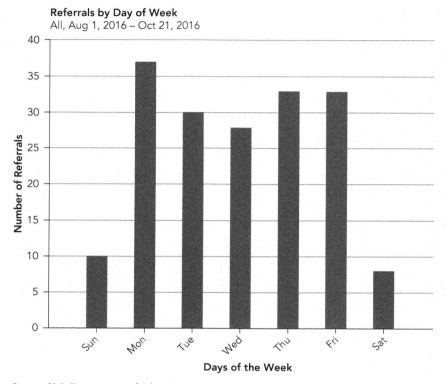

Referrals by Day of Week
All, Aug 1, 2016 – Oct 21, 2016

What sense can you make of these data? Monday has the highest number of referrals; what hypotheses can you make about why that might be the case?

Source: U.S. Department of Education

you're in the hallway again after Period 2, you can earn two points by keeping your hands to yourself."

At the end of the day, the student takes the goal card back to the assigned adult mentor; the adult reviews the card, totals the points, acknowledges the positive behaviors, and provides encouragement for continued improvement. Then the adult gives the card back to the student, who takes it home for a parent/caregiver signature. That card is turned in the next morning when the student checks in with her mentor, and the process starts over again. The mentoring adult keeps data on the student's progress with CICO and uses the data to help make determinations about how well it's working and whether its use can be discontinued or should be modified.

CICO has been shown to be effective in numerous investigations; students engaged in CICO tend to show a decrease in inappropriate behavior and an increase in prosocial behavior. CICO is generally reported by teachers, students, and parents to be effective and efficient (Lewis, Mitchell, Trussell, & Newcomer, 2015).

A second Tier 2 intervention is the use of Social Skills Instructional Groups. In this intervention, social skills are taught directly to students. The

Figure 12.9

This graph is fictitious, but it seems to show that there are some students whose behavior is significantly more concerning than that of their peers. Do you see how this data could lead a PBIS behavior team to differentiate among students who need supports at the different levels of the PBIS model?

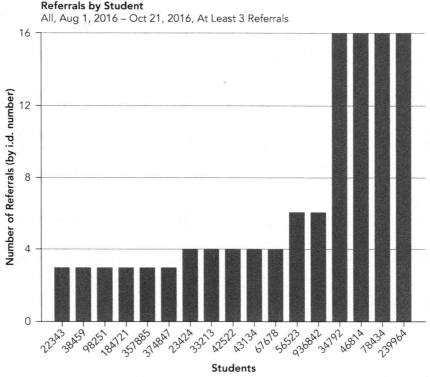

Referrals by Student
All, Aug 1, 2016 – Oct 21, 2016, At Least 3 Referrals

Source: U.S. Department of Education

idea is that students are taught the skill, then work with teachers and peers to practice the skill. Ultimately, social skills instruction is considered successful when students reduce their inappropriate behavior and use the new skill in novel situations.

Commentary From Anonymous Teacher 2

My kindergarten students participated in these social skills groups last year and they were very beneficial to learning skills to apply in class. Sharing, communication of feelings, kindness to others, and listening were among these skills. Empowerment education was used in conjunction with these social skills groups to help students self-regulate their own emotions.

Figure 12.10 ■ Sample CICO Goal Card

Student Name:			Date:						Adult Initials
GOAL	**Responsibility**			**Respect**		**Safety**			
	Complete and turn in my work; do what I should be doing			Use polite language		Sit quietly with my hands to myself			
Period 1	2	1	0	2	1	0	2	1	0	
Hallway	2	1	0	2	1	0	2	1	0	
Period 2	2	1	0	2	1	0	2	1	0	
Hallway	2	1	0	2	1	0	2	1	0	
Period 3	2	1	0	2	1	0	2	1	0	
Hallway	2	1	0	2	1	0	2	1	0	
Cafeteria	2	1	0	2	1	0	2	1	0	
Period 4	2	1	0	2	1	0	2	1	0	
Hallway	2	1	0	2	1	0	2	1	0	
Total Points									
CICO Mentor Signature									
Parent Signature									

Source: U.S. Department of Education

A social skills lesson might look something like this:

> The teacher introduces and defines the particular social skill goal. Then the teacher describes the skill, explains why it's useful, and identifies steps involved in demonstrating the skill. The teacher follows the telling with "showing" the students—modeling the skill for them, providing both examples and non-examples. The teacher and students might talk about the purpose of the skill, and why it's preferable to other (less appropriate) behaviors that they might use.

> The teacher and students might then move into a "Do" phase of the lesson, where the students define the skill and identify the steps in demonstrating it. Then the students role-play use of the new behavior/skill, and other students provide feedback on the demo. The teacher monitors their progress as they practice the skill, and perhaps even lets them move into pairs to continue to practice and provide feedback to one another. At the conclusion of the lesson, the teacher gives the students an assignment that involves practice of the skill, and then quickly gives feedback on the day's session.

So, how might this look? Well, let's say that Mr. Tejera has a small group of students who are struggling to find ways to connect with their peers; despite the school's focus on being responsible and respectful, students in this little group don't initiate interactions appropriately with classmates. In fact, the students in this group are a little socially awkward, and they tend to seek attention by annoying others in the class. A social skills lesson with these students might go like this:

So, today, we're going to talk about one way to get along with other people. Sometimes it's difficult for us to find positive ways to get other people to be our friends, but you know what? There are some things you can do to show other people that you're interested in getting along with them, and to get to know them in ways that don't annoy them.

One of the things you can do to start growing a friendship is that when you see someone you'd like to get to know better, you can start a conversation with them. And one of the best ways to get other people to talk is to ask them questions about themselves. Almost everybody likes it when other people are interested in them, so today we're going to practice our best "getting to know you" skills. We're going to learn to ask people questions about themselves and practice using those conversations to start building friendships.

When you're trying to make a new friend, or even become better friends with someone you already know a little bit, it's nice to ask them questions about themselves. I can think of some questions that I would like people to ask me, like, "What is your favorite thing to do on the weekends?" or "What is something you'd really like to learn to do?" When we ask people questions about themselves, we show them that we're interested in them, and it gives us a starting point for more conversation.

Now, when you're asking questions to make friends, it's good to ask questions that don't just have yes or no answers. If I say, "Do you like dogs?" then the person I'm talking to can just say yes or no, and that's not a very interesting conversation. But if I say, "Out of all the animals you could have for a pet, which is your favorite and why?," I'm likely to hear not only about which animal they like, but also about what they think is cool about that animal. I might be able to ask them more about what they know about that sort of animal . . . what does it eat? Have they ever had one as a pet? What was that like? Pretty soon we're having a conversation about animals, and that's one topic I love!

Now, of course, your questions don't just have to be about animals. Let's make a list of some other questions we can ask when we want to start a conversation with someone.

After the list has been made, the teacher might say, "Okay, Now I want to practice using my question-asking skills. I'm going to show you how I'd do this. Cynthia, will you pretend we don't know each other at all? I'm going to go up to Cynthia, and I'm going to say, 'Hi. My name is Mr. Tejera, and I saw you were sitting here by yourself, so I decided to come talk with you. I was wondering, what is your very favorite book you have read so far this year?'" Cynthia would, we hope, answer, and Mr. Tejara might continue the conversation by asking more questions.

Once that role-play is done, Mr. Tejera might put the students into pairs and tell one student in each pair that they're going to practice asking questions. He would likely remind them that they could choose a question from the list generated earlier, or come up with some others. Students would practice in pairs, and Mr. Tejera would listen and give some feedback. Students could give each other feedback, too. For instance, Felix might say, "It was fun to talk about my favorite comic book character!" and Natalie might say, "I asked a yes or no question, so it didn't work out as well."

At the end of the lesson, Mr. Tejera might review the idea that asking questions is a good way to start conversations, and that starting conversations is a good way to start making friends. He might say, "Your homework assignment for today is to start a conversation, using one of our questions, with at least one person in our school. Then tomorrow, we'll talk about how those conversations went. You all did a good job of listening and generating questions today. Each of you participated in the role-playing and in discussing the new skill we're learning."

What might a social skills lesson look like for older, more sophisticated students? What higher-level prosocial skills are teachers of upper-grade students likely to teach?

Tier 3 in Depth

It happens, with a small number of students (roughly 5% of the school population, if you'd like a number), that neither Tier 1 nor Tier 2 supports are enough to move them toward behaving appropriately with any degree of consistency. When a student has not responded to Tier 2 supports, the teacher and PBIS behavior team may decide that it is appropriate to move the student to Tier 3 supports. Tier 3 supports are targeted and intensive; they're designed to help change the behavior of students with serious, chronic behavior problems.

When a student is referred to the behavior team to identify appropriate Tier 3 supports, the team member conducts a functional behavior assessment and then develops an individualized plan, often relying on the principles of applied behavior analysis (a systematic way of providing and evaluating the effectiveness of interventions). After gathering data from teachers, parents, and other appropriate stakeholders, the team summarizes the findings, identifying the problem behaviors and the context(s) in which they occur. They identify the desired behaviors and decide upon the reinforcers (positive and negative) that they will use as they implement the behavioral plan. Further, they identify the strategies that they will use to move the student toward the desired behaviors.

On the pbis.org site, there is a case study of a student named Hannah (pbis. org/school/tier3supports/case-examples, n.d.; U.S. Department of Education). Hannah was a fourth-grader whose disruptive behaviors did not respond to interventions at the universal (Tier 1) and targeted (Tier 2) levels. The school's action team met several times to make a plan for helping Hannah move toward more desirable behavior; they gathered data that led them to the conclusion that Hannah engaged in off-task behavior as a means of getting attention from her peers.

The team chose to begin moving Hannah toward higher levels of work completion and lower levels of inappropriate interactions with peers; they decided to use interaction with peers as a reinforcer when Hannah completed work and self-managed her behavior.

As part of the intervention, the team settled on some structural/environmental strategies to support Hannah's progress; they decided to use a picture schedule with Hannah, making a visual representation of the work she needed to complete. They used pre-correction strategies to help point Hannah toward appropriate behavior preventively, and they also used pre-correction strategies with Hannah's classmates in an effort to reduce the attention they gave Hannah when she behaved inappropriately. (Pre-correction strategies are those actions teachers use to prevent inappropriate behavior and facilitate acceptable behavior.) They also encouraged Hannah's peers to respond positively when her behavior was appropriate.

The team also recommended some particular instructional strategies in Hannah's case: directly teaching Hannah what on-task behavior "looks like" in both group and independent work settings; enhancing her self-monitoring skills by teaching her a system designed for that purpose; and teaching Hannah unobtrusive strategies for seeking teacher assistance and for waiting quietly. And in addition to being a structural strategy, the picture schedule used with Hannah serves as an instructional tool.

The next piece of the intervention is to identify consequence strategies to encourage Hannah's investment in the process. The team recommended the use of a self-management card; when Hannah was demonstrating self-management, she'd earn a plus (+) on her card. She was also encouraged to record a zero for herself if she found that she was off task.

Hannah could trade in her plusses for class points, which would increase her status among her peers, as the additional points moved the group toward a preferred activity. Another outcome option for Hannah was to be able to spend free time with a friend.

Finally, the team developed monitoring and evaluation strategies for Hannah. She met weekly with the teacher at first, and as she gained skill and consistency, these meetings were set farther apart. At each meeting, Hannah and her teacher would review her progress. The teacher used a weekly record to monitor progress and then Hannah took the record home to share with her family.

This all sounds like a great plan, right? And it was . . . but it didn't permanently solve the issues about Hannah's behavior. Interestingly, the team met to review how well the plan was working, and they realized that Hannah's behavior was still problematic, but for different reasons. Her instructional situation had changed, and she was working frequently with a one-on-one instructional assistant. As the instructional setting changed, the nature of the inappropriate behavior also shifted. Hannah's new behavioral aim seemed to be escaping instructional demands. So the team revised the goal of the plan to encourage on-task, engaged behavior. The written plan was updated to reflect the new focus.

This case is a great example of the sort of planning/implementation/data collection/evaluation/revision that is at the core of the PBIS framework. We recommend you access the full case and read it to deepen your understanding of how all the pieces fit together.

Commentary From Anonymous Teacher 3

I am currently working with a student on Tier 3. He has a Positive Behavior Plan and Functional Behavior Assessment. I have his schedule listed for him each day with three positive goals along with reminders of what to do in the Calm Down Spot. He has a three color traffic light of behaviors on red, yellow, and green that relate to what color he lands on. (He can always move back up on the traffic light when moved down.) These systems have been successful Tier 3 interventions.

The Role of Rewards in PBIS

One topic that has generated a great deal of discussion in education circles over the last several decades is that of rewards and their effects (or lack thereof) on intrinsic motivation. Some researchers argue that using rewards (generally thought of as positive experiences/outcomes that influence behavior) undermines intrinsic motivation; others argue strongly that rewards, when used effectively, can be instrumental in promoting desired learning and behavioral outcomes. A full discussion of the pros and cons of reward use is, unfortunately, beyond the scope of this book, but the authors acknowledge that the use of rewards in educational settings is controversial. If you're interested in reading more about the controversy, you'll be able to find many, many articles that argue one view or the other.

Within the PBIS arena, rewards are generally thought of as tools that, when used well, can effectively influence student behavior without undermining intrinsic motivation. A hallmark of PBIS schools is a commitment to acknowledging and encouraging positive behavioral choices; many schools have designed a system of rewards used to recognize students who are demonstrating the behaviors built into the school's implementation plan. PBIS organizers insist that "giving kids stuff" is not the object of the system; instead, it is to teach students to focus on the behaviors we want them to exhibit, and to acknowledge those behaviors when they're on display.

So, how might a schoolwide incentive system work? Many schools using the PBIS framework identify a schoolwide method for recognizing positive behavior. Often, these systems involve the use of some sort of token that can be given to students when they are seen demonstrating desirable behavior. For instance, if the expectation is that students entering the band hall get out their instruments and music folders and sit down immediately with no talking or horseplay, Mrs. Tomlinson might pass out "Scholar Dollars" to each student who complies with that expectation. Or, if one of the prosocial behaviors that Case Elementary School has adopted is "Be respectful," Mr. Ellison, a cafeteria worker, might choose to give Elmira a "High Five" coupon because she waited patiently for her turn in line. This sort of reinforcement is aligned with the PBIS framework because it is immediate, can occur in any setting within the school, and recognizes appropriate behavior. (Did you already figure out that the use of High Five coupons or Scholar Dollars is a Tier 1 support?)

Students who receive tokens such as High Five coupons or Scholar Dollars can typically exchange them for a reward of some sort. For instance, some schools collect all tickets earned by students and then hold a Friday raffle for some sort of reward. Some schools allow students to trade tickets immediately for small reinforcers, such as pencils or time to do a preferred activity. And some schools allow students to collect tickets over time, essentially "banking" them and trading them later for "bigger" rewards. In fact, we've heard of one high school that allows their students to bank their tokens, and, when they've earned a particular number of them, the school will make a small donation to a charity of the students' choice.

Commentary From Anonymous Teacher 4

At my school we use BEARS bucks that students earn from any staff member in the school. Intrinsic motivation is applied to this system as they purchase nonmaterialistic rewards, like pajama day, wear a hat to school, lunch with the principal, or handprints with their name on the wall. We have a BEARS bookstore as well to encourage literacy; students can purchase books or trade in books with BEARS bucks.

Figure 12.11 ■ A Bears Buck

What Does Research Say About the Effectiveness of PBIS?

Evaluating the effectiveness of PBIS programs as a whole is complicated, because each program is, in and of itself, multifaceted and complex. Research continues to emerge; however, preliminary results of various studies indicate that implementing PBIS in schools reduces the number of behavioral problems that students exhibit in school. Further, PBIS implementation has been associated with academic gains for students and an increase in the amount of time actually used for instruction during the school day (Lewis, Mitchell, Trussell, & Newcomer, 2015).

Applying PBIS Ideas: What Might They Look Like in Action?

CASE 1 Kristina Will Not Work

Mr. Jake works in a school that has implemented a PBIS program. The members of the school community, under the direction of the PBIS team, have agreed to a shared set of Tier 1 interventions designed to prevent misbehavior and recognize positive choices. Throughout the school, students are expected to demonstrate the key behaviors of respect and responsibility. They are awarded Star Points for positive behavior; Star Points can be redeemed for a variety of experiential reinforcers.

Kristina, a student in Mr. Jake's class, is quite docile. She socializes little with other students and never disrupts lessons. However, despite Mr. Jake's best efforts and the Tier 1 interventions in place to encourage students to complete their work in a timely fashion, Kristina will not do her work. She rarely completes an assignment. She is simply there, putting forth no effort at all. *How might this scenario be addressed in a PBIS school?*

After careful data collection and analysis about the scope of the problem, and after reflecting to make sure that he has been implementing his Tier 1 interventions with fidelity, Mr. Jake would consult with the PBIS team. The team would examine the data about Kristina's performance and consider Tier 2 supports for her. They would consider a variety of possibilities and match the intervention to Kristina's specific situation, considering what seems to be driving the behavior, and then planning for interventions in structure/context, instructional strategies, consequences, and data collection/follow-up. As part of the Tier 2 supports, Kristina might be given a Check In-Check Out mentor who could help her begin to be more accountable for completing her work. The agreed-upon interventions would be implemented over time, and the results carefully evaluated. If Kristina's behavior doesn't respond as hoped/expected, the team would revisit her situation and develop alternatives. They might consider Tier 3 supports, but they also might try a different Tier 2 support. Either way, they would carefully set out a plan, make sure Mr. Jake is confident in implementing it, collect data, evaluate results, and modify as needed.

CASE 2 Sara Will Not Stop Talking

Sara is a pleasant girl who participates in class activities and does most, though not all, of her assigned work. She cannot seem to refrain from talking to classmates, however. Her teacher, Mr. Gonzales, has to speak to her repeatedly during lessons, to the point that he often becomes exasperated and loses his temper. *What might intervention look like in Sara's case in a PBIS school?*

CASE 3 Joshua Clowns and Intimidates

Joshua, larger and louder than his classmates, always wants to be the center of attention, which he accomplishes through a combination of clowning and intimidation. He makes wise remarks, talks back (smilingly) to the teacher, utters a variety of sound-effect noises such as automobile crashes and gunshots, and makes limitless sarcastic comments and put-downs of his classmates. Other students will not stand up to him, apparently fearing his size and verbal aggression. His teacher, Miss Pearl, has come to her wit's end. *What Tier 1 interventions might Miss Pearl already be trying with Joshua? What purpose do you believe this behavior is serving for Joshua? What would happen next if Joshua were in a PBIS school? What interventions might assist Miss Pearl in shaping Joshua's behavior?*

CASE 4 Tom Is Hostile and Defiant

Tom has appeared to be in his usual foul mood ever since arriving in class. On his way to sharpen his pencil, he bumps into Frank, who complains. Tom tells him loudly to shut up. Miss Baines, the teacher, says, "Tom, go back to your seat." Tom wheels around, swears loudly, and says heatedly, "I'll go when I'm *&$#^ good and ready!" *How would Tom's behavior be handled in a PBIS classroom?*

You Are the Teacher

IN THE HIGH SCHOOL CAFETERIA

The high school in which you work is in the beginning stages of implementing a PBIS model. Careful analysis of the data collected about student behavior indicates that the cafeteria is a site where students quite regularly engage in teasing, verbal put-downs, and low-level harassment of their peers. The PBIS team has set out Respect and Integrity as core school values. Desirable behaviors associated with respect include behaving kindly and treating others in ways they themselves would like to be treated; desirable behaviors for integrity include acting appropriately when no one is watching and exhibiting behaviors that produce feelings of pride.

Lexie is one of your students who sometimes behaves inappropriately in the cafeteria by teasing others. Though her target varies from incident to incident, you're pretty sure that she finds the attention she receives from others when she teases her peers be very rewarding. You've spoken with her about this twice already; her behavior doesn't rise to the level of bullying (yet), but you're concerned that if it is not stopped, it will have very negative effects over time.

A TYPICAL OCCURRENCE

You are in the cafeteria having your own lunch, and you notice that Bethany moves away from the group to sit by herself. Her posture is drooping; you can't read her facial expression, because she has her head down, but you are pretty sure that her body language communicates hurt and dejectedness. You look around and see Lexie laughing with another group of girls; they are looking over in Bethany's direction and cackling.

CONCEPTUALIZING A STRATEGY

If you were on the collaborative PBIS team in a school that utilized a PBIS framework (or one that was beginning to, since some of these behaviors would be much less likely if a fully developed program were in place), what would you do or recommend with regard to the following?

- Instituting Tier 1 supports to prevent the problems from occurring in the first place
- Putting an end to the misbehavior in the moment
- Maintaining student dignity and good personal relations
- Intervening if the behavior did not change with universal supports in place
- Helping the students involved develop increased responsibility and self-control

REFLECTING ON PBIS: WHAT YOU HAVE LEARNED IN THIS CHAPTER

Predominant Themes in the PBIS Framework

Behavioral intervention should be data-driven and should rely on evidence-based strategies.

Learning should be a meaningful, engaging, and cooperative activity.

Classrooms work better when students experience success. All students (not just those who frequently misbehave) benefit from attention to their academic, social, and behavioral growth.

Effective managers spend a significant amount of time actively teaching rules and procedures.

Teachers' interpersonal skills and methods for communicating with students are critical to the class experience; teachers and students should interact in ways that are positive, civil, and humane.

Effective managers focus on preventing, not just reacting to, misbehavior.

Students benefit from learning how to manage themselves and their emotions.

Clarity of expectations supports good behavior.

Student needs impact their behavior.

Students grow in important ways when they realize that their behaviors are the results of choices they make and that they can make better choices when the situation calls for it.

Punishments and threats should be avoided, as they're ineffective; enhancing students' intrinsic motivation is critically important.

Reinforcement can shape behavior, but should be carefully considered.

The theme correlations in this chapter are, perhaps, a little broader than they are in others in this book, in part because PBIS is such a comprehensive way of structuring management. In fact, one could argue that a majority of the themes we discussed in Chapter 4 would be expected to be evident in PBIS schools; however, because the framework allows for flexibility, they might be apparent to a greater or lesser degree depending on the school's focus.

Table 12.1 shows the potential positives and questions associated with the main tenets of the PBIS model. Remember to take notes in your planning guide as you reflect.

Table 12.1

PBIS Ideas	Potential Positives	Questions to Consider
Schools should base their management programs on data reflecting multiple aspects of the school context.	School personnel can gain insight into management targets on macro and micro levels, allowing more focused interventions with particular students at particular times and in particular places.	• What additional considerations must be made in order to use data as the foundation for a schoolwide program?
Interventions should be evidence-based.	Interventions that have been shown through research to be effective have a higher chance of success in shaping student behavior.	• Which interventions are most reliable? • What are the costs/benefits of foregoing the use of strategies that don't have research support?
The school should create a PBIS team to facilitate program functioning.	A multidisciplinary team will enhance integrity of implementation, facilitate consistency, and develop significant expertise that can be of service to all members of the school.	• Who should be on the team? What size is ideal? • How long should team members serve? Is there benefit to rotating members? • What if there are interpersonal issues on the team?

(continued)

Table 12.1 (*continued*)

PBIS Ideas	Potential Positives	Questions to Consider
Directly teaching students how to behave appropriately is necessary.	Just as students need to learn academic skills and content, they need to learn how to behave; direct teaching prevents misbehavior that results from ignorance of expectation.	• What effect might the direct teaching of behavioral/self-management skills have on classroom time? • How do teachers help students whose out-of-school lives follow a very different values system regarding behavior? • How can teachers keep behavioral instruction from being perceived as condescending or reflective of low expectations? • How does one deliver behavioral instruction to older students who may be more resistant to the idea that they don't know how to do something?
School personnel should pay attention to individual student needs with regard to classroom management; some students will need much more intensive intervention than others.	A whole-school focus on prevention and consistency allows teachers to exert minimal effort to address the behavior of most students and to focus on helping those who demonstrate less productive behaviors.	• What are the benefits of the tiered system in terms of teacher effort? In terms of potential outcome? • How do teachers prevent some students from being scapegoated or painted as "the bad students"?
Setting a positive tone and consistent expectations throughout the school facilitates all students' behavior.	Students benefit from knowing how to act in all school contexts; having all school personnel involved in the program facilitates consistency.	• What should happen if a school staff member doesn't follow the PBIS program? • What effect might PBIS implementation have on teacher autonomy and individuality?

MyLab Education **Self-Check 12.1**
MyLab Education **Self-Check 12.2**
MyLab Education **Application Exercise 12.1** Considering Behavior Plans
MyLab Education **Application Exercise 12.2** A PBIS System in Action

13

Classroom Management for Students With Learning and Behavioral Challenges

How Do Teachers of Students With Disabilities and Other Challenges Manage the Classroom?

LEARNING OUTCOMES:

13-1 Identify and describe student characteristics that may affect classroom management

13-2 Consider classroom management accommodations that might support students with learning differences.

The information you explored in previous chapters pertained primarily to students who are *able* to control their behavior, whether they choose to do so or not. Unfortunately, not all students can reliably control themselves. Some students—currently about 13% of the school-aged population—are eligible for services under the Individuals with Disabilities Education Act; among that group, students with some particular categories of disabilities are more likely to have difficulty controlling their own behavior. As you can imagine, this population of students can require extra problem solving on the part of the teacher; effective teachers think carefully about how best to manage students who face learning and behavior challenges.

WHAT MANAGEMENT STRATEGIES DO I USE WITH ATYPICAL LEARNERS?

The Common Goal of All Approaches to Management
Responsible, Civil Classroom Behavior That Becomes Habitual and Lasts over Time.
Responsible means paying attention, making a strong effort, and doing what is proper without being told.
Civil means respectful, polite, cordial, and well mannered.

↑

Management for Atypical Learners

↓   ↑

Overarching Management Strategy
Provide conditions and support that allow each student to feel secure and have the best possible access to learning.

↓   ↑

Principal Tactics
- Attempt to provide each and every student the best learning opportunities possible.
- Assess each student's particular needs and provide the specific support they require.
- Avoid the tendency to diagnose students.
- Work toward helping each student develop the self-control needed for successful participation in group settings.
- Reduce or eliminate distractions in the classroom environment.

↓   ↑

↓ ——————— → ——————— ↑

WHAT DO WE KNOW ABOUT STUDENTS WITH LEARNING AND BEHAVIORAL CHALLENGES?

You're undoubtedly aware that there is tremendous variation in students' abilities and experiences, and it's common sense that these differences would affect classroom learning and behavior. Some students demonstrate atypical or erratic behavior; in some cases, the students' cerebral processes do not function typically and thus their behavior is also atypical (Kranowitz, 2005). In school, almost all classes contain one or more students with a learning difference or exceptionality. Teachers find some of these students to be especially challenging because their behavior may be difficult to understand or predict; further, it often does not respond reliably to ordinary management tactics.

Scenario 1 Tyler

Tyler began the morning by refusing to participate in opening activities. He chose instead to make beeping sounds. After the opening activities, the class was to read quietly on their own for 10 minutes, but Tyler decided to sing loudly. When asked to stop, he began to hoot. He was belligerent and noisy for some time. He poked Jackie with his pencil, chewed the eraser off the pencil and swallowed it, and insisted on writing on his math sheet with a tiny piece of pencil lead moistened with spittle. He refused to comply with academic instructions until it was almost time for recess. During recess, Tyler pushed, poked, hit, and tried to choke other students. He laughed when they protested. He engaged in violent play fantasies and was extremely argumentative with the teachers on duty, swearing at them and insisting they could not make him do anything he didn't want to do. Finally, Tyler had to be led physically back to the classroom. He screamed that his rights were being violated and that he would sue the school.

Tyler worked the rest of the morning alone in the resource room with the resource teacher. In the afternoon, he returned to the regular classroom and was well behaved, compliant, and willing and able to participate and learn.

Students such as Tyler behave erratically or inconsistently for reasons that are mysterious to many teachers, sometimes even to those who have been specially trained. The behavior in question may result from: a compromised ability to process information correctly; chemical imbalances in the brain; congenital brain differences; brain injuries; or brain diseases, among others (Greene, 2001; Hall & Hall, 2003; Kranowitz, 2005; Papolos & Papolos, 2002). Because these types of learning differences are not always easily diagnosed, affected students sometimes do not receive the help they need for several years after their symptoms first appear.

Indicators: What Would Suggest That a Student Might Have a Learning or Behavioral Difference?

Three indicators—behavior difficulties, language difficulties, and academic difficulties—can each signal the possibility that a student might be experiencing a learning challenge.

Behavior difficulties are frequently the first indication that something unusual is occurring in the student, especially if the behavior is atypical, inconsistent, compulsive, or immune to normal behavior management. Throughout this chapter, you'll read about strategies for addressing behavioral challenges among atypical learners.

Language difficulties include problems in understanding, processing, and expressing information verbally. Classroom interactions operate on the assumption that language is understood in more or less the same way by all students and teachers. But such is not the case for some students, who may not interpret, understand, process, respond to, or use language in a typical manner (Cook, Kellie, Jones, & Goossen, 2000; Greene, 2001; Hall & Hall, 2003).

Suggestion: If you notice students who seem to have difficulty understanding, or who are not complying with expectations or requests, try using fewer words and increasing the time in which you expect them to comply. Make your directions clear, concrete, and consistent. You may need to show directions physically as well as explain them verbally. Ask students to repeat the directions or show you they understand what they are supposed to do.

Academic difficulties vary among students with exceptionalities. Some difficulties are easily recognized and dealt with; some are not. Memory may be compromised, resulting in variable gaps in learning. Difficulties with fine and gross motor skills, comprehension, language, and mathematics are often evident.

Suggestion: As you work with students who are receiving special services, take note of what the special education teachers do. You can adapt and use some of their strategies in your normal teaching; teaching practices that support students with learning challenges are often effective with the general school population as well.

TWO COMMON DIAGNOSES THAT CAN AFFECT LEARNING AND BEHAVIOR

Two prevalent diagnoses include learning disabilities (*LD*) and attention-deficit hyperactivity disorder (*ADHD*). *Learning disabilities* are associated with student struggles in a particular area of the school curriculum, such as reading or mathematics. *Attention-deficit hyperactivity disorder* is characterized by student restlessness, short attention span, impulsivity, and poor organizational skills, among other behaviors.

Learning Disabilities: What Are They and How Can I Help Students with This Diagnosis?

A learning disability (commonly abbreviated as LD) interferes with learning in specific subjects or topics. Though the term "learning disability" has often been used generically to describe any situation in which a student struggles to learn, its technical definition is much more specific. A learning disability is *not* the same as an attention disorder, although the two may occur together. Developmental delays, autism, auditory or visual impairments, physical disabilities, and emotional disorders are also not learning disabilities. Learning disabilities are *not* caused by lack of educational opportunities, frequent changes of schools, poor school attendance, or lack of instruction in basic skills, though of course those conditions can make progress even harder for students with learning disabilities.

Learning disabilities *are* difficulties in learning in certain areas, especially reading, writing, and mathematics. Students with learning disabilities typically have average to above-average intelligence, but struggle with processing language or numbers; learning disabilities can affect students' abilities "to listen, think, speak, read, write, spell, or do mathematical calculations" (IDEA, 2004). It's typical that a student with a learning difficulty might struggle in one particular area (reading, writing, math, etc.) but perform typically or even exceptionally well in other curricular areas. Students do not outgrow learning disabilities, but with support and intervention, they can be successful in learning and life.

Learning disabilities are categorized by the academic areas in which difficulties are identified. Some common learning disabilities are *dyslexia*, which is difficulty in processing language; *dyscalculia*, difficulty with basic mathematics; *dysgraphia*, difficulty with handwriting and spelling; and *dyspraxia*, difficulty with fine motor skills (National Council for Learning Disabilities [NCLD], 2005).

Indicators of learning disabilities include the following (NCLD, 2005), though it's important to note that the presence of one or more of these behaviors doesn't mean that a student definitely *has* a learning disability:

- Inability to discriminate between/among letters, numerals, or sounds.
- Difficulty sounding out words; reluctance to read aloud; avoidance of reading and/or writing tasks.
- Poor grasp of abstract concepts; poor memory; difficulty telling time.
- Confusion between right and left.
- Distractibility, restlessness, impulsiveness; trouble following directions.
- Inappropriate responses; saying one thing but meaning another
- Slow work pace; short attention span; difficulty listening and remembering.
- Eye–hand coordination problems; poor organizational skills.

Specialized psychological and academic testing is needed to confirm a suspected learning disability. In some countries, the law requires that the diagnosis be made by a multidisciplinary group, including the teacher, student, other school staff, family members, and professionals such as psychologists, reading clinicians, and speech and language therapists. Based on their assessment and on the availability of resources, special services may be provided to the student at school.

You can do a number of things to promote success among students with learning disabilities; many of the strategies listed in the next section will be effective with all students in your class. The lists that you'll encounter in this chapter are by no means exhaustive. They're designed to get you thinking about the ways you can best support your students, but you'll have to individualize your choices to fit any given student's needs.

Suggestions for supporting students with learning disabilities:

- Consult with special educators in your school for recommendations about addressing any curricular struggles that students face. Find out what is in the student's Individualized Education Program (IEP) and make plans to work toward those goals.
- Ensure that materials are at an appropriate level of challenge for students' abilities. Remember that inability to meet an expectation is likely to be demotivating.
- Directly teach academic skills that may support students' academic behavior: taking notes, marking the text, creating visual organizers, and so forth.
- Provide advance organizers to help students understand how the pieces of lessons go together. Provide study guides to help them focus on what is important, especially if their disability is in reading.
- Evaluate work to see when a struggle in one curricular area (e.g., math) might affect a student's ability to succeed in other curricular areas (e.g., science or economics). Consider ways to modify assignments or provide scaffolding to reduce the negative impact of the disability.
- Teach students, when appropriate, the use of memory aids such as mnemonics or imagery.
- Utilize technology as appropriate to support students; consider, for instance, allowing a student with dysgraphia to utilize a keyboard and printer instead of relying on writing things out by hand.
- Assign collaborative partners who are good facilitators.

Scenario 2 Justin

The class had just finished a discussion of a chapter in the book they were reading. Justin actively participated in the discussion, making correct and well-thought-out responses. Mr. Gatta, the teacher, then instructed the class to complete a chapter summary sheet at their desks. Justin needed to be told a second time to get started. Justin put his feet up on his desk and began to belch loudly. The students laughed. Mr. Gatta asked Justin to stop belching

In other chapters, we've talked about students who misbehave because they have unmet needs. This description of Justin's behavior *could* simply reflect a behavioral choice made in attempt to meet a need; however, it's also true that Justin might have a learning disability or other exceptionality that might be affecting his behavior. Teachers who encounter students like Justin (and others mentioned in this chapter) must be careful not to "diagnose" the student; instead, they should consult with others in the school if a student's behavior doesn't change when typical classroom management strategies are used.

and take his feet off his desk, whereupon Justin put his feet down and wrapped his legs around the legs of his desk. He then leaned back and made himself fall backwards, pulling his desk on top of him.

When Mr. Gatta came to help disentangle Justin from the furniture, Justin grabbed the desk, wrapped his legs tighter around it, squealed loudly, and laughed uncontrollably.

Commentary: Justin shows great reluctance to write down answers, even though he can say them correctly. His behavior may be linked to a learning disability, and there may also be other neural issues involved.

Attention Deficit Hyperactivity Disorder: What Is It and How Can I Help Students With This Diagnosis?

Attention-deficit hyperactivity disorder (ADHD) is also common among school-age children. It affects about 10% of the school population (Kahn & Faraone, 2006) and is characterized by short attention span, weak impulse control, and hyperactivity, all of which inhibit learning and often promote misbehavior. ADHD can begin in infancy and extend into adulthood, with negative effects on the individual's life at home, in school, and in the community. ADHD is not a separate category qualifying a student for services under IDEA, but many students with ADHD do receive accommodations, either because their ADHD exists concurrently with another disability eligible for IDEA accommodations, or because they are eligible for services under Section 504 of the Rehabilitation Act of 1973.

The cause of ADHD is not known. Maternal alcohol consumption or drug use during pregnancy is often associated with ADHD, as are childhood maladies such as viral infections, meningitis, encephalitis, head injury, and epilepsy (Millichap, 2008). More males than females have the condition. ADHD often occurs in combination with other diagnoses.

Many of the strategies that will support students with learning disabilities will also be helpful for students with ADHD. In fact, these two conditions often occur simultaneously. *Suggestions for supporting students with ADHD:*

- Maintain a highly structured classroom. Use a written schedule augmented with pictures to support the structure. Keep assignment folders and equipment in specific and consistent places with specific locations for all materials (pencil pouches, tabs in notebooks, etc.).
- Build small sequential steps into the classroom routine.
- Examine the class environment when the student is on-task, and when the student is off-task. Look for differences that might help or hinder the student.
- Keep at hand extra pencils, texts, and other materials for students to use when they cannot find their own.

- Give written/pictorial directions whenever possible rather than auditory prompting.
- Give fewer problems/questions on worksheets and consider using "window boxes," which are pieces of paper with a hole cut in them. The hole exposes only the question the student is to work on, but covers the rest of the questions on the page.
- Use a visual timer to help the student understand time constraints.
- Limit distractions as much as possible.
- Color code materials. Cover the textbook for one course in the same color as the notebook for that subject.
- Be aware of where the student is seated. Sit at the student's desk and observe the environment. Understand that stimulation and variety in the classroom often adversely affect students with ADHD. You may also wish to seat the student at an individual desk rather than a table and have separate work areas for different activities, which seems to help some students with ADHD work better.
  - Give advance warning of when a transition is going to take place ("Now we are completing the worksheet, next we will . . .") and the expectation for the transition ("and you will need . . ."). Visual timers are good for transitions.
  - Allow students to doodle or manipulate quiet fidget items, such as stress or foam balls, or small plastic items; this can improve their attention level. If students begin to tap their pencils on their desks, ask them to tap their thighs instead.
  - Tape a large piece of coarse sandpaper on the top inside of the student's desk, for the student to rub when he or she needs to pay attention.
  - Decrease auditory and visual distractions during difficult or new tasks. Study carrels or corners away from the group can be beneficial.
  - Specifically say and display lists of materials needed. List steps necessary to complete each assignment.
  - Allow the student to get into a comfortable position while learning.
  - Have lists, calendars, charts, pictures, and finished products in the classroom for students to refer to.
  - Provide short movement breaks, such as allowing the student with ADHD to pass out papers, run errands, or go for a drink of water.

Fidget spinners are extremely popular among students, even students who do not have learning or attention problems. If you're going to allow some students to have a fidget item, you'll need to make plans to (a) keep it from becoming a distraction to others and (b) explain why you may choose not to allow every student to have a fidget item (unless, of course, you'd be agreeable to that).

WHAT OTHER STUDENT EXCEPTIONALITIES AM I LIKELY TO ENCOUNTER?

It is very likely you will, over the course of your teaching career, interact with students with many sorts of physical, behavioral, and learning differences. You can expect at one time or another to work with students who have sensory integration dysfunction (SID), bipolar disorder, oppositional defiant disorder (ODD), autism spectrum disorder (ASD), fetal alcohol spectrum disorder (FASD), and brain injuries. Information is presented here to alert you to these diagnoses and their implications.

It is important to recognize that students with disabilities cannot overcome their difficulties through willpower. Their conditions are not related to their character or capacity to learn. Some disorders can be treated successfully with medication, but in some cases, the medication adversely affects attention, concentration, and stamina (National Institute of Mental Health, 2008).

Sensory Integration Dysfunction: What Is It and How Can I Help Students Who Have This Diagnosis?

Sensory integration dysfunction (SID)—also called *sensory processing disorder (SPD)*—reflects abnormalities in organizing, interpreting, and responding to information taken in through the senses. Sensory integration occurs automatically to keep us informed, ready to act, and able to protect ourselves. For some people, flaws in the process result in incorrect perception and interpretation of information. Impaired processing of information may lead in turn to inappropriate behavior and poor learning.

Most teachers know little about SID, even though it is suspected of being a major cause of hyperactivity, inattention, fidgety movements, inability to calm down, impulsivity, lack of self-control, disorganization, language difficulties, and learning difficulties (Cook, 2008a; Kranowitz, 2005; Kranowitz, Szkut, Balzer-Martin, Haber, & Sava, 2003). Some students' sensory processing systems seem to be easily overwhelmed by excess visual and auditory stimulation.

Suggestions for supporting students with SID: You can help these students by reducing distractions and lessening incoming stimuli. For example, you can

- keep the classroom neat and tidy
- remove sources of loud or unpredictable noise
- enlarge printed questions or directions
- stand in front of a solid white overhead screen when giving instructions and directing lessons
- give directions slowly and distinctly, checking that students have understood them
- maintain a sense of calm.

Scenario 3 Jimmy

Jimmy entered kindergarten in September. By January, his behavior was worse than when he began school. Every day he had a series of tantrums, usually beginning when he arrived at school. He sometimes complied with

As you see, Jimmy did not have to have an official diagnosis of SID for his teacher to try out strategies to help him behave more appropriately. Though it's entirely possible that a full-scale evaluation would have led to a diagnosis of Sensory Integration Disorder, the teacher did not wait for an official determination before trying strategies to reduce the sensory stimulation Jimmy was encountering. Similarly, when you have students in class, you don't have to "wait" for a diagnosis to begin trying different interventions.

directions, but more often, especially during changes of activity, he might scream, cry, kick, flail his arms, fall to the floor, or run out of the classroom. During his "episodes," he sometimes kicked and hit staff members and students who were in his way.

Jimmy's home life was unremarkable. He lived in a quiet neighborhood with both parents and an older sibling. His family environment was loving and stable. His parents were very concerned about his behavior.

Jimmy did not have any diagnosed neurological conditions. His mother did not drink or use illicit substances during her pregnancy. The pregnancy and his birth were deemed typical.

Commentary: This child, with no diagnosis other than his behavior to suggest neurological dysfunction, was having a terrible experience in school. His teacher ultimately changed the classroom environment to cut down sensory stimulation, after which Jimmy's behavior improved considerably.

Bipolar Disorder: What Is It and How Can I Help Students Who Have This Diagnosis?

Bipolar disorder is an affective condition characterized by severe mood swings that occur in cycles of mania and depression, or highs and lows. Individuals with bipolar disorder can change abruptly from irritable, angry, and easily annoyed to silly, goofy, giddy, and disruptive, after which they return again to low-energy periods of boredom, depression, and social withdrawal (AACAP, 2004c). These abrupt swings of mood and energy, which in some individuals occur several times a day, are often accompanied by poor frustration tolerance, outbursts of temper, and oppositional behavior. Students with bipolar disorder are also frequently diagnosed with sensory integration dysfunction (Papolos & Papolos, 2002).

The cause of bipolar disorder is not known. The disorder was once thought to be rare in children, but recent research shows it can begin very early in life and is much more common than previously believed. Proper drugs can stabilize mood swings, and cognitive therapy and counseling can often help. Indicators of bipolar disorder in school students include the following (Papolos & Papolos, 2002):

- episodes of hysterical laughing and infectious happiness for no evident reason, followed by periods of lethargy or "being down"
- belligerence and argumentation, often followed by self-recrimination
- jumping from topic to topic in rapid succession when speaking.

Suggestions for supporting students with bipolar disorder:

- Adapt lessons and assignments as appropriate for the student's particular situation.
- To the extent possible, follow a consistent schedule.
- Identify a safe space where a student can go when overwhelmed.
- Patiently teach students to work toward self-control.
- Communicate with caregivers and with school experts to identify strategies for each student.

Oppositional Defiant Disorder: What Is It and How Can I Help Students Who Have This Diagnosis?

You expect some of your students to talk back to you, argue, and disregard your directives now and then. You don't enjoy such behavior, but probably realize it is a normal occurrence in human development. However, an occasional student will behave in a manner so uncooperative and hostile that it not only drives you to distraction but also damages the student's social, academic, and family life. That sort of behavior is characteristic of **oppositional defiant disorder (ODD)**.

The American Academy of Child and Adolescent Psychiatry (2004b) lists the following as symptoms of ODD:

- frequent temper tantrums
- excessive arguing with adults
- active defiance and refusal to comply with adult requests and rules
- belligerent and sarcastic remarks
- deliberate attempts to annoy or upset people
- blaming others for one's own mistakes or misbehavior
- being touchy or easily annoyed by others
- speaking hatefully when upset
- seeking revenge

Suggestions for supporting students with ODD: If you have a student who displays the characteristics of ODD, you might consider using positive reinforcement when the student shows flexibility or cooperation. Indirect or earshot praise sometimes works well, such as when the student "overhears" two adults talking positively about him or her (intending to be overheard).

It is also helpful to reduce the number of words you use when speaking to a student with ODD (Hall & Hall, 2003). A suggested procedure is to say and show what you mean, just once, and then do not explain yourself further. Students will ask for more information if they need it, and then you can provide what they need. If you feel your responses are about to make the conflict worse, take a personal time-out. This allows you to calm down, and it also presents a good model for the student.

Autism Spectrum Disorder: What Is It and How Can I Help Students Who Have This Diagnosis?

Autism spectrum disorder (ASD) includes various diagnoses of atypical development in verbal and nonverbal communication, along with impaired social development and restricted, repetitive, and stereotyped behaviors and interests (Faraone, 2003). It also includes delays in the development of socialization and communication skills and Asperger syndrome, which is a pattern of behavior among students of normal intelligence and language development who also exhibit autistic-like behaviors and marked deficiencies in social and communication skills.

Autism affects four times as many males as females. Students with ASD may show extreme hyperactivity or extreme passivity in relating to people around them. In its milder form, autism may resemble a learning disability. Indicators of ASD include the following:

- self-stimulation, spinning, rocking, and hand flapping
- obsessive compulsive behaviors such as lining objects up evenly
- repetitive odd play for extended periods of time
- insistence on routine and sameness
- difficulty dealing with interruption of routine schedule and change
- monotone voice and difficulty carrying on social conversations
- inflexibility of thought and language (e.g., one student with autism refused to wear his winter jacket during subzero weather in early December because he had learned winter did not officially begin until December 21).

Manifestations of autism vary enormously in severity. Sensory integration dysfunction is also common in students with ASD, and sensory overload can lead to behavior problems in school.

Suggestions for supporting students on the autism spectrum: Modifying the physical environment can do much to improve behavior and academic achievement of students with ASD. Some people with autism never develop language and need full-time care, whereas others become fully functioning, independent members of society. Teachers of students with autism often find benefit from having a consistent schedule and actively preparing students for any instance in which a change will occur (e.g., fire drills). Many people with autism respond well to visual information (directions given as a set of pictures, to-do lists, etc.). Being mindful of each individual's unique combination of preferences and behaviors is also very helpful in working with students with autism.

Scenario 4 Tay

Tay is extremely noisy. Even during quiet work time, she taps, hums, or makes other noises. When the teacher asks her to stop, she denies doing anything. She talks very loudly. When classmates ask her to be quiet, she ignores them.

Tay wears three pairs of socks all the time and adjusts the cuffs on each pair a number of times a day. She cannot settle down and focus until her socks are just right. She will not change shoes for gym class. When the gym teacher tried to make her do so, Tay swore at her and ran out of the gym and away from school, crying hysterically. When dashing across the street, Tay ran into the side of a parked car, then fell to the road and sobbed until a teacher came to get her.

Commentary: Tay is diagnosed with ASD with extreme SID. Outside noise bothers her greatly, so she makes her own noise to drown it out. It is speculated that she wears the three pairs of socks to put extra pressure on her feet, which would be an indicator of SID, as is her continual cuff adjustment. Things that have been done to help her benefit more from school include (a) providing ear covers to block outside noise, (b) using a portable radio/CD player with headphones to drown out other noise, (c) giving her chewing gum or mints to help keep her mouth quiet, (d) overlooking her sock rituals, which are not a major issue, and (e) compromising by allowing Tay to decide whether she will change shoes for gym class or move to an alternate activity arranged for her, which includes instruction in social skills in her individualized education program.

Fetal Alcohol Spectrum Disorder: What Is It and How Can I Help Students Who Have This Diagnosis?

FASD is a group of neurobehavioral and developmental abnormalities that includes fetal alcohol syndrome (FAS), alcohol-related neurodevelopmental disorder (ARND), and partial fetal alcohol syndrome (pFAS).

The disorder results from the fetus being exposed to alcohol from the mother's blood. Ingestion of even small amounts of alcohol by mothers, as little as 1 ounce per week, has been linked to delinquent and aggressive behavior in children. The Centers for Disease Control and Prevention (CDC) contend that alcohol consumption by pregnant mothers is a significant contributor to brain impairment and that no level of alcohol consumption during pregnancy is considered to be safe (CDC, 2004). This conclusion was challenged, however, by findings in a large study in the United Kingdom that showed no ill effects in offspring whose mothers were "light drinkers" during pregnancy (Kelly, Sacker, Gray, Kelly, Wolke, & Quigley, 2009).

Most individuals with FAS and other diagnoses on the FASD continuum have normal intelligence (Streissguth, Barr, Kogan, & Bookstein, 1997). At the same time, many of them have compromised adaptive and social skills, including poor impulse control, poor judgment, a tendency to miss social cues, learning difficulties, and difficulty with the tasks of daily living. ADHD frequently occurs in association with FASD, and behavior difficulties are common (Kellerman, 2003).

Suggestions for supporting students with FASD:

■ Use clear, step-by-step instructions free of figurative language.
■ Provide multisensory learning activities.
■ Be prepared for a student who has seemingly mastered a concept, skill, or behavior one day to have forgotten it the next.
■ Modify assignments as needed (length, outcome mode).
■ Monitor for signs of increasing stress and provide a respite period.

Scenario 5 Sam

Sam, age 10, never sits still in class. He is always talking and calling out answers in class even though they are usually wrong. Yesterday he pushed a classmate when they were coming in from recess. The teacher spoke to him, reminded him of the rules, and told him he could not go out for recess that afternoon. This morning, Sam was reminded to keep his hands to himself or he would lose recess again. Sam repeated word for word what he was told: "I will keep my hands to myself and if I don't I won't be able to go out for recess this afternoon." Fifteen minutes later Sam pushed Jonathan. When the teacher spoke to him, Sam claimed he didn't do anything and it wasn't his fault.

Commentary: Sam has been diagnosed with FASD and ADHD. His repeating back the words and consequences indicates language-processing difficulties common to FASD. Like other students with the condition, he reacts automatically to situations without always remembering what he did. Calling out and inability to sit still are associated with ADHD.

Brain Injuries: What Are They?

Brain injuries, traumatic and nontraumatic, often inhibit the brain's ability to function in a normal manner. Traumatic injuries result from blows to the head incurred during events such as accidents, sporting events, or assaults. Nontraumatic injuries result from disrupted blood flow to the brain (as in strokes), or from tumors, infections, drug overdoses, and certain medical conditions (Brain Injury Society of Virginia, 2012). The effects of severe injuries are readily apparent, but mild injuries may go unrecognized even when they have a significant effect on behavior. Because brain injuries affect behavior in so many different ways, students' resultant limitations must be diagnosed and special instruction devised to help with particular difficulties.

Rage: How Can I Recognize and Respond to It?

You may never experience an episode of rage in your classroom, but the following information will help you if you do.

Rage is an extreme behavior. Puzzling and frightening, it displays as an explosion of temper that occurs suddenly, with little warning, and may turn violent

(Packer, 2005). The process is traumatic for everyone and may best be understood as a neurological event that involves behavior over which the student has little control.

Rage differs from tantrums, which are goal-directed with the purpose of getting something or getting somebody to do something. Rage is not goal-oriented. Rather, it is a release of built-up tension or frustration. (Tantrums sometimes evolve into rage.) Once a rage episode has begun, there is little one can do to stop it. It may only last for a few minutes, or may continue for hours. Although it usually has to run its course, it can be softened and controlled somewhat by teachers and other adults.

Four phases comprise the *rage cycle*: (1) triggering, (2) escalation, (3) rage, and (4) post-rage. These phases, their characteristics, and how you can help in each of them are described in the following observations and suggestions (Cook, 2008b; Echternach & Cook, 2004; Greene, 2001; Hill, 2005; Packer, 2005).

Phase 1: Triggering

Triggers are precipitating events that provoke or set in motion episodes of rage, apparently by initiating neurochemical changes in the brain that greatly heighten the self-protective responses commonly called fight/flight/freeze reactions. In classrooms, triggering conditions seem to be associated at times with work transitions, sensory overload, being told "No," fatigue, frustration, confusion, hunger, anxiety, and mood swings. For students with ADHD, triggers tend to be related to sensory and/or emotional overstimulation. For students with bipolar disorder, triggers are often related to having limits set on their behavior (Papolos & Papolos, 2002). In the triggering phase, students may appear angry, confused, frustrated, dazed, tense, or flushed, and they may swear and use other rude language.

Suggestions: When a student is in this phase:

- Recognize that a rage episode has begun and you may not be able to prevent it.
- Understand that this is a neurological event. The student's flight/fight/freeze responses are strongly activated.
- Understand that the rage is not intentional or personal toward you.
- Stay calm. Use a quiet tone of voice. Do not become adversarial.
- Use nonthreatening body language. Stand at an angle off-center to the student, at least a long stride away. Make sure the student can see your hands.
- Use empathic verbal support ("It sounds like you're upset." "That would upset me too.").
- Deflect control elsewhere ("The clock says it's time to clean up." "The big rule book in the office says . . .").
- Calmly, quietly, and succinctly use logical persuasion to provide the student an alternative behavior.

Phase 2: Escalation

Following the triggering, the rage may escalate mildly or rapidly. In *mild escalations*, the student may begin to get angry, call names, swear, exhibit startled verbal or physical responses, talk rapidly, increase the volume and cadence of speech, and show tension in the arms, hands, and body. *Rapid escalations* are characterized by violent temper, hostility, aggressive comments ("Leave me alone!" "I'm going to kill you!"), profanity, flushed face, and clammy body. The student may show fists and throw objects or furniture.

Suggestions: When a student is in this phase:

- Remain calm.
- Ensure the safety of others by clearing them from the room or supporting them to ignore the escalation.
- If the student threatens you, walk away.
- Calmly direct the student to a safe place (e.g., quiet room or designated area) to allow the energy to dissipate.
- Continue to use short and direct phrases, nonemotional language, and body language that is nonthreatening and nonconfrontational.
- Praise the student as soon as the student begins to respond to your direction.
- Do not address the student's inappropriate language, threats, or other behavior at this time. The student cannot process the information and may only become further inflamed.

Phase 3: Rage or Meltdown

Here, the student is fully caught up in the rage.

Suggestions: When a student is in this phase:

- Allow the student space to go through the physical manifestations.
- Do not restrain the student unless there is an immediate threat to physical safety.
- Do not question, make sarcastic comments, or try to talk the student out of the rage.
- Do not try to make the student understand instructions.
- While the student is going through the cycle of reactions, support others in the room and help ensure that their interpretations of the rage event are correct.

Phase 4: Post-Rage or Post-Meltdown

After a rage event, the student may or may not remember the behavior or the triggering causes. This is a low point because the student has expended a great amount of energy and is left confused and often embarrassed. The student will now be tired, passive, headachy, and sometimes remorseful and apologetic. The student may need sleep.

Suggestions: When a student is in this phase:

- Reassure the student that they are is all right now.
- When ready, help the student put language to the event.
- Help the student plan what to do the next time a rage occurs—such as finding a sensory-friendly refuge (a safe place or room in which to rage), using words to get what is needed, and remaining in a safe place until able to calm down.

■ After the rage event and when the student is calm, take care of yourself. Relax, drink water, and remind yourself that it was not personal and that you did the best you could. Meanwhile, document your observations, hold debriefing conversations with a colleague, and listen to reflections made by anyone involved.

■ Note any evident triggers, sensory influences, or other environmental characteristics that may have precipitated the rage.

Scenario 6 Michael

Ms. Brant sees Michael begin to scribble all over his math worksheet. Ms. Brant calls out from across the room, "Stop that, you're making a mess" or says in an accusatory tone of voice, "And what do you think you are doing, young man?"

Those accusatory statements attract attention of all students in class and thereby set up a power struggle between Ms. Brant and Michael. Michael begins to scream, "I hate this f----- s-----! I'm going to kill myself!" His screaming threatens the teacher and affects the functioning of the class.

Ms. Brant responds, "Michael, you cannot swear in this classroom. As for killing yourself, don't be ridiculous." Michael thinks Ms. Brant has called him ridiculous, which further inflames him. Other students in the class are now alert and waiting to see what happens.

A more effective response would be for Ms. Brant to walk calmly to Michael, bend down, and quietly ask, "Do you need some help?" When Ms. Brant stoops down, she is not vulnerable to being kicked and is not physically intimidating to Michael. Ms. Brant knows never to scold students for swearing at the time they swear. The time to deal with profanity is after the student has settled down, not in the middle of the incident.

Ms. Brant suggests to Michael that the two of them talk in the private area of the classroom. She says, "It is nobody else's business, so let's talk privately about this." Ms. Brant may say, pointing to Michael's scribbles, "Boy, Michael, I used to have a dress that looked like that." The issue of profanity is then dealt with privately, and Michael apologizes later to the class for swearing. Ms. Brant might further defuse the situation by asking Michael to go to the photocopy room to get more paper.

What Are Some Specific Suggestions for Preventing Misbehavior Among Students With Special Needs?

To increase the likelihood of student success, consider the following suggestions.

■ Establish a positive and nurturing rapport with the students. Warmly greet them when they arrive at class. Show interest in them and talk about pop culture or something they are interested in.

■ Modify the classroom to make it sensory friendly. Sit in the student's seat and look at the room from the student's perspective. See if there are things that might be distracting or annoying. It is far more productive to change the classroom than try to change the student.

■ Add structure to time periods that are ordinarily unstructured, such as recess and free time. Many students, regardless of ability or disability, have difficulty with unstructured time.

■ Make appropriate use of humor, which is effective with all students. Avoid sarcasm.

■ Keep in mind that students with disabilities and/or behavioral challenges are not predestined to fail. Look for their many qualities and strengths that can be nurtured and built into important life competencies.

■ All small improvements should be celebrated as important steps to a better-quality life, now and in the future.

What Are Suggested Ways of Redirecting Misbehavior?

When misbehavior does occur, keep your reactions as positive as possible. Here are some suggestions:

■ Be careful about eye contact. It can stimulate upper-cortex activity, which is good for academic thinking, but can at times trigger episodes of misbehavior. Eye contact combined with a stern tone of voice is often interpreted as a threat.

■ Be careful how you use your voice. If you raise your voice, students will often raise their voices in return.

■ When giving students a choice of behaviors, provide two alternatives you can live with and let the students select the one they prefer.

■ Remain positive. Your positive attitude can greatly improve the quality of service you provide to students and their families. Remember that students with learning and behavioral challenges are human beings first and foremost, and you have the opportunity to help them.

As to what you can say, specifically, to individual students who break class rules of conduct:

■ Tell them, using unemotional language, that the rule was broken.

■ Using very few words, tell them what to do to fix the mistake. Reduce public attention; stand close to shield them from the view of others and speak as quietly/privately as you can.

■ Provide praise and encouragement when they begin to comply.

■ If they begin to argue, say, "Wrong tone of voice . . . you're not ready to fix your mistake . . . I'll wait." Then wait, not staring at them and not making eye contact. You may have to wait a few seconds or even a few minutes.

■ When they have made progress in resolving the situation, provide them with recognition.

Scenario 7 Abraham

Abraham, a 10-year-old student with severe behavior issues, was brought back from gym class. An educational assistant had Abraham by his wrist, escorting him to a private area in the back of the classroom as Abraham loudly spewed a tirade of profanities and threats. To ensure everyone's safety, teachers used the "separate and supervise" strategy to isolate Abraham from his peers. He was put in a back room adjacent to the classroom, where he continued to scream profanities and threats. As the other staff members helped the other students carry on the daily classroom routine, Ms. Snell walked toward the back area of the room where a staff member stood in front of the closed door. Abraham had a history of running away. Ms. Snell opened the door just a fraction and saw Abraham standing with a chair over his head in a threatening pose.

Ms. Snell quietly called in, "You sound angry at me, Abraham." Ms. Snell was deliberately trying to deflect and divert Abraham's attention to herself in an attempt to engage another part of Abraham's brain.

Abraham shrieked, "I'm not f---ing angry at you, I'm angry at Billy!"

"Excellent, Abraham! You put other words to this, way to go!" Ms. Snell said this in an encouraging, sincere, but soft tone. "Why are you angry at Billy?"

Abraham was still shouting and still had the chair over his head. "Because Conrad is my friend!" he screamed.

"Oh, I'm glad Conrad is your friend, but what does Billy have to do with this?" Ms. Snell gently put her index finger to her lips in a shhhing motion.

"Billy told Conrad to f--- off, and that's not nice," Abraham replied indignantly, at a lower volume but still with the chair over his head.

"Great, Abraham, you put words to this! Hey, Abraham, let's add other words to this so you can respectfully tell Billy why you're upset. Billy doesn't even know you are mad at him, and he and Conrad are already eating lunch together. Put the chair down so I can come in."

"NOOOOO!" Abraham screamed. "You'll try to put me in the Quiet Room if I put the chair down."

Ms. Snell answered quietly, "Abraham, as long as you are safe, I'm safe, and the class is safe, you don't need to go to the Quiet Room. Put the chair down so we can plan to get out of here."

Abraham put the chair down, but removed the detachable plastic seat, holding it ready to strike anyone who came close.

"Great, Abraham, you put down the chair, good for you! Now let me help you fix the chair where the seat has come off." Ms. Snell slowly approached from his left, walking at an angle and off-center from him, so he could see her coming and not be startled by any sudden movements. Ms. Snell positioned herself between the chair and Abraham, with him on the inside of the room, and herself near the door. Although the screaming had subsided, Ms. Snell was still concerned about her safety.

Together, Ms. Snell and Abraham snapped the seat back on the chair and Abraham quickly sat down. "Thanks, Abraham," Ms. Snell said. "I always have trouble getting those blasted seats back on those chairs."

Abraham was now calm. He was then able to articulate why he was upset, without using profanity, and he found a way to let Billy know he was upset and tell Conrad that he was his friend. Within four minutes, Abraham had fixed things up, made amends, and was with his peers having lunch. Abraham did not have any more big explosions after this. Perhaps he began to understand he had other options when he was confused or upset. This situation appeared to provide an invaluable learning experience.

Commentary From Anonymous Teacher 1

When I first began teaching, I knew nothing about students with learning differences and behavioral challenges. To my knowledge it was never mentioned in my teacher education program. I learned no special techniques or strategies for helping these students. I learned from whomever I could and just did my best.

One of my students I remember well was a boy who had fallen from a balcony at age 2 and suffered a traumatic brain injury. He exhibited some of the characteristics and behaviors I read about in this chapter. He was frequently off task, wouldn't stay in his seat, made noises, scribbled on his desk, and hit, slapped, and pushed kids on the playground. For some time, no form of discipline I tried helped change his behavior.

Finally, after much collaboration with the principal and the school psychologist, I did the following: Each day, if my student failed twice to control himself, I would send him to a special desk in the classroom separated from the others. There he would work until the completion of activities in a particular subject area. After that, he could return to "the group," as we called it. The process would start all over at that point. This young man did not like the isolation from the group, and generally his disruptive behavior would stop. As the year progressed, I came to realize that oftentimes this boy could not fully control his behavior.

In this chapter, I found the scenarios especially helpful. They gave me a new perspective on the behavior I sometimes encountered. I think all prospective teachers should be aware of challenges like these and recognize that the number of students who display them is increasing. Such is certainly the case at my school.

Commentary From Anonymous Teacher 2

Before I read this chapter, I had received no pre-service training in recognizing, identifying, understanding, or helping students with any of the diagnoses described here. I knew my subject matter and the basics of curriculum design but very little about working with the amazing variety of students I would encounter. I wasn't far into my first year when it became evident I needed help if I were going to survive.

I didn't like admitting my ignorance, but I had to go to colleagues for help. The special education teachers opened their trove of ideas, techniques, and strategies to help me. My fellow teachers offered tips that had worked for them. Often I just asked the students directly, "What can I do to help you succeed?" I attended inservice sessions when appropriate and researched when necessary. I spoke with parents about my hopes for their child. I learned by experience, sometimes the hard way.

Now, many years later, I have had my share of successes in helping students and regret that I never could find the key for others. Although I have taught many students with ADD/ADHD, learning disabilities, and other diagnoses, I never had to deal with violent, threatening, profane, or raging students, although I know many teachers who have.

As we all know, overcoming strong challenges does not happen quickly or easily. We all want to prepare our students to live successful lives. I think I got better at it as I learned to do the following: (1) *Retain patience* to allow students to think, make mistakes, and be patient with themselves and others; (2) *show persistence* in going the distance with students and doing what it takes to help them keep trying and not give up; (3) *keep a positive attitude*, expect good things, maintain hope, and help students look on the bright side; and (4) *search for strengths* by helping students recognize that we all have our strengths and weaknesses and can find many strengths in ourselves and others.

REFLECTING ON TEACHING STUDENTS WITH LEARNING AND BEHAVIORAL DIFFERENCES: WHAT YOU HAVE LEARNED IN THIS CHAPTER

You have learned that you can be successful in helping students with learning and behavioral challenges—those students whose individual circumstances may require more problem solving and flexibility on your part. You've learned a little bit about some of the more prevalent disabilities and challenges students face, and you've learned how strategies that make school success more attainable for students with special needs can also work for and with more typical students. You've learned that consulting with others, modifying your expectations, providing clarity and structure, and carefully considering your interaction patterns are all important factors in moving toward successful classroom management for all students.

MyLab Education **Self-Check 13.1**

MyLab Education **Self-Check 13.2**

MyLab Education **Application Exercise 13.1** Strategies for Supporting Individual Students

MyLab Education **Application Exercise 13.2** What Do Teachers Say About Meeting Individual Students' Needs?

14

Striving for Personal Excellence in Classroom Management

You are now on the verge of achieving every teacher's aspiration, which is to be able to teach classes of cooperative, courteous, and nondisruptive students. The previous chapters in this book have provided you with a great deal of information and many skills for doing so; by now, you should be seeing your own classroom management plan coming into focus. Though you'll continue to refine it and develop new skills throughout your teaching career, we're hopeful that you have a firm grasp on the considerations that will be necessary as you plan your management decisions and actions.

Remember that we started this text with some fundamental questions about classroom management:

- What is the purpose of classroom management?
- What kinds of behavior should I expect of students?
- What is classroom misbehavior?
- Why does it happen, and how does it affect teaching and learning?
- What does effective management require of me legally, professionally, and ethically?
- What attitude/approach toward classroom management will serve me best?
- What are the most effective things I can do to support proper behavior and social-emotional growth in my classes?
- What are the most effective things I can do to prevent or reduce the likelihood of misbehavior?
- What are the most effective things I can do to redirect misbehavior humanely and effectively?

By now, you should be comfortable articulating, at least in part, your own answers to these questions. Remember that your classroom and school contexts will affect how, exactly, your classroom management plan plays out; if you're not currently serving as a classroom teacher, you will need to be ready to modify your preliminary thoughts to fit the reality of your first teaching assignment. And remember, what works one year in one school may need to be modified to be effective in another year or in another setting; learning to be an effective manager requires constant reflection and continued professional development.

Are you still worried about classroom management? Stop and think for a moment; you already know a great deal about the topic. Remember, as you've progressed through this text, you've learned about why it's critical for you to develop and hone your classroom management skills. You have learned about teacher and student factors that affect the smoothness with which classrooms operate, and you have developed an understanding of the professional obligations of teachers as they work with students and manage their classrooms. You've learned about communication skills that support effective classroom management, and about how to build community among the members of your class.

You've explored teacher-centered, student-centered, and schoolwide approaches to management. You've studied the terminology used to describe classroom management, and you've learned about the contributions and recommendations of many, many professionals who have done work in fields that directly relate to classroom management. You've also learned about potential causes of misbehavior, ways to prevent it, ways to respond to it when it happens, and ways to support positive behavior among your students. You've begun to examine your own personal beliefs and values as they relate to classroom management. And through all this study, you have explored the main themes that have recurred over time as educators and other professionals have tried to figure out how to establish and maintain effective learning environments.

Let's revisit these themes, originally presented for your consideration in Chapter 4 of this text.

Themes	
Meaningful, Successful Learning	Learning should be a meaningful, engaging, and cooperative activity. Classrooms work better when students experience success. All students (not just those who frequently misbehave) benefit from attention to their academic, social, and behavioral growth.
Effective Communication	Teachers' interpersonal skills and methods for communicating with students are critical to the class experience; teachers and students should interact in ways that are positive, civil, and humane.

Themes	
Teaching Self-Management	Students benefit from learning how to manage themselves and their emotions. Teachers and students who view themselves as being on the same team are likely to have smoother relationships; teachers who run democratic classrooms (as opposed to autocratic or permissive ones) are more likely to be successful classroom managers.
Fostering Positive Interpersonal Relationships	Classrooms work better when teachers attend to group dynamics and cooperative, supportive interpersonal relationships.
Motivation, Rewards, and Punishment	Punishments and threats should be avoided, as they're ineffective; enhancing students' intrinsic motivation is critically important. Reinforcement can shape behavior, but should be carefully considered.
Making Appropriate Choices	Students grow in important ways when they realize that their behaviors are the results of choices they make and that they can make better choices when the situation calls for it.
Class Meetings	Class meetings are a useful way of building relationships and involving students in the problem-solving process. Reflection and problem solving are tools that not only help teachers and students change behavior, but also build community.
Normalizing Mistakes	Students benefit when teachers normalize error and help students understand the role mistakes play in the learning process.
Focus on Prevention	Effective managers focus on preventing, not just reacting to, misbehavior. Attending to management logistics when delivering instruction is critical to avoiding wasted time in classrooms.
Identifying Needs	Student needs impact their behavior. Students can learn to meet their needs without negatively affecting others.
Clarifying Expectations	Clarity of expectations supports good behavior. Helping students understand the relationship between behaviors and consequences is one aspect of clarity.
Using Data and Research	Behavioral intervention should be data-driven and should rely on evidence-based strategies.
Establishing and Teaching Rules and Procedures	Effective managers spend a significant amount of time actively teaching rules and procedures.
Impact of Testing	Testing and accountability measures have strongly impacted teachers' approaches to curriculum, often to the detriment of student behavior and motivation.

By now, you should be relatively comfortable explaining why each theme has been identified as important to classroom management; you should also be able to identify which of the authorities we've studied would be most likely to support each theme. You'll likely embrace some of the themes wholeheartedly as part of your own system of beliefs about classroom management. Some you may opt to exclude from your initial management system; others you may need to investigate further. Remember that effective teachers are reflective teachers, and effective classroom managers can identify not only what they believe about how classrooms should operate, but also why they believe that those things are important.

IDENTIFYING THEMES IN ACTION: TWO ILLUSTRATIVE MANAGEMENT PLANS

Many prospective and beginning teachers are hungry for models of how other teachers have decided to manage their own classrooms. For your perusal, here are two classroom management approaches constructed and used by experienced teachers. One is for use at the primary-grade level, and the other is for use with secondary students. We suspect you'll be interested to read the teachers' efforts at devising management systems for their classes; however, we're not suggesting that you emulate either plan, or even that you'll agree with everything in them. You will have your own way of doing things, and you'll reflect upon your own beliefs and values, the context in which you teach, the needs of your students, and many other factors as you determine what your management plan will be. As you read these two plans, refer back to the Themes Table and determine which ones are present; are any themes missing from either plan?

Example 1. An Approach That Emphasizes Rules and Consequences

Many teachers use management plans built around rules and consequences. They feel this approach provides maximum clarity and allows students to learn in a supportive environment. Management plans of this type involve good teaching combined with (1) a set of *rules* concerning what students are allowed and not allowed to do in class; (2) *consequences*—what happens when students follow the rules and when they violate them; and (3) *procedures* for invoking consequences. This approach has served hundreds of thousands of teachers for many years and is still popular. To see how a present-day teacher uses the rules-consequences-procedures protocol, examine the following program developed by third-grade teacher Deborah Sund.

Deborah Sund's Third-Grade Classroom Management Plan

Deborah Sund, who had been teaching for two years when she devised this program, wanted a management approach that provided structure for class members while meeting the needs of all concerned. Here is her plan.

My Philosophy of Classroom Management

Purpose of Management: I believe the purpose of classroom management is to provide a safe, supportive, calm environment in which students are able to learn to the best of their abilities. To make that possible, I believe teachers should strive to meet the needs of everyone in the class, students and teacher alike.

Students' needs I will keep foremost in mind are:

- To feel safe and personally valued in the group.
- To learn interesting and useful information, especially skills in reading, math, and language.
- A learning environment that is attractive, stimulating, and conducive to productive work.
- A teacher who is helpful, attentive, and kind.
- The opportunity to interact and work cooperatively with other students.
- To learn how to relate to others humanely and helpfully.
- To have the opportunity to excel.

My own needs that I hope will be met are:

- To be respected and valued as a teacher.
- To be able to teach without unwarranted disruptions.
- To have an orderly classroom appearance: good room arrangement; materials neatly stored; interesting, well-thought-out displays.
- To have structure and routines that provide comfort and security with flexibility.
- To have students who are considerate of others, attentive, and willing to participate and follow directions.
- A class sense of warmth, enthusiasm, responsibility, and mutual regard.

My Particular Dislikes: I want to be upfront with my students about my particular dislikes, which are:

- Inattention to speaker, teacher, other adult, or class member.
- Excessive noise: loud voices, inappropriate talking and laughing.
- Distractions such as toys, unnecessary movement, poking, teasing.
- Abuse of instructional materials: misusing, wasting, or destroying.
- Unkind and rude conduct: ridicule, sarcasm, bad manners, and physical abuse.

My Theory of Classroom Management I believe good classroom management must maintain a focus on learning, which in turn is supported by persistent helpfulness and kindness by all class members. I believe the desired behavior is best promoted through preventing misbehavior, supporting proper behavior, practicing class rules, responsibly fulfilling roles and requirements, and relying on instructional tactics that assist students in abiding by the rules.

What I Will Do Proactively to Limit Misbehavior I will familiarize myself further with the known causes of misbehavior and try to attend to all of them in advance. I will make sure to maintain proper lighting, temperature, traffic patterns, and room attractiveness so students won't feel strained, tired, or inconvenienced. I will endeavor to meet students' needs for safety, belonging, and interesting activities. I will plan carefully for modeling, teaching, and practicing good manners and courtesy. I will discuss with my students the meaning and practice of responsibility and why it is so important in learning. And I will carefully plan out an active curriculum that includes interesting activities, physical movement, and singing, along with times of quiet listening and resting.

What I Will Do to Support Proper Behavior *Establish Class Rules.* On the first day of school I will ask my students to tell me how they would like to be treated by others in the room. I will also ask them what kinds of behavior they especially dislike. We will discuss their contributions at length, making sure through examples that we have a clear understanding of everyone's wishes. By the next day, I will have written out some statements that summarize what they have said. I'll then ask if these ideas seem good ones to live by in the class. I anticipate students' agreeing with the ideas, which we will then call our class rules.

Practice Abiding by Rules. We will spend time practicing how we will conduct ourselves in accordance with the rules. I will demonstrate the prompts, cues, hints, and other assistance I will give to help students abide by the behaviors we have agreed on. I expect the following to emerge as class rules:

- Be considerate of others at all times. (We will discuss and practice speaking kindly, behaving helpfully, and not bothering others.)
- Do our best work. (We will discuss the importance of getting as much done as possible, not wasting time, and doing neat work we are proud of.)
- Use quiet voices in the classroom. We will discuss and practice using regular speaking voices during class discussions, speaking quietly during cooperative work, and whispering at other times. I will inform students which volume of voice is appropriate until they learn to use the proper volume automatically.
- Use signals to request permission or receive help. I will explain and have students practice the signals for assistance, movement, and restroom pass.

Recognize and Comply with Roles and Responsibilities. We will identify and practice the "job descriptions" expected of both teacher and students.

I will describe my role, with examples, as including:

- Having main responsibility for what we will learn and making sure we learn it.
- Being as helpful as I can to each and every student, without exception.
- Always treating everyone with kindness and consideration.

I will describe students' roles, with examples, as:

- Paying attention, participating, and doing one's best to learn.
- Always being polite and behaving the way you know is best.
- Helping keep the classroom neat and orderly.

Help Students Learn to Behave Responsibly. To support students' efforts to behave responsibly, I will routinely do many of the things suggested by Fred Jones, such as:

- Circulate among class members to remind them I am attentive and available.
- Interact with individual students to provide acknowledgment and support.
- Provide help immediately as it is needed.
- Show I am genuinely pleased when students follow the rules and behave responsibly. I will make use of winks, nods, and pats. Sometimes I will say aloud how pleased I am with the way they are working or behaving toward each other.
- Keep their caregivers informed about the class activities and their child's progress, and invite them to be involved with the class.
- Begin and end each day on a positive note, with fond greetings or good-byes and expectations of happy and productive days in class.

How I Will Redirect Students When They Break Rules Earlier, when first discussing the class rules, I will ask students what they think should happen when someone breaks a rule. I expect them to suggest punishment, but I will tell them that instead of punishment, I will probably do one of the following:

- Look at them with "pirate eyes" (a stern glance with disappointed or puzzled expression) that lets them know they need to behave properly.
- Point out that a rule is being broken by saying: "I hear noise." "Some people are not listening."
- Tell them exactly what they have done wrong and ask them to do it properly: "Gordon, you did not use the signal. Try again and use the signal this time."
- Have them take "time out" from the group until they can conduct themselves properly.

My Attention to Professionalism I believe the established standards of the teaching profession provide reliable guidance and safeguards for working effectively with colleagues and young learners. I take those standards seriously, none more so than those affecting the physical and psychological safety of the students in my care. I will also check continually to make sure I am complying with the ethical standards of the profession and with normal human decency as well. It is very important to me to present myself as a good teacher, a valued colleague, and a good person.

Example 2: An Approach That Combines Prevention of Misbehavior and Cooperation Between Teacher and Students

The following approach emphasizes preventing misbehavior by meeting students' needs and building personal relationships. It is designed to gain student cooperation and reduce student inclination to disregard or try to outwit the teacher. It emphasizes the following:

- Attending continually to students' needs for security, hope, acceptance, dignity, power, enjoyment, and competence.
- Making class activities consistently enjoyable and worthwhile, with abundant attention, encouragement, and support for students.
- Discussing and practicing manners, courtesy, and responsibility.
- Reducing misbehavior by attending to its causes.

Gail Charles's Classroom Management Plan for Her English Classes

My Philosophy of Classroom Management I think classroom management in a school setting should focus on responsibility and respect for others. I will emphasize to my students why we benefit from getting along with others, why we need to limit some of our personal actions for the good of the group, and why and how classmates and school personnel should be treated with respect and civility. I also believe students can benefit greatly by learning how to speak respectfully with adults, including making eye contact, using a pleasant tone of voice, and making use of courteous expressions such as "please" and "thank you." I agree with Tom Daly that it is beneficial for students to behave in ways that cause teachers to like them. It is highly desirable that students learn to relate respectfully with classmates, as well.

My Theory of Classroom Management I consider there to be four necessary components of an effective system of management. The first component is a set of class rules or agreements that places limits on behavior and informs students how they are to manage their behavior and interact with each other. The second, third, and fourth components are, respectively, preventive tactics that forestall misbehavior, supportive tactics that reinforce proper behavior and help students persevere, and redirective tactics that cause misbehaving students to return to proper behavior. My preventive tactics will include providing a suitable learning environment and preparing lessons with student needs in mind. My supportive tactics will feature positive interactions with students, much student participation in lessons, and quick attention and help to students when they need it. My redirective tactics for most misbehavior will involve body language, physical proximity, and asking students to redo misbehavior correctly. I believe these efforts will maintain good interpersonal relations, increase student self-control, and increase student productivity.

The Professional and Ethical Behavior I Will Display Here are matters of professionalism I will endeavor to live by:

First, I will give my best to my students and the profession. I will provide the best learning environment I can and will teach using the best methods known to me. I will show the high value I place on education. I will model responsibility and self-control. I will laud effort and accept mistakes as a natural part of learning.

Second, I will supervise and safeguard the well-being of my students at all times. I will always be mindful of due diligence and my obligations associated with *in loco parentis*.

Third, I will value and respect my students as social equals and friends. I will keep my promises and commitments to them, be helpful in all situations, and strive to be fair and consistent. I will do my best to remain positive and optimistic. And as William Glasser suggests, I will do my best to replace my "deadly habits" of blaming, complaining, criticizing, nagging, punishing, rewarding to control, and threatening with the "connecting habits" of befriending, caring, contributing, encouraging, listening, supporting, and trusting in all of my interactions with students, their families, and my colleagues.

Fourth, I will treat my students' families as valued partners. I will maintain a class website to inform families of class policies, assignments, and upcoming events. I will update students' grades weekly. I will support PTA projects and keep lines of communication open.

Fifth, I will maintain a network of mutual support with my colleagues. I will express interest in their personal lives. I will show myself as open to new ideas and suggestions, and will offer support by sharing supplies, experiences, ideas, and lessons when asked. I will contribute to the school by volunteering to help with extracurricular activities and programs.

And sixth, I will show I am trustworthy by keeping confidences, following through on commitments, and not gossiping. I will behave in a way that reflects well on me, my family, my school, my district, and the profession. I will comply with state and federal regulations and school district policies, and I will do my best to be truthful, compassionate, and kind in my dealings with others.

The Behavior I Will Endeavor to Promote and the Rules That Support It Here's what I will try to promote in my students:

I want them to share my enthusiasm for learning. I want them to show self-discipline and persistence in learning. And I want them to be respectful, patient, and tolerant in their dealings with others.

I will use the following rules to support proper behavior:

■ Treat others in this classroom the way you would like to be treated.
■ Pay attention and complete assignments on time.
■ Do your best. When you make mistakes, learn from them, and don't give up.
■ Do your part to keep the classroom running smoothly.
■ Always behave in a way that shows the kind of person you want to be.

What I Will Do Proactively to Prevent or Reduce Misbehavior I will do my best to address, in advance, conditions that are likely to promote misbehavior. I will do the following:

First, I will ensure that the classroom is comfortable and conducive to learning, as concerns lighting, ventilation, temperature, seating, and the availability of ample textbooks and materials for various lessons.

Second, I will endeavor to devise lessons that keep students involved, including topics of interest to students, skills that have value and relevance, and activities that call for much student participation.

Third, I will teach in an engaging style. I will bring energy and enthusiasm to the classroom. I will inject humor, novelty, challenge, and fun to keep things lively. And I will personally interact a great deal with students in all phases of the lesson.

Fourth, I will be continually mindful of meeting students' needs, ensure they experience a sense of belonging, and find ways for them to make choices and participate in class decisions.

Fifth, I will do my best to create routines and procedures that facilitate a highly functional classroom. I will teach the routines to students, have students rehearse them, and reteach the routines as needed until all students become familiar with them.

How I Will Support My Students' Efforts to Participate and Persevere I will support my students' efforts to learn through my physical presence and the ways I speak.

Physical Presence: I will be conspicuous in the classroom rather than inconspicuous. I will circulate, use proximity, and be quickly alongside students who seem to need help. I will use eye contact, facial expressions, gestures, and posture to show I am attentive to them.

Manner of Speaking: I will speak to students in ways that show caring, appreciation, kindness, and encouragement. I will notice and comment on new hairstyles, clothing, braces on/off, and so forth. I will ask students how they are feeling and listen to their responses. I will acknowledge accomplishment, and I will offer help and hope. I will speak with kindness, as I would speak to a friend and, if necessary, teach students to speak to me in the same way.

At the same time, I will avoid speaking to students in ways that nag, threaten, intimidate, criticize, humiliate, or belittle. I will not ask them "why" they did something. I will not raise my voice to them or pronounce judgments on them.

How I Will Make Sure Students Know What They Are Expected to Do As indicated previously, I will establish procedures for classroom routines and carefully teach the procedures and provide practice. I will make plain what students are to do at the beginning of the class period, how to put headings on their papers, how papers will be collected, how students are to prepare for dismissal, and what they are to do when they hear the fire alarm.

Further, I will provide oral and written instructions for each assignment and check to make sure students understand. I will monitor students as they begin independent work. When necessary, I will provide visual instructional plans for students to follow as Fred Jones suggests. I will also post assignment directions on my classroom website for student reference.

Finally, I will teach students how to engage and participate in various types of exercises I like to emphasize, such as those that call upon a variety of learning modalities, involve teamwork, and permit choices and creative thinking.

How I Will Engage Students Actively When I Am Providing Instruction Any time I use large-group instruction, I want to keep my students actively engaged. Here are some things I will use toward that end: I will use Fred Jones's Say, See, Do teaching. I will frequently check for understanding. I will build novelty and fun into the lesson. I will relate the lesson to the students' lives. I will incorporate media when possible. I will pace the lesson carefully and make adjustments to keep it moving forward.

How I Will Monitor Students During Independent Work I will use Fred Jones's "interior loop" seating arrangement for quick access to all students. I will circulate among students to help them stay on task and to provide help as needed. I will use body language such as proximity, posture, eye contact, gestures, and facial expressions. I will use smiles, nods, winks, and thumbs-up, but will refrain from head shaking, eye rolling, and scowls. I will attempt to show confidence and energy.

How I Will Influence Students to Do High-Quality Work I will provide students specific examples of high-quality work by former students and explain why it is good. I will also provide rubrics for guidance and self-evaluation. I will have students keep portfolios of their work and compile a "showcase portfolio" of their best work over a given grading period.

How I Will Redirect Students When They Misbehave When students misbehave, here's what I will do:

In a positive manner, I will stop the misbehavior and take an appropriate action to help students return to appropriate behavior. Here are some of the tactics I will use:

Low-key options: (1) Eye contact, facial expression, body language, and proximity. (2) Using Marshall's Hierarchy, ask the student to describe the current level of behavior. (3) Mention to the class that a rule is being broken and ask them to behave as they know they should.

Mid-level options: (1) Ask the student to repeat the behavior correctly. (2) Choose a technique such as "picture it right" as suggested by Spencer Kagan. (3) Ask the student to reflect on the misbehavior and take responsibility for finding a solution, as suggested by Barbara Coloroso.

Stronger options: (1) Engage the student in thinking responsibly as suggested by Ed Ford (2004), who asks students, when necessary, in a calm voice (a) What are you doing? (b) Is that against the rules? (c) What could you do that would be better? (2) Apply leverage such as after-school detention as suggested by Craig Seganti to ensure compliance. (3) Have the student take "time out" and sit alone in a designated area or in a colleague's classroom. (4) In cases of absolute refusal to comply with my directions, I will very calmly tell the student I know I can't make him or her comply, but it is absolutely necessary that students follow my directions; those who are unwilling to do so will have to be placed elsewhere. I will tell the student that I am genuinely sorry we could not work this out, but I will ask the principal to proceed with finding another placement for the student (for this, I will have previously made sure of the principal's approval and support).

How and When I Will Communicate My Management Approach to Students, Administrators, and Students' Caregivers Here are some of the things I am considering for explaining my classroom management plan to students. I will cover the plan thoroughly at the beginning of a term and review it periodically thereafter.

- Create a PowerPoint presentation to share with students.
- Prepare note-taking sheets for students to use during my initial presentation for later feedback.
- Print rules and "My Job—Your Job" lists on a single sheet of paper to distribute to students.
- Post classroom management plan and rules sheet on the class website.
- Post charts of rules in the classroom.

- Review, rehearse, and reteach as many times as necessary.
- Ask students to sign a form indicating they understand and will abide by the classroom management plan.

I will share this plan in its entirety with my principal before the year or term begins. I will ask for feedback, suggestions, and support. I will make suggested modifications if needed.

Once the principal has approved my plan, I will post it on the classroom website. I will print out rules and "My Job—Your Job" on single sheets of paper and send them home for families to review. I will request that caregivers sign a form indicating they have read and understood the plan and support it. I will cover the plan again with them on Back to School Night.

END WORD

And so we come to the end. We are confident that you are now prepared to develop and implement an effective system of classroom management that is compatible with your personality, values, and beliefs; we also believe that your system will be optimized for inviting students' cooperation, meeting their needs, supporting their efforts, and helping them become better and more successful people.

As you put your plan into effect, you can expect to make some mistakes. That's nothing to worry about because mistakes, when corrected, enhance quality, and those corrections or improvements are long remembered. Talk with your peers. Continue your professional development. Ask for feedback from your students, their caregivers, and your administration. Enjoy the puzzle that is teaching; we're confident that you're well on your way to becoming not just an effective manager, but an effective teacher.

MyLab Education Self-Check 14.1

MyLab Education Application Exercise 14.1 Putting It All Together: Making Classroom Management Decisions

MyLab Education Application Exercise 14.2 Evaluating a Lesson for Management Strengths and Weaknesses

Glossary

The following terms are given special emphasis in this book. When appropriate, authorities who originated and/or helped popularize a given term are indicated.

ABCD of disruptive behavior (Kagan): Aggression, breaking rules, confrontations, disengagement.

Academic difficulties Problems with learning that may be associated with compromised memory, fine and gross motor skills, comprehension, and language or mathematics abilities.

Acceptable behavior Student conduct that is consistent with class expectations. It does not interfere with learning, demean others, or violate moral codes of society.

Accountability Showing responsibility in discharging expected tasks.

ADHD Attention-deficit hyperactivity disorder. The second most common diagnosis in NBB, characterized by short attention span, weak impulse control, restlessness.

Aggression (Kagan; others): Behavior in which hostility or unwanted attention is directed toward others.

Appraising reality (Redl & Wattenberg): Having students acknowledge what they are doing wrong.

Appreciative praise (Ginott): Praise that expresses gratitude or admiration for effort.

Appropriate behavior Student conduct that is consistent with class expectations. It does not interfere with learning, demean others, or violate moral codes of society.

Assertive response style (Canter & Canter): Responding to student behavior in a helpful manner while insisting that class rules be followed.

Assertive teachers (Canter & Canter): Teachers who clearly, confidently, and consistently reiterate class expectations and attempt to build trust with students.

At-risk, behaviorally Refers to students who are likely to fail in school because of unacceptable behavior.

Attention-seeking (Dreikurs): A mistaken goal of student behavior, involving disruption and showing off, to gain attention from the teacher and other students.

Authority without punishment (Marshall): Methods of exerting authority in the classroom without resorting to threat or punishment.

Autism spectrum disorder (ASD): A range of disorders in which individuals fail to develop normal speech patterns or personal relationships.

Autocratic classrooms (Dreikurs): Classrooms in which the teacher makes all decisions and imposes them upon students.

Autocratic teachers (Dreikurs): Teachers who command, demand cooperation, dominate, and criticize.

Backup system (Jones): The planned action teachers take when students misbehave seriously and refuse to comply with positive teacher requests—often involves being sent to the principal's office.

Basic needs Psychological requirements for normal functioning.

Basic student needs

(Charles): Security, association belonging, hope, dignity, power, enjoyment, and competence.
(Dreikurs): Belonging.
(Glasser): Security, belonging, power, freedom, fun.

Behavior The totality of one's physical and mental activities.

Behavior as choice (Glasser; others): The contention that students choose their behavior at any given time.

Behavior difficulties Generally, student behavior that breaks rules or disrupts learning.

Behavior management Organized efforts to influence students to behave in particular ways.

Behavior modification (Skinner's followers): The use of Skinnerian principles of reinforcement to control or shape behavior.

Behavior shaping (Skinner): The process of gradually modifying behavior through application, or withdrawal, of reinforcement.

Bell work (Jones; Wong & Wong): Work students do to begin a class period that does not require instruction from the teacher, such as reading, writing in journals, or completing warm-up activities.

Belonging (Dreikurs; Glasser; others): A basic human need for legitimate membership in groups, with attendant security and comfort. For Dreikurs, the primary need that motivates social behavior in school.

Big Three of discipline (Kagan): (1) Establish an interesting curriculum. (2) Provide meaningful cooperative activities. (3) Be an interesting teacher; adapt curriculum to student needs.

Bipolar disorder   A mental health diagnosis characterized by alternating cycles of euphoria and depression.

Body carriage   (Jones): Posture and movement—can indicate to students whether the teacher is well, ill, in charge, tired, disinterested, or intimidated.

Body language   (Jones): Nonverbal communication transmitted through posture, eye contact, gestures, and facial expressions.

Boss managers   (Glasser): Teachers who set the tasks, direct the learning activities, ask for little student input, and grade student work. (Contrasted with *lead managers.*)

Brain injuries, nontraumatic   Cerebral injuries resulting from disrupted blood flow to the brain (as in strokes), or from tumors, infections, drug overdoses, and certain medical conditions.

Brain injuries, traumatic   Cerebral injuries resulting from blows or other physical damage to the brain, incurred during events such as accidents, sporting events, assaults, or birth.

Breach of duty   A teacher's failure to comply with one or more legal obligations at school.

Causes of misbehavior   (Charles): Factors known to foster misbehavior, such as boredom and threat to personal dignity. Charles identifies 26 such factors, most of which can be minimized or eliminated in the classroom.

Charisma, teacher   (Charles): Teacher personal allure that attracts student attention and cooperation.

Choice theory   (Glasser): Theory that we all choose how to behave at any time, cannot control anyone's behavior but our own, and that all behavior is purposeful in meeting basic needs.

Class agreements   Agreements or codes formalized by teachers and students that indicate how class behavior, instruction, and other matters are to occur.

Class code of conduct   See **Class agreements.**

Class roles   Roles that students play in the classroom, either unintentionally (Dreikurs) or because they are stipulated as "jobs" in the class agreements (Gossen; others).

Class rules   Written statements that specify acceptable and unacceptable behavior in the classroom.

Classroom management   Everything teachers do to establish and maintain conditions wherein teachers can teach, students can learn, students cooperate with one another, and teacher and students experience satisfaction.

Classroom meetings   (Glasser; others): Planned, regularly scheduled sessions for all class members and teacher to promote communication, allow for feedback on activities and policies, and address and solve problems.

Classroom procedures   Detailed instructions that show students how to perform all activities in class—effective use can eliminate a number of discipline problems.

Communities, classroom   (Kohn): Classrooms and schools where students feel cared about and care about each other, are valued and respected, are involved in decision making, and have a sense of "we" rather than "I."

Community building   Intentional efforts to develop and communicate a sense of belonging, trust, and respect among class members.

Compliance training   (Morrish): Efforts to cause students routinely to abide by teacher requests and directions—an important element in Morrish's approach to discipline.

Conferring dignity   (Ginott; Curwin & Mendler; others): Showing respect for students by putting aside their past history, treating them considerately, and being concerned only with the present situation.

Confrontation   (Kagan): One of four basic types of classroom misbehavior featured in Win-Win Discipline; occurs when parties involved vie for control and/or attempt to show dominance.

Congruent communication   (Ginott): A style of communication in which teachers acknowledge and accept students' feelings about situations and themselves.

Culturally responsive teaching   An approach to education that calls for teachers to recognize and dispose of their own cultural biases, to consider and learn about students' cultural contexts, and to honor and include students' cultural identities as a foundation for instruction.

Democratic classrooms   (Dreikurs): Classrooms in which teachers give students responsibility and involve them in making decisions.

Democratic teachers   (Dreikurs): Teachers who show friendly guidance and encourage students to take on responsibility, cooperate, and participate in making decisions.

Discipline   (Charles): What teachers do to help students conduct themselves appropriately in class. (Jones): Efforts to engage students in learning, with teachers using the most positive, unobtrusive tactics possible.

Discipline, preventive   (Charles): Steps teachers take in advance to prevent or reduce the occurrence of misbehavior.

Discipline, redirective   (Charles): Steps teachers take to stop misbehavior and redirect it in a positive manner.

Discipline, supportive   (Charles): Tactics teachers use in an ongoing manner to help students remain attentive and on-task.

Discipline structures (Kagan): Discipline tactics that are designed for addressing types of disruptive behavior.

Disengagement Withdrawing from an activity or not paying attention; "D" of Kagan's ABCD of disruptive behavior.

Displaying inadequacy (Dreikurs): Student withdrawal and failure to try.

Disruptive behavior Actions that disrupt teaching or learning. Often used interchangeably with "misbehavior."

Doorway tactics (Seganti): Tactics teachers use as students enter the room to help ensure that students do not misbehave.

Do-over (Morrish): A tactic in which teachers ask students to repeat, in a correct manner, a behavior that has not been acceptable.

Due diligence A responsibility of all school personnel to pay close and reasonable attention to students under supervision; reasonable care must be taken to protect students from harm.

Dyscalculia Learning difficulty characterized by difficulties with mathematics.

Dysgraphia Learning difficulty characterized by difficulties with handwriting and spelling.

Dyslexia Learning difficulty characterized by struggles in word recognition, spelling, word decoding, and occasionally with the phonological (sound) component of language.

Dyspraxia Learning difficulty characterized by difficulty with fine motor skills.

Empowerment of choice (Marshall): Allowing students to select from acceptable choices how they will conduct themselves—a tactic that empowers students to succeed.

Essential virtues, seven (Borba): Empathy, conscience, self-control, respect, kindness, tolerance, and fairness, all of which can and should be taught in school.

Ethical concerns The professional requirement that teachers conduct themselves in accordance with moral and legal codes of conduct.

Ethics Behavior considered in terms of what is right and what is wrong.

Evaluative praise (Ginott): Praise that expresses judgment about students' character or quality of work. Considered to be detrimental by Ginott and various other authorities.

External motivation Synonymous with *extrinsic motivation*—that which comes from outside the individual.

Extinction (Skinner): In behavior management, the gradual removal of a given behavior, accomplished by withholding reinforcement.

Fetal alcohol spectrum disorder (FASD): A mental health diagnosis in which students show poor impulse control, poor judgment, lack of common sense, and learning difficulties; caused by alcohol consumption by the mother during pregnancy.

Fidelity The extent to which members of a PBIS school staff are applying the core features of the PBIS model.

15-minute detention (Seganti): The requirement that misbehaving students must attend after-school detention for 15 minutes; provides strong leverage in ensuring that students comply with class rules.

Five A's (Albert): Acceptance, attention, appreciation, affirmation, and affection. Used for establishing and strengthening interpersonal connections.

Follow-up structures (Kagan): A discipline tactic used to help students develop proper behavior over the long run; used when students need additional assistance in behaving responsibly.

Four classical virtues (Marshall): Prudence, temperance, justice, and fortitude. Should be emphasized in the process of helping students develop desirable behavior.

Four essential skills (Nelson & Lott): 1. Intrapersonal. (I understand my emotions and can control myself.) 2. Interpersonal. (I can communicate, cooperate, and work well with others.) 3. Strategic. (I am flexible, adaptable, and responsible.) 4. Judgmental. (I can use my wisdom to evaluate situations.)

Frame of reference (Covey): Point of view. To communicate effectively, it is important to understand the other's perception of reality.

Freedom (Glasser): A basic student need that can be met when the teacher allows choices in subject matter and in methods of study.

Fun (Glasser): A basic student need that can be met when the teacher provides opportunities for students to work and talk with others, engage in interesting activities, and share accomplishments.

General rules (Jones): Rules that define class standards and expectations that apply at all times, as distinct from specific rules related to certain activities.

Genuine incentives (Jones) Incentives that truly motivate students to work or behave appropriately, as contrasted with vague incentives such as "become a better person."

Grandma's rule (Jones): "First eat your vegetables, then you can have your dessert," or, "First finish your work, then you can do something you especially enjoy."

Group alerting (Kounin): Quickly getting students' attention to advise them of what they should be doing or do next.

Group behavior (Redl & Wattenberg): Behavior occurring in groups that is different from the ways individuals typically behave—more conforming in some ways, combined with more risk-taking.

Group concern (Jones): A condition in which every student has a stake in the behavior the group uses to earn preferred activity time.

Group dynamics (Redl & Wattenberg): Psychological forces that occur within groups and influence the behavior of group members.

Guided choices (Marshall): Eliciting from students a consequence or procedure to help redirect inappropriate or impulsive behaviors.

Habits Patterns of willful behavior ingrained to the point that we repeat them without having to think.

Helpless handraisers (Jones): Those students who sit with hands raised, not working unless the teacher is hovering nearby.

Hidden asset, the teacher's (Ginott): Sincerely asking students, "How can I help you?"

Hidden rules (Payne): Seldom-recognized values and guidelines that strongly affect behavior in various ethnic and socio-economic groups.

Hierarchy of Social Development (Marshall): A hierarchy of four levels used to help students reflect on their chosen behaviors. From lowest to highest, the four levels are: (A) anarchy, (B) bossing/bullying, (C) cooperation/conformity, and (D) democracy (inseparable from responsibility). Levels A and B are unacceptable in the classroom. Level C is the expected level of behavior and is essential for a civil society. Level D connotes taking the initiative to do the right thing without supervision.

I-messages (Ginott): Teachers' expressing their personal feelings and reactions to situations without addressing student behavior or character: Example, "I have trouble teaching when there is so much noise in the room."

Inappropriate behavior Any behavior that through intent or thoughtlessness interferes with teaching or learning, threatens or intimidates others, or oversteps society's standards of moral, ethical, or legal behavior.

In loco parentis Teachers' exercising care over students as if they were the students' parents—in place of parents.

Incentive (Jones): Something outside of the individual that can be anticipated and that entices the individual to act.

Incentive, genuine (Jones): An incentive that motivates all members of the class rather than just a few.

Individual supports (PBIS): Tailored support designed to meet the needs of individual students whose inappropriate behavior persists after Tier 1 and Tier 2 interventions.

Influence techniques (Redl & Wattenberg; others): Helping students behave properly by providing attention and support, rather than punishment.

Insistence (Morrish): A discipline tactic teachers should use when students show reluctance to comply with directions.

InTASC The Interstate New Teacher Assessment and Support Consortium that has described competencies teachers require for professional teaching.

Interior loop (Jones): A classroom seating arrangement with wide aisles that allows teachers to move easily among students at work.

Internal motivation (Marshall): The desire to behave responsibly without having to be told to do so, because of innate needs or beliefs rooted in ethics and values.

Interventions (Kagan & others): What teachers do to deal with misbehavior at the moment of disruption, for follow-up, and for the long term.

Inviting cooperation (Ginott): Encouraging and enticing students into activities and giving them choices, rather than demanding their participation.

Irresponsible behavior (Kagan & others): Synonymous with *misbehavior*.

Laconic language (Ginott): Brevity of teacher's comments about misbehavior. Example: "This is work time."

Language difficulties Problems in understanding, processing, and expressing information verbally.

Lead managers (Glasser): Teachers who involve students in exploring topics and activities for learning. Lead teachers also provide necessary help and encourage students to do quality work. (Contrasted with *boss managers*.)

Learning communities (Kohn): See **Communities, classroom.**

Learning disabilities (LD): Unusual difficulties students exhibit in learning certain subjects in school. A mental health diagnosis, not simply a teacher observation.

Leverage (Seganti): Something that teachers can use to ensure student compliance with rules. In Seganti's approach, leverage exists in the form of the 15-minute detention after school.

Limits The imaginary boundaries that separate acceptable/appropriate behavior from misbehavior/inappropriate behavior.

Long-term structures (Kagan): Plans for helping students get along with others, become more self-directing, and control their behavior.

Massive time wasting (Jones): A condition Jones found prevalent in classrooms where discipline was not done efficiently.

Metacognition Being able to think about and actively control one's thought processes.

Misbehavior Behavior that is considered inappropriate for the setting or situation in which it occurs. Any behavior that, through intent or thoughtlessness, interferes with teaching or learning, threatens or intimidates others, or oversteps society's standards of moral, ethical, or legal behavior.

Misbehavior, causes of (Charles): Factors that reside in students, the class environment, school personnel, and elsewhere that tend to promote student misbehavior. (Charles identifies 26 such factors.)

Misbehavior, teacher (Charles): Anything teachers do in the classroom that adversely affects learning or human relations, or that is unprofessional in any way.

Misbehavior, types of

(Charles): Inattention, apathy, needless talk, moving about the room, annoying others, disruption, lying, stealing, cheating, sexual harassment, aggression and fighting, malicious mischief, and defiance of authority.
(Coloroso): Mistakes (unintentional), mischief (intentional light misbehavior), and mayhem (more serious misbehavior).
(Dreikurs): Attention-seeking, power-seeking, revenge-seeking behaviors, and feigned helplessness.
(Kagan): Aggression, breaking rules, confrontation, and disengagement.

Mistaken goals (Dreikurs): Goals of attention, power, revenge, and avoidance of failure that students seek in the mistaken belief they will bring positive recognition and sense of belonging.

Momentum (Kounin): Refers to teachers' getting activities started promptly, keeping them moving ahead, and bringing them to efficient transition or closure.

Moral intelligence (Borba): The ability to distinguish right from wrong, the establishment and maintenance of strong ethical convictions, and the willingness to act on those convictions in an honorable way.

Need A mental construct (an imaginary "something") we use to explain motivation and behavior; a desire that is long-lasting and recurrent.

Needs of students, basic

(Charles): Security, association, belonging, hope, dignity, power, enjoyment, competence.
(Dreikurs): Belonging.
(Glasser): Security, love and belonging, power, freedom, fun.

Neglected 50% (Charles): The aspect of teaching that exerts positive influence on students to cooperate and make an effort in class. Tactics involve persuasion, personal charisma, skillful communication, intriguing questions, personal attention, helpfulness.

Negligence A teacher's failure to maintain a careful watch over students under supervision.

Nonassertive teachers (Canter & Canter): Teachers who fail to take charge and instead assume a passive, hands-off approach in dealing with students.

Noncoercive tactics (Glasser; Marshall; many others): Discipline in which teachers invite, encourage, and otherwise influence students to behave properly, without using demands or threats.

Omission training (Jones): An incentive plan for an individual student who, by cutting down on undesired behavior, can earn preferred activity time for the entire class.

Oppositional defiant disorder A mental health diagnosis in which students regularly oppose and defy the teacher and others.

Overlapping (Kounin): Refers to teachers' attending to two or more issues in the classroom at the same time.

Ownership of behavior problem (Coloroso; Ford): Students taking responsibility for their improper actions in advance of working out appropriate solutions.

Permissive classrooms (Dreikurs): Classrooms in which teachers overlook students' failure to comply with rules, which suggests teacher acceptance of misbehavior.

Permissive teachers (Dreikurs): Teachers who put few if any limits on student behavior and do not invoke consequences for disruptive behavior.

Perspective taking (Kohn): Doing one's best to see and understand a situation from another person's point of view.

Philosophy of discipline The beliefs one has about the nature, purpose, and value of discipline.

Physical proximity (Redl & Wattenberg; others): The teacher's moving close to a student who is becoming restive or is misbehaving.

Picture it right (Kagan): A tactic in which students are asked to picture how they would like the class to be and verbalize what they need to do to make it that way.

Positive Behavior Interventions and Supports (PBIS): A schoolwide systems change process designed to promote positive, prosocial behavior throughout all areas of the school. PBIS is an implementation framework that relies on data to inform management decisions.

Positive influence What teachers do to invite or entice students to cooperate, through providing helpful assistance rather than criticism.

Positivity (Marshall): Maintaining an inclination toward optimism.

Poverty Term used to describe a family that has to spend more than one-third of its disposable income for food adequate to meet the family's nutritional needs is said to be living in poverty.

Power (Glasser): A basic student need for control, satisfied when students are given significant duties in the class and are allowed to participate in making decisions about class matters.

Power-seeking behavior (Dreikurs): Behaviors such as temper tantrums, backtalk, disrespect, and defiance that students use to try to show they have power over the teacher.

Praxis A series of tests published by the Educational Testing Service for assessing the competency of teachers.

Preferred Activity Time, or PAT (Jones): Time allocated for students to engage in activities of their preference; used as an incentive to encourage responsible behavior.

Preventive discipline (Charles): The aspect of discipline in which one removes or otherwise controls factors likely to lead to misbehavior.

Procedures (Wong & Wong): Detailed instructions that show students how to perform all activities in class—effective use can eliminate a number of discipline problems.

Professionalism For teachers, displaying the fairest, most considerate, and most ethical ways of fulfilling the duties of the teaching profession.

Providing help efficiently (Jones): A technique in which the teacher quickly provides enough help to get a student working again, then moves away. To be accomplished in 20 seconds or less.

Proximity Moving close to a student who is misbehaving.

Quality curriculum (Glasser): A program of study that emphasizes excellence in learning in topics that students consider useful.

Quality teaching (Glasser): Instruction in which teachers help students become proficient in knowledge and skills the students consider important. This is usually done via "lead teaching."

Quality World (Glasser): A mental image of what an individual would like his or her life to be like.

Rage Extreme behavior, sometimes exhibited by students with NBB, manifested as an explosion of temper that occurs suddenly with no real warning and may turn violent.

Rage cycle (Cook): Progression of rage episode through four phases—triggering, escalation, rage (or meltdown), and post-rage (or post-meltdown).

Real Discipline (Morrish): An approach to discipline that makes use of teacher insistence and careful teaching of expectations and procedures.

Real Discipline, three phases of (Morrish): Training, teaching, and management.

Reconciliation (Coloroso): A human relations skill in which individuals who have been in a dispute take steps to resolve and smooth over their differences.

Reflective questions (Marshall): Questions posed to students to help them make better behavioral choices and assume responsibility.

Reinforcing stimuli (Skinner): Stimuli received by an organism immediately following a behavior that increase the likelihood the behavior will be repeated.

Resolution (Coloroso): Identifying and correcting whatever caused a behavior problem—one of the follow-up steps in dealing with misbehavior.

Responsible behavior Student behavior consistent with class expectations—does not interfere with learning, demean others, or violate the moral codes of society. Synonymous with *proper behavior*.

Restitution (Gossen; Coloroso): Repairing or replacing damage done when one behaves irresponsibly—one of the steps in resolving the problem.

Right to learn (Canter & Canter): The contention that students have a right to learn in classrooms that are safe and free from threat.

Right to teach (Canter & Canter): The contention that teachers have a right to teach in classrooms that are free from disruptions, with backing from administrators and caregivers.

Rule A firm expectation for students' behavior; in most classroom management models, rules govern time, space, materials, and safety, among other areas.

Sane messages (Ginott): Teacher messages that address situations rather than students' character.

Satiation (Kounin): Getting all one can tolerate of a given activity, resulting in frustration, boredom, or listlessness.

Say, See, Do teaching (Jones): A teaching method of repeated short cycles of teacher input, each followed by student response. Keeps students attentive and involved.

Scaffolding Teachers provide as much framing and assistance as is needed to move the student toward a learning goal, then fade the guidance as students gain independence in the new concept or skill.

Self-diagnostic referral (Marshall): A self-diagnosis done by a student who has violated class rules and submitted as a plan for improvement—includes description of what was done wrong and the steps that will be taken to improve.

Self-discipline, for teachers (Ginott): When working with students, being careful to not display behaviors that should be eradicated in students, such as raising the voice to end noise and reacting rudely to impolite students.

Self-restitution (Gossen): An activity in which students who have behaved inappropriately are encouraged to reflect on their behavior, identify the need that prompted it, and create a new way of behaving as the responsible person they want to be. This was the first system to ask misbehaving students to make things right within themselves and improve from the experience.

Sense of community (Kohn): A condition in classrooms where students feel safe and are continually brought into making judgments, expressing their opinions, and working cooperatively toward solutions that affect themselves and the class.

Sensory integration dysfunction (SID): Irregularities in the process we use to take in information from our senses, organize it, interpret it, and respond to it.

Sensory processing disorder Same as *sensory integration dysfunction*.

Setting limits Clarifying with the class exactly what is expected of them.

Seven connecting habits vs. seven deadly habits (Glasser): Seven habits that help teachers connect with students are *caring, listening, supporting, contributing, encouraging, trusting,* and *befriending*. They should replace the seven deadly habits of *criticizing, blaming, complaining, nagging, threatening, punishing,* and *rewarding students to control them*.

Shaping behavior (Skinner): The process of using reinforcement to produce desired behavior in students.

Significant seven (Nelsen & Lott): Within a positive classroom environment, students develop three empowering perceptions about themselves: (1) personal capability, (2) significance in primary relationships, (3) personal power. They develop four essential skills: (1) intrapersonal, (2) interpersonal, (3) strategic, (4) judgmental.

SIR (Glasser): An acronym standing for the process of self-evaluation, improvement, and repetition, used to promote quality.

Smoothness (Kounin): Absence of abrupt changes or interruptions by the teacher that interfere with students' activities or thought processes.

Social interest (Dreikurs): The concept that one's personal well-being is dependent on the well-being of the group. This encourages individuals to behave in ways that benefit the group.

Specific rules (Jones): Rules relating to procedures and routines that detail exactly what students are to do in various learning activities.

Structures (Kagan): Discipline approaches designed for use with particular combinations of disruptions and student needs; specific plans of action that teachers use to teach the curriculum and to address misbehavior.

Student needs
(Charles): Security, association belonging, hope, dignity, power, enjoyment, competence.
(Dreikurs): Belonging.
(Glasser): Security, love and belonging, control, freedom, fun.

Student positions (Kagan): Conglomerates of factors that leave students uninformed or dispose them to seek attention, show anger, avoid failure, become bored, seek control, or be overly energetic.

Student responsibility (Jones; Glasser; Marshall; others): The contention that students have the obligation to reflect on their behavior choices, recognize how they affect themselves and others, and deal with whatever consequences occur.

Student roles (Redl & Wattenberg): Roles students assume in the classroom, such as instigator, clown, leader, and scapegoat.

Successive approximations (Skinner): Behavior that, through reinforcement, moves progressively closer to the desired goal.

Support buddies (Wong & Wong): Students assigned to help or support each other; members of cooperative learning groups.

Support groups (Wong & Wong): Groups of students who help and support each other; cooperative learning groups.

Survival (Glasser): A basic need that motivates self-protective behavior.

Synergetic teaching (Charles): Teaching in a manner that energizes the class. Done by putting in place combinations of elements known to produce heightened classroom energy.

Targeted supports (PBIS): Interventions for students whose behavior indicates that they would benefit from more in-depth teaching of effective behaviors. Targeted (Tier 2) supports are typically delivered in small groups and are of short duration.

Teacher misbehavior (Charles): Anything teachers do in the classroom that adversely affects learning or human relations, or that is unprofessional in any way.

Teacher roles (Redl & Wattenberg): Various roles students expect teachers to play, such as surrogate parent, arbitrator, disciplinarian, and moral authority.

Teacher self-discipline (Ginott): Teacher self-control, of paramount importance in helping students conduct themselves appropriately.

Teacher–student same-side collaboration (Kagan): A "we" approach that gives teachers and students a joint interest in maintaining responsible behavior.

Teachers at their best (Ginott): Teachers, when using congruent communication that addresses situations rather than students' character, invites student cooperation, and accepts students as they are.

Teachers at their worst (Ginott): Teachers, when they name-call, label students, ask rhetorical *why* questions, give long moralistic lectures, and make caustic remarks to their students.

Teachers' hidden asset (Ginott): Showing willingness to help any given student at any given moment.

Theory of discipline An overall explanation of the elements that comprise discipline and how they work together to produce particular outcomes.

Theory X and Theory Y (Marshall): Theories of managing people. Theory X holds that people must be directed and controlled, whereas Theory Y holds that people should be encouraged and given responsibility.

Three C's (Albert): To help students feel that they have an important place in class; focus on helping students (1) feel capable, (2) connect with others, (3) make contributions to class and to others.

Three facets of discipline (Charles): (1) Preventive discipline, to forestall misbehavior. (2) Supportive discipline, to encourage appropriate behavior. (3) Redirective discipline, to stop misbehavior and help students move to appropriate behavior.

Three perceptions (Nelson & Lott): 1. Perception of *personal capability*. (I have ability; I can do this.) 2. Perception of *significance in primary relationships*. (I am needed; I belong.) 3. Perception of *personal power* to influence one's own life. (I have control over how I respond to what happens to me.)

Three phases of Real Discipline (Morrish): (1) Training for compliance, (2) teaching students how to behave, and (3) managing student choice.

Three pillars of Win-Win Discipline (Kagan): (1) Same side—students and teachers work together for benefit of students. (2) Collaborative solutions—teachers and students work together to solve discipline problems. (3) Learned responsibility—students develop desire to behave appropriately, practice self-management, and get along with others.

Traditional teaching (Glasser): Teaching in which the teacher states expectations, strives for student compliance, makes and enforces rules of conduct, directs almost all aspects of lessons, and evaluates student performance.

Types of classroom misbehavior

(Charles): Inattention, apathy, needless talk, moving about the room, annoying others, disruption, lying, stealing, cheating, sexual harassment, aggression and fighting, malicious mischief, and defiance of authority.

(Coloroso): Mistakes (unintentional), mischief (intentional light misbehavior), and mayhem (more serious misbehavior).

(Dreikurs): Attention-seeking, power-seeking, revenge-seeking, and feigned helplessness.

(Kagan): Aggression, breaking rules, confrontation, and disengagement.

Universal supports (PBIS): Preventive methods implemented schoolwide to establish and maintain, to the greatest extent possible, a positive and productive learning environment.

Unobtrusive tactic (Jones): A discipline tactic directed at a particular student that is unnoticed by most of the class members, such as facial expression, eye contact, hand signal, or physical proximity.

Useful work (Glasser): Schoolwork that deals with skills and information that students deem valuable in their lives.

Value judgments (Glasser): Students evaluate their own work in terms of quality—a step in moving toward high-quality work.

Value systems Overall, what members of particular cultures and segments of society believe to be right, proper, and worthwhile, and, conversely, what they believe to be wrong, improper, and of no worth.

Visual instructional plans (VIPs) (Jones): Graphic prompts that guide students through the process of the task or performance at hand.

Why questions (Ginott): Counterproductive questions that teachers put to students, asking them to explain or justify their behavior, e.g., "Why did you . . . ?"

Win-Win Discipline (Kagan): A "together, same-side" approach to discipline in which teachers and students work collaboratively to promote good classroom behavior—both teachers and students are deemed to "win."

Withitness (Kounin): The teacher's knowing what is going on in all parts of the classroom at all times.

Work the Crowd (Jones): Moving about the class while teaching and interacting with students.

You-messages (Ginott): Teacher messages that attack students' character, such as "You are acting like barbarians." These messages are put-downs that can convey heavy blame and guilt.

References

Albert, L. (2004/2002/1996/1989). *Cooperative discipline*. Boston: Pearson.

American Academy of Child and Adolescent Psychiatry. (2004a). Children with oppositional defiant disorder. Retrieved from http://www.aacap.org/publications/factsfam/72.htm

American Academy of Child and Adolescent Psychiatry. (2004b). Bipolar disorder in children and teens. Retrieved from www.aacap.org/publications/factsfam/72.htm

Bear, G. G. (2015). Preventive and classroom-based strategies. In E. T. Emmer & E. J. Sabornie (Eds.), *Handbook of classroom management* (pp. 25–39).

Borba, M. (2001). *Building moral intelligence: The seven essential virtues that teach kids to do the right thing*. San Francisco: Jossey-Bass.

Borba, M. (2004). *Don't give me that attitude! 24 rude, selfish, insensitive things kids do and how to stop them*. San Francisco: Jossey-Bass.

Borba, M. (n.d.). [See various articles, from 2005–2009, posted on the Borba website: http://www.micheleborba.com]

Brophy, J. (2006). History of research on classroom management. In C. M. Evertson & C. S. Weinstein (Eds.), *Handbook of classroom management: Research, practice, and contemporary issues* (pp. 17–43). Mahwah, NJ: Lawrence Erlbaum Associates.

Brophy, J. (2010). Classroom management as socializing students into clearly articulated roles. *The Journal of Classroom Interaction*, *45*(1), 41–45. Retrieved from http://0-www.jstor.org.wncln.wncln.org/stable/23869182

Brain Injury Association of Virginia. 2012. *Brain Injury 101*. http://www.biav.net/brain-injury-101.htm

Brown, D. F. (2003). Urban teachers' use of culturally responsive management strategies. *Theory into Practice*, *42*, 277–282.

Canter, L., & Canter, M. (1976). *Assertive discipline: A take-charge approach for today's educator*. Seal Beach, CA: Lee Canter & Associates. [The second and third editions of the book, published in 1992 and 2001, are entitled *Assertive discipline: Positive behavior management for today's classroom*.]

Carnegie, D. (1981 revision). *How to win friends and influence people*. New York: Pocket Books.

Cartledge, G., Gardner, R., & Ford, D. (2009). *Diverse learners with exceptionalities: Culturally responsive teaching in the inclusive classroom*. Upper Saddle River, NJ: Merrill.

Cartledge, G., & Johnson, C. T. (2004). School violence and cultural sensitivity. In J. C. Conoley & A. P. Goldstein (Eds.), *School violence intervention: A practical handbook* (2nd ed.) (pp. 441–482). New York: Guilford Press.

Cartledge, G., Lo, Y., Vincent, C. G., & Robinson-Ervin, P. (2015). Culturally responsive classroom management. In E. T. Emmer & E. J. Sabornie (Eds.), *Handbook of classroom management* (pp. 411–430). Boston: Pearson.

Cartledge, G., Singh, A., & Gibson, L. (2008). Practical behavior management techniques to close the accessibility gap for students who are culturally and linguistically diverse. *Preventing School Failure*, *52*(3), 29–38.

Centers for Disease Control and Prevention (CDC). (2004). Alcohol consumption among women who are pregnant or who might become pregnant—United States, 2002. Retrieved from http://www.acbr.com/fas/

Chamberlain, S. P. (2005). Recognizing and responding to cultural differences in the education of culturally and linguistically diverse learners. *Intervention in School and Clinic*, *40*(4), 195–211. Retrieved from http://0-search.proquest.com.wncln.wncln.org/docview/211738862?accountid=8388

Charles, C. (1974). *Teachers' petit Piaget*. San Francisco: Fearon.

Charles, C. (2000). *The synergetic classroom*. Boston: Allyn and Bacon.

Charles, C. (2008). *Today's best classroom management strategies: Paths to positive discipline*. Boston: Allyn & Bacon.

Collaborative for Academic, Social, and Emotional Learning, Chicago. (n.d.) [This organization has a goal to make social and emotional learning an essential part of education. Numerous resources are provided at its website: http://www.casel.org/]

Coloroso, B. (1994/2002). *Kids are worth it!: Giving your child the gift of inner discipline*. New York: Quill.

Cook, P. (2008a). Sensory integration dysfunction: A layperson's guide (2nd ed.) [Booklet]. Available from the author, Paula Cook. Internet contact: pcook59@shaw.ca

Cook, P. (2008b). A layperson's guide to what to do when someone begins to rage (2nd ed.) [Booklet]. Available from the author, Paula Cook. Internet contact: pcook59@shaw.ca

Cook, P., Kellie, R., Jones, K., & Goossen, L. (2000). *Tough kids and substance abuse*. Winnipeg, MB, Canada: Addictions Foundation of Manitoba.

Council of Chief State School Officers. (2013). Model standards for beginning teacher licensing, assessment, and development. Retrieved from http://www.ccsso.org/projects/Interstate_New_Teacher_Assessment_and_Support_Consortium

Covey, R. (1989). *The 7 habits of highly effective people*. New York: Simon and Schuster.

Covey, R. (2004). *The 7 habits of highly effective people: Restoring the character ethic*. New York: Free Press.

Crone, D. A., Hawken, L. S., & Horner, R. H. (2010). *Responding to problem behavior in schools: The behavior education program* (2nd ed.). New York: Guilford Press.

Curwin, R. L., Mendler, A. N., & Mendler, B. D. (2008). *Discipline with dignity: New challenges, new solutions*. Alexandria, VA: ASCD.

Delpit L. (1995). *Other people's children: Cultural conflict in the classroom*. New York: New Press.

Diamond, M., & Hopson, J. (1998). *Magic trees of the mind: How to nurture your child's intelligence, creativity, and healthy emotions from birth through adolescence*. New York: Dutton.

Dreikurs, R., & Cassel, P. (1995). *Discipline without tears*. New York: Penguin-NAL. (Originally published in 1972.)

Drye, J. (2000). *Tort liability 101: When are teachers liable?* Atlanta, GA: Educator Resources. Retrieved from http://www.Educator-Resources.com

Dykeman, C., Nelson, J. R., & Appleton, V. (1995). Building strong working alliances with American Indian families. *Social Work in Education, 36*, 103–112.

Echternach, C., & Cook, P. (2004). The rage cycle [Paper]. Available from the author, Paula Cook. Internet contact: pcook59@shaw.ca

Emmer, E. T., & Evertson, C. M. (2012). *Classroom management for middle and high school teachers* (9th ed.). Boston: Pearson.

Evertson, C. M, & Emmer, E. T. (2012). *Classroom management for elementary teachers* (9th ed.). Boston: Pearson.

Everston, C. M. & Weinstein, C. S. (2006). Classroom management as a field of inquiry. In C. M. Evertson & C. S. Weinstein (Eds.), *Handbook of classroom management: Research, practice, and contemporary issues* (pp. 3–15). Mahwah, NJ: Lawrence Erlbaum Associates.

Faraone, S. (2003). *Straight talk about your child's mental health*. New York: The Guilford Press.

Ford, D. Y., & Key, C. D. (2009). Creating culturally responsive instruction: For students' sake and teachers' sake. *Focus on Exceptional Children, 41*, 1–18.

Ford, E. (1999). *Discipline for home and school, Book Two* (revised and expanded). Scottsdale, AZ: Brandt Publishing.

Ford, E. (2004). *Discipline for home and school, fundamentals*. Scottsdale, AZ: Brandt Publishing.

Forni, P. (2006). The other side of civility. Retrieved from http://www.jhu.edu

Gay, G. (2010). *Culturally responsive teaching: Theory, research, and practice* (2nd ed.). New York: Teachers College Press.

Ginott, H. (1971). *Teacher and child*. New York: Macmillan.

Ginott, H. (1972). I am angry! I am appalled! I am furious! *Today's Education, 61*, 23–24.

Glasser, W. (1965). *Reality therapy*. New York: Harper & Row.

Glasser, W. (1969). *Schools without failure*. New York: Harper & Row.

Glasser, W. (1986). *Control theory in the classroom*. New York: HarperCollins.

Glasser, W. (1990). *The quality school: Managing students without coercion*. New York: HarperCollins.

Glasser, W. (1992). The quality school curriculum. *Phi Delta Kappan, 73*(9), 690–694.

Glasser, W. (1993). *The quality school teacher*. New York: HarperCollins.

Glasser, W. (1998a). *Choice theory in the classroom*. New York: HarperCollins.

Glasser, W. (1998b). *The quality school: Managing students without coercion*. New York: HarperCollins.

Glasser, W. (1998c). *The quality school teacher.* New York: HarperCollins.

Glasser, W. (2001). *Every student can succeed.* Chatsworth, CA: William Glasser Incorporated.

Glavac, M., (2005). Summary of major concepts covered by Harry K. Wong. The Busy Educator's Newsletter. Retrieved from http://www.glavac .com/

Goorian, B., & Brown, K. (2002). Trends and issues: School law. ERIC Clearinghouse on Educational Management. Retrieved from http://eric.uoregon .edu/trends_issues/law/index.html

Gorski, P. (2008). The myth of the culture of poverty. *Educational Leadership*, 65(7), 32–36. Retrieved from http://www.ascd.org/publications/educational- leadership/apr08/vol65/num07/The-Myth-of-the- Culture-of-Poverty.aspx

Gorski, P. (2011). Unlearning deficit ideology and the scornful gaze: Thoughts on authenticating the class discourse in education. *Counterpoints*, 402, 152– 173. Retrieved from http://0-www.jstor.org.wncln .wncln.org/stable/42981081

Gorski, P. (2013). Building a pedagogy of engagement for students in poverty. *The Phi Delta Kappan*, 95(1), 48–52. Retrieved from http://0-www.jstor .org.wncln.wncln.org/stable/23617759

Gossen, D. (1992). *Restitution: Restructuring school discipline.* Chapel Hill, NC: New View Publications.

Gossen, D. (2004). *It's all about we: Rethinking discipline using restitution.* Saskatoon, SK, Canada: Chelsom Consultants Limited.

Greene, R. (2001). *The explosive child.* New York: Harper Collins.

Hall, P., & Hall, N. (2003). *Educating oppositional and defiant children.* Alexandria, VA: Association for Supervision and Curriculum Development.

Hill, P. (2005). Pharmacological treatment of rage. Retrieved from http://www.focusproject.org.uk/ SITE/UPLOAD/DOCUMENT/Hill.

Hinder, T. (2006). An overview of seven Glasser Quality Schools in the USA. NSW Department of Education and Training Leadership Fellowship 2005–2006. A Report of a Study Tour to the USA—April 2006. Therese Hinder. Principal. Epping West Public School. 96 Carlingford Road. Epping NSW 2121. Australia. [Use title of the article to locate this report on the Internet.]

Hirschfield, P. J. (2008) Preparing for prison? The criminalization of school discipline in the USA. *Theoretical Criminology*, 12(1), 79–101.

Individuals with Disabilities Education Act, 20 U.S.C. § 1400 (2004). Retrieved from https://sites.ed.gov/ idea

Interstate New Teacher Assessment and Support Consortium (InTASC). (2013). [See InTASC's website at: http://www.ccsso.org]

Jones, F. (1987a). *Positive classroom discipline.* New York: McGraw-Hill.

Jones, F. (1987b). *Positive classroom instruction.* New York: McGraw-Hill.

Jones, F.. (2007b). *The video toolbox.* Santa Cruz, CA: Fredric H. Jones & Associates.

Jones, F. (2012/2007a). *Tools for teaching.* Santa Cruz, CA: Fredric H. Jones & Associates.

Jones, F. (n.d.). PAT bank. [Jones's and various teachers' suggestions for PAT activities.] Retrieved from http://www.fredjones.com/PAT/ index.html

Kagan, S. (2001). Teaching for character and community. *Educational Leadership*, 59(2), 50–55.

Kagan, S. (2003, Spring). A brief history of Kagan structures. *Kagan Online Magazine*. Retrieved from http://www.kaganonline.com [Other articles on structures are posted on this site as well.]

Kagan, S., Kyle, P., & Scott, S. (2004/2007). *Win-win discipline.* San Clemente, CA: Kagan Publishing.

Kaufman, J. S., Jaser, S. S., Vaughan, E. L., Reynolds, J. S., Di Donato, J., Bernard, S. N., & Hernandez Brerton, M. (2010). Patterns in office discipline referral data by grade, race/ethnicity, and gender. *Journal of Positive Behavior Interventions*, 12, 44–54.

Kelly, Y., Sacker, A., Gray, R., Kelly, J., Wolke, D., & Quigley, M. A. (2009). Light drinking in pregnancy, a risk for behavioural problems and cognitive deficits at 3 years of age? *International Journal of Epidemiology*, 38(1), 129–140.

Khan S. & Faraone, S. 2006. The genetics of attention-deficit/hyperactivity disorder: A literature review of 2005. *Current Psychiatry Reports*, 2006 Oct; 8:393–397.

Kohn, A. (1993/1999). *Punished by rewards: The trouble with gold stars, incentive plans, A's, praise, and other bribes.* Boston: Houghton Mifflin.

Kohn, A. (1999). *The schools our children deserve: Moving beyond traditional classrooms and "tougher standards."* Boston: Houghton Mifflin.

Kohn, A. (1996/2001). *Beyond discipline: From compliance to community.* Upper Saddle River, NJ: Merrill/Prentice Hall. [1996 edition—Alexandria, VA: Association for Supervision and Curriculum Development.]

Kounin, J. (1971). *Discipline and group management in classrooms.* New York: Holt, Rinehart & Winston. (Reissued in 1977.)

Kranowitz, C. (2005). *The out-of-sync child.* New York: Skylight Press.

Kranowitz, C., Szkut, S., Balzer-Martin, L., Haber, E., & Sava, D. (2003). *Answers to questions teachers ask about sensory integration.* Las Vegas, NV: Sensory Resources LLC.

Ladson-Billings, G. (1995). Toward a theory of culturally relevant pedagogy. *American Educational Research Journal, 32,* 465–491.

Ledlow, S. (1992). Is cultural discontinuity an adequate explanation for dropping out? *Journal of American Indian Education, 31*(3), 21–36.

Lewis, T. J., Mitchell, B. S., Trussell, R., & Newcomer, L. (2015). School-wide positive behavior support. In E. T. Emmer & E. J. Sabornie (Eds.), *Handbook of classroom management* (pp. 40–59). New York: Routledge.

Marshall, M. (2001). *Discipline without stress® punishments, or rewards: How teachers and parents promote responsibility & learning.* Los Alamitos, CA: Piper Press.

Marshall, M. (2005a). A letter worth reading. Retrieved from http://www.marvinmarshall.com/aletterworthreading.html

Marshall, M. (2005b). A principal's experience. Retrieved from http://www.marvinmarshall.com/principal.htm

Marshall, M. (2005c). Classroom meetings. Retrieved from http://www.disciplinewithoutstress.com/sample_-chapters.html

Marshall, M. (2005d). Collaboration for quality learning. Retrieved from http://www.disciplinewithoutstress.com/sample_chapters.html

Marshall, M. (2005e). Promoting positivity, choice, and reflection. Retrieved from http://www.MarvinMarshall.com/promoting_positivity.htm

Marshall, M. (2005f). Reducing perfectionism. Retrieved from http://www.disciplinewithoutstress.com/sample_chapters.html

Marshall, M. (2005g). Samples of hierarchies for promoting learning. Retrieved from http://www.marvinmarshall.com/hierarchy.htm

Marshall, M. (2007). *Discipline without stress® punishments, or rewards: How teachers and parents promote responsibility & learning* (2nd ed.). Los Alamitos, CA: Piper Press.

Marshall, M. (2008). A system is superior to talent. Retrieved from http://teachers.net/gazette/MAR08/marshall/

Marshall, M. (2010, September). A response from Dr. Marshall to a letter received. *Promoting Responsibility & Learning, the Monthly Newsletter by Marvin Marshall, 10*(9). Retrieved from http://www.marvinmarshall.com

Maslow, A. (1954). *Motivation and personality.* New York: Harper.

Millichap, G. (2008, February). Etiologic classification of attention deficit/hyperactivity disorder. *Pediatrics, 121,* e358–e365.

Morgan, H. (2010). Improving schooling for cultural minorities: The right teaching styles can make a big difference. *Educational Horizons, 88*(2), 114–120.

Morrish, R. (1997). *Secrets of discipline: 12 keys for raising responsible children.* Fonthill, Ontario, Canada: Woodstream Publishing.

Morrish, R. (2000). *With all due respect: Keys for building effective school discipline.* Fonthill, Ontario, Canada: Woodstream Publishing.

Morrish, R. (2003). *FlipTips.* Fonthill, Ontario, Canada: Woodstream Publishing.

Morrish, R. (2012). What is real discipline? Retrieved from http://www.realdiscipline.com

National Center for Children in Poverty. (n.d.). Basic facts about low income children. Retrieved from http://www.nccp.org/publications/pub_1145.html.

National Council for Learning Disabilities. (2005). The ABCs of learning disabilities. Retrieved from http://www.ncld.org/

National Education Association. (1975). Code of ethics of the education profession. Retrieved from www.nea.org/aboutnea/code.html

National Institute of Mental Health. (2008). Health information quick links. Retrieved from www.nimh.nih.gov

Nelsen, J., & Lott, L. (2000/1993). *Positive discipline in the classroom.* Rocklin, CA: Prima.

Papolos, D., & Papolos, J. (2002). *The bipolar child.* New York: Broadway Books.

Payne, R. (2001). *A framework for understanding poverty*. Highlands, TX: Aha! Process, Inc.

Positive Behavioral Intervention & Supports: OSEP Technical Assistance Center. (n.d.). Positive behavioral interventions and supports. Retrieved from https://www.pbis.org/

Positive Behavioral Intervention & Supports: OSEP Technical Assistance Center. (n.d.). Case examples. Retrieved from pbis.org/school/tier3supports/case-examples

Positive Behavioral Intervention & Supports: OSEP Technical Assistance Center. (n.d.). Tier 1 Supports. Retrieved from https://www.pbis.org/school/tier1supports

Positive Behavioral Intervention & Supports: OSEP Technical Assistance Center. (n.d.). Tier 2 FAQs. Retrieved from https://www.pbis.org/school/secondary-level/faqs

Piaget, J. (1951). *Judgment and reasoning in the child*. London: Routledge & Kegan Paul.

Rebell, M., & Wolff, J. (2012). Educational opportunity is achievable and affordable. *The Phi Delta Kappan*, 93(6), 62–65. Retrieved from http://0-www.jstor.org.wncln.wncln.org/stable/41497552

Redl, F., & Wattenberg, W. (1951). *Mental hygiene in teaching*. New York: Harcourt, Brace & World. (Revised and reissued in 1959.)

Reeve, J. (2006). Extrinsic rewards and inner motivation. In C. M. Evertson & C. S. Weinstein (Eds.), *Handbook of classroom management: Research, practice, and contemporary issues* (pp. 645–664). Mahwah, NJ: Lawrence Erlbaum Associates Publishers.

Seganti, C. (2008a). Classroom discipline 101: How to get control in any classroom. Retrieved from http://www.classroomdiscipline101.com

Seganti, C. (2008b). *Ezine*. [See articles on the Seganti approach to discipline.] Retrieved from http://ezinearticles.com/?expert=Craig_Seganti

Skinner, B. (1953). *Science and human behavior*. New York: Macmillan.

Skinner, B. (1954). The science of learning and the art of teaching. *Harvard Educational Review*, 24, 86–97.

Starr, L. (1999). Speaking of classroom management—an interview with Harry K. Wong. *Education World*. Retrieved from http://www.educationworld.com/a_curr/curr161.shtml

Sugai, G., Horner, R. H., Algozzine, R., Barrett, S., Lewis, T., Anderson, C., Bradley, R., Choi, J. H., Dunlap, G., Eber, L., George, H., Kincaid, D., McCart, A., Nelson, M., Newcomer, L., Putnam, R., Riffel, L., Rovins, M., Sailor, W., & Simonsen, B. (2010). *School-wide positive behavior support: Implementers' blueprint and self-assessment*. Eugene, OR: University of Oregon.

Sugai, G., Horner, R. H., Dunlap, G. Hieneman, M., Lewis, T. J., Nelson, C. M., Scott, T., Liaupsin, C., Sailor, W., Turnbull, A. P., Turnbull, H. R., III, Wickham, D. Reuf, M., & Wilcox, B. (2000). Applying positive behavioral support and functional behavioral assessment in schools. *Journal of Positive Behavioral Interventions*, 2, 131–143.

Sugai, G., & Simonson, B. (2012). *Positive behavioral interventions and supports: History, defining features, and misconceptions*. Retrieved from www.pbis.org/common/cms/files/pbisresources/PBIS_revisited_June19r_2012.pdf

U.S. Census. (n.d.). Retrieved from https://www.census.gov/topics/income-poverty/poverty.html

William Glasser Institute. (2005). Control theory. Retrieved from http://www.wglasser.com/whatisct.htm

William Glasser Institute. (n.d.). Quality schools. Retrieved from http://wglasser.com/our-approach/quality-schools/

Wong, H., & Wong, R. (2000a). The first five minutes are critical. Teachers.net *Gazette*. Retrieved from http://teachers.net/gazette/NOV00/wong.html

Wong, H., & Wong, R. (2000b). The problem is not discipline. Teachers.net *Gazette*. Retrieved from http://teachers.net/gazette/SEP00/wong.html

Wong, H., & Wong, R. (2000c). Your first day. Teachers.net *Gazette*. Retrieved from http://teachers.net/gazette/JUN00/covera.html

Wong, H., & Wong, R. (2004a). A well-oiled learning machine. Teachers.net *Gazette*. Retrieved from http://teachers.net/wong/MAR04/

Wong, H., & Wong, R. (2004b). *The first days of school: How to be an effective teacher*. Mountain View, CA: Harry K. Wong Publications.

Wong, H., & Wong, R. (2004c). His students are all certified. Teachers.net *Gazette*. Retrieved from http://teachers.net/wong/MAY04.

Wong, H., & Wong, R. (2005a). The first ten days of school. Teachers.net *Gazette*. Retrieved from http://teachers.net/wong/JAN05/

Wong, H., & Wong, R. (2005b). The power of procedures. Teachers.net *Gazette*. Retrieved from http://teachers.net/wong/FEB05

Wong, H., & Wong, R. (2005c). His classroom is a real life office. Teachers.net *Gazette*. Retrieved from http://teachers.net/wong/MAR05

Wong, H., & Wong, R. (2007). *The first days of school: How to be an effective teacher* (2nd ed.). Mountain View, CA: Harry K. Wong Publications.

Wong, H., & Wong, R. (2009). *The first days of school: How to be an effective teacher* (3rd ed.). Mountain View, CA: Harry K. Wong Publications.

Wong, H., & Wong, R. (n.d.). [Teachers.net *Gazette* articles from 2000–2009 are available at this site: http://teachers.net/wong/]

Wong, H., Wong, R., Rogers, K., & Brooks, A. (2012) Managing your classroom for success. *Science and Children*, 49, 60–64.

Yell, M. L., Rozalski, M., & Miller, J. (2015). Classroom management and the law. In E. T. Emmer & E. J. Sabornie (Eds.), *Handbook of classroom management* (pp. 431–445).

Name Index

Albert, Linda, 73, 85–87
Algozzine, R., 279–280
Appleton, V., 39

Barr, H., 309
Bear, G. G., 1, 2
Bookstein, F., 309
Borba, Michele, 74
Brophy, J., 1, 199
Brown, D. F., 40, 41
Brown, K., 17

Canter, Lee, 73, 84–85
Canter, Marlene, 73, 84–85
Carnegie, Dale, 65
Cartledge, G., 36, 37, 39, 40
Cassel, Pearl, 34, 73
Chamberlain, S. P., 38, 39, 40
Charles, C. M., 31, 34, 74
Coloroso, Barbara, 74, 89–90, 329
Cook, P., 300, 305, 311
Covey, S., 23–24
Crone, D. A., 281–282
Curwin, Richard, 73

Delpit L., 40, 41
Diamond, M., 235–236
Dreikurs, Rudolf, 34, 73, 83–84, 87
Drye, J., 17
Dunlap, G., 279–280
Dykeman, C., 39

Echternach, C., 311
Emmer, Edmund, 51–52
Evertson, Carolyn, 51–52

Faraone, S., 303, 308
Ferguson, Eva Dreikurs, 73
Ford, D., 36, 39, 40
Ford, Ed, 74
Forni, P. M., 74

Gardner, R., 39, 40
Gay, G., 39, 40, 41, 42
Gibbs, Nathan, 154
Ginott, Haim, 19, 21–23, 73, 81–83
Glasser, William, 24–25, 34, 72–73, 75, 78–80, 196–220
Glavac, M., 148
Goorian, B., 17
Goossen, L., 300

Gorski, Paul, 44–46
Gossen, Diane, 66, 74
Gray, R., 309
Greene, R., 299, 300, 311

Hall, N., 299, 300, 307
Hall, P., 299, 300, 307
Hambacher, E., 49
Hawken, L. S., 281–282
Hill, P., 311
Hopson, J., 235–236
Horner, R. H., 279–280, 281–282

Jaser, S. S., 38
Johnson, C. T., 37
Jondahl, Sarah, 158–159
Jones, Fred, 25–26, 54, 73, 75–76, 171–195
Jones, K., 300
Jones, Patrick T., 172

Kagan, Spencer, 75, 249–270, 253–254, 265, 329
Kahn, S., 303
Kaufman, J. S., 38
Kellerman, T., 309
Kellie, R., 300
Kelly, J., 309
Kelly, Y., 309
Key, C. D., 36
Kogan, J., 309
Kohn, Alfie, 74, 90–92
Kounin, Jacob, 73, 80–81
Kranowitz, C., 299, 305
Kyle, Patricia, 75, 253–254, 265

Ladson-Billings, G., 38
Ledlow, S., 39
Levine, 58–59
Lewis, T. J., 93, 276–277, 285, 292
Lo, Y., 36
Lott, Lynn, 74, 87–88
Lucero, Ed, 164

Marshall, Marvin, 66, 75, 226–232
Maslow, Abraham, 34
McGregor, Douglas, 226
Mendler, Allen, 73
Mendler, B. D., 73
Miller, J., 13–14

Millichap, G., 303
Mitchell, B. S., 93, 276–277, 285, 292
Morgan, H., 41
Morrish, Ronald, 74, 76, 97–120, 143–144

Nelsen, Jane, 74, 87–88
Nelson, J. R., 39

Packer, 310, 311
Pantoja, Melissa, 161–162
Papolos, D., 299, 306–307, 311
Papolos, J., 299, 306–307, 311
Pavlov, Ivan, 72
Payne, Ruby, 43–46
Piaget, Jean, 31–33

Quigley, M. A., 309

Rebell, M., 43
Redl, Fritz, 72, 76–77
Reeve, J., 184
Reynolds, J. S., 38
Robinson-Ervin, P., 36
Rozalski, M., 13–14

Sacker, A., 309
Scott, Sally, 75, 253–254, 265
Seganti, Craig, 76, 121–145
Seroyer, Chelonnda, 163–164
Simonson, B., 75, 93
Skinner, B. F., 72, 77–78
Slovenske, Jane, 162–163
Smith, Jeff, 164
Streissguth, A., 309
Sugai, G., 75, 93, 279–280
Sund, Deborah, 322–325
Szkut, S., 305
Trussell, R., 93, 276–277, 285, 292
Vaughan, E. L., 38
Vincent, C. G., 36

Wattenberg, William, 72, 76–77
White, Byron, 13
Wolff, J., 43
Wolke, D., 309
Wong, Harry, 74, 75, 146–170
Wong, Rosemary, 74, 75, 146–170

Yell, M. L., 13–14

Subject Index

ABCD of disruptive behavior (Kagan), 252
Academic difficulties, 300
Acceptable behavior, 53, 275
Acceptance (Albert), 86
Accountability
    Kounin on, 81
    Seganti on, 76
Achievement (Albert), 86
Actions, versus words in discipline, 323
    Ginott on, 22
    Seganti on, 124
ADHD (attention-deficit hyperactivity disorder), 300, 303–304
    individual condition for misbehavior, 58
Adolescence/teen stage (Marshall), 230
Adult/grown-up stage (Marshall), 230
Adult-to-child relations, 37
Affection (Albert), 86
Affirmation (Albert), 86
Aggression (Kagan), 252
Aimlessness (Jones), 174
Alcohol-related neurodevelopmental disorder (ARND), 309
American Academy of Child and Adolescent Psychiatry, 307
Anarchy (Marshall), 227, 230
Anger (Kagan), 252
    interventions for, 258–259
Appreciation (Albert), 86
Appreciative praise
    Dreikurs on, 84
    Ginott on, 82
Appropriate behavior, definition, 53
ASD (autism spectrum disorder), 308–309
Asperger syndrome, 308
Assertive Discipline (the Canters), 73, 84–85
Assertive Discipline: A Take-Charge Approach for Today's Educator (the Canters), 84–85
Assessment, three purposes (PBIS), 276
Attention (Albert), 86
Attention-deficit hyperactivity disorder (ADHD), 300, 303–304
Attention seeking (Dreikurs), 83
Attention seeking (Kagan), 252
    interventions for, 257–258

Authority
    in academics and discipline, 18
    in training for compliance (Morrish), 101, 103, 105–106
    without punishment (Marshall), 237
Autism spectrum disorder (ASD), 308–309
Autocratic classrooms (Dreikurs), 84
Avoidance, cause of misbehavior, 57–58

Baby/infant stage (Marshall), 230
Backup systems for misbehavior (Jones), 186, 188
Basic needs of students
    Charles on, 34, 326
    Dreikurs on, 34
    Glasser on, 34, 201
    Maslow on, 34
Befriending, as connecting habit, 24
Behavior
    affect of economic realities, 42–43
    appropriate vs. inappropriate, 53–54
    as choice, 53, 72–73, 201, 206–207
    defined, 34, 52, 275
    definition of expected behaviors (PBIS), 280
    emphasized by schools, 37–38
    high school grades, 33
    intermediate grades, 32
    irresponsible, 252
    middle school grades, 32–33
    modification (Skinner), 78
    motivations for, 34 (*See also* Basic needs of students)
    poor choices, as cause of misbehavior, 57
    primary grades, 31–32
    redirecting students with special needs, 314
    shaping (Skinner), 78
    sociocultural influence, 36–37
    three types (Seganti), 136
    total (Glasser), 199
    typical, at various stages (Charles), 31–33
Behavioral intervention, 272–275, 294, 320
Behavior difficulties, 300
Behavior management. *See also* Discipline
    Morrish on, 100
Behavior matrix, 273

Behavior modification (Skinner), 72, 78
Bell work
    Jones on, 178
    the Wongs on, 160
Belonging, need for
    Charles on, 34, 327
    Dreikurs on, 73, 83–84
    Glasser on, 201
Big Three of Win-Win Discipline (Kagan), 263–264
Bipolar disorder, 306–307
Blaming, habit (Glasser), 210, 211
Body carriage (Jones), 26, 181
Body language (Jones), 25–26, 180–181, 189
Boredom (Kagan), 253
    interventions for, 260
Bossing (Marshall), 227
Boss management (Glasser), 197
Boss teachers, boss managers (Glasser), 200, 203, 204–206
Bothering (Marshall), 227
Brain injuries, 310
Breach of duty, teachers, 17
Breathing, as management tactic (Jones), 181
Bullying, 17, 27, 227
Butterfly analogy, to teach hierarchy of social development (Marshall), 230–232

Calm, as management tactic (Jones), 181
Capability (Albert), 86
Caring, as connecting habit (Glasser), 24, 211
Center on Positive Behavioral Interventions and Supports, 93
Charisma, 20, 328
Check In, Check Out (CICO), 281, 283
    sample goal card, 286
Child-to-adult relations, 37
Child/youth stage (Marshall), 230
Choice
    behavior as (Glasser), 72–73, 78–80
    empowerment of (Marshall), 226, 228, 232, 242, 246
    guided (Marshall), 237–239
    making appropriate, 320
    management, third phase of real discipline (Morrish), 107–108
    managing (Marshall), 75

Choice management (Morrish), 107–108
Choice theory (Glasser), 73, 78–80, 197, 201
   connecting place in classrooms, 216
   reality therapy (CT/RTC) certification, 209
Choice Theory in the Classroom (Glasser), 197
Choice Theory/Reality Therapy (CT/RTC) certification, 209
Chores, in the classroom, 178
Civil classroom behavior (Morrish), 99
Civility, establishing in the classroom (Forni), 74
Class agreements (Glasser), 206
Classroom Discipline 101: How to Get Control of Any Classroom (Seganti), 121, 126
Classroom factors, classroom management, 27
Classroom learning communities (Kohn), 74
Classroom management
   in the big picture, 27–28
   building personalized system of, 4–6
   defined, 50
   five realities of, 6–8
   legal basis for, 13–14
   legal obligations associated with, 16–18
   main objectives of, 8–13
   student diversity in, 29–49
   timeline of developments in, 72–76
   vs. discipline, 1–2
Classroom meetings, 95, 320
   Glasser on, 79, 208
   Kohn on, 92
   Marshall on, 236
   Nelson and Lott on, 88
Classroom procedures, 35
   the Wongs, 74, 149, 151–152, 152–158
Classroom roles (the Wongs), 74
Classroom seating arrangement
   Jones on, 176, 187
   Seganti on, 132, 136–137
   the Wongs on, 151
Class rules (Kagan), 261
Coercion, avoiding, 196, 224, 225
Coercive discipline, 1
Collaboration (Marshall), 234
Collaborative solutions (Kagan), 254, 261
Communication
   Carnegie on, 65
   congruent (Ginott), 21–23, 73, 81–83
   frames of reference for (Covey), 23–24

importance for teachers, 19, 21–26
   inviting cooperation (Ginott), 22, 82
   nonverbal (Jones), 25–26
   teachers' responsibility, 23
   teaching effective, 95, 319
Community, classroom (Kohn), 74, 90–92
Community alliances and schoolwide programs (Kagan), 262–263
Competence and self-esteem
   Morrish on, 114
   Seganti on, 124
Complaining, habit (Glasser), 210, 211
Compliance (Morrish), 103–106
   students who fail to comply, 114–115
   training, 98
Concrete operational stage (Piaget), 31
Conferring dignity (Ginott), 81–83
Confidence building (Albert), 86
Conflict resolution (Marshall), 236
Conformity (Marshall), 227–228
Confrontation (Kagan), 252
Congruent communication (Ginott), 21–23, 73, 81–83
Connecting habits (Glasser), 198, 210–212, 326
Connecting place, for choice theory, 216
Connect with others (Albert), 86
Consequences for misbehavior, 321
   the Canters on, 85
   Coloroso on, 89–90
   Gossen on, 74
   Kagan on, 255, 256
   Marshall on, 224
   Morrish on, 112–113
   Seganti on, 125
   strategies (PBIS), 289
Constant reinforcement (Skinner), 77
Contagious group behavior, cause of misbehavior, 59–60
Contracts, agreement between student/teacher (Kagan), 256
Contributing, as connecting habit, 24
Contributions (Albert), 86
Control-seeking (Kagan), 252
Control-seeking, intervention strategies for (Kagan), 259
Control Theory in the Classroom (Glasser), 197
Cooperation
   Marshall on, 227–228
   between teacher and students, 325
   teachers' responsibility, 19
   in work groups (the Wongs), 150, 157, 163
Cooperative activities (Kagan), 263
Cooperative discipline (Albert), 73, 85–87

Core principles of PBIS, 275–276
Criticism vs. positive influence, 66–69
   Morrish on, 111–112
Criticizing, habit (Glasser), 210, 211
CT/RTC (Choice Theory/Reality Therapy) certification, 209
Culturally responsive teaching, 36
Culture of poverty (Payne), 43–44
Curiosity (Marshall), 234
Curriculum (Kagan), 263, 270
Cyberbullying, 27

Damaging practices, teachers' (Marshall), 223–224
Data
   used for decision making (PBIS), 276, 280
   using for behavioral intervention, 320
Deadly habits (Glasser), 24, 198, 210–212, 326
Decisions, policymakers', 27
Defiance (Seganti), 137
Deficit ideology (Gorski), 44–45
Democracy
   Dreikurs on, 73, 83–84
   Marshall on, 228
Democratic classrooms (Dreikurs), 73, 83–84
Department of Education Office of Special Education Programs Technical Assistance Center, 272
Dignity
   conferring and maintaining (Ginott), 81–83
   maintaining students' (Curwin and Mendler), 73
Directions (Seganti), 126
Discipline
   Albert's approach to, 73, 85–87
   the Canters'; assertive approach, 73, 84–85
   coercive approach vs. positive influence, 1–2, 224–225
   Coloroso's approach to, 89–90
   developing a personal plan for, 321, 329–330
   development of modern, 71–76
   with dignity (Curwin; Mendler), 73
   Dreikurs's approach to, 83–84
   flow chart, 279
   Ginott's approach to, 21–23, 81–83
   Glasser's approach to, 25–26, 78–80
   Gossen's approach to, 74
   Jones's approach to, 73
   Kagan's approach to, 249–270
   Kohn's approach to, 90–92
   Kounin's approach to, 73, 80–81

Discipline (*Continued*)
Marshall's approach to, 221–248
Morrish's approach to, 97–120
nine fundamental questions in, 3
noncoercive (Glasser; Marshall), 196, 199–200
objectives of, 2–3
personal philosophy of, 322
personal theory of, 322–323
real, vs. behavior management (Morrish), 100–101
redirective, 314
Redl and Wattenberg's approach to, 72, 76–77
Seganti's approach to, 121–145
self-discipline, 2, 89–90
supportive discipline (Charles), 327–328
Theory X and Theory Y (McGregor), 226–227
win-win approach, 75
without stress (Marshall), 75, 221, 240, 246
Discipline and Group Management in Classrooms (Kounin), 80
Discipline without Stress, Inc. (Marshall), 222
Discipline without Stress, Punishments, or Rewards (Marshall), 221, 240, 246
Discipline without Tears (Dreikurs and Cassel), 73
Disengagement (Kagan), 252
Disrespect (Seganti), 138
Disruptions, 53, 264
intervention structures for various types, 257–260
preventing (Kagan), 254
repeated (Seganti), 138
responding to (Kagan), 253–254
Diversity
classroom management, 29–49
culture of poverty (Payne), 43–44
differing group values, 38–42
working effectively with societal and economic groups, 46–48
Doorway tactics (Seganti), 135–136
Do-over (Morrish), 114
Due diligence, 17
Dyscalculia, 301
Dysgraphia, 301
Dyslexia, 301
Dyspraxia, 301

Early intervention, 272, 275
Economic disadvantage, 42
Economic groups
affect on student behavior, 42–43
working effectively with, 46–48

Education World, 172
The Effective Teacher (Wong), 148
Effort, teachers' responsibility, 19
Egocentric personalities, 58
Empathetic listening (Covey), 24
Empowering students (Marshall), 222
Empowerment of choice (Marshall), 226, 232
Encouraging, as connecting habit, 24, 211
Energetic (Kagan), 253
interventions for, 259
Enjoyment (Seganti), 124
Escalation of rage, phase 2 (Cook), 311–312
Ethics in the classroom, 20–21, 325–327
Evaluation
Glasser on, 203–204, 213
the Wongs on, 150
Evaluative praise (Glasser), 82
Every Student Can Succeed (Glasser), 197
Exceptionalities, student, 304–317
autism spectrum disorder (ASD), 308–309
bipolar disorder, 306–307
brain injuries, 310
fetal alcohol spectrum disorder (FASD), 309–310
oppositional defiant disorder (ODD), 307
rage, 310–313
sensory integration dysfunction (SID), 305–306, 309
External motivation
fallacy of (Marshall), 224
internal vs. (Marshall; Glasser), 199, 200, 201, 225, 232
Eye contact (Jones; Seganti), 25, 132, 181

Facial expressions (Jones; Seganti), 26, 182
Failure, avoiding
Glasser, 79–80, 197, 219
Kagan, 252, 258
Fetal alcohol spectrum disorder (FASD), 309–310
Fidelity, 276
15-minute detention (Seganti), 127, 130, 137, 329
First Day of School Action Plan (the Wongs), 158–160
First days of class, suggestions for (the Wongs), 150–151, 158–163
first five minutes of, 160–161
first ten days of school, 162–163
The First Days of School: How to Be an Effective Teacher (Wong), 75, 148, 163

Five A's (Albert), 86
Five realities of classroom management, 6–8
FlipTips (Morrish), 98, 101
Follow-up structures (Kagan), 254–255
Formal operations stage (Piaget), 32
Four classical virtues (Marshall), 236
Four Essential Skills (Nelsen and Lott), 88
Four stages of social development (Marshall), 230
Frames of reference (Covey), 23–24
Freedom, students' need (Glasser), 201
Fun, students' experience (Glasser), 201
Functional behavior assessment, 288

General rules (Jones), 177
Generational poverty (Payne), 43
Genuine discipline (Ginott), 82–83
Genuine incentives (Jones), 183–184
Glasser, William, 196–219, 246, 261
Goals, genuine vs. mistaken (Dreikurs), 83
Golden rule, the (Glasser), 213
Goss v. Lopez, 13
Grandma's rule (Jones), 182–183
Greeting students (the Wongs), 161
Group alerting (Kounin), 81
Group behavior, dynamics of (Redl and Wattenberg), 72, 76–77
Group concern, PAT management (Jones), 185
Group values, differing, 38–42
Guided choice (Marshall), 237–239

Habits
connecting (Glasser), 24–25, 78, 198, 210–212
deadly (Glasser), 24–25, 78, 198, 210–212
defined, 35
inappropriate, cause of misbehavior, 56–57
Helpfulness, teachers', 19
Helpless handraising (Jones), 174–175
Hidden asset of teachers (Ginott), 82
Hidden Rules (Payne), 43–44, 46
Hierarchy of social development (Marshall), 75, 227–230, 239, 241, 246, 329
using the butterfly analogy, 230–232
High school
typical behavior in, 33
using the Wongs' approach in, 163–165
Hopson, Janet, 235
How to Win Friends and Influence People (Carnegie), 65

Humaneness, emphasizing (Nelson and Lott), 74, 87–88

Identifying causes of misbehavior, 55–63
If-then statements, 114
I-messages vs. you-messages (Ginott), 22
Immoral activities, of teachers, 16
Implementation framework, 93
Improvement (Glasser), 204
Incentives (Jones), 182, 189
Independent work, help during (Jones), 186–187, 328
Individual factors, classroom management, 27–28
Individualized education plan (IEP), 302
Individual supports, 94
Individuals with Disabilities Act of 1997 (IDEA), 75, 93, 273, 297
  and ADHD, 303
Influence (Marshall), 224, 227, 236
Influence tactics, 29, 328–329
Influence techniques (Redl and Wattenberg; Glasser), 77
In loco parentis, 17–18, 326
Inner discipline (Coloroso), 74, 89–90
Insistence (Morrish), 104, 115
InTASC, 21
Interior loop (Jones), 176, 187, 328
Intermediate grades, typical behavior in, 32
Intermittent reinforcement (Skinner), 77
Internal motivation, versus external, 232
  Glasser on, 199, 200, 204
  Marshall on, 224, 225, 227–229, 231, 232
Interpersonal relationships, fostering, 95, 233, 320
Interstate Teacher Assessment and Support Consortium (InTASC), 21
Interventions (Kagan), 257
  for anger, 258–259
  for attempts to avoid failure/ embarrassment, 258
  for attention-seeking behavior, 257–258
  for boredom, 260
  for control-seeking behavior, 259
  for overly energetic behavior, 259
  for the uninformed, 260
Inviting cooperation (Ginott), 22, 82
Irresponsible behavior (Kagan), 252
"It is my job" (Moorish), 106

Justice, 236

Kagan, Spencer, 249–270

Kids Are Worth It: Giving Your Child the Gift of Inner Discipline (Coloroso), 89–90
Kyle, Patricia, 253

Lack of stimulation, cause of misbehavior, 60–61
Laconic language (Ginott), 22
Language difficulties, 300
LD (learning disabilities), 300–302
  indicators of, 302
  individualized education plans for (IEPs), 302
Lead management (Glasser), 198, 204–206
Lead managers, lead teachers (Glasser), 198, 200, 204–206
Learned responsibility (Kagan), 261
Learning, meaningful and successful, 319
Learning communities (Kohn), 74, 90–92
Learning disabilities (LD), 300–302
  indicators of, 301
  individual condition for misbehavior, 58–59
  individualized education plans for (IEPs), 302
Legal responsibilities of teachers, 13–14, 16–18
Lesson management (Kounin), 73, 80–81
"A Letter Worth Reading" (Marshall), 231
Leverage (Seganti), 76, 127, 129–131, 329
LGBTQI students, 28
Lifelong responsible behavior, 260
Life skills, structures for promoting (Kagan), 257
Limits
  defined, 53
  Jones on, 177
  Morrish on, 103, 105
Listening
  as connecting habit (Glasser), 24, 211
  in order to influence others (Marshall), 235
Living in poverty (Payne), 42
Long-term structures (Kagan), 254, 255
Low-key options, misbehavior redirection, 329

"Make a Better Choice" (Kagan), 254
Management plan (the Wongs), 151–152
Management tactics (Seganti), 124–125
Manipulation by students (Seganti), 127, 134

Marshall, Marvin, 221–248
Marvin Marshall Teaching Model, 242
Massive time wasting (Jones), 73, 173
McGregor, Douglas, 226
Meaninglessness, cause of misbehavior, 60
Medication, learning and behavioral difficulties and, 305
Meltdown (Cook), 312
Mental health among children and adolescents, 28
Metacognitive, 32
Middle school grades, typical behavior in, 32–33
Mid-level options, misbehavior redirection, 329
Mild escalations, 311
Misbehavior
  backup systems for (Jones), 186, 188
  causal conditions in individual students, 55–59
  conditions in instructional environments, 60–61
  conditions in peers/groups, 59–60
  conditions in teachers and other personnel, 61–63
  consequences for (Morrish), 112–113
  defined, 53
  five realities of, 6–8
  frequency in classrooms (Jones), 186
  identifying causes of, 54–63
  as ineffective behavior (Kagan), 253
  prevention among students with special needs, 313–314
  proactively limiting, 323, 327
  teacher, 61
  types of, 53–54, 252–253
Mistaken goals (Dreikurs), 84
Mistakes, normalizing, 95, 320
Moment of disruption, structures for (Kagan), 254
Momentum of lessons (Kounin), 81
Monitoring frequently, PBIS, 275–276
Moral intelligence (Borba), 74
Motivation, 95, 320
  importance of (Glasser), 199, 220
  internal vs. external (Glasser; Marshall), 200, 204, 224, 225, 227–229, 231
  Theories X and Y (McGregor), 226–227
"My job, your job," 329, 330
  Moorish on, 106
  Seganti on, 124
  the Wongs on, 148–149

Nagging
  Glasser on, 210, 211
  Jones on, 175
National Center for Children in
    Poverty (NCCP), 42
National Council for Learning
    Disabilities (NCLD), 301
National Education Association (NEA),
    20
NBB. See Neurological-based behavior
Needs, 95, 320, 322
  Charles on, 34, 326
  defined, 33–34
  discussing with students, 36
  Dreikurs on, 34, 73, 83–84
  Glasser on, 34, 201
  Kagan on, 253, 261
  meet without harming others (Ford),
    74
  Sund on, 322
  unmet needs and misbehavior, 55
Negligence, teacher, 17
Negotiating differences, connecting
    habit (Glasser), 211
Neurological-based behavior (NBB)
  autism spectrum disorder (ASD),
    308–309
  bipolar disorder, 306–307
  brain injuries, 310
  fetal alcohol spectrum disorder
    (FASD), 309–310
  medication for, 305
  oppositional defiant disorder
    (ODD), 307
  rage, 310–313
  sensory integration dysfunction
    (SID), 305–306
Noncoercive discipline (Glasser; Mar-
    shall), 196, 199–200
Nonthinking activity, compliance
    (Morrish), 103
Nontraumatic brain injuries, 310
Nonverbal communication, 25–26
Numbers, assigning to students (the
    Wongs), 162

Obedience vs. responsibility,
    (Marshall), 224
Offer rule (Kagan), 261
Omission training (Jones), 185
Opportunity, valued by schools, 37
Oppositional defiant disorder (ODD),
    307
Outside factors, classroom
    management, 27
Overarching strategy (Morrish), 99
Overlapping (Kounin), 81
Ownership of problem (Coloroso), 89

Parents (caregivers)
  establishing alliances with (Kagan),
    262–263
  establishing relationships with (the
    Wongs), 159
  as partners (Morrish), 110
  sample letter to (Marshall), 243
  Seganti on, 131, 139
Partial fetal alcohol syndrome (pFAS), 309
PBIS. See Positive Behavioral
    Interventions and Supports
Permissive classrooms, 84
Personal achievement and competition, 37
Personal behavior, 37
Personal improvement plan (Kagan), 255
Personal system of classroom discipline
  communicating the plan, 329–330
  developing a plan for, 4–6, 322
  philosophy of, 322
  preventive tactics, 327
  redirective tactics, 324, 329
  rubric for, 321–330
  supportive tactics, 323–324,
    327–328
  theory of, 322–323
  two illustrative plans, 321–330
Perspective taking (Covey), 23–24
pFAS (Partial fetal alcohol syndrome),
    309
Physical contact, with students, 18
Physical discomfort, as misbehavior
    cause, 60
Physical proximity (Jones), 25, 181–182
"Picture It Right" (Kagan), 254, 329
Pictures, quality world (Glasser),
    201–202
Planning ahead, valued by schools, 37
Planning and organizing (the Wongs), 152
Positions, of students (Kagan), 252–253
Positive attitude, importance of, 64
Positive Behavioral Interventions and
    Supports (PBIS), 75, 93–94,
    272–296
  collaboration, 276
  core principles, 275–276
  research on effectiveness, 292
  rewards, 290–291
  three-tiered structure of, 277–290
Positive Classroom Discipline (Jones),
    172
Positive Classroom Instruction (Jones),
    172
Positive Discipline in the Classroom
    (Nelson and Lott), 87
Positive images (Marshall), 224
Positive influence, suggestions for,
    53–54, 64–69, 196
  Glasser on, 199–200

Positive relationships with students
    (Morrish), 111–112
Positivity, and humaneness (Nelson
    and Lott), 74, 87–88
Positivity, nature and value of, 74, 224,
    226, 232, 234–235, 242
Post-rage, phase 4 (Cook), 312–313
Poverty, effect on students (Payne),
    43–44
Power, students' senses of (Glasser),
    201
Praise
  Ginott on, 82
  Marshall on, 233
  Morrish on, 112, 113
Preferred activity time (Jones), 182
  educational value, 184
  group concern, 185
Preoperational stage (Piaget), 31
Prevention of misbehavior,
    95, 320
  and cooperation between teacher
    and student, 325
  as facet of discipline, 272
  Jones on, 193
  Kagan on, 254, 255
  for students with special needs,
    313–314
Preventive discipline, guide for,
    313–314
Primary grades, typical behavior in,
    31–32
Procedures
  Emmer and Evertson, 51–52
  instead of rules (Marshall), 222,
    224–225
  teaching, 320
  the Wongs, 152–158, 163
Professionalism
  achieving higher levels of, 325,
    326–327
  Code of Conduct (NEA), 20–21
  dressing professionally, 132
  ethical behavior, 18
Promoting Responsibility & Learning
    (Marshall), 239
Provocation as a cause of misbehavior, 59
Prudence, 236
Punishment
  avoiding, 320
  Ginott on, 82
  Glasser on, 210, 211
  Marshall on, 225
  Morrish on, 104–105
  in PBIS, 295
  Redl and Wattenberg on, 77
  Skinner on, 78
  as teacher misbehavior, 3

Quality classrooms, establishing (Glasser), 202–204, 212–214
Quality curriculum, (Glasser), 199, 202
Quality education (Glasser), 199, 200–201
Quality learning (Glasser), 200
The Quality School: Managing Students Without Coercion (Glasser), 197
Quality Schools (Glasser), 24, 196, 209–210
The Quality School Teacher (Glasser), 197
Quality teaching (Glasser), 203–204, 207–208
Quality world (Glasser), 201–202
Quiet, cultivating, 132

Rage (Cook), 310–313
    escalation, 311–312
    post-meltdown, 312–313
    triggering, 311
Rage cycle, 311
Raise Responsibility System (Marshall), 232, 242
Rapid escalations, 311–312
Ready rule (Kagan), 261
Real Discipline (Morrish), 74, 76, 97–120
    applying, 116–118
    choice management, 107–108
    defined, 100–101
    mindset for teachers, 105–106
    motivation and rewards in, 113
    teaching students to behave, 106
    three phases of, 102–108
    training for compliance, 103–106
Reality therapy (Glasser), 196
Reality Therapy: A New Approach to Psychiatry (Glasser), 78–80
Reconciliation (Coloroso), 89–90
Redirective facet of discipline, 314, 324, 329
Redo misbehavior properly (Morrish), 98
Redo properly (Morrish), 106
Reestablishing expectations (Kagan), 256
Reflective questions (Marshall), 222, 227, 232, 235, 242
Reinforcing stimulus (Skinner), 77
Relations with others, 37
Replacement behavior, identifying (Kagan), 256
Request rule (Kagan), 261
Resolution (Coloroso), 89–90
Respect
    as connecting habit (Glasser), 211
    teachers' responsibility, 19

Respect rule (Kagan), 261
Responsibility, stimulating in students (Jones; Marshall), 75, 183, 224, 225, 232–233
Responsibility rule (Kagan), 261
Responsible behavior, 53, 264, 324
Responsible thinking (Kagan), 256
Responsible Thinking Process (RTP) (Ford), 74
Restitution
    Coloroso on, 89–90
    Gossen on, 74
    Kagan on, 256–257
Rewards, 320
    Marshall on, 225
    Morrish on, 113
    role of in PBIS, 290–291
    Seganti on, 124
    using to control students, 210, 211
Routines (the Wongs), 152
Rules, teaching, 320, 323, 327
Rules in discipline
    Canter on, 85
    Evertson and Emmer on, 51
    Glasser on, 207–208
    Jones on, 176–178
    Kagan on, 252, 261
    Marshall on, 223–224, 224–225, 234
    Morrish on, 103–105, 108–110
    Seganti on, 125–126, 126–131
    the Wongs on, 150, 151–152, 161

Safety, student needs (Glasser), 201
Same-side chat (Kagan), 256
Same-side collaboration (Kagan), 75, 251, 253, 256, 261
Sane messages (Ginott), 22, 82
Satiation, lesson quality (Kounin), 81
Say, See, Do teaching (Jones), 178, 328
Scaffolding, 47
School factors, classroom management, 27
Schools' obligations to students, 14
Schools Without Failure (Glasser), 78, 197
School-Wide Positive Behavior Supports (SWPBS), 93, 272
Science and Human Behavior (Skinner), 77
Scott, Sally, 253
Seats, assigning
    Seganti on, 132, 136–137
    the Wongs on, 150
Seat work, providing help during (Jones), 186–187
Secondary students, the Wongs' approach, 163–165

Secrets of Discipline (Morrish), 98
Secrets of Discipline: 12 Keys for Raising Responsible Children (Morrish), 107
Self-assessment (Seganti), 133
Self-control (Marshall's Hierarchy of Social Development), 228–229
Self-diagnostic referral (Marshall), 238–239
Self-evaluation (Glasser), 204
Self-evaluation, improvement, and repetition (SIR), 204
Self-management, 95, 289, 320
Self-manager application (Slovenske), 162–163
Self-manager plan (Slovenske), 162–163
Self-restitution theory (Gossen), 74
Sensory integration dysfunction (SID), 304–305, 309
Sensory processing disorder (SPD), 304–305, 309
Setting limits (Jones), 177
Seven connecting habits (Glasser), 24–25, 198, 210–212
Seven deadly habits (Glasser), 198, 210–212
Shaping behavior (Skinner), 72, 78
Sharing vs. telling (Marshall), 235
Showcase portfolio, of student work, 329
Significant Seven (Nelsen and Lott), 88
Silence (Seganti), 134
SIR (self-evaluation, improvement, and repetition), 204
Smoothness, of lesson (Kounin), 81
Social interest (Dreikurs), 83
Social skills instructional groups (PBIS), 285–288
Societal groups
    influence on behavior, 36–37
    working effectively with, 46–48
Societal trends, 27
Specific rules (Jones), 177
Statement of purpose (PBIS), 279
Step-by-step graphic plan (Jones), 180
Structures (Kagan)
    for follow-up, 254–255
    intervention for various types of disruptions, 257–260
    for life skills, 257
    for long-term success, 255–257
    for preventing disruptions, 253–254
    for responding to disruptions, 254
Student positions (Kagan), 252–253
Student roles (Redl and Wattenberg), 76

Students
  accountability (Kounin, Seganti),
    76, 81, 125–129
  complying with expectations, 50–52
  with learning and behavioral
    challenges, 299–317
  obligations, 15, 17, 30
  passivity (Jones), 174
  positions (Kagan), 252–253
  responsibilities in class (Jones), 183
  responsibilities in class (Marshall),
    75
  responsibilities in class (Seganti), 75
  roles in classroom (Redl and
    Wattenberg), 76
  self-esteem (Morrish; Seganti), 76,
    114
  success (Glasser), 75
  wants, needs, dislikes in school,
    35–36
Study group activity (Jones),
    188–189
Success, valued by schools, 37
Successive approximation (Skinner), 78
Summary graphic, 179
Support groups, support buddies (the
    Wongs), 163
Supporting, as connecting habit
    (Glasser), 24, 211
Supportive discipline, 321–325
Survival, students (Glasser), 201
Suspension, Seganti's reasons for,
    130–131, 137–138
SWPBS (School-Wide Positive Behavior
    Supports), 93
Synergetic teaching (Charles), 74

Tangible progress (Albert), 86
Targeted supports, 94
Teach, rehearse, reinforce (the Wongs),
    153
Teacher and Child (Ginott), 81–82
Teacher roles (Redl and Wattenberg), 76
Teachers
  assertive (the Canters), 73, 85
  attitudes of (Seganti), 123–125, 328
  capability, importance of, 149
  effective, 75
  ethical obligations of, 18–21,
    326–327
  hidden asset of (Ginott), 83
  importance of, 83
  influence techniques of, 328–329
  lead vs. boss teachers/managers
    (Glasser), 200–201, 204–206
  misbehavior of, 61–63
  motivating tactics (Marshall),
    233–234

  multiple roles of (Redl and
    Wattenberg), 76
  obligations to students, 15
  professional competencies of
    (InTASC), 21, 31
  professional obligations, 15, 19–20
  reactive vs. proactive (Marshall),
    223
  responsibilities of, 18–20
  at their best (Ginott), 22, 83
  at their worst (Ginott), 22, 83
Teacher–student same-side collabora-
    tion (Kagan), 251, 253–254,
    256, 261
Tedium, as cause of misbehavior, 60
Temperance, 236
Temptation, cause of misbehavior, 56
Testing. See Evaluation
Testing and accountability procedures,
    28, 96, 320
  Glasser on, 213
The First Days of School: How to Be an
    Effective Teacher (Wong), 164
Theory of discipline, personal,
    322–323, 325–326
Theory X and Theory Y (McGregor),
    226–227
"The Science of Learning and the Art
    of Teaching" (Skinner), 77
Threatening, habit (Glasser), 210, 211
Three C's (Albert), 86
Three perceptions (Nelson and Lott), 88
Thwarted desires, cause of misbehavior,
    55
Tier 1 supports of PBIS, 277, 278–280
Tier 2 interventions (PBIS), 277–278,
    281–288
  Check in, Check out (CICO), 281,
    283, 286
  Social skills instructional groups,
    285–288
Tier 3 supports (PBIS), 277, 278,
    288–290
  functional behavior assessment, 288
  structural/environmental strategies,
    289
Time orientation, 37
Time wasting (Jones)
  avoiding, 173, 175–176
  massive, 73
Tools for Teaching (Jones), 171, 190
Total learning competency (Glasser),
    210
"To you . . . to me," (Kagan), 254
Traumatic brain injuries, 310
Trends, in behavior, 39
Triggering rage, phase 1 (Cook), 311
Trust, 211, 233, 326

Trusting, as connecting habit (Glasser),
    24, 211
Tutoring students (Marshall), 234
Types of students (Seganti), 136

Uninformed (Kagan), 253
  interventions for, 260
Universal supports, 93, 277,
    278–280
Unobtrusive tactics (Jones; Marshall),
    177, 236–237
Urge to transgress, cause of
    misbehavior, 56
U.S. Census Bureau, 42
Useful class work (Glasser), 203

Value judgments (Glasser), 203
Values
  effect on behavior, 36–37
  emphasized in school, 37–38
Value systems, 38–42
Variety (Marshall), 234
Verbal learning, 37
The Video Toolbox (Jones),
    172, 188
Visual instructional plans (VIPs)
    (Jones), 179–180, 187, 189
Voluntary control, 52

Warnings (Seganti), 124
Why questions (Ginott),
    22–23, 82
The William Glasser Institute, 209
Win-Win Discipline (Kagan), 250,
    253–257
  attention to needs, 261
  Big Three essentials to teaching,
    263–264
  class rules, 261
  community alliances and schoolwide
    programs, 262
  goal of, 260–261
  introducing to classroom,
    264–265
  three pillars of, 250, 254, 261
Win-Win Discipline (Kagan, Kyle,
    Scott), 253
Win-Win Discipline, Three Pillars of
    (Kagan), 75
With All Due Respect (Morrish), 98
Withitness (Kounin), 81
"Work the crowd" (Jones),
    176, 189

You-messages (Ginott), 22

Zero tolerance policies, 27, 28